MW00814316

The Communicati‹
And How to Fix It

Mark Lloyd • Lewis A. Friedland
Editors

The Communication Crisis in America, And How to Fix It

palgrave
macmillan

Editors
Mark Lloyd
University of Southern California
Los Angeles, California, USA

Lewis A. Friedland
University of Wisconsin-Madison
Madison, Wisconsin, USA

ISBN 978-1-349-95030-0 (soft cover)   ISBN 978-1-349-94925-0 (eBook)
DOI 10.1057/9781349949250

Library of Congress Control Number: 2016947005

Cover illustration Moodboard/Getty Images

Printed on acid-free paper

This Palgrave Macmillan imprint is published by Springer Nature
The registered company is Nature America Inc. New York

Foreword

In his 1822 letter to the then Lieutenant Governor of Kentucky William Taylor Barry, James Madison wrote that:

> "A popular Government, without popular information, or the means of acquiring it, is but a Prologue to a Farce or a Tragedy; or, perhaps both. Knowledge will forever govern ignorance: And a people who mean to be their own Governors, must arm themselves with the power which knowledge gives."

This Enlightenment Era belief in the crucial nexus of democratic governance and an informed public is captured more formally in the US Bill of Rights' First Amendment and its protection of the freedoms of speech, the press, peaceable assembly, and petitioning the government for a redress of grievances. The linking together of these four positive freedoms is no coincidence, as the quote from Madison makes clear. For citizens "to be their own governors" in the kind of representative system constructed by the Founders, they required the right to express their views individually and collectively, even if those views were in opposition to people in power. But to do so in a way that avoided "a farce or a tragedy; or, perhaps both," citizens required "information, or the means of acquiring it," through institutions such as public education (the subject of his letter to Barry) and a free press.

Based on my own work and that of many other scholars, it appears that Madison had it right. All else being equal, "politically informed" citizens are more accepting of democratic norms, such as political tolerance, are more efficacious about politics, and are more likely to participate in political and civic life in a variety of ways. They are also more likely to have opinions about public issues, to hold stable opinions over time, and to hold opinions that are ideologically consistent with each other. They are less likely to change their opinions in the face of new but tangential or misleading information, yet more likely to change in the face of new relevant or compelling information. Political information also affects the opinions held by different socioeconomic groups (e.g., groups based on race, class, gender, and age differences). More-informed citizens within these groups hold opinions that are both significantly different from less-informed citizens with similar demographic characteristics and that are arguably more consistent with their values and/or material circumstances. Political information increases citizens' ability to connect their policy views to evaluations of public officials and political parties, and to their political behavior. For example, informed citizens are more likely to identify with the political party, approve of the performance of officeholders, and vote for candidates whose policy stands are most consistent with their own views. Finally, and also consistent with Madison's view, it is clear that while being informed is driven by a number of factors, attention to the news media (i.e., the means of acquiring "popular information") is among the most important of these factors. Of course, information and the means of acquiring it do not, in and of themselves, assure a well-functioning democracy. There are instances where more information, if unbalanced or biased, can lead to less sanguine outcomes, or where ideology or partisanship can trump "the facts." Nonetheless, taken as a whole, the research strongly suggests that information and the means of acquiring it, if equitable, are crucial if people are to effectively be their own governors.

It was the importance of an informed citizenry and the central role played by the press in creating and maintaining one that gave the practice of journalism, in its different and evolving forms, its special status in the USA for most of our existence as a nation. As Victor Pickard notes in his essay in this volume, journalism is both a private and a public good, and "Like many public goods exhibiting positive externalities, journalism has never been fully supported by direct market transactions; it always has been subsidized to some degree." These subsidies have been both private (e.g., advertising) and public (e.g., reduced postal rates for the circulation of newspapers). The special status of journalism has also been reflected in both the regulations imposed on (e.g., the equal time provision, the fairness doctrine, and limits on cross ownership) and rights granted to (e.g., shield laws) journalists and the organizations they work for. And it has been reflected in the real, albeit not fully successful, efforts over time to create and support a public media system that is independent of traditional market forces.

Driven by changes in the contemporary cultural, political, economic, and technological environments, this special status has eroded dramatically over the past several decades, at great expense to the profession and the institutions of journalism. In the last three decades, over 300 daily newspapers have closed, newspaper circulation has dropped by 35 percent, the number of professional journalists has declined by over 40 percent, and revenues are at the same level as 1950, when the population was half what it is today and the economy was one seventh its current size. Over this period the trends for local and national television news are equally grim, with nightly viewership dropping by over 50 percent and the average age of viewers rising to over 60. And public trust in the news media in general is at an all-time low. These are changes certainly worthy of being called a "crisis." At the same time, however, the very cultural, political, economic, and technological changes responsible for journalism's impending demise have arguably led to a plethora of new sources of public information and analyses, beginning with cable news and talk and extending to online news, blogs and microblogs, citizen journalists (and random acts of citizen journalism), crowd sourcing, online access to international media, and popular culture genres such as satirical news.

It is also important to remind ourselves that even at its best, twentieth-century journalism was only partially successful in doing its part in the education of the American citizen. Public knowledge about political institutions and processes, substantive policies and socioeconomic conditions, and political and economic actors has been generally low in the USA, with a great deal of variance in what Americans know and which Americans know it. Of particular significance is the fact that sociocultural differences in the opportunities to access and process information have led to substantial knowledge gaps across demographic groups, with men, whites, older citizens, and wealthier citizens significantly more informed than women, non-whites, younger citizens, and poorer citizens, reinforcing other socioeconomic inequities in the material and political resources available to citizens. To the extent that information matters for citizens' ability to effectively advocate for their individual and collective self-interest and their conceptions of the public interest, large segments of the public are and have been disadvantaged.

Viewed in this light, the current crisis also affords a rare opportunity to rethink journalism's role in American democracy, salvaging the best of the past while remedying some of its significant shortcomings. So what are we to do? While the answer to this question is complicated, a sensible starting point is to better understand the current state of affairs by answering two more specific questions. What *are* the information needs of the numerous communities—of geography and of interests—to which we belong? And how well and for whom do the complex, multifaceted information environments in which we now live—including but not limited to professional journalism—meet those needs? These are both empirical and normative questions that we as scholars are particularly well suited to help answer, but with two important caveats. First, understanding what citizens' need requires input from multiple voices. These voices should include scholars, information providers of various stripes, policymakers, and so forth, but it is crucial that citizens themselves have a voice in constructing this answer. After all, it is *their* information needs that we are trying to divine. And second, understanding both citizens' information needs and our media ecologies' ability to meet them will require a multi-disciplinary and multi-method approach. These are questions the answers to which reside at the micro-, meso-, and macro-levels. That will require insights from disciplines such as communication; political science; law; history; economics; sociology; anthropology; and gender, race, and ethnicity studies. That will require data and methods running the gamut from ethnography, in-depth interviews, community-based case studies, and discourse analysis, to historiography, policy, and legal analyses, to survey research, to computational science approaches to content, behavioral, and geospatial analyses of "big data."

Collectively, the essays in this volume take just such a multi-disciplinary and multi-methodological approach to understanding the current crisis in journalism, and its implications for information inequality in the USA. In doing so, they point the way to how we might take advantage of this crisis to better understand the information needs of the nation's various publics, and use this knowledge to improve both the quality of popular information and our means of acquiring it.

Annenberg School for Communication   Michael X. Delli Carpini
University of Pennsylvania
Philadelphia, PA, USA

ACKNOWLEDGMENTS

We gratefully acknowledge the following people, without whom this project could not have been accomplished.

A special thanks to Ernest J. Wilson III, Dean of the Annenberg School for Communication at the University of Southern California, and Carola Weil, Dean of the School of Professional & Extended Studies at American University. Much of this book grew out of their work on the Literature Review on the Critical Information Needs of American Communities, and their continuing engagement and support made this book possible. We also extend a special thanks to Phil Napoli, Katya Ognyanova, and Danilo Yanich, who have been with us and ahead of us from the beginning along with the other members of the Communications Policy Research Network.

We would also like to thank the many colleagues whose prior work deeply informed this project, especially Sandra Ball-Rokeach, Michael Delli Carpini, Hemant Shah, Greg Downey, Dhavan Shah, Hernando Rojas, Wick Rowland, and Jorge Reina Schement. And we feel obliged to acknowledge our many contributors who took time out from very busy schedules to meet what some would consider impossible deadlines to get this work out. We know you would have liked to have had more time to write and a larger word count.

Friedland would also like to acknowledge the School of Journalism and Mass Communication, UW-Madison, his lifelong intellectual home. Carmen Sirianni has been a colleague and partner in matters civic and democratic for more than 40 years. The project could not have been completed without the support of Stacey Oliker.

Sandra Knisely expertly edited and shepherded the manuscript from its earliest stages through submission (even on her honeymoon) and we thank her.

And last, but not least, we thank our editor, Shaun Vigil, who immediately embraced this work, as well as Erica Buchman and Michelle Smith who worked to see it through completion.

CONTENTS

Section 1   Preface: New Approaches to Solving the
            Communications Challenge   1

1   America's Critical Community Information Needs   3
    Lewis A. Friedland

2   Understanding Our New Communications Economy:
    Implications for Contemporary Journalism   17
    Philip M. Napoli

3   Researching Community Information Needs   31
    Katherine Ognyanova

Section 2   Preface: Communication Challenges in a Changing
            America   47

4   Understanding a Diverse America's Critical
    Information Needs   49
    Mark Lloyd, Jason Llorenz, and Jorge R. Schement

5   Feminist Perspectives on Critical Information Needs   65
    Carolyn M. Byerly and Alisa Valentin

6 Ethnic Media and the Social Incorporation
of New Americans 81
Matthew D. Matsaganis and Vikki S. Katz

7 Do Spanish-Language Broadcast Media Serve a
Changing America? 95
Federico Subervi

8 The Whole Community Communication Infrastructure:
The Case of Los Angeles 107
Minhee Son and Sandra Ball-Rokeach

Section 3 Preface: Government Capture and Market Failure 125

9 Confronting Market Failure: Past Lessons Toward
Public Policy Interventions 127
Victor Pickard

10 Tripartite Regulation in the Public's Interest: The
Overlapping Roles of the DOJ, FCC, and FTC in
Consolidation of the Communications Industry 143
Allen S. Hammond IV

11 Same ol', Same ol': Consolidation and Local Television
News 165
Danilo Yanich

12 Bridging the Content Gap in Low-Income Communities 183
James T. Hamilton and Fiona Morgan

13 The Online Participation Divide 199
Eszter Hargittai and Kaitlin Jennrich

14 Media Deserts: Monitoring the Changing Media
    Ecosystem   215
    Michelle Ferrier, Gaurav Sinha, and Michael Outrich

Section 4   Preface: Net Neutrality is Not Enough   233

15 The Constitutional Case for Addressing Critical
    Information Needs   235
    Mark Lloyd and Michael Park

16 A Provocation on Behalf of the Excluded   249
    *Ernest J. Wilson III, Sasha Costanza-Chock,
    and Michelle C. Forelle*

17 A Public Trust Unrealized: The Unresolved Constraints
    on US Public Media   267
    Willard D. "Wick" Rowland

18 Addressing the Information Needs of Crisis-Affected
    Communities: The Interplay of Legacy Media
    and Social Media in a Rural Disaster   285
    Dharma Dailey and Kate Starbird

19 Conclusion: The Fierce Urgency of Now   305
    Mark Lloyd and Lewis Friedland

Index   311

NOTES ON CONTRIBUTORS

Sandra Ball-Rokeach is a professor in the Annenberg School for Communication and Journalism at the University of Southern California. She is the founder and principal investigator of the Metamorphosis Project. Ball-Rokeach is the author or editor of seven books, including *Understanding Ethnic Media: Producers, Consumers and Societies* (with Matthew Matsaganis and Vikki Katz), *The Great American Values Test: Influencing Belief and Behavior Through Television* (with Milton Rokeach and Joel Grube), and *Media, Audience and Social Structure* (with Muriel G. Cantor). The Metamorphosis Project is an in-depth inquiry into the transformation of urban community under the forces of globalization, population diversity, and new communication technologies.

Carolyn M. Byerly is a professor and chair of the Department of Communication, Culture & Media Studies at Howard University. She is a feminist critical scholar who conducts research on gender and race in media. Her recent research in political economy of women's employment in newsrooms around the world was published in the *Global Report on the Status of Women in News Media* (2011) and *The Palgrave International Handbook of Women and Journalism* (2013). She is co-author of *Women and Media: A Critical Introduction* (2006) and co-editor of *Women and Media: International Perspectives* (2004). Her book chapters and articles have appeared in *Critical Studies in Media and Communication, Journalism: theory & practice, Feminist Media Studies*, and others. She received her PhD and MA from the University of Washington and her BS from the University of Colorado.

Sasha Costanza-Chock is a researcher and mediamaker who works on social movement media, co-design, media justice, and communication rights. He is the Associate Professor of Civic Media at MIT's Comparative Media Studies program and is a faculty associate at the Berkman Center for Internet & Society at Harvard University. His book *Out of the Shadows, Into the Streets: Transmedia Organizing*

xvi NOTES ON CONTRIBUTORS

and the Immigrant Rights Movement was published in 2014. He sits on the board of Allied Media Projects and is a cofounder of Research Action Design. He received his AB from Harvard University, MA from the University of Pennsylvania, and PhD from the Annenberg School for Communication & Journalism at the University of Southern California, where he was a postdoctoral research associate.

Dharma Dailey researches how people get information in crisis contexts. She has an MS in Human Centered Design & Engineering (HCDE) from the University of Washington and BS in Interdisciplinary Studies from SUNY Empire State College. Prior to graduate school she spent over a decade working on accessibility of communications technologies to underserved populations in the USA. She is a PhD student in HCDE.

Michael X. Delli Carpini is Dean of the Annenberg School for Communication. His research explores the role of the citizen in American politics, with particular emphasis on the impact of the mass media on public opinion, political knowledge, and political participation. He is author of five books and a number of articles, including *What Americans Know about Politics and Why It Matters* (1996, winner of the 2008 American Association of Public Opinion Researchers Book Award), *A New Engagement? Political Participation, Civic Life and the Changing American Citizen* (2006), *Talking Together: Public Deliberation and Political Participation in America* (2009), and *After Broadcast News: Media Regimes, Democracy, and the New Information Environment* (2011), as well as numerous articles, essays, and edited volumes on political communications, public opinion, and political socialization. Dean Delli Carpini was awarded the 2008 Murray Edelman Distinguished Career Award from the Political Communication Division of the American Political Science Association. Dean Delli Carpini is the former Director of the Public Policy Program at The Pew Charitable Trusts.

Michelle Ferrier is the Associate Dean for Innovation for Ohio University's Scripps College of Communication. Ferrier is the principal investigator for and founder of The Media Deserts Project **and is** the president of Journalism That Matters, a nonprofit organization focused on helping professionals and educators navigate the new media landscape. Ferrier has received grant funding for a platform to deal with online harassment and a hyperlocal online news project. She has also convened sponsored regional and national conferences around media entrepreneurship and community needs. She received a PhD in Texts and Technology from the University of Central Florida and a master's degree in journalism from the University of Tennessee.

Michelle C. Forelle is a doctoral student of communication at the University of Southern California's Annenberg School of Communication and Journalism. Originally from Venezuela, her dissertation work examines how the "Internet of Things" is changing legal interpretations of property, contract, and labor. She has presented and published on a wide variety of topics, ranging from the use of games in national electoral get-out-the-vote efforts, to the epistemological obstacles in the way of media ownership diversity policy, to the emergence of the interactive music video genre online.

Lewis Friedland is the Vilas Distinguished Achievement Professor in the School of Journalism and Mass Communication and Departments of Sociology and Educational Psychology (affiliated), University of Wisconsin-Madison, where he directs the Center for Communication and Democracy and holds the Leon Epstein Fellowship in Letters and Sciences. Friedland is author or co-author (with Carmen Sirianni) of five books on civil society, the public sphere, and civic innovation in America. He is completing a book on civic communication in a network society (for Polity Press) and writing on the communication ecologies of American communities, most recently in the *American Behavioral Scientist*.

James T. Hamilton is the Hearst Professor of Communication and Director of the Journalism Program at Stanford University. His books on media markets and information provision include *Democracy's Detectives: The Economics and Impacts of Investigative Reporting* (forthcoming); *All the News That's Fit to Sell: How the Market Transforms Information into News*; and *Regulation Through Revelation: The Origin, Politics, and Impacts of the Toxics Release Inventory Program*. Through research in the field of computational journalism, he is exploring how the costs of story discovery can be lowered through better use of data and algorithms.

Allen S. Hammond IV is the Phil and Bobbie Sanfilippo Chair and Professor of Law at Santa Clara University and Director of the Broadband Institute of California. Hammond has a publication record spanning 30 years. He is co-author of a forthcoming casebook on Regulation of Broadband Communications. His prior positions include attorney, White House Office of Telecommunications Policy; program manager, NTIA; counsel, WJLA-TV, MCI Communications and Satellite Business Systems; attorney, Media Access Project; and professor, Syracuse University College of Law and the New York Law School.

Eszter Hargittai is the Delaney Family Professor in the Communication Studies Department and Faculty Associate of the Institute for Policy Research at Northwestern University, where she heads the Web Use Project. Her research looks at how people may benefit from their digital media uses with a particular focus on differences in people's web-use skills. She is editor of *Research Confidential: Solutions to Problems Most Social Scientists Pretend They Never Have* (2009) and co-editor with Christian Sandvig of *Digital Research Confidential* (2015), both on the realities of doing empirical social science research.

Kaitlin Jennrich is an undergraduate student at Northwestern University majoring in Communication Studies with a certificate in Integrated Marketing Communications.

Vikki S. Katz is an associate professor in the School of Communication and Information at Rutgers University. She is author of *Kids in the Middle: How Children of Immigrants Negotiate Community Interactions for their Families* (2014), and second author of *Understanding Ethnic Media: Producers, Consumers and Societies* (2011). Her research addresses challenges that immigrant parents and their children face as they integrate into US society, with particular interest in how media and technology are implicated in these experiences. Her work has been published in a variety of academic journals, and she has authored multiple policy briefs related to digital equity initiatives for low-income and immigrant children and families. She received her PhD from the University of Southern California.

Jason Llorenz is a part-time lecturer at the Rutgers University School of Communication & Information and staff member at the Rutgers University Office of Diversity & Inclusion (OIDI). His research and teaching focus on telecommunications and Internet policy, as well as the role of digital and social media in the innovation economy. Llorenz holds a BA from Cazenovia College and juris doctor from the State University of New York at Buffalo School of Law. His writing often appears in the *Huffington Post*.

Mark Lloyd is a Professor of Professional Practice of Communication at the University of Southern California – Annenberg School, where he teaches communication policy. He was an associate general counsel at the FCC, served as the general counsel of the Benton Foundation, and was as an attorney at the law firm Dow, Lohnes & Albertson. Lloyd has conducted research at the Civil Rights Forum on Communication Policy, the Center for American Progress and at MIT. An Emmy Award–winning journalist, including work at NBC and CNN, and an author and contributor to several books and articles, Lloyd graduated from the University of Michigan and the Georgetown University Law Center.

Matthew D. Matsaganis is an associate professor in the Communication Department at the University at Albany, State University of New York. He is first author of *Understanding Ethnic Media: Producers, Consumers and Societies* (2011, with Vikki Katz and Sandra Ball-Rokeach). His research addresses issues of ethnic media consumption, production and sustainability, the role of communication in building community capacity, health disparities, and the social determinants of health, as well as the social impact of technology. His research has also been published in *Journalism: Theory, Practice, & Criticism*, the *Journal of Health Communication*, the *Journal of Applied Communication Research*, the *International Journal of Communication*, and the *Journal of Information Policy*, among other outlets. He received his PhD from the University of Southern California.

Fiona Morgan is the Journalism Program Director at Free Press. She began her journalism career at Salon.com, and then reported for *Indy Week*, the alternative newsweekly in Durham, North Carolina. She received a master's degree in public policy from Duke University in 2011. She authored a report for the New America Foundation's Media Policy Initiative on the media ecology of North Carolina's Research Triangle region. She was a research associate at Duke's Sanford School of Public Policy before joining Free Press in 2015. Her work focuses on the information needs of underserved local communities.

Philip M. Napoli (PhD, Northwestern University) is the James R. Shepley Professor of Public Policy in the Sanford School of Public Policy at Duke University. His research interests focus on media institutions and media policy. His books include *Foundations of Communications Policy: Principles and Process in the Regulation of Electronic Media* (2001); *Audience Economics: Media Institutions and the Audience Marketplace* (2003); and *Audience Evolution: New Technologies and the Transformation of Media Audiences* (2011). His research has been funded by organizations such as the Ford Foundation, the New America Foundation, and the Democracy Fund.

Katherine Ognyanova is an assistant professor in the Communication Department at the School of Communication and Information, Rutgers University. She does work in the areas of computational social science and network analysis. Her research has a broad focus on the impact of technology on social structures, political and civic engagement, and the media system. Prior to her appointment at Rutgers, Ognyanova was a postdoctoral researcher at the Lazer Lab, Northeastern University, and a fellow at the Institute for Quantitative Social Science, Harvard University. She holds a doctoral degree in communication from the University of Southern California.

Michael Outrich is a senior at Ohio University studying Geographic Information Sciences and pursuing a minor in meteorology and a certificate in wealth and poverty. He has plans on pursuing a master's degree in urban planning with a social equity focus and is passionate about empowering economically disadvantaged and marginalized communities. As a GIScience analyst/cartographer PACE Fellow with the geography department at Ohio, he processes the geographic data and generates maps and statistics for the Media Deserts Project under the direction of Michelle Ferrier and Gaurav Sinha.

Michael Park is an Assistant Professor of Communication at the S.I. Newhouse School of Public Communications, Syracuse University. He specializes in media law, communications policy, and sports communication. His research interests include critical media studies in race and masculinity. Michael's writing has appeared in communication and law journals. His professional experience includes stints at William Morris Endeavor, in Beverly Hills, California; and the Federal Communications Commission, in the office of FCC

Commissioner Michael J. Copps. Michael completed his doctorate at the Annenberg School for Communication & Journalism at the University of Southern California and is also a graduate of the University of California, Hastings College of the Law.

Victor Pickard is an associate professor at the Annenberg School for Communication at the University of Pennsylvania. Previously he taught at NYU and the University of Virginia, and he worked on media policy in Washington, DC, at Free Press, the New America Foundation, and Congresswoman Diane Watson's office. He has written over 50 scholarly articles and book chapters, and his op-eds have appeared in *The Guardian*, *The Huffington Post*, and *The Atlantic*. He has authored or edited several books, including *Will the Last Reporter Please Turn Out the Lights* (with Robert McChesney), *The Future of Internet Policy* (with Peter Decherney), and *America's Battle for Media Democracy*.

Willard D. "Wick" Rowland is dean and professor emeritus of the School of Journalism and Mass Communication at the University of Colorado and is president and CEO emeritus of Colorado Public Television (KBDI-12). He has held appointments at the University of Illinois and at PBS in Washington, DC. Rowland writes in communication policy history, media institutions, and communications studies, and he lectures and conducts research internationally. He has lobbied frequently on behalf of public media and is the recipient of national public television advocacy and Colorado broadcaster awards. He also has been a leader of several national journalism and communications academic associations and public television and Colorado broadcaster groups.

Jorge R. Schement became Rutgers Vice President of Institutional Diversity and Inclusion on July 1, 2013. He is also professor II in the Bloustein School of Public Policy and in the Department of Latino-Hispanic Caribbean Studies. Previously, he was dean of the School of Communication & Information at Rutgers University. A PhD from Stanford University, he is author of over 200 papers and articles, with eight book credits including *Global Networks* (1999/2002). A Latino from South Texas, his research focuses on the social and policy consequences of the production and consumption of information, especially as they relate to ethnic minorities. Schement is editor-in-chief of the *Encyclopedia of Communication and Information*.

Gaurav Sinha is an Associate Professor of Geographic Information Science and Geography in the Department of Geography at Ohio University. He has a BSc degree in Geological Sciences from the Indian Institute of Technology (IIT), Kharagpur, India, and MA and PhD degrees in Geography (GIScience) from the University at Buffalo. He teaches courses in GIScience and conducts research on cognition-driven semantic modeling of landscape features. He was also engaged for several years on an NSF-funded project on climate change adaptation in rural

Tanzania, and also collaborates on research projects related to geospatial health science and geospatial media analytics.

Minhee Son received her PhD in communication from the Annenberg School for Communication and Journalism at the University of Southern California and is a postdoctoral research associate with the Metamorphosis Project. Her most recent work identifies the communication and church participation factors shaping civically oriented attitudes and behaviors among Korean-born immigrants in Los Angeles. She has conducted research and written on communication ecologies, migration, civic engagement, and intergroup communication.

Kate Starbird is an assistant professor at the Department of Human Centered Design & Engineering (HCDE) at the University of Washington (UW). Kate's research is situated within human-computer interaction (HCI) and the emerging field of crisis informatics—the study of the how information-communication technologies (ICTs) are used during crisis events. Specifically, her work seeks to understand and describe how affected people, emergency responders, and remote individuals come together online to respond to major crisis events, often forming emergent collaborations to meet unpredicted needs. Kate received her PhD from the University of Colorado at Boulder in Technology, Media and Society and holds a BS in Computer Science from Stanford University.

Federico Subervi has been teaching, conducting research, publishing, and consulting on issues related to Latinos and the media in the USA since 1982. He is author and editor of *The Mass Media and Latino Politics. Studies of U.S. Media Content, Campaign Strategies and Survey Research: 1984–2004* (2009). In fall 2015, he retired from Kent State University but remains active in his research, consulting and travel as president of the Association for Latino Media & Markets Communication Research, secretary of the Board of Directors of the Latino Public Radio Consortium, and member of the Advisory Board for Hispanic Child Trends.

Alisa Valentin is a doctoral student in the Communication, Culture and Media Studies Program at Howard University. She is also a teaching assistant in Howard's principles of speech program, a graduate assistant for the *Howard Journal of Communications*, and a member of the Howard Media Group, a faculty-student research collaborative focused on communication policy. Her research interests include communication policy and social media in social movements. She received her MS in journalism from Northwestern University and BS in telecommunications from the University of Florida. She is a former broadcast journalist specializing in urban affairs reporting.

Ernest J. Wilson III is the Walter Annenberg Chair in Communication and Dean of the Annenberg School for Communication and Journalism at the University of Southern California. He is also a Professor of Political Science and a faculty fellow at the USC Center on Public Diplomacy at the Annenberg School. He has worked in government at the White House National Security Council and served on the board of the Corporation for Public Broadcasting from 2000 to 2010, the last year as chairman. His most recent books are *Governing Global Electronic Networks* and *Negotiating the Net: The Politics of Internet Diffusion in Africa*. Wilson received a PhD and MA in political science from the University of California, Berkeley, and a BA from Harvard College.

Danilo Yanich is an associate professor and director of the MA program in Urban Affairs & Public Policy in the School of Public Policy & Administration at the University of Delaware. He leads the Local TV Media Project and focuses on the nexus of the media, citizenship, and public policy. Recent research has examined the effect of consolidation on local television news content, political ads, and news and citizen information needs. His work has been consistently cited by media reformers and policy makers, including the Federal Communications Commission. Yanich is also a charter member of the Communications Policy Research Network.

LIST OF FIGURES

Fig. 8.1   Anglos vs. Latinos vs. Armenians in Glendale   112
Fig. 8.2   Latinos in Glendale vs. Pico Union   113
Fig. 10.1   Comcast/NBCU timeline   151
Fig. 10.2   AT&T's proposed merger with T-Mobile   154
Fig. 11.1   Percentage of duplicated stories on the SA/LMA/duopoly
             stations   173
Fig. 11.2   Distribution of the use of same script/video on the SA/
             LMA/duopoly stations   175
Fig. 11.3   Distribution of the use of the same anchor/reporter on the SA/
             LMA/duopoly stations   177
Fig. 14.1   Change in total number of daily newspapers serving a ZIP
             code between 2007 and 2014   225
Fig. 14.2   Change in circulation penetration of daily newspapers
             serving a ZIP code between 2007 and 2014   227
Fig. 18.1   Examples of information needs in the Catskills over the
             course of the Irene crisis   288

LIST OF TABLES

Table 11.1 % who got news about politics and government in the
previous week from...   169
Table 14.1 Change in number of newspapers serving a ZIP code
between 2007 and 2014   225
Table 14.2 Total number of newspapers serving a ZIP code in 2014   226
Table 14.3 Newspaper circulation penetration for a ZIP code in 2014 227
Table 14.4 Change in newspaper circulation penetration for a ZIP code
between 2007 and 2014   228
Table 16.1 Data gathered from: U.S. Census Bureau 2007; Federal
Communications Commission 2014; Corporation for
Public Broadcasting 2011[a]   252
Table 16.2 Data gathered from: American Society of News Editors 2014;
Papper 2015; and Corporation for Public Broadcasting 2011[b]   252
Table 16.3 Wilson–Tongia Formulation   258

INTRODUCTION

SOLVING AMERICA'S COMMUNICATION CRISIS

Mark Lloyd and Lewis A. Friedland

The critical information needs of the diverse American public are not being met. There was a clear instance of failure when Hurricane Sandy hit in 2012. Inadequate warnings and other communication problems led, in part, to billions of dollars in damages and over a hundred deaths. But communications failures are also evident in both the loud political battles filled with hateful rhetoric and soaked in dark money, and in the too-quiet local elections in far too many cities where far too few turn out to vote. Rather than addressing haphazard communication in the face of an environmental disaster, or the often ugly and apathetic nature of our democratic conversation, policymakers are too often focused on the latest gadget or proposed merger or some other passing interest of the powerful. It is long past time that we begin addressing the critical information needs of all Americans.

But this is not simply an indictment of policymakers. A vast majority of Americans with real political influence and power are stuck in an old way of thinking about how we communicate and why that way of communicating matters so much. We push against the idea that legacy media (newspapers, movies, radio, television) do not matter. We push against the notion that we should only be concerned about the new coming media, or with the dominant media. This way of thinking is not new; it is too simple, and it has not worked very well in the past.

There is little question that the operation of communications markets has changed. This change is not only about the dwindling circulation of newspapers or the struggle to make money from the Internet. It is also about the way the Internet has sped up decisions on Wall Street and how once-private information is now gathered and archived and marketed by by "Silicon Valley" corporations which remain largely unaccountable for their decisions to the public. Our struggle with change is also about how new digital technologies have altered the fundamentals of funding media—that is, how media funding has altered the way communities get information. Our struggle is with what this change means for marginalized communities.

Too many think they are imagining the future of all Americans as they wrestle with the rules regarding digital technologies or work toward getting everyone online. They are treating digital communication just like society once treated television, forgetting that other media also matter and continue to play an important part in how we communicate with each other. The Internet is not another stand-alone communication system; it is not another silo. The idea that getting everyone broadband is the answer to the problem of information inequality is simplistic. The new world is bigger and broader and much harder. To understand it as citizens and policymakers we need to begin thinking about our complex, interactive, interdependent, and dynamic communications ecology.

Moreover, our rapidly increasing diversity adds to this complexity. And by diversity, we are not referring only to what has been called the digital divide, or the separate and unequal status of black and white. It is not even just about acknowledging the full range of ethnicities in America. Our concern with diversity is also about Americans of all colors struggling to make ends meet, including those Americans with disabilities and those Americans who do not live in cities rich with fiber-optic cable; it is about those Americans who live on tribal lands, or who farm the land, or work on the energy platforms off our coasts—all far from robust Internet service. It is also about older Americans, and Americans who do not speak English.

Even as this book is being finalized, the impact of our communications crisis on the US political conversation is front and center. A few see it, with most of the handwringing focused on the media's role in the political success of the businessman and TV reality show star, Donald Trump. And as happens in almost every presidential campaign, some blame the horserace coverage of the media and the failure to examine issues in any real depth. A few focus on the 24-hour news cycle of cable combined with social media. Some decry the rise of partisan cable channels. But we have not found anyone who has bothered to note that most of the crude and substantive national "debates" have aired on pay TV, limiting the access of the roughly 12 million households (mostly minority and poor and rural and increasingly young) who do not get pay TV.

When asked about the 2016 national presidential campaign, CBS president and chief executive officer Leslie Moonves was perhaps more honest than he intended when he said, "It may not be good for America, but it is damn good for CBS. The money's rolling in and this is fun." Political ads, spin, and "Tweets" may be fun, but they do not substitute for a place where *all* Americans can make a serious choice about the serious challenges ahead and how best to meet those challenges.

There is a communications crisis in America. The lives of all Americans and the very fabric of our society are at risk if we do not address it. Our communication infrastructure does not serve our nation not because we lack the technology. Our communication markets do not serve our nation not because the markets have failed to generate profit for investors. Our communication ecology is not meeting the critical information needs of the public because our public policies are badly made and misinformed.

This work is an attempt to sound the alarm; we hope to be heard not only by our students and other teachers but also by our fellow citizens and those who represent us in the halls of government. While we understand many challenges in communication are global in nature, this is a book about the problems in the USA. We believe that the best approach to understanding our complex communication environment is to draw on multiple disciplines. Network theory, gathering stories from our fellow citizens, and crunching data all have a place in clarifying the current crisis in communication. And so, this is a multi-disciplinary work of media studies, economics, sociology, history, political science, and law. We do not put one branch of social science above another nor do we place social science above legal analysis or solid journalism. Each of these disciplines has something to teach us, and together they provide a well-rounded way to understand our complex world. And, even at that, we understand that we cannot adequately cover all the perspectives or issues that need to be addressed in solving the communications crisis in America.

We acknowledge the limits of our efforts but seek to reach you, the reader, despite them, at least in part because we believe scholarship must begin to reach beyond the walls of academia and try to communicate with the public's servants and the public…and that this crisis requires immediate attention. We have asked each scholar to hold on to the depth and rigor of her or his discipline but to write in such a way that other experts and the general public might better understand their various insights. We have tried to keep it somewhat short…but not simple.

Book Organization

A short preface begins each major section in an attempt to pull each section together and help the reader understand how each essay contributes to the whole. We have divided the work into four main sections:

- Section 1 establishes a foundation for approaching our communications challenge, defining critical information needs, examining the current market impact on journalism, and surveying different research methods employed to better understand our communications ecology.
- Section 2 shifts focus to the public and looks at the challenges of understanding critical information needs in an era of rapid demographic change. This section focuses especially on the different ways racial/ethnic groups and women interact with our communication ecology.
- Section 3 turns to the problems of government capture and market failure. This section brings together historical, sociological, legal, and economic perspectives to examine the inability or unwillingness of regulators to confront the failure of communication markets to adequately serve the public interest.
- Section 4 directly confronts the rationale for the failure to develop policy on the critical information needs of all Americans with the tools of constitutional analysis, network analysis, historical analysis, and empirical research.

The public and policymakers, and even perhaps you, the reader, are impatient for solutions about how to fix the crisis we are in. We have heard: "Yes, we all know there is problem; how do we fix it? What policies do you propose?" We understand the urgency of our current situation. We believe another environmental disaster is imminent; we see not only our crumbling bridges and vulnerable levees but also our frail communications infrastructure. We do not believe these public problems will be solved by the market or new technologies. Informed public policy is necessary. We know smart public policy is hard when our political environment is part of the problem. While solutions are proposed throughout the book, we pull a few of them together in our conclusion. But more importantly, we seek to speak directly to our fellow citizens to urge them to demand a statement of action from their party and candidate of choice. We believe that the communication crisis in America can be fixed.

Preface: New Approaches to Solving the Communications Challenge

Our first section sets out the foundation of our broad thesis. In order to clearly understand the communications challenge and how to begin to think about it, we must begin to answer: What are critical information needs? What is happening in our communication markets today? And what research is necessary for us to find solutions?

Friedland proposes eight critical information needs of American communities and argues that both their severity and potential solutions vary greatly by community and neighborhood. Napoli demonstrates that the explosive growth of new media has undermined the business model for traditional information, but that new media still depend on "old" media for much of their content, particularly content that addresses critical information needs. Ognyanova reviews the range of approaches and methods that have been used to model community communication ecologies and discusses why these community-based methods are still necessary in a new media era.

While much of the following chapter draws on the Review of the Literature Regarding Critical Information Needs of the American Public written for the Federal Communications Commission and the work of the Aspen/Knight Commission on the Information Needs of Communities in a Democracy, neither this chapter nor this book repeats those efforts. This chapter captures recent research and analysis necessary to understand the new approaches to solving the communications challenge in America.

CHAPTER 1

America's Critical Community Information Needs

Lewis A. Friedland

Americans need information to govern themselves, to participate effectively in society, and to be safe. Even as the American public remains divided on so many issues, this proposition should generate near-universal agreement. In order to understand what critical community information needs are and how they are delivered, two points stand out. The first is that our mixed system under-delivers information (public goods) that the public needs to survive and thrive. These public goods are systematically under-produced, penalizing both individuals and whole communities. The second, mirroring the first, is that public policy for the democratic provision of community information needs *can* make a difference.

For example, without civic information, we cannot know what laws our elected officials are proposing, who may be supporting those laws, and who is contributing to political campaigns. We cannot monitor whether laws are being implemented well or fairly. As fewer and fewer American communities have regular sources of news that cover political campaigns at the local level, we often cannot even know who our candidates are or what they stand for.

Information flows are also the lifeblood of our economic system. But the provision of information by and about markets is uneven at

L.A. Friedland (✉)
University of Wisconsin, Madison, WI, USA

© The Editor(s) (if applicable) and The Author(s) 2016   3
M.I. Lloyd, L.A. Friedland (eds.), *The Communication Crisis in America, And How to Fix It*, DOI 10.1057/978-1-349-94925-0_1

best. Although it is true that information might be more transparent in competitive markets, many information markets really are not competitive. For example, most Americans have no choice in their cable provider or what kind of cable service they receive. Similarly, in the twenty-first century, the "market" for broadband service, the very gateway to an information society, effectively consists of a series of local monopolies enforced by state legislators who too often limit competition, especially from local governments. As a result, large swaths of Americans are squeezed out from real participation in an information society. Our economic system has left us with a fast lane, a slow lane, and an "entrance closed" lane.

In addition to civic and commercial economic information flows, the American system for providing information even in emergency situations lacks transparency and consistent access. The provision of content is often from government (the National Weather Service or the National Centers for Disease Control, for example) via privately owned and operated media, over a delivery infrastructure owned by the public (spectrum and public streets).

This chapter first establishes the concept of critical community information needs. It then offers eight sets of critical needs that individuals and communities need to thrive. We next discuss how critical community information needs are embedded in local communication ecologies, and drawing from authors in this volume, argue that they need to be studied ecologically. Finally, we discuss the failure to develop public policy toward critical community information needs and point to some new directions.

DEFINING CRITICAL INFORMATION NEEDS

Critical information needs of local communities are those that must be met for citizens and community members to live safe and healthy lives; have full and fair access to educational, employment, and business opportunities; and to fully participate in the civic and democratic lives of their communities.

In 2012, the University of Southern California (USC) was funded by the Federal Communications Commission (FCC) to examine a wide range of social sciences from multiple disciplines to propose a set of critical information needs (Friedland et al. 2012). USC reached out to a team of scholars collectively identified as the Communication Policy Research Network (CPRN). That group identified more than 1000 articles drawing from the disciplines of communication and journalism, economics, sociology, geography, urban studies, urban planning, library and information science, education, health sciences, transportation, environmental science, and emergency and risk management.

CPRN found that communities need access to eight categories of critical information. Further, this critical information is needed in a timely manner; it must be accessible in an interpretable language; and it must be available through media that diverse communities can reasonably access.

The eight categories of critical needs include information about:

(1) Emergencies and risks, both immediate and long-term;
(2) Health and welfare, including specifically local health information as well as group-specific health information where it exists;
(3) Education, including the quality of local schools and choices available to parents;
(4) Transportation, including available alternatives, costs, and schedules;
(5) Economic opportunities, including job information, job training, and small business assistance;
(6) The environment, including information about air and water quality; environmental threats to health; and access to restoration and recreation;
(7) Civic information, including information on civic institutions and opportunities to associate with others;
(8) Political information, including information about candidates at all relevant levels of local governance, and about relevant public policy initiatives affecting communities and neighborhoods.

Everyday and Quality-of-Life Needs

Emergencies and Public Safety

Perhaps the most fundamental need of all is for access to emergency information that allows individuals, neighborhoods, and communities to protect themselves and their families. This should be fundamental to policymakers, but unfortunately, even after Hurricane Katrina and the shootings at Sandy Hook and San Bernardino, there are no clear national standards for the provision of information about dangerous weather alerts, environmental and other biohazardous outbreaks, or human-caused events. Despite public safety threats, including terrorism, child abduction, mass shootings, and other threats to public order and safety, uniform standards for alerting the public simply do not exist. Further, it is abundantly clear that all citizens need access to local (including neighborhood) information on policing and public safety. However, neither the platforms, nor data, or even data standards, exist in most cities, much less a basic level of interoperability across platforms that would be necessary to ensure the equitable provision of information in situations of high risk.

Even with the spread of cell and smartphones, it should not be assumed that everyone has access to social media (or that information found there in time of disaster is accurate). Seniors are much more likely to depend on radio and television. Even in large cities with large concentrations of immigrants, emergency and risk information is not universally and uniformly available via these most basic regulated media that operate on the public spectrum.

Further, in a nation as diverse as the USA, it seems self-evident that emergency information has to be universally accessible in languages that are understood by the large majority of local populations when a natural or human disaster approaches. New York City public schools recognize 176 languages spoken by its students; the borough of Queens alone contains at least 138. It is estimated that 224 languages are spoken in Los Angeles. But despite this linguistic diversity—part of our heritage of immigration— even the needs of Spanish speakers, the largest linguistic minority in the USA, are generally not being met.

Health

Information on local health and healthcare, including information on family and public health is of vital importance. Broadly, we can distinguish three types of healthcare information. The first is information about health risk, disease, and infirmity. While it is widely assumed that this information is available on the Internet (and a great deal is), this doesn't mean that all populations have equal access to digital services. Nor, as Hargittai and Jennrich argue here, do all members of communities have the *skills* to find and navigate these sources.

The second category is information about health insurance. While much political furor has been expended on the information exchanges created by the Affordable Care Act, these clearly work unevenly, depending on whether a state has created its own exchange, done it well or poorly, or drawn on the federal exchanges. Regardless, as Hamilton and Morgan make clear, the life skills necessary to navigate information about insurance, whether through the exchanges or Medicaid, are far from equally distributed. Information intermediaries have been shown to be important in assisting many Americans to navigate these sites, but again, there is no uniform policy, provision, or even clear knowledge about where they exist and how well they work.

The third type of healthcare information is the availability of *local health services*. CPRN found few examples of local, accessible information about which doctors and hospitals accept Medicaid; where prenatal or well-baby care can be obtained; or about chronic illnesses that affect local populations and their treatment. While there is much research on healthcare information systems, and many studies are devoted to specific local and environmental health problems, very little research has been devoted to understanding the critical health information needs of citizens, especially at the local level (Friedland et al. 2012).

Finally, the same issues of accessible languages and platforms exist for healthcare as for emergency and risk. Information is needed on the availability, quality, and cost of local healthcare for accessibility, lowering costs, and ensuring that markets function properly, including variations by neighborhood and city region; the availability of local public health, programs, and services, including wellness care and local clinics and hospitals; timely information in accessible language on the spread of disease and vaccination; and timely access to information about local health campaigns and interventions.

Education

Education is central to the social well-being of all American families. Where children attend school in our US educational system is primarily determined by their parents' residence. Families reside in communities offering a wide range of educational choices, including public schools, religious schools, charter schools, and even home schooling. Parents need trustworthy information about these choices to judge where or whether to enroll their children. However, we found that there is little information at the local level about local schools presented in ways that all parents can easily navigate and understand, and little research about the choices that exist, despite the widespread installation of charter school and other "choice-systems." This means that, effectively, educational information is too often locked into the personal networks of middle- and upper-middle-class citizens who have the means to obtain and share it privately.

Local communities need access to information on all aspects of the local educational system, decision-making, and resource allocation, including: the quality and administration of local school systems at a community-wide level; the quality of schools within specific neighborhoods and geographic regions; information about educational opportunities, including school performance assessments, enrichment, tutoring, after-school care and programs; information about school alternatives, including charters; information about adult education, including language courses, job training, and GED programs, as well as local opportunities for higher education.

Transportation Systems

If you cannot get to school or the health clinic or the job, you cannot participate effectively in society. We need to know what routes are available or which may be congested during an emergency. We need to know what public transportation is available. We need to know about the safety of our transportation infrastructure. Of course, this is where private communication often works best: radio is saturated with traffic information and Google and other apps provide timely routing. But for those who depend on public transportation for work, finding out routes, times, safety, and other essential information in a clear and timely manner is much more difficult. While real-time transit apps are being developed in many metro systems, these frequently do not work well and generally require a smartphone.

All members of local communities need timely information about local transportation across multiple accessible platforms, including: information about essential transportation services; mass transit at the neighborhood, city, and regional levels; traffic and road conditions, such as those related to weather and closings; and timely access to public debate on transportation at all layers of the local community, including roads and mass transit.

Environment and Planning

The environmental information needs of local communities are vast and complex. At the most basic level, communities need to know about air and water quality in their neighborhoods and urban regions. They need timely alerts of hazards that may not rise to the issue of emergencies, for example, access to the location of nearby brownfields and other potential environmental hazards. In many rural communities, activities such as fracking or farming can have significant local environmental effects, but even when this data is available from public agencies, it is usually not easily accessible and clearly explained. One of the most important environmental information needs is for clear, accessible, and interoperable data, but much of it remains locked in government or private silos.

Beyond hazards, communities need information on their environmental regions: the conditions of local watersheds and habitat for monitoring, but also for opportunities for civic participation in environmental restoration (Fisher et al. 2015). And, of course, communities need access to information about environmental recreational opportunities for children and adults.

While a great deal of this information exists, its availability is often determined by underfunded public agencies. Some states and localities do a much better job than others, but there is insufficient attention to how these kinds of complex, interlocking databases can be pulled together in publicly accessible ways.

Economic Development

Individuals, neighborhoods, and communities need access to a broad range of economic information to find jobs, training, and business opportunities. Private providers appear to have stepped into the partial void left by the decline of classified ads in the past decade. But there is no clear evidence that an online search for employment is as robust for lower-skilled employment, nor, as we have discussed, is access to the broadband and search skills necessary to find jobs equal among job-seekers (in this volume, see Hamilton and Morgan (Chapter 12); Hargittai and Jennrich (Chapter 13)). Employment information and opportunities vary, depending on where one lives. In a comprehensive review, Ionnnides and Loury (2004) demonstrated that finding a job is strongly linked to personal networks in location. So, job search varies by region, as does job training and retraining, apprenticeship opportunities, and other sources of reskilling and advancement. These different contexts call forth different employment information needs by community and neighborhood.

Further, neighborhood boundaries change the information pool about small business opportunities, including startup assistance and capital resources. Redlining (the unethical practice of some financial institutions to make it extremely difficult or impossible for residents of targeted communities to borrow money, gain approval for a mortgage, or become insured) is discrimination that is difficult to prove without recourse to underlying information that could show neighborhood effects or patterns. As banks withdraw from neighborhoods, and as financial activity moves online, important sources of capital based on local knowledge and reputation have dried up, particularly in low-income neighborhoods (Bates and Robb 2015).

Finally, as local journalism continues to shrink, information on economic development initiatives affecting all levels of the local community becomes harder to find, and when it exists, it is often pitched at a general level of city-wide programs, rather than specifying neighborhood opportunities and risks.

CIVIC AND DEMOCRATIC LIFE

Civic Information

Civil society continues to lie at the heart of American democracy in an information age, but the forms of civic association and how we connect with others is changing rapidly. Despite the growing tendency for Americans to associate online, face-to-face organizations in local communities are still the backbone of civic life. In a study of more than 4000 civic events in Chicago, Robert Sampson and colleagues (2005) found that event information is strongly rooted in neighborhood and community organization, and that 85 percent of events concern charity, children, the arts, education, the environment, and local government policy. Clearly, communities need information about these civic institutions, nonprofit organizations, and associations, both major and minor. But local journalism is providing less every year.

There is very little evidence that local Internet services are filling this gap. And even when information is formally available, it is now disbursed over many sources and sites, subject to search, rather than common forms of information provision. Citizens have an ongoing need for information about libraries and community-based information services; cultural and arts information; recreational opportunities; nonprofit groups and associations; community-based social services and programs; and religious institutions and programs. We simply don't know whether and how the local Internet is providing this information because there is very little research on local civic ecologies.

One case study conducted by Friedland in Seattle (2014a) shows that where government policy builds civic communication infrastructure, it is indeed used and leads to a broader distribution not just of hardware, but of community information provision of all types. But the failure of the

FCC, NSF, and others to fund basic and baseline research means that we simply don't know how much civic information is being lost, who navigates, what does exist, and how.

Political Life

Our democracy is multilayered, local, and complex. Citizens need information on every layer of government—local, county, regional, and state—in order to make informed decisions. Historically, this role was played by newspapers first, and then, more widely publicized (at a superficial level) by television. But, as we have discussed, this is increasingly not the case. When most newspapers cover candidates for city council and aldermanic elections, the positions of candidates are rarely developed beyond a few information boxes. Of course, this is even more true for information on elected and voluntary neighborhood councils, school boards, and even county elections.

Beyond elections, citizens need timely information on public meetings and issues, including their outcomes. They need information on where and how to register to vote, including requirements for identification and absentee ballots. And they need information on state-level issues where they impact local policy formation and decisions.

But much of this information is disappearing from political life. As Ferrier shows in this volume, some communities are "news deserts," suffering from little or no news at all. But even those middle- and upper-middle-income communities do not generate sufficient mass to create a demand for political news that markets can satisfy. As Pickard shows, this is leading to a systematic under-production of the news necessary for democracy, a market failure.

LOCATION, LOCATION, LOCATION

Neither these eight critical information needs nor the way that they are met are distributed equally across American communities. Literature from demography in sociology and policy studies shows that American communities vary widely by size (metropolitan [367], micropolitan [576], or rural); racial and ethnic composition; percentage of immigrants; rates of population growth or loss; density; and income distribution (Frey 2015). The overall composition of a given community across these dimensions is a significant determinant of both its overall pattern of community information needs and of the degree to which these needs are likely to be met.

Communities are primarily defined by their geo-spatial and demographic boundaries, but they also represent common sets of identity, cultures, and beliefs that contribute to significant variations within and across communities. Such in-group variations must be taken into account in assessing and responding to critical information needs.

Within a given region (defined as a number of city-regions, sometimes cutting across states), low-income, women, minorities, the disabled, non-English speaking, or other at-risk communities, especially, continue to be disadvantaged in the meeting of community information needs, although existing research makes it difficult to demonstrate precise patterns of disadvantage and how they vary within and across communities. The literature points to several challenges in particular, such as *reduced access to basic information infrastructure* (lower rates of home computer ownership; reduced access to broadband and lower speed broadband; greater reliance on mobile phones, but lower rates of smartphone use; and poorly equipped libraries in low-income communities, despite heavy use); and *fewer opportunities for learning advanced computer skills*, even while these skills are growing in importance for job-seeking, health information, information on local schools, and other basic, everyday needs.

There is evidence of fewer regional and local media, hyperlocal news websites, information blogs, and online sources of neighborhood news in low-income communities, although the evidence is not yet systematic. Although much has been made about the ability of new media to fill the gap left by the decline of traditional reporting, it seems likely that there will be significant gaps, or even "news deserts" in some low-income communities (see Ferrier et al. (Chapter 14)). This may be partly offset in some non-English speaking neighborhoods, although there is no robust general evidence that non-English news fills the local news gap (see Katz and Matsuganis (Chapter 6)).

As low-income communities become information islands, partly cut off from both surrounding neighborhoods and the larger community information system, this can have systematic consequences for larger resource systems, e.g., negative *perceptions* of a neighborhood as stronger predictors of long-term poverty than actual poverty indices (Sampson 2012). For example, there is evidence of growing re-segregation of many local communities. Community information needs are met through a mixture of private and public goods. But lower-income communities are particularly dependent on informational public goods, which are systematically under-produced. Limited case evidence demonstrates that where communities have systematically invested in the information needs of low-income communities, as in Seattle, gaps can be at least partially bridged (Friedland 2014).

We have argued that economic and social differentiation within communities yields differences in the information needs of sub-populations. But, in a nation as varied as the USA, there are differences in information needs and how they are met *across* geographic or metropolitan areas as well. Increasingly, in an information society, those communities that thrive are those with a highly educated population and superior access to both information infrastructure and more developed local news ecologies. Metropolitan typologies (which include rural communities) developed in the past several years, ranging from the Brookings Institution (2012) to those of Gimpel and Chinni (2004, 2010), demonstrate that community information status operates as one of the most significant independent variables predicting economic growth. Those that thrive score high on multiple indicators of information access and robustness; those that struggle are low. Thus, information inequalities within communities can have both short- and medium-term consequences for individuals' access to basic opportunities, and potential long-term consequences for community development. While causality is difficult to determine, some scholars argue that ready access to high-quality actionable information in many domains is an important determinant of economic and societal outcomes (Moretti 2012; Katz and Bradley 2013).

Public Policy

A central premise of this volume is that there must be a public policy for democratic communication and that administrations of both parties have avoided this need for too long. While Republicans have long believed that the market will resolve all information inequalities (ironically, to the point of leading the fight to stifle broadband competition in local communities through state laws passed at the behest of cable and telephone companies), Democrats have failed to address community information needs by omission. Although the FCC under the Obama administration has, as of 2015, made limited moves to override the stifling of broadband in the states, its focus has largely been on network neutrality. While we believe this fight to keep the Internet open is important, it also obscures the failure of the FCC to address the critical community information needs of Americans that we outline in this book.

Federal communications policy, of both parties, is dominated by the combined interests of cable-telephone providers and Silicon Valley. The former seek to preserve their broadband monopolies, the latter to ensure that ever larger numbers of people around the world subscribe to their services with the minimum of government regulation. Silicon Valley has powerful allies in the young and Internet savvy, who famously melted the FCC's servers down after television satirist John Oliver's call to comment on Net Neutrality went viral. But this obscures a real fault line in the information needs of Americans as perceived by both parties.

When the FCC was considering *research* into the critical information needs of Americans in order to determine whether its policies were enabling a communications environment that addressed those needs, the CPRN's comprehensive review showed that while the research record was incomplete, there was strong evidence that the critical information needs of the public were not being met (Friedland et al. 2012). The National Association of Broadcasters strongly opposed the FCC's research plans, and soon after, what Kathleen Hall Jamieson calls the right-wing echo chamber was in full attack mode in an attempt to kill any research into whether local communities were getting their critical information needs met. Republicans threatened investigations, and finally, the small independent research group hired to test the potential of a study design withdrew. Given the firestorm from the right, and the confused and relatively tepid response from both progressive communication policy advocates and the academic community, the FCC moved on to the much more popular concern over net neutrality (Friedland 2014, 92–126).

But the problem of determining whether the public is getting its critical information needs met has not gone away. If anything, this problem is getting worse. More and more newspapers atrophy or go under, leaving gaping holes at the center of American communities' civic communication ecologies. News deserts are growing, and not just in low-income communities. The idea that local websites would open a world of hyperlocal information is being exposed as yet another utopian promise, at least beyond the consumption needs of the young, hip, and well-to-do. So-called "civic coding" (Cohen 2015) may crowdsource potholes, but does nothing to bring basic broadband or information literacy to lower- and middle-income Americans or to shed light on local achievement gaps. The needs of communities for information during emergencies and about healthcare, education, transportation, jobs, and the environment—and not least, for the basic knowledge necessary to fully and freely associate across the growing separation lines of race, ethnicity, and income and to govern ourselves—only grow as we become a plural nation. This volume is a first attempt to put critical community information needs squarely at the center of the agenda for public policy for communication democracy.

REFERENCES

Bates, Timothy, and Alicia Robb. 2015. Impacts of owner race and geographic context on access to small-business financing. *Economic Development Quarterly* 30: 159–170.

Cohen, Rachael. 2015. Pushing civic tech beyond its comfort zone. *The American Prospect* 26: 76.

Fisher, Dana R., Erika S. Svendsen, and James Connolly. 2015. Urban environmental stewardship and civic engagement; how planting trees strengthens the roots of democracy. *Human Ecology* 43(5): 783–784.

Frey, William. 2015. *Diversity explosion: How new racial demographics are remaking America*. Washington, DC: Brookings Institution Press.

Friedland, Lewis. 2014a. Civic communication in a networked society: Seattle's emergent ecology. In *Varieties of civic innovation: Deliberative, collaborative, network, and narrative approaches*. Nashville: Vanderbilt University Press.

Friedland, Lewis. 2014b. The real story behind the FCC's study of newsrooms. *Washington Post*, February 28.

Friedland, Lewis, Philip Napoli, Katherine Ognyanova, Carola Weil, and Ernest J. Wilson III. 2012. *Review of the literature regarding critical information needs of the American public*. Washington, DC: Federal Communications Commission.

Gimpel, James G., and Dante Chinni. 2010. *Our patchwork nation: The surprising truth about the "real" America*. New York: Penguin.

Gimpel, James G., and Jason E. Schuknecht. 2004. *Patchwork nation: Sectionalism and political change in American politics*. Ann Arbor: University of Michigan Press.

Ioannides, Yannis M., and Linda Datcher Loury. 2004. Job information networks, neighborhood effects, and inequality. *Journal of Economic Literature* 42: 1056–1093.

Katz, Bruce, and Jennifer Bradley. 2013. *The metropolitan revolution: How cities and metros are fixing our broken politics and fragile economy*. Washington, DC: Brookings Institution Press.

Moretti, Enrico. 2012. *The new geography of jobs*. Boston: Houghton Mifflin Harcourt.

Sampson, Robert J. 2012. *Great American city: Chicago and the enduring neighborhood effect*. Chicago: University of Chicago Press.

Sampson, Robert J., Doug McAdam, Heather MacIndoe, and Simon Weffer-Elizondo. 2005. Civil society reconsidered: The durable nature and community structure of collective civic action1. *American Journal of Sociology* 111(3): 673–714.

CHAPTER 2

Understanding Our New Communications Economy: Implications for Contemporary Journalism

Philip M. Napoli

INTRODUCTION

Working to ensure that the American public's critical information needs are being met requires developing a comprehensive understanding of how today's increasingly complicated communications economy operates. Over the past two decades, we have seen new media platforms develop alongside established media platforms, with effects that have been difficult to disentangle. For instance, while new media have, to some extent, undermined the business models of traditional news media, they have also provided new avenues for the production and dissemination of news and information. New media platforms are, in many ways, reliant on traditional media for content, yet at the same time, they foster means of content production and dissemination that are largely freed from the traditional bottlenecks associated with legacy media. However, these newer platforms operate as gatekeepers in their own right, often employing algorithmic curation and filtering systems that are increasingly important to new outlets' efforts to reach audiences.

P.M. Napoli (✉)
Duke University, Durham, NC, USA

© The Editor(s) (if applicable) and The Author(s) 2016   17
M.I. Lloyd, L.A. Friedland (eds.), *The Communication Crisis in America, And How to Fix It*, DOI 10.1057/978-1-349-94925-0_2

This complex interplay between emerging and legacy media, and how they are managed and operated in the production and dissemination of news and information, needs to be better understood in terms of the positive and negative effects on the extent to which communities' information needs are being met (Picard 2014). However, the bottom line is that today's communications economy is fundamentally different from the communications economy that characterized the "mass media era" that preceded it, in ways that can dramatically affect the production, dissemination, and consumption of news and information that are critical to the effective functioning of democracy.

In addressing this economic transformation, the first section of this chapter reviews how technological changes have undermined some of the fundamental aspects of the traditional business models for organizations involved in the production and dissemination of news. The second section explores new mechanisms for the production and dissemination of news that have emerged from these technological changes, and the alternative economic models that have accompanied them. Throughout these discussions, connections will be drawn between the technological and economic changes taking place and some of the fundamental economic characteristics of news and the audiences that consume news.

THE DECLINE OF THE TRADITIONAL BUSINESS MODEL FOR NEWS

It is hard to imagine a topic that has been more comprehensively chronicled and analyzed than the dramatic effect that technological changes have had on the economics of the US news industry (see, e.g., Anderson et al. 2012; Downie and Schudson 2009; Knight Commission 2009). This narrative typically starts with the rise of the Internet in the 1990s and the quick decision by many local newspapers to make their content available online for free. Some still point to this decision (driven largely by a lemming-like mentality to follow suit with what other papers were doing) as a key strategic error that contributed to the economic decline of the traditional business model for news—one in which the revenues from the sale of newspapers to consumers and revenues from the sale of news audiences to advertisers were both vitally important to newspapers' bottom lines (Tofel 2012). According to this perspective, the established expectation among news consumers that news costs money was quickly undermined. Search engines, portals, other aggregators, and of course, the rise of user-generated content, contributed to this process by further establishing the web as a place where news could be found for free (Downie and Schudson 2009).

However, there were additional factors that undermined the traditional news economy. Accounts of the ways that the Internet undermined the economics of news also point to the loss of advertising revenues that newspapers have been experiencing over time (Downie and Schudson 2009). Part of the issue here is, of course, that the Internet has provided a much more competitive audience marketplace, in which there is an expansive array of options for audiences and for advertisers looking to reach consumers. The result has been a reconfiguring of the supply and demand dynamics for audiences in such a way that supply exceeds demand to a greater extent than was ever possible within traditional media. Partially as a reflection of this dynamic, it has also been the case that advertisers have demonstrated a persistent unwillingness to pay as much, on a cost-per-thousand basis for audiences reached online as for audiences reached via other platforms, such as print and television (though this has started to change) (Grueskin et al 2013).

The measurement of online audiences has been another key factor that has undermined the online audience marketplace (Napoli 2011). To this day, the measurement of online audiences is considered unreliable, given the difficulties in tracking audience demographics across so many online sources and growing evidence that many of the online "exposures" are in fact not humans at all, but rather various bots and web-crawling engines mistakenly being registered as legitimate "impressions" (White Ops 2014).

From a measurement standpoint, the irony is that the Internet has presented a more measurable (more "accountable," to use the industry parlance) environment for placing advertisements, given that audiences' direct responses can be measured via click-through rates and subsequent purchasing behaviors. What this has meant, though, is a significant shift in the online audience marketplace in comparison to traditional media. Specifically, instead of all audiences exposed to the content being monetized (a convention that has characterized most traditional media), advertisers now frequently only pay for those members of the audience who either click on an advertisement or go one step further and make a purchase. This has meant that, in many cases, the bulk of audience "impressions" are not monetized (Napoli 2011).

This shift would not be fundamentally problematic if a sufficient premium were being paid for those audiences who click-through and/or make a purchase, to compensate for all the many others who are merely exposed to an ad and don't take any subsequent action. But this has not yet turned out to be the case (Napoli 2011). And so, in migrating their content online, and initially making it available for free, news outlets found themselves relying on the revenues from an audience marketplace that have thus far proven inadequate compensation for the revenues lost through the more traditional exposure-based model that characterized print and the early days of the web.

The dynamics of this decline accentuate a key characteristic of the traditional business model for news, and one of the key ways that technology has transformed the contemporary communications economy. Specifically, when we look back at the relatively vibrant economics for news that characterized the pre-Internet era, we need to recognize that one of the defining aspects of the legacy model was that news was effectively bundled with other potentially higher-value products and services (coupons, classifieds, horoscopes, comics). This is important in that we can't look at the revenues of news organizations in the pre-Internet era as any kind of meaningful indication of a higher level of demand for news. News benefited from consumer demand for the wide range of information products and services that accompanied news—a subsidy model of sorts that helped to provide a stable and robust economic foundation for the production of news.

The irony is that some of these highly valued bundled products were the advertisements (classifieds, coupons, etc.); so much so that, in the digital age, many of the most successful online enterprises were essentially based upon disaggregating these advertising categories from local newspapers and offering them as stand-alone services (e.g., Ebay, Craigslist, Monster, etc.).

This unbundling, or disaggregation of content into discrete units, is a defining characteristic of the contemporary media economy (McCann 2015). Whether it is albums being disaggregated into digital singles in the music industry or the bundling of multiple cable networks into large, costly packages straining under the pressures of increased "cord-cutting" and "over-the-top" programming options, the availability of content through digital, high-bandwidth, interactive, and on-demand platforms results in an environment in which consumers increasingly demand and receive content in discrete, disaggregated forms.

And so, news readers are less likely to even visit an online news site, with its bundle of news stories on different topics presented on the site's home page and on subsequent pages. Rather, they are more likely to first encounter an individual story in isolation from the rest of the news site's content, on their social media feeds, where content that has been disaggregated from its original source is reaggregated into a more personalized, algorithmically curated mix, across a wide range of online sources (Pew Research Center 2015). This process of reconfiguring the dynamics of news distribution and consumption has been accompanied by a redistribution of revenues, with social media platforms and other aggregators inserting themselves in between the relationship between news producers and news consumers and extracting a significant portion of the advertising revenue that could potentially have found its way to the originating news site instead (Hof 2012).

The Evolving News Ecosystem

This latter example brings us to the issue of the evolving news ecosystem of today, in which alternative modes of producing, distributing, and monetizing news (and news audiences) are being pursued, and in which some new realities about how news and information production can be sustained are beginning to be recognized.

Algorithms and Automation

First, it is important to recognize the increasingly important role that algorithms are playing in the production, distribution, and consumption of news (see, e.g., Napoli 2015). On the production side, algorithms and big data are serving as an increasingly important mechanism for analyzing and predicting demand for news and information (see, e.g., Napoli 2014a). In some cases, such as Patch, AOL's failed hyper-local news venture, algorithms were used to analyze demographic, social, and political variables related to specific geographic communities and their anticipated demand for local news, in order to determine where local news outlets are established (Tartakoff 2010). So, for instance, the presence of Starbucks in a community was utilized as a relevant input in determining whether a Patch venture should be initiated. In this way, the very existence of local news operations is, to some extent, being algorithmically dictated.

In addition, news organizations are increasingly relying on analyses of various forms of user behavior and feedback data to more precisely calibrate their newsgathering and reporting activities (Bockzkowski and Mitchelstein 2013). Many newsrooms now operate with comprehensive and immediate feedback related to various aspects of online news consumption, ranging from page views to time spent on a site/story, to ratings, to volume and valence of comments. Today, there is a growing array of data sources and analytical tools that can be used to analyze local news audiences (see, e.g., Ellis 2015), all of which take advantage of the inherent interactivity of online news consumption and the variety of data footprints that news consumers leave online. A growing body of literature is exploring how various quantitative forms of audience analytics are being integrated into newsroom decision-making, to both positive and negative effect (see, e.g., Anderson 2011; McKenzie et al. 2011; Tandoc and Thomas 2015).

Many of these newer analytical tools (such as Chartbeat and the multitude of purveyors of social media analytics) offer the opportunity to conduct highly detailed, granular analyses of the audiences of individual online news stories, how long they spend on individual stories, and how these stories are circulating—and being responded to—in the larger media ecosystem. Such data are proving increasingly influential to how news is produced.

"Content farms" represent an extreme case of this type of demand-driven journalistic production. Content farms mine search-engine data to estimate demand for content on various topics, and then produce that content rapidly and cheaply in order to meet that demand (Bakker 2012). Once again, the process is algorithmically driven. Leading content farm Demand Media, for instance, feeds its algorithm three types of data: (a) popular search terms from search engines; (b) the ad market for keywords (i.e., which keywords are currently being sought and how much is being paid for them); and (c) the competitive environment (in terms of content that's already available online) (Roth 2009). The output then represents a prediction of the type of content for which there is the highest unmet audience and advertiser demand, and Demand Media produces that content accordingly.

Algorithms play a role not only as a means of predicting and estimating audience demand for various types of news stories, but also, increasingly, as a means of producing the actual journalism to meet these demands (Napoli 2014a). This model is at the core of firms such as Narrative Science, a start-up based around a software package that can generate complete news stories once it is fed the core data on which the stories will be based (e.g., sporting event scores and statistics, company financial reports, housing data, survey data) (Lohr 2011).

All of these examples of the role that algorithms are playing in the new communications can be seen as reflections of the changing economic climate for news. Here, we see an industry desperately in search of tools that will allow for a tighter congruence between news supply and news demand. Of course, one of the long-standing ethical debates in journalism involves the extent to which the dynamics of consumer demand should dictate news production (see, e.g., McCollough et al. 2015; McManus 1994). This debate revolves around questions about whether efforts to achieve better congruence between what news outlets produce and what news consumers want is beneficial from a broader public interest standpoint. We're also witnessing efforts (through algorithmic news generation) to dramatically reduce the costs of producing journalism by essentially automating the process as much as possible, allowing for the substituting of relatively expensive and less productive human employees with relatively cheap and more productive news story-generating software packages; a process that also theoretically allows for reporting on a greater range of topics and issues to take place.

As was noted above, audiences' consumption of news is also being dramatically affected by what we might call algorithmic intermediaries—search engines and (increasingly) social media platforms that curate and filter news audiences' exposure to news (Bucher 2012; Napoli 2014b, 2015). In many ways, this rise of algorithmic intermediaries is understandable as a means of assisting audiences navigating an increasingly complex and fragmented media environment. To some extent, one could argue that content has become commodified, with the real value residing in the systems that users can employ to navigate through and select from the wealth of available content. The bottom line, however, is that the new news economy is increasingly dominated by a new type of intermediary that has been inserted into the process and has the capabilities to perform many of the gatekeeping functions that long have been associated with traditional media (Gillespie 2014).

This is a position that not only provides these intermediaries with the potential for tremendous political influence (see, e.g., Gillespie 2014; Napoli 2014b, 2015), but that also puts them in a position to dramatically reconfigure the dynamics of the contemporary news economy. Facebook, for instance, has used its increasingly influential position as intermediary in the contemporary news ecosystem to launch a service called Instant Articles for its mobile platform. Online publishers that participate in the

Instant Articles program allow the entirety of their article to be hosted by—and accessed via—Facebook, rather than the reader being linked back to the originating source's website (Marshall 2015a). The fact that publishers such as the *New York Times* and the *Washington Post* are participating in this program highlights the centrality of Facebook to contemporary news distribution and consumption, and the leverage that the platform holds over news outlets. And perhaps it is not surprising that concerns are already being raised about whether publishers are receiving their fair share of the advertising revenue generated through Instant Articles (Marshall 2015b).

Single-Subject News

Another direction in which the contemporary news economy is evolving is a reflection of the processes of disaggregation and reaggregation discussed above. Specifically, as news has been disaggregated from its traditional multi-topic and multi-interest bundles, a key characteristic of the reaggregation process has been the rise of specialized, targeted, single-issue news services that focus exclusively on specific topics such as education, politics, or the environment. This "single subject news model" may very well become a defining characteristic of the modern news economy (Nolan and Setrakian 2014). This model essentially reflects the extent to which a diversity of interests can be served online, with the reach of online media making it possible to develop news and information services that aggregate audiences with a strong interest in a particular topic from across the country (or even the world). Put in terms that long have been used to describe the nature of the diversity of news and information available to consumers (see, e.g., Napoli 1999), the evolving model appears to be one of horizontal diversity (subject matter diversity *across* news sources) rather than vertical diversity (subject matter diversity *within* news sources).

Audience Engagement

In this fragmented media ecosystem, in which attracting and retaining audiences is increasingly difficult, given the range of options available to news consumers, one of the perhaps most significant shifts that has taken place in the communications economy—and in the news economy in particular—is a rethinking by content providers and advertisers of how to assess and value audiences (Napoli 2011). In a media environment in which small audiences are the rule rather than the exception, it has proven necessary for content providers such as news organizations to explore dimensions of their audience beyond their size and demographic characteristics that advertisers might find valuable. Conveniently, it so happens that the contemporary media environment also is one in which there is an increasing flow of audience data from a variety of sources (see above). From this confluence of circumstances, we have the contemporary emphasis on audience engagement in journalism (Batsell 2015).

Audience engagement seems to be functioning both as a means and an end in the contemporary communications economy. That is, news organizations have accumulated a growing body of evidence that more engaged audiences are more likely to be frequent visitors to their sites. From this standpoint, engagement is a means of audience expansion and retention. At the same time, advertisers are increasingly embracing notions of audience engagement as an alternative or supplementary source of audience value. That is, higher levels of engagement are being seen as a reason for valuing one site's audience more than another's (Napoli 2011).

Shifting Dynamics Between Large and Small Market Journalism

Another characteristic of the contemporary communications economy is the shifting of journalistic resources away from smaller markets and towards larger markets. For instance, one recent report noted that large cities such as New York, Washington, D.C., and Los Angeles are employing an increasing proportion of the country's professional journalists, with smaller cities experiencing dramatic declines (Tankersley 2015).

In many ways, this pattern is a reflection of how technological change is accentuating some of the fundamental characteristics of media content such as news. Specifically, news is what economists call a "public good" (see Hamilton 2004). Public goods are not used up in consumption. That is, once someone consumes a news story, that news story is still available to be consumed by many other people without the producer incurring additional cost—unlike, say, cars, where each car sold requires that another car be manufactured in order for the next car to be sold. Public goods thus also have very low variable costs, which means there can be tremendous economies of scale in their production, as producers try to spread the production costs across as large an audience as possible. And, of course, public goods such as news (or movies, or music) have always been inherently vulnerable to piracy, along with basic sharing, which makes it challenging for producers to recoup revenues that reflect the true level of demand for the content. And finally, research tells us that budgets are an excellent predictor of audience's media consumption patterns (Owen and Wildman 1992). That is, given a choice, media consumers will gravitate to higher-budget content over lower-budget content.

One of the key ways the Internet has transformed the communications economy involves how content can so easily be shared (think about the ease of pirating or sharing digital content today, compared to hard copies in the pre-digital era) and move across geographic boundaries (think, for instance, of the ease of having a news site with a national or international audience reach, versus distributing a print publication nationally or globally). This, of course, makes it more difficult for news producers to capture revenues that even begin to approximate the true level of demand for their content.

Further, these dimensions of the Internet have exacerbated the prominence of "one way flows"—a term that refers to the phenomenon in which content flows from large markets to small markets and not vice versa, given audiences' general preference for higher-budget content, and that content in larger markets generally has larger production budgets than content produced for smaller markets. We know, for instance, that the 100 most popular online news sources have a larger share of the total online news audience than the 100 most popular print newspapers have of the total print news audience (Hindman 2008). Once the geographic boundaries to distribution are removed, audiences' natural tendency to gravitate toward larger-market, higher-budget content becomes more pronounced. And so, as the example reported above about the migration of journalism jobs to large markets illustrates, we seem to be witnessing the evolution of a news economy that more strongly favors the production, dissemination, and consumption of national content over local content.

The end result of these conditions appears to be what some have termed a "mega-site effect," in which more and more audience attention migrates away from local news sources to larger market news sources, whether they be focused on the state, national, or international levels. This creates something of a vicious circle as the economic base for local journalism erodes. This erosion, in turn, undermines investment in local journalism. This decline in investment diminishes the relative appeal of local journalism to mega-sites, or to single-subject news sites (which also tend to have a national or international orientation), which further exacerbates audience erosion and thereby circles us back to further declines in investment.

Given, as other chapters in this volume discuss, that diminished attention to local news can disengage residents from their communities (culturally, politically, and in civic terms), the end result is an economic phenomenon with potentially dramatic social and political repercussions.

CONCLUSION

Today, the contemporary news industry is in the midst of a wide-ranging search for alternative means of staying viable. Given that, in the USA, the political culture is still one in which any notion of substantial public funding for journalism can not find its way onto the public agenda, the focus remains on finding viable commercial models. Even the growing number of foundations that are fortunately devoting resources to a wide range of journalism enterprises are doing so generally with the expectation that at least some of these enterprises will become self-sustaining. These foundations are not committing themselves to supporting journalism in perpetuity; nor is it realistic to expect them to do so. Similarly, there remain a host of unanswered questions about whether various forms of citizen and participatory journalism can function as an effective and sustainable substitute for the diminished capacity of professional news organizations.

And so, as was illustrated above, we see a range of approaches by news organizations to navigate the contemporary communications economy. These approaches involve dramatic changes to how news is produced and distributed, how news audiences are valued, and even to which types of communities are likely to receive robust news and information and which types are not (see, e.g., Napoli et al. 2016). The danger here, of course, is that local news will increasingly be oriented primarily around the dwindling number of communities in which the financial resources of consumers and producers, and/or the economic value of news audiences, are sufficient to support its production. In an environment in which the economics of local journalism is increasingly challenging, the future of local journalism may be increasingly focused on those communities in which there are individuals and organizations that are in the position to invest in local journalism as more of a public service than a business enterprise (Napoli et al. 2016).

The news economy remains very much in a state of flux. It seems reasonable to expect continued change to how audiences are valued and measured, and in how news content is produced, disseminated, and consumed. But, as this chapter has hopefully illustrated, the nature of the technological changes that have affected the news industry have had such dramatic effects because of the fundamental ways that these technological changes have interacted with certain fundamental economic characteristics of news content, news audiences, and the news marketplace as a whole.

REFERENCES

Anderson, Chris W. 2011. Deliberative, agonistic, and algorithmic audiences: Journalism's vision of its public in an age of audience transparency. *International Journal of Communication* 5: 529–547.

Anderson, Chris W., Emily Bell and Clay Shirky. 2012. *Post-industrial journalism: Adapting to the present.* Tow Center for Digital Journalism. Available at http://towcenter.org/research/post-industrial-journalism/.

Bakker, Piet. 2012. Aggregation, content farms, and huffinization: The rise of low-pay and no-pay journalism. *Journalism Practice* 6(5–6): 627–637. doi:10.1080/17512786.2012.667266.

Batsell, Jake. 2015. *Engaged journalism: Connecting with digitally empowered news audiences.* New York: Columbia University Press.

Boczkowski, Pablo J., and Eugenia Mitchelstein. 2013. *The news gap: When the information preferences of the media and the public diverge.* Cambridge, MA: MIT Press.

Bucher, Taina. 2012. A technicity of attention: How software 'makes sense'. *Culture Machine* 13: 1–23.

Downie, Leonard Jr., and Michael Schudson. 2009. The reconstruction of American journalism. *Columbia Journalism Review.* Available at http://www.cjr.org/reconstruction/the_reconstruction_of_american.php.

Ellis, Justin. 2015. Deciphering what the next generation of public radio listeners wants through NPR One. *Nieman Lab*, May 7. Retrieved from http://www.niemanlab.org/2015/05/deciphering-what-the-next-generation-of-public-radio-listeners-wants-through-npr-one/.

Gillespie, Tarleton. 2014. The relevance of algorithms. In *Media technologies*, ed. Tarleton Gillespie, Pablo J. Boczkowski, and Kirsten A. Foot, 167–194. Cambridge, MA: MIT Press.

Grueskin, Bill, Ava Seave, and Lucas Graves. *The story so far: What we know about the business of digital journalism.* Tow Center for Digital Journalism. Available at http://academiccommons.columbia.edu/download/fedora_content/download/ac:144480/CONTENT/The_Story_So_Far.pdf.

Hamilton, James T. 2004. *All the news that's fit to sell: How the market transforms information into news.* Princeton: Princeton University Press.

Hindman, Matthew. 2008. *The myth of digital democracy.* Princeton: Princeton University Press.

Hof, Robert. 2012. How tech firms steal all the ad dollars from news media. *Forbes*, March 19. Available at http://www.forbes.com/sites/roberthof/2012/03/19/how-tech-companies-steal-all-the-ad-revenues-from-news-media/.

Knight Commission. 2009. Informing communities: Sustaining democracy in the digital age. In *The report of the Knight Commission on the information needs of communities in a democracy*. Available at http://www.knightcomm.org/read-the-report-and-comment/.

Lohr, Steve. 2011. In case you wondered, a real human wrote this. *New York Times*, September 10. Available at http://www.nytimes.com/2011/09/11/business/computer-generated-articles-are-gaining-traction.html?pagewanted=all&_r=0.

Marshall, Jack. 2015a. Facebook's instant articles could mean less traffic for websites. *Wall Street Journal*, October 28. Available at http://www.wsj.com/articles/facebooks-instant-articles-could-mean-less-traffic-for-websites-1446028207.

Marshall, Jack. 2015b. Facebook mulls ad changes for Instant Articles after publisher pushback. *Wall Street Journal*, November 11. Available at http://www.wsj.com/articles/facebook-mulls-ad-changes-for-instant-articles-after-publisher-pushback-1447281399.

McCann, Joe. 2015. The unbundling of everything. *TechCrunch*, April 18. Available at http://techcrunch.com/2015/04/18/the-unbundling-of-everything/.

McCollough, Kathleen, Jessica Crowell, and Philip M. Napoli. 2015. *Portrait of the online local news audience*. News Measures Research Project. Available at http://mpii.rutgers.edu/wp-content/uploads/sites/129/2015/06/Portrait-of-the-Online-Local-News-Audience_Nov-2015.pdf.

McKenzie, Carly T., Wilson Lowrey, Hal Hayes, Jee Young Chung, and Chang Wan Woo. 2011. Listening to news audiences: The impact of community structure and economic factors. *Mass Communication & Society* 14: 375–395.

McManus, John H. 1994. *Market-driven journalism: Let the citizen beware?* Thousand Oaks: Sage.

Napoli, Philip M. 1999. Deconstructing the diversity principle. *Journal of Communication* 49(4): 7–34.

Napoli, Philip M. 2011. *Audience evolution: New technologies and the transformation of media audiences*. New York: Columbia University Press.

Napoli, Philip M. 2015. Social media and the public interest: Governance of news platforms in the realm of individual and algorithmic gatekeepers. *Telecommunications Policy* 39: 251–760.

Napoli, Philip M. 2014a. On automation in media industries: Integrating algorithmic media production into media industries scholarship. *Media Industries Journal* 1(1): 33–38.

Napoli, Philip M. 2014b. Automated media: An institutional theory perspective on algorithmic media production and consumption. *Communication Theory* 24: 340–360.

Napoli, Philip M., S. Stonbely, K. McCollough, and B. Renninger. 2016. Local journalism and the information needs of local communities: Toward a scalable assessment approach. *Journalism Practice.*

Nolan, Kristin, and Lara Setrakian. 2014. *Seeking the single-subject news model.* Tow Center for Digital Journalism. Available at http://towcenter.org/wp-content/uploads/2013/11/Seeking-The-Single-Subject-News-Model.pdf.

Owen, Bruce M., and Steven S. Wildman. 1992. *Video economics.* Cambridge, MA: Harvard University Press.

Pew Research Center. 2015. *The evolving role of news on Twitter and Facebook.* Pew Research Center. Available at http://www.journalism.org/files/2015/07/Twitter-and-News-Survey-Report-FINAL2.pdf.

Picard, Robert G. 2014. Twilight or new dawn of journalism? Evidence from the changing news ecosystem. *Digital Journalism* 2(3): 273–283.

Roth, Daniel. 2009. The answer factory: Demand media and the fast, disposable, and profitable as hell media model. *Wired*, October 19. Available at http://www.wired.com/2009/10/ff_demandmedia/.

Tandoc Jr., Edson C., and Ryan J. Thomas. 2015. The ethics of web analytics: Implications of using audience metrics in news construction. *Digital Journalism* 3(2): 243–258.

Tankersley, Jim. 2015. Why the PR industry is sucking up Pulitzer winners. *The Washington Post*, April 23. Available at http://www.washingtonpost.com/blogs/wonkblog/wp/2015/04/23/why-the-pr-industry-is-sucking-up-pulitzer-winners/.

Tartakoff, Joseph. 2010. AOL's Patch aims to quintuple size by year-end. *paidContent*, August 17.

Tofel, Richard. 2012. *Why American newspapers gave away the future.* Santa Monica: Now and Then Reader.

White Ops, Inc. 2014. *The bot baseline: Fraud in digital advertising.* Association of National Advertisers. Available at https://www.ana.net/getfile/21853.

CHAPTER 3

Researching Community Information Needs

Katherine Ognyanova

The complex processes of information packaging, dissemination, and consumption in a contemporary communication ecology have been examined in a variety of disciplines employing a wide range of theoretical and methodological frameworks. This chapter provides a brief overview of major theory-driven approaches contributing to the evaluation of community information needs (CIN) and the extent to which those needs are met in a given context. The frameworks outlined here are grounded in: (1) communication ecology and multilevel approaches; (2) economics research, market, and audience analyses; (3) information inequality and digital exclusion; (4) mass communication and content analysis; and (5) computational social science and network analysis. While this list is by no means exhaustive, much of the relevant academic, industry, and policy research falls into one or more of those five categories.

COMMUNICATION ECOLOGIES AND COMMUNITY RESEARCH

Understanding a community is a critical step in identifying and evaluating individual and group information needs. Research in that area builds on a long tradition of studies exploring the social fabric of neighborhoods and

K. Ognyanova (✉)
Rutgers University, New Brunswick, NJ, USA

© The Editor(s) (if applicable) and The Author(s) 2016   31
M.I. Lloyd, L.A. Friedland (eds.), *The Communication Crisis in America, And How to Fix It*, DOI 10.1057/978-1-349-94925-0_3

its implications for civic engagement (Putnam 2000)—a theoretical focus that has retained its relevance in the age of digital communication.

A defining feature of studies in this tradition is the multilevel approach examining nested structures—from individuals, through families, to neighborhoods and cities, combined with a high-level view on the forces that shape an urban environment. Those investigations often use multifaceted mixed-method designs combining quantitative and qualitative analysis.

Mixed-method studies of metropolitan, neighborhood, and interpersonal communication processes are at the core of major ecological projects conducted in a wide range of communities. Research efforts in the USA have explored communication and media ecologies in large metropolitan areas, including Los Angeles (Chen et al. 2013), Philadelphia (Schaffer 2010), Seattle (Friedland 2013), and Baltimore (Pew Research 2010) as well as mid-sized and smaller cities like Madison, Wisconsin (Friedland et al. 2007); Macon, Georgia (Mitchell et al. 2015); New Brunswick, Newark; and Morristown, New Jersey (Napoli et al. 2015).

Sampson's *Great American City* (2012), grounded in the Chicago School tradition of urban sociology, provides one of the most comprehensive recent examples of ecological community research. The analyses reported in the volume are based on eight years of cohort studies, community surveys, systematic social observation, experiments, and multiwave network analysis seeking to identify community leaders.

Another set of studies explicitly adopting the multilevel ecological approach to urban neighborhoods is grounded in *communication infrastructure theory* (Ball-Rokeach and Jung 2004; Chen et al. 2013). This framework examines CIN in the context of larger social systems, incorporating demographic and institutional processes. The media ecology of residents is seen as a subset of their total connections to communication resources, both interpersonal and organizational. A central concept in that research is the *neighborhood storytelling network*, a system encompassing residents, local media, and organizations, as well as the connections within and among them (Kim et al. 2006). A strong storytelling network was found to enhance civic outcomes including engagement, collective efficacy, and neighborhood belonging.

Focusing on the interplay between social relations and space in an urban environment, Friedland (2001) advances the *communicatively integrated community* framework, which encompasses power relations and communicative action at global, regional, metropolitan, and local levels. His follow-up works in this ecological line of research examine the interplay between community and media over time (Friedland et al. 2007), as well as the interactions between civic and communication ecologies (Friedland 2013).

Some recent efforts to explore the information needs of communities have focused on an ecological understanding of journalism. One example comes from *The Media + the Public Interest Initiative*, which explores three cities in the state of New Jersey (Napoli et al. 2015). The parameters examined in that research include the local journalism infrastructure, encompassing news sources and their social media presence—as well as journalistic output and performance, measuring the number of news stories and posts and their ability to address the critical information needs of the community.

The efforts to examine CIN through ecological studies expand beyond the realm of academia. In a high-profile report, the Knight Commission (2009) urged researchers, policymakers, and organizations to pursue three key objectives: (1) making relevant and credible information available to all, (2) strengthening the capacity of individuals to engage with information by providing access to needed tools and skills, and (3) promoting engagement with both local information and the public life in communities, leading to a more effective self-governance. Following that call, the Federal Communications Commission (FCC) commissioned two comprehensive reports exploring the US media landscape and the critical information needs of Americans (Waldman 2011; Friedland et al. 2012).

The Pew Research Center is another organization evaluating the local news ecologies in a diverse set of US communities (Rosenstiel et al. 2011; Mitchell et al. 2015). Their most recent project focusing on local news in three metro areas includes six studies that: (1) identified local news providers; (2) surveyed local residents about their news consumption; (3) analyzed and coded news stories produced in the target areas; (4) conducted interviews with residents, journalists, local officials, and businesses; (5) explored the news and information carried by social media platforms; and (6) examined city-level variables including geography, population size, demographics, and broadband penetration.

One important aspect of community research that deserves to be mentioned separately involves the role of technology. Online and mobile platforms, social media, and participatory digital spaces have become a crucial part of the communication infrastructure of American communities. Scholars have developed a variety of conceptual frameworks explaining the profound changes in social networks and information flows in a digital age

(Hampton 2015; Wellman and Rainie 2012; Castells 1996). Reflecting the critical importance of digital communication patterns, recent works evaluating the health of community news and information systems, almost without exception, incorporate investigations of the availability and access to digital content.

ECONOMIC RESEARCH: MARKET AND AUDIENCE ANALYSES

Works in this tradition explore the demand and supply dynamics that influence the availability of news and information in local communities. Economic studies of the media system have examined the effects of audience preferences, advertising demands, and competition (Dimmick 2003; McManus 1994). Media outlets vary in size, location, projected identity, social context, target audiences, political orientation, production technologies, available resources, and ties to other organizations. All of those characteristics—and more—affect content production (Allern 2002). This has clear implications for an informed citizenry, as mainstream media still have a leading role in producing current affairs news and shaping public opinion (Shehata and Stromback 2013).

The economic approach has been used to examine the factors that cause underproduction of local, political, and public affairs coverage. In a comprehensive investigation of the market forces underpinning the media business, Hamilton (2004) describes the economic characteristics of news products as information goods. His book discusses the complicated realities of commercial media models that need to satisfy both advertiser demands and consumer preferences. Story coverage is tailored to maximize its appeal to key demographic groups: those who are most likely to buy the advertised products. When target audiences place low value on hard news, media outlets have an incentive to reduce current affairs and political reporting in favor of entertainment and sports coverage.

Works in that line of research have explored the impact of economic factors like ownership and market structure on a variety of outcomes, including individual news consumption (Althaus et al. 2009), political behavior and election turnout (Althaus and Trautman 2008), the availability of local news (George and Waldfogel 2006), the quality of political coverage (Dunaway 2008), and the political slant of news sources (Gentzkow and Shapiro 2010).

One central theme in economic studies of the media system is the relationship between markets and media diversity. Diversity is a major regulatory concern, as maintaining a pluralism of voices in the media is essential for a healthy democracy. The diversity principle can be seen as comprising three separate measurable components: *source, content,* and *exposure* diversity (Napoli 1999).

The *source* dimension refers to the ownership and workforce diversity of media organizations and program producers. The *content* component examines the range of programming available to audience members, and its diversity in terms of type, target audience, and represented viewpoints. The *exposure* dimension shifts the focus from the content that is made available to the content that people actually consume. Metrics of that type evaluate the number and type of outlets and programs selected by the public, as well as the range of viewpoints presented by those outlets.

The FCC has launched a number of efforts to evaluate media diversity. One such effort involved the development of a Diversity Index for local media markets meant to serve as an evaluation instrument in media ownership regulation. The index sparked controversy. It was eventually challenged in court, and its use was suspended (Lloyd and Napoli 2007). The FCC's further efforts to examine the critical information needs of US communities were put on indefinite hold after coming under strong criticism from several media outlets and members of Congress.

Another key theme here is audience fragmentation (Napoli 2011): the idea that as information gets increasingly personalized, mass audiences may dissolve into small, isolated groups. Scholars have predicted a coming era of *cyberbalkanization* (Sunstein 2007) and filter bubbles (Pariser 2011). Empirical research, however, has found no conclusive evidence to support those predictions. In a set of studies unpacking audience fragmentation across traditional and online news sources, Webster (2014) finds high levels of duplication across media outlets and no evidence of isolation in like-minded consumption groups.

Information Inequality and Digital Exclusion Research

Evaluating information inequalities is crucial for any effort seeking to identify the complex social, economic, and technological factors that come together to produce informed communities. Contemporary debates of inequality in this context incorporate three major aspects: (1) predictors and patterns of disparity in the production of information relevant to different social groups; (2) inequalities in the quantity and quality of access to information and participation; and (3) differences in training, skills, and digital literacy levels. Some of the major parameters defining the information divides in the USA today include geography, language, age, income, education, race and ethnicity, immigration status, disability, gender, and sexual orientation.

Works evaluating the inequality in content production systems have often focused on the role of female and minority ownership and employment in media organizations. Policy-relevant research has demonstrated a link between the quality and quantity of content directed at different demographic groups and their presence in the workforce and management of news companies (Bachen et al. 2007). Nonetheless, women and ethnic minorities remain underrepresented in many areas of the media industry, especially at the higher levels (Hunt 2014; American Society of News Editors 2015; Papper 2015). Discussing the costs of exclusion, Costanza-Chock and Wilson (2012) examine disparities in ownership in print, broadcast, and online media. While they find more diversity of ownership on the Internet as compared to offline outlets, their results suggest that even online sources are infrequently owned by people of color to a disproportionate degree.

Early research on information inequality was focused on the *digital divide*, individual and community-level disparities in access to information and communication technologies. Today, the gap in access to devices and Internet connection is narrower, though recent reports still show lower penetration in rural communities and among the elderly, people with disabilities, and those in the lowest education and income brackets (Rainie 2015). Even larger disparities remain with regard to the quality of access and technology used across groups. A recent report by the White House (Council of Economic Advisers 2015) describes a *broadband gap* in the USA: high-speed Internet services still have much lower availability, market competitiveness, and end-user penetration in rural and low-income communities.

Perhaps more importantly, inequalities remain in the areas of digital literacy, skills, and types of use. Different online activities have different outcomes, some more beneficial than others. Internet use can focus on entertainment, or it can provide a chance for advancing one's education, career, and financial status by accruing economic, social, and cultural capital (van Deursen and van Dijk 2014).

Examining differences in digital participation, Wei (2012) found that people with lower income and education have a narrower scope of online activities and use the Internet primarily for entertainment and socializing. Women and senior citizens also take part in fewer online activities. Büchi,

Just, and Latzer (2015) similarly found systematic differences in types of Internet use across gender, age, and socioeconomic groups.

These digital inequalities are also associated with participation gaps. Studies examining the general impact of Internet use on political and civic engagement have reported mixed results (Boulianne 2009). We do know, however, that specific online activities and goals are linked to higher political participation (Dimitrova et al. 2014) and efficacy (Ognyanova and Ball-Rokeach 2015). This makes the demographic disparities in online activity patterns particularly consequential.

MASS COMMUNICATION RESEARCH AND CONTENT ANALYSIS

Compared to ecological, economic, and inequality studies, classic mass communication research has been less prominent in the policy conversations around CIN. Works in that tradition, however, can make substantive contribution to the debate by illuminating important aspects of media production and content. This section provides a few select examples of relevant theoretical frameworks and discusses the use of media content analysis across research traditions.

While economic studies investigate the market forces behind news production, the mass communication literature explains how media content is shaped by journalistic standards and practices. For instance, the *gatekeeping theory* explores how the vast number of potential news stories gets selectively narrowed down to the coverage actually carried by news media. A major contribution of gatekeeping research is the identification of multiple critical points where news selection happens. Shoemaker and Vos (2009) describe five levels where gatekeeping processes may occur. The *individual level* refers to effects coming from the demographic and personal characteristics of news workers. The *routine level* deals with the prevailing practices and standards of journalistic work. The *organizational level* captures properties of media companies, including their ownership, structure, and size. The *social institutions level* looks into external factors relevant to the media industry—audiences, advertisers, political institutions, and interest groups. Studies at the *social system* level explore gatekeeping controls imposed by a country's economic, political, or cultural system.

Among other themes, that line of research has explored media coverage patterns under different economic conditions. Soroka (2012), for instance, uses the framework to examine the relation between the state of the economy, inflation and interest rates, unemployment, and their coverage in mainstream media. Recent gatekeeping work has also examined the content diversity and systematic bias in reporting on cable and online news (Gonzalez-Bailon et al. 2014).

Agenda-setting research is similarly relevant, as it explores the information priorities of individuals, social groups, and media sources. In one representative study from that tradition, Tan and Weaver (2013) investigate the diversity of issues that received public and media attention over time. Other works have explored the influence of online content and social media on journalism and news reporting, especially in the context of political information (Conway et al. 2015; Quandt 2008).

Agenda-setting studies have traditionally relied on content analysis to measure the priority of different themes in news coverage and on opinion polls to evaluate the public interest in a variety of topics. With the increasing importance of digital platforms, scholars have started exploring new ways of assessing audience priorities. Bastos (2015) examines the diffusion of stories through social media to identify the types of content favored by online consumers. Lee et al. (2015) propose using search engine requests as a proxy for individual interest in news topics. Their study finds the volume of Google searches for economic information over time is associated with the salience of economic issues measured through opinion polls.

A content analysis of media stories is often used to determine their topic, valance, geographic focus, political slant, and other key parameters. This classic analytical strategy of mass communication is now routinely employed by other research traditions discussed here. Scholars have used content analysis to evaluate, for instance, the relationship between ownership structure and local news content (Yanich 2010), as well as the extent to which broadcast news serve the public interest (Kaplan and Hale 2010).

While the bulk of studies using content analysis have focused on newspaper and broadcast stories, researchers increasingly use this analytical strategy to process online content, often comparing it to traditional media coverage (Carpenter 2010). The Pew Research Center has been at the forefront of these efforts, with a number of projects collecting newspaper, broadcast, blog, and social media stories over time and coding them into thematic categories (Mitchell et al. 2015; Pew Project for Excellence in Journalism 2010).

Comprehensive content analysis, whether at the local or national level, has been difficult to maintain and scale, as it required a large number of human coders. New methods discussed in the next section of this chapter have vastly expanded the viability of that option in large longitudinal projects.

COMPUTATIONAL SOCIAL SCIENCE RESEARCH AND NETWORK ANALYSIS

Advances in computational social science provide sophisticated analytical techniques that can illuminate the social, technological, and economic processes underpinning the information systems of communities. New methodological tools facilitate the examination of large-scale digital trace data. One feature of particular relevance here is the capacity to conduct automated text, image, audio, and video analysis. While still inferior to human coding in terms of precision and flexibility, automated content analysis can work at a very large scale, producing consistent results across a variety of unstructured content. One obvious application is a thematic categorization of news stories and social media posts, facilitating the analysis of content diversity for multiple outlets over time.

In one recent example, scholars analyzed 30,000 news stories produced over the span of 30 years to determine how media coverage and public perceptions about the economy influenced each other (Soroka et al. 2015). Another study used a computational approach to examine one million news articles and over five million tweets, unpacking different aspects of the public conversation around mass shootings (Guggenheim et al. 2015). In a high-profile paper assessing the way people share and view political news on social media, Bakshy et al. (2015) examined the content streams of over ten million Facebook users. The analysis found three major factors reducing the political diversity of news consumed by Facebook users: the individual preference for friends who share your political views; the individual propensity to click on links that align with your political views; and Facebook's news feed algorithm, which selectively filters and orders the posts and stories that users see.

This brings up another point of critical importance for research exploring patterns of information-seeking and consumption on the Internet. Today, the content we see online is rarely curated by humans. Instead, it is selected and organized by sophisticated computer algorithms. They filter and order search results, social media posts, and news stories. We are presented with personalized information based on our location, device, demographics, and past behavior. This is useful and necessary as it helps us navigate the vast oceans of online content. As Bakshy et al. (2015) demonstrate, however, personalization can also reduce the diversity of the information we see, decreasing our exposure to a variety of viewpoints. Algorithms can also perpetuate inequalities as they learn, for instance, to show ads for lower-paying jobs to women compared to men (Datta et al. 2014). The lack of transparency in those systems presents a key challenge to our understanding of individual and group interactions with online information.

One important set of methods and theoretical constructs within computational social science comes from network analysis. Network thinking enables us to study the complex interactions between media and social systems (Ognyanova and Monge 2013). Network strategies have been used to examine the structure of the media industry, a sector increasingly characterized by trends toward consolidation, collaborations, and local and global partnerships (Arsenault and Castells 2008). Researchers have also explored the interplay between social ties and information consumption. Friemel (2015), for instance, uses actor-based models to examine the networks of high-school students and the influence of social contacts on individual preferences for TV programs.

Studies taking a network approach have also explored the diversity of media content and audiences. Ognyanova (2013) measures the levels of media fragmentation in a network of mainstream US news outlets. Her work finds an increase in media content homogeneity over time. Webster (2014) examines how individuals connect to broadcast and online sources and finds relatively low levels of audience fragmentation.

Network methods also allow us to track the complex patterns of message diffusion through multiple channels (Aral et al. 2009). Research has examined, for instance, the spread of political and civic information over social media, and the factors predicting a user's ability to distribute messages to a large audience (González-Bailón et al. 2013). Understanding the patterns of content flow across platforms is a key step in the process of evaluating the information sources and distribution channels that individuals and communities rely on.

Conclusion

Each of the frameworks discussed in this chapter has well-understood advantages and drawbacks. Ecological projects provide rich information about the focal community, often highlighting key mechanisms and processes that may generalize beyond the local case. Unfortunately, multilevel, mixed-method studies are also very resource-intensive and difficult to do at a large scale.

Relevant economic research has had a fairly narrow focus on ownership and market structure, overlooking key social and cultural processes. It has been, however, particularly useful in the context of policy, as its main predictor variables are most amenable to regulation.

Digital exclusion works give us a much needed look at the problematic areas and information gaps that we need to address. Yet the field is still facing serious challenges when it comes to finding consistent and relevant metrics and reliable sources of information.

Traditional mass communication frameworks throw light on important aspects of news production and content, though the discipline is still struggling to redefine itself in a digital age.

Computational methods are scalable and allow us to address complex questions—though it is not always clear whether and how answers obtained through digital trace data map onto offline concepts and activities. A computational approach, furthermore, tends to work best in combination with deep qualitative domain understanding.

Many of the interesting research efforts evaluating CIN combine usefully multiple approaches. Economic works have occasionally taken an ecological perspective (Dimmick 2003), mass communication authors have considered ownership and market structure (Shoemaker and Vos 2009), and all frameworks include some studies using content analysis, computational, and network methods. As we seek to understand content production, dissemination, and consumption in a new information environment, combining existing frameworks with new analytical tools provides one promising direction for exploration.

References

Allern, Sigurd. 2002. Journalistic and commercial news values. News organizations as patrons of an institution and market actors. *Nordicom Review* 23(1/2): 137–152.

Althaus, Scott L., and Todd C. Trautman. 2008. The impact of television market size on voter turnout in American elections. *American Politics Research* 36(6): 824–856.

Althaus, Scott L., Anne M. Cizmar, and James G. Gimpel. 2009. Media supply, audience demand, and the geography of news consumption in the United States. *Political Communication* 26(3): 249–277.

American Society of News Editors. 2015. *ASNE newsroom employment census.*
Columbia: American Society of News Editors.

Aral, Sinan, Lev Muchnik, and Arun Sundararajan. 2009. Distinguishing influence-
based contagion from homophily-driven diffusion in dynamic networks.
Proceedings of the National Academy of Sciences 106(51): 21544–21549.

Arsenault, Amelia H., and Manuel Castells. 2008. The structure and dynamics of
global multi-media business networks. *International Journal of Communication*
2: 707–748.

Bachen, Christine M., Allen S. Hammond IV, and Catherine J.K. Sandoval. 2007.
Serving the public interest: Broadcast news, public affairs programming, and
the case for minority ownership. In *Media diversity and localism: Meaning and
metrics*, ed. Philip M. Napoli, 269–308. Mahwah: Lawrence Erlbaum
Associates.

Bakshy, Eytan, Solomon Messing, and Lada Adamic. 2015. Exposure to ideologically diverse news and opinion on Facebook. *Science* 348(6239): 1130–1132.

Ball-Rokeach, Sandra J., and Joo-Young Jung. 2004. From media system dependency to communication infrastructure: A review on the evolution of MSD
theory and proposals for a new concept. *Journal of International Communication*
2: 001.

Bastos, Marco Toledo. 2015. Shares, pins, and tweets. *Journalism Studies* 16(3):
305–325.

Boulianne, Shelley. 2009. Does internet use affect engagement? A meta-analysis of
research. *Political Communication* 26(2): 193–211.

Büchi, Moritz, Natascha Just, and Michael Latzer. 2015. Modeling the second-
level digital divide: A five-country study of social differences in Internet use.
New Media & Society. doi:10.1177/1461444815604154.

Carpenter, Serena. 2010. A study of content diversity in online citizen journalism
and online newspaper articles. *New Media & Society* 12(7): 1064–1084.

Castells, Manuel. 1996. *Rise of the network society: The information age: Economy,
society, and culture.* Cambridge: Blackwell Publishers.

Chen, Nien-Tsu Nancy, Katherine Ognyanova, Nan Zhao, Wenlin Liu, Daniela
Gerson, Sandra Ball-Rokeach, and Michael Parks. 2013. Communication and
socio-demographic forces shaping civic engagement patterns in a multiethnic
city. In *Communication and community*, ed. Patricia Moy, 207–232. New York:
Hampton Press.

Conway, Bethany A., Kate Kenski, and Di Wang. 2015. The rise of twitter in the
political campaign: Searching for intermedia agenda-setting effects in the presidential primary. *Journal of Computer-Mediated Communication* 20: 363–380.

Costanza-Chock, Sasha, and Ernest J. Wilson. 2012. New voices on the net? The
digital journalism divide and the costs of network exclusion. In *Race after the
internet*, ed. Lisa Nakamura and Peter Chow-White, 246–268. New York:
Routledge.

Council of Economic Advisers. 2015. *Mapping the digital divide*. Washington, DC: Executive Office of the President.

Datta, Amit, Michael Carl Tschantz, and Anupam Datta. 2014. Automated experiments on ad privacy settings: A tale of opacity, choice, and discrimination. *arXiv preprint* arXiv:1408.6491.

Dimitrova, Daniela V., Adam Shehata, Jesper Strömbäck, and Lars W. Nord. 2014. The effects of digital media on political knowledge and participation in election campaigns: Evidence from panel data. *Communication Research* 41(1): 95–118.

Dimmick, John W. 2003. *Media competition and coexistence: The theory of the niche*. Mahwah: Lawrence Erlbaum Associates.

Dunaway, Johanna. 2008. Markets, ownership, and the quality of campaign news coverage. *The Journal of Politics* 70(04): 1193–1202.

Friedland, Lewis A. 2001. Communication, community, and democracy: Toward a theory of the communicatively integrated community. *Communication Research* 28(4): 358–391.

Friedland, Lewis A. 2013. Civic communication in a networked society: Seattle's emergent ecology. In *Varieties of civic innovation: Deliberative, collaborative, network, and narrative approaches*, ed. Jennifer Girouard and Carmen Sirianni. Nashville: Vanderbilt University Press.

Friedland, Lewis A., Christopher C. Long, Yong Jun Shin, and Nakho Kim. 2007. The local public sphere as a networked space. In *Media and public spheres*, ed. Richard Butsch, 43–57. New York: Palgrave Macmillan.

Friedland, Lewis, Philip Napoli, Katherine Ognyanova, Carola Weil, Ernest J. Wilson, and III. 2012. *Review of the literature regarding critical information needs of the American public*. Washington, DC: Federal Communications Commission.

Friemel, Thomas N. 2015. Influence versus selection: A network perspective on opinion leadership. *International Journal of Communication* 9: 1–20.

Gentzkow, Matthew, and Jesse M. Shapiro. 2010. What drives media slant? Evidence from U.S. daily newspapers. *Econometrica* 78(1): 35–71.

George, Lisa M., and Joel Waldfogel. 2006. The 'New York Times' and the market for local newspapers. *The American Economic Review* 96(1): 435–447.

González-Bailón, Sandra, Javier Borge-Holthoefer, and Yamir Moreno. 2013. Broadcasters and hidden influentials in online protest diffusion. *American Behavioral Scientist* 57(7): 943–965.

Gonzalez-Bailon, Sandra, Gianmarco De Francisci Morales, Marcelo Mendoza, Nasir Khan, and Carlos Castillo. 2014. Cable news coverage and online news stories: A large-scale comparison of digital media content. In *Annual Meeting of the International Communication Association (ICA)*, Seattle, Washington, DC.

Guggenheim, Lauren, S. Mo Jang, Soo Young Bae, and W. Russell Neuman. 2015. The dynamics of issue frame competition in traditional and social media. *The ANNALS of the American Academy of Political and Social Science* 659(1): 207–224.

Hamilton, James T. 2004. *All the news that's fit to sell: How the market transforms information into news*. Princeton: Princeton University Press.

Hampton, Keith N. 2015. Persistent and pervasive community: New communication technologies and the future of community. *American Behavioral Scientist*. doi:10.1177/0002764215601714.

Hunt, Darnell. 2014. Turning missed opportunities into realized ones. In *The 2014 Hollywood Writers Report*. Los Angeles: Writers Guild of America, West.

Kaplan, Martin, and Matthew Hale. 2010. *Local TV news in the Los Angeles media market: Are stations serving the public interest?* Los Angeles: Norman Lear Center.

Kim, Yong-Chan, Joo-Young Jung, and Sandra J. Ball-Rokeach. 2006. 'Geoethnicity' and neighborhood engagement: A communication infrastructure perspective. *Political Communication* 23(4): 421–441.

Kinght Commission. 2009. *Informing communities: Sustaining democracy in the digital age*. Washington, DC: The Aspen Institute.

Lee, ByungGu, Jinha Kim, and Dietram A. Scheufele. 2015. Agenda setting in the Internet Age: The reciprocity between online searches and issue salience. *International Journal of Public Opinion Research*. Advance Access published September 1, 2015: 1–16.

Lloyd, Mark, and Philip N. Napoli. 2007. *Local media diversity matters: Measure media diversity according to democratic values, not market values*. Washington, DC: Center for American Progress.

McManus, John H. 1994. *Market-driven journalism: Let the citizen beware?* Thousand Oaks: Sage Publications.

Mitchell, Amy, Jesse Holcomb, Paul Hitlin, Jeff Gottfried, Katerina E. Matsa, Michael Barthel, and Kenneth Olmstead. 2015. *Local news in a digital age*. Washington, DC: Pew Research Center.

Napoli, Philip M. 1999. Deconstructing the diversity principle. *Journal of Communication* 49(4): 7–34.

Napoli, Philip M. 2011. *Audience evolution: New technologies and the transformation of media audiences*. New York: Columbia University Press.

Napoli, Philip M., Sarah Stonbely, Kathleen McCollough, and Bryce Renninger. 2015. *Assessing the health of local journalism ecosystems, a comparative analysis of three New Jersey communities*. New Brunswick: Media + the Public Interest Initiative.

Ognyanova, Katherine. 2013. Intermedia agenda setting in an era of fragmentation: Applications of network science in the study of mass communication. PhD dissertation, Annenberg School for Communication and Journalism, University of Southern California.

Ognyanova, Katherine, and Peter Monge. 2013. A multitheoretical, multilevel, multidimensional network model of the media system: Production, content, and audiences. *Communication Yearbook* 37: 66–93.

Ognyanova, Katherine, and Sandra J. Ball-Rokeach. 2015. Political efficacy on the internet: A media system dependency approach. In *Communication and information technologies annual: Politics, participation, and production*, ed. Laura Robinson, Shelia R. Cotten, and Jeremy Schulz, 3–27. Bingley: Emerald Group Publishing.

Papper, Bob. 2015. *RTDNA / Hofstra university annual survey: Women and minorities data*. Washington, DC: Radio-Television News Directors Association.

Pariser, Eli. 2011. *The filter bubble: How the new personalized web is changing what we read and how we think*. New York: Penguin Press.

Pew Project for Excellence in Journalism. 2010. *New media, old media: How blogs and social media agendas relate and differ from the traditional press*. Washington, DC: Pew Research Center.

Pew Research Center. 2010. How news happens: A study of the news ecosystem of one American city. Available at www.journalism.org/analysis_report/how_news_happens.

Putnam, Robert D. 2000. *Bowling alone: The collapse and revival of American community*. New York: Touchstone Books.

Quandt, Thorsten. 2008. (No) news on the world wide web? *Journalism Studies* 9(5): 717–738.

Rainie, Lee. 2015. Digital Divides 2015. Pew Research Center. Available at http://www.pewinternet.org/2015/09/22/digital-divides-2015/.

Rosenstiel, Tom, Amy Mitchell, Kristen Purcell, and Lee Rainie. 2011. *How people learn about their local community*. Washington, DC: Pew Research Center and The Knight Foundation.

Sampson, Robert J. 2012. *Great American city: Chicago and the enduring neighborhood effect*. Chicago: University of Chicago Press.

Schaffer, Jan. 2010. *Exploring a networked journalism collaborative in Philadelphia: An analysis of the city's media ecosystem with final recommendations*. Washington, DC: J-Lab.

Shehata, Adam, and Jesper Strömbäck. 2013. Not (Yet) a new era of minimal effects a study of agenda setting at the aggregate and individual levels. *The International Journal of Press/Politics* 18(2): 234–255.

Shoemaker, Pamela J., and Timothy P. Vos. 2009. *Gatekeeping theory*. New York: Routledge.

Soroka, Stuart N. 2012. The gatekeeping function: Distributions of information in media and the real world. *The Journal of Politics* 74(2): 514–528.

Soroka, Stuart N., Dominik A. Stecula, and Chirostpher Wlezien. 2015. It's (change in) the (future) economy, stupid: Economic indicators, the media, and public opinion. *American Journal of Political Science* 59(2): 57–474.

Sunstein, Cass R. 2007. *Republic.com 2.0*. Princeton: Princeton University Press.

Tan, Yue, and David H. Weaver. 2013. Agenda diversity and agenda setting from 1956 to 2004. *Journalism Studies* 14(6): 773–789.

van Deursen, Alexander J.A.M., and Jan van Dijk. 2014. The digital divide shifts to differences in usage. *New Media & Society* 16(3): 507–526.

Waldman, Steven. 2011. *The information needs of communities: The changing media landscape in a broadband age.* Washington, DC: Federal Communications Commission.

Webster, James G. 2014. *The marketplace of attention: How audiences take shape in a digital age.* Cambridge, MA: MIT Press.

Wei, Lu. 2012. Number matters: The multimodality of internet use as an indicator of the digital inequalities. *Journal of Computer-Mediated Communication* 17(3): 303–318.

Wellman, Barry, and Lee Rainie. 2012. *Networked: The new social operating system.* Cambridge, MA: MIT Press.

Yanich, Danilo. 2010. Does ownership matter? Localism, content, and the federal communications commission. *Journal of Media Economics* 23(2): 51–67.

Preface: Communication Challenges in a Changing America

America has always been a country rich in diversity. The Powhatans who greeted the English Captain John Smith were only one of many "tribes" who had to deal with strangers from various parts of Eurasia. The English, the Spanish, the French, the Germans, the Dutch, and others, including Africans, came and settled and conquered diverse peoples. This early American plurality was not only a diversity of peoples, but also a diversity of languages and cultures. America has long been home to a diversity of religions and a diversity of rich and poor. The classless melting pot that was also somehow "white" and Christian has long been recognized as a myth. American diversity has always been a fact; it has also always been a source of bitter violent struggle, shameful intolerance, and political inequality. Diversity has always presented challenges regarding our ideals of freedom and equality, and it has always presented challenges regarding how we communicate with each other. Not only are communications technologies and market shifts disrupting the old ways of doing things, but also the very public is changing ... and faster than ever.

In this section, we examine the rapidly changing demographic landscape of American communities, with a focus on the relationship between these dramatic shifts and how we communicate with one another. Do our communications policies bake in American inequality? Is our present communication infrastructure capable of serving the needs of our nation where women and so-called racial and ethnic "minorities" are clearly the new majority? In the midst of this altered landscape, we examine the challenges of how this new America communicates in three ways. First, Jorge Reina Schement and Jason Llorenz look at the way and the reasons diverse communities create their own distinct media and telecommunications environments. Carolyn Byerly and Alisa Valentin examine the unique needs and contributions of women in a communication ecology dominated by men. Vikki Katz and Matthew Matsuganis explore the complex landscape and too-often unappreciated contributions of ethnic media in our society. Federico Subervi offers a blunt challenge to Spanish-language media to address the critical information needs of America's growing Latino communities. And finally, Sandra Ball-Rokeach and Minhee Son give us sharp anthropological detail of the communication patterns of neighborhoods, the organizations that serve them, and how they interact with local media in Los Angeles ... and how policymakers need to begin to conduct better research into how our diverse populations communicate.

These few chapters cannot possible address all the diversity of our nation. The original Americans living in Indian territory and the newest American immigrants from Asia and Eastern Europe and Africa all face very real challenges in getting information they need to participate effectively in our society. This is also still true of those who are blind or deaf, or unable to press the same buttons or sometimes not-so-smart screens as the fully able among us. This section is not meant to cover all the strands of the American quilt, it is meant, however, to suggest that all, and we mean all, Americans matter. To address the communications crisis in America, we must begin to see and appreciate these differences and to conduct the research and establish policy to meet the critical information needs of our proudly diverse nation.

CHAPTER 4

Understanding a Diverse America's Critical Information Needs

Mark Lloyd, Jason Llorenz, and Jorge R. Schement

INTRODUCTION

America is a richly diverse nation. We are made up of different economic classes and ages and religions and customs and abilities. Much has been written about the rapidly changing American demographic, but too little attention has been paid to the effect of these demographic changes on whether all Americans get the critical information to protect themselves in emergencies or to participate as equal members in our society.

To address the critical information needs of this diverse nation, we must first come to a better understanding of our diversity and what it means to both convey and accept information to and from different groups. It is essential to understand that one method or means of communication does not and will not meet the needs of all of us. Different communities and households have strong reasons for creating their particular

M. Lloyd (✉)
University of Southern California, Los Angeles, CA, USA

J. Llorenz
Rutgers University, New Brunswick, NJ, USA

J.R. Schement
Rutgers University, New Brunswick, NJ, USA

© The Editor(s) (if applicable) and The Author(s) 2016   49
M.I. Lloyd, L.A. Friedland (eds.), *The Communication Crisis in America,*
And How to Fix It, DOI 10.1057/978-1-349-94925-0_4

communication environment. The young have strong reasons for relying upon social media, older Americans have good reasons to rely on newspapers, recent immigrants have good reason to rely upon ethnic media, and the poor have strong reasons not to purchase Internet service at home. Understanding these reasons is the first step in establishing smart public policies aimed at protecting the needs and rights of America's diverse community.

In this chapter, we focus on the critical information needs of an evolving polyracial/multiethnic America—an America of pluralities. We argue here that policymakers and scholars must begin to delve more deeply into the reasons different communities address their unique information needs, and we must look more critically at the categories currently used to identify difference.

ADDRESSING RACE AND ETHNICITY

The challenge of American diversity is sometimes thought of as the changing racial demographic. But the challenge of diversity is much more complex than that. The concept of race conceals our complex diversity. For example, thinking of Black Americans as a race with fixed tendencies, cultural habits, and capabilities obscures the fact that Black Americans are included in a wide range of economic classes, ethnicities, and cultural affiliations. There are Black Americans who are Hispanic, some are more closely connected to the Caribbean, some have recently migrated from the former slave states of the South, others have been in the North or the West since well before the Civil War, some Black Americans are recent immigrants from Somalia or Tanzania. While some may see all Black Americans as one dangerous and potentially criminal race, this clearly ignores real and important differences.

The same observation is clearly true of Cubans, Puerto Ricans, South Americans, Mexicans, and others categorized as Hispanic or Latino. The same observation is true of the hundreds of First Nations people misnamed as Indians. The same observation is true of the wide variety of people who are identified as Asian, including Indians from India, or the Hmong community or the Chinese or Japanese or Korean or Vietnamese or Filipino community. The fact that recent Russian immigrants and Persians and Israelis and Poles and Italians and Irish, all speaking different languages, with different religious beliefs and habits of thought, are all considered White demonstrates the pernicious power of the concept of race.

There has long been broad scientific agreement that racial categories should be tossed into the junk heap of history. And yet, *racism* is still alive and well. The impact of racism *is* captured in census data, when the categories of "race" are correlated with other categories such as income or education. The correlation of this data reveals the persistence of inequality (i.e., unequal treatment) between "races" and suggests the vestiges of American racism continue to impact the diverse Black community. Thus, the categories of race, used by the U.S. Census Bureau and other surveys, hold a kind of utility, even as they validate an insidious concept and encourage its continued circulation (Sussman 2014).

Those of us attempting to understand whether all Americans have the information they need to protect themselves in emergencies or to participate as equal members of our society must understand the problems that come with the collection of data about "race." Race as a category comes packaged in racism, since it collapses a range of cultures and ethnicities into a single group or "other" and, as Sussman argues, enables stereotypic bundling resulting in exclusion (Sussman 2014). And as Yanow argues, when social scientists, policymakers, and journalists fail to acknowledge the fluid and transitory nature of race as a category, it may seem as if we understand something that, in fact, we do not fully understand. The latest survey on the disparate use of "social media" by Blacks, Whites, and Latinos tells us far less than we think. The use of these categories may indeed do more harm than good (Yanow 2015).

Ethnicity is another matter. While the terms "race" and "ethnicity" are too often used interchangeably, these concepts are not at all the same. All Americans are "ethnics." Whether arriving on the *Mayflower* with its "First Families," or the American brig *Creole* with its cargo of slaves, or the SS *Westphalia* with its manifest of Poles, Slavs, and Russian Jews, every American comes with cultures of origin. Native American "Indians" are Choctow and Mohawk and Apache and Eskimo and so many other peoples, far too many long lost, but still distinct and separate "ethnicities," each with their own language, foods, and customs. Ethnicity is about the identity that one learns from one's family, while the (mis)identity of race comes from historical confusions.

We are all ethnic Americans. But information about our ethnicity is rarely properly gathered or understood in the USA. Even in acknowledging Hispanic or Latino as ethnicities, rarely do we acknowledge the cultural differences between Salvadorans and Puerto Ricans or Mexicans and Cubans. Nor do we acknowledge the different challenges faced by dark-skinned Latinos as compared to Latinos with a lighter complexion; that is, the lumping together of these different cultures obscures the challenges faced by certain "Latinos" resulting from the "racism" most usually associated with Blacks, or the privilege enjoyed by other "Latinos" most usually associated with Whites (Hunter 2016).

Complicating all this confusion is the fact that ever more people are identifying themselves as belonging to more than one racial/ethnic group. There exist today multiple variations of Americans across racial/ethnic lines, socioeconomic statuses, origins, religious beliefs, and commitments (Yanow 2015).

And the terms "majority" and "minority" are not particularly insightful either. After the 2010 decennial counting of the public, the U.S. Census Bureau reported that by 2042, there will be no single majority group, as we currently understand the concept (U.S. Census Bureau 2004). Indeed, as of 2010, many American communities have more "racial/ethnic" households than "White" households. The list of major cities where Whites are already in the minority includes: Baltimore, Boston, Buffalo, Charlotte, Chicago, Cincinnati, Cleveland, Dallas, Detroit, El Paso, Houston, Los Angeles, Memphis, Milwaukee, Philadelphia, Phoenix, New Orleans, New York City, St. Louis, San Antonio, San Diego, San Francisco, San Jose, Tampa, and Washington, D.C. In four states, there are more "minorities" than Whites: California, Hawaii, New Mexico, and Texas. To describe this, some have adopted the nonsensical term "majority-minority" communities.

Even before the New Orleans levees broke after Hurricane Katrina, studies found that "racial and ethnic communities" in the USA were more vulnerable to natural disasters, due to factors such as language, housing patterns, building construction, community isolation, and the insensitivities of those in power who did not consider themselves part of those communities (Fothergill et al. 1999). It is then of special importance that policymakers focus on these vulnerable communities to make sure all Americans have the critical information they need.

THE INTERNET ALONE IS NOT THE ANSWER

Historical Gaps Resulting from the Nature of the Exchange

The gap in access to critical communications will not be spanned by sole reliance on Internet-only, mobile phone-centric technologies. Even as we challenge the current use of the so-called racial/ethnic categories (White, Black, Asian, Hispanic, American Indian), we have long observed gaps in access to information technology among these broad groups. In 2000, Schement and Forbes looked at the gaps in telephone penetration and asked: "What are the characteristics of the persistent gaps in information technology among the nation's majority whites and minority blacks and Hispanics?" (Schement and Fobes 2000; see also Schement 1995). The answers illuminate how we might look at the gaps to critical information today across all media and telecommunications service, including legacy and emerging communications.

Immediately after the breakup of AT&T in the early 1980s, it became clear that the lack of telephone service in households resulted largely from poverty-related factors (Perl 1983; Hausman et al. 1993; Schement 1995, 1998; Schement et al. 1997; Mueller and Schement 1996; Williams and Hadden 1991, 1992). Other studies suggested that those at the margins of society were particularly "vulnerable to the socioeconomic consequences of isolation as a result of phonelessness" (Schement 1995, 1998; Schement et al. 1997). Too few studies examined the causes of the telephone gap (NTIA 1995, 1998). In 2000, Schement conducted an analysis of historical gaps in some earlier information technologies and found them instructive (Perl 1983; Hausman and Belinfante 1993; Mueller and Schement 1996; Williams and Hadden 1991; Schement 1995, 1997, 1998).

Compare the adoption of radio, television, and telephone service: In the mid-1920s, only 10 percent of US households owned radios, but by 1930, ownership had increased to 46 percent, and ten years later (during the Great Depression), Americans ownership of radios had increased to 82 percent. Assuming a gap existed between the white majority and ethnic minorities, that gap vanished by 1950, when radio achieved nearly universal household saturation.

In 1950, less than 10 percent of households owned a television, but only 15 years later, over 90 percent of household owned a television. During the first seven years of television adoption, lower-income groups lagged behind wealthier ones, but by 1970, nearly 90 percent of households owned a television. The adoption gap closed.

The telephone presents a stark contrast. The first practical telephone exchange was established around 1878; eighty years later, three-quarters of US households owned a telephone (Brooks 1975). By 1970, 93 percent of households owned telephones, advancing to 94 percent in 1990 (Belinfante 1993). Through the 1990s, there was an 8 percent adoption gap between "minorities" (Blacks and Hispanics) and Whites in nation-wide telephone penetration.

The key to the contrast among the three technologies lies in the nature of the exchange. Radio and television constitute goods requiring one single lump-sum payment, while the telephone constitutes a service that requires monthly installment payments. More specifically, continuous telephone service requires a decision to pay a monthly fee, and the building and maintenance of an infrastructure in order for the connection to function. For households on the margin, the payment structure of telephone service means a hard choice every month, especially when the option of long-distance calling is added to basic local phone service. Research suggests that such a choice may result in the rejection of telephone service in favor of other purchases deemed more essential, perhaps a main reason why the gap between majority and minority populations exists 120 years after the telephone first entered American life (Horrigan and Rhodes 1995; Mueller and Schement 1996; Schement et al. 1997). By comparison, the one-time cost characteristic of radio and television—which allows them to circulate second- and third-hand—facilitates rapid diffusion, and, thereby, the (Schement and Forbes 2000) closure of whatever gaps might have arisen in the early stages of their diffusion.

Simply put, a one-time purchase, or a purchase that can be reliably budgeted over time, is more attractive than an expense that may increase radically from month to month. Research, whether it is conducted in New Jersey, Texas, or Kansas, consistently shows that people are driven off the phone network by the costs that result from using the phone and not by the costs of basic service. The results from these three places show that eight of the twelve households surveyed in Camden lost telephone service because they incurred large phone bills, which they were unable to pay; 57 percent of the 172 people surveyed in Texas said that the cost of long-distance calls made service difficult to afford; and 37 percent of the people surveyed in

Kansas strongly agreed that long-distance charges were the reason their phone service was disconnected (Mueller and Schement 1995). Similar studies performed in Washington, D.C. and California are consistent with these results (Chesapeake and Potomac Telephone Company 1993).

Different Groups Create Different Media Environments at Home

In a study of media use in Camden, Mueller and Schement found that four of the eight households without telephone service had cable service, and six of the eight households had video cassette recorders (VCRs) (Mueller and Schement 1995). Other studies made similar findings. In Texas, 40 percent of the people without phones had cable service, and 95 percent owned televisions (Horrigan and Rhodes 1995).

We have evidence that, in some instances, households have rejected telephone service because incurred toll charges over-stressed their ability to pay. The telephone represents one more unbearable cost. In addition, for some households, the telephone offers a channel whereby undesirable peers may contact a child in the household and encourage some criminal activity, such as the use of drugs. And threats to the household from agencies with either real or bogus claims against the household are often delivered by telephone.

On the other hand, our research indicates that some heads of households are willing to invest in cable—sometimes instead of telephone service—because of cable's high-use value, given their circumstances. Cable offers relatively inexpensive entertainment that is viewed by some communities as more cost-effective than any other comparable expenditure. Some cable customers report that cable provides more members of the household entertainment than the phone calls to individual family members. In addition, cable service is an enticement to keep children at home and away from the dangerous streets of the neighborhood; and to households with few comforts, cable offers a visible sign of material well-being (Mueller and Schement 1995).

That some households decide to forego telephone service in favor of cable television has led newspaper columnists, social critics, and academics to wonder if such choices represent cultural irrationality and dysfunction; after all, can the banality of cable ever hold greater value than the utility of the telephone? The answer to this question usually results in exasperation.

But as the respondents themselves have indicated, they see their choices as "forced"—choices which must be seen against a context of survival options.

Furthermore, family members combine the information environments of their homes. Especially among some youth, media multitasking has become a way of life. For example, a majority of teenagers multitask "most" or "some" of the time while listening to music (73 percent of respondents), using a computer (66 percent), watching TV (68 percent), and reading (53 percent) (Rideout et al. 2010). As Napoli reports in this volume, this is, at least in part, due to altered media marketing strategies and the increasing prevalence of convergent technologies, including mobile, in the household. There may be significant differences between youth dependent upon financial, cultural, language, and geographic differences.

The decline in the sum total of household members and the multiplication of single person households means that the cohesiveness of the "average" family no longer holds in growing numbers of living situations (Vespa et al. 2013). In households with small children, media are often employed as babysitters. Research suggests that neighborhoods, parental limits, and family conflict/stability are significant predictors of children's media use within time or over time (Lee et al. 2009). Similarly, Lenhart et al. (2001) reported that teenagers in single-parent households were more likely to use the Internet for entertainment purposes, compared to adolescents from two-parent households. Vittrup et al. speculate that the computer in these families may be used more as a babysitter or "companion" when the parent is busy (Vittrup et al. 2014). In other words, the different stresses different cultures/ethnic groups endure and the different habits they embrace make a difference in their media adoption and use. The broad categories of White, Black, Latino, Asian-American, and Native American simply do not capture these differences.

Despite evidence that different ethnic groups construct media environments differently, there remains in some quarters an insistence that uniform adoption of one technology (broadband) is the answer. However, our research makes it clear that broadband (or advanced telecommunications) access alone is not the answer. Closing what some call the "digital divide" will not necessarily ensure that the critical information needs of all Americans are addressed. As Schement (2003) captured: "rather than drop the newspaper in favor of the television (or the Internet online news service), many Americans have shifted their reliance on the traditional newspaper to reframe it as a source of local information. Nor are Americans moving toward a national homogeneity of media. For one thing, diffusion rates vary" (Schement 2003, 403–422). Today's data on broadband access varies widely—with poverty, age, disability, and Spanish-language dominance among several factors associated with lack of broadband access. Still, about 15 percent of Americans do not use the Internet at all (Anderson and Perrin 2015).

We have much to learn about the complex reasons for non-Internet use among that 15 percent. While broadband adoption rates among seniors, for example, are rising, they remain well below the national average (Smith 2014). The least likely to be connected to broadband are seniors, the poor, Spanish-dominant, newer immigrants, and people with disabilities (Rainie 2015). The cost of connection continues to be a factor for non-adopters, but it is not the only factor. "In April 2009, Pew asked adults who had dial-up Internet at home what it would take for them to switch to a broadband connection. A plurality (35 percent) said the price would have to fall, 17 percent said it would have to become available where they live, and one in five (20 percent) said nothing would get them to change" (Zickuhr and Smith 2013). By 2015, nearly a third of non-Internet users (32 percent) said the Internet was too difficult to use, including 8 percent of this group, who said they were "too old to learn." The cost was also a barrier for some adults who were offline; 19 percent cited "the expense of Internet service or owning a computer" (Anderson and Perrin 2015). Whatever the variety of factors for Internet non-adoption, it is clear that the Internet is not yet the universal medium, and we should have serious concerns about whether a largely privately controlled communication service should be relied upon as the sole information source for any community.

We suggest holding to the long-standing US policy of promoting diverse sources of information for a diverse American community. Let each community, each culture, and ethnicity choose for themselves how to construct their own media environment while encouraging the proliferation of critical information for all.

Conducting Research on American Diversity and Diversity of Media Use

If we are to determine whether all Americans are actually acquiring, or have the opportunity to acquire critical information, we will have to move beyond what Dvora Yanow calls the racial "category making in public policy" (Yanow 2015). We will have to conduct better research on our complex diversity. We will have to demand reflection and continue to critique those who blindly use racial categories, and we will have to take a truly scientific approach to understanding difference and what different human characteristics matter to the public policy we are creating. And it starts with the Census Bureau.

The first U.S. census was conducted by Secretary of State Thomas Jefferson in 1790. Jefferson ordered a counting of the heads of households and the numbers in each household in the original 13 states, plus the districts of Kentucky, Maine, and Vermont, and the Southwest Territory (Tennessee) and included five categories:

- Free White males of 16 years and upward
- Free White males under 16 years
- Free White females
- All other free persons
- Slaves

Thus, the category of race (as in Free White) was introduced as a public policy tool to meet the Constitutional requirement set out in Article I, Section 2:

> Representatives and direct Taxes shall be apportioned among the several States which may be included within this Union, according to their respective Numbers, which shall be determined by adding to the whole Number of free persons, including those bound to Service for a Term of years, and excluding Indians not taxed, three fifths of all other Person.

Who was White was left to those charged with taking census. While the category may seem obvious today, who was "White" was very much in flux in the early days of the US republic, and it was not at all clear at the time that Spaniards, Italians, French, Russians, Swedes, or Germans (all labeled "swarthy" by Benjamin Franklin) should be considered White (Jacobson 1998). The categories of race gained a little more specificity in 1820, when the term "colored" was introduced. By the mid-1800s, the now-controversial "racial science" of eugenics was having a profound influence on public policy, and the assumption of racial hierarchies was subtly (and sometimes, not so subtly) introduced into US policymaking, including how the government counted the diverse American community (Snipp 2003; Frederickson 2002).

Social scientists and public policymakers have for far too long propped up the long discredited notion that certain ugly stereotypes could be sensibly aligned with skin tone, hair texture, and bone structure to constitute a "race." The "drunken Irishman," the "hot-blooded Italian," and the "stingy Jew" were all thought to be distinct races, as was the "inscrutable Oriental," the "lazy Mexican," and the "primitive Black."

In 1998, the Executive Board of the American Anthropological Association issued a statement that read in part:

> Racial beliefs constitute myths about the diversity in the human species and about the abilities and behavior of people homogenized into "racial" categories. The myths fused behavior and physical features together in the public mind, impeding our comprehension of both biological variations and cultural behavior, implying that both are genetically determined. Racial myths bear no relationship to the reality of human capabilities or behavior. Scientists today find that reliance on such folk beliefs about human differences in research has led to countless errors. (AAA 1998)

And yet, too many of the hateful racist ideas persist as a given in our national conversation. Sometimes they persist not because of hate but because of ignorance, and sometimes they exist because they are convenient. How *do* we address the impact of racism without using the false categories of "race"? As Hodgkinson notes: "We need the categories in order to eliminate them. Without knowing who our oppressed minorities are, how can we develop remedies so that they will no longer be oppressed?" (Hodgkinson 2001). The challenge of "racial profiling" demonstrates this very real tension. Asking police officers or real estate agents or school officials to identify people by race allows government to address discrimination even while it perpetuates, indeed encourages, the false notion that race is a valid category. Of course, much of the conversation about a "digital divide" also reveals this tension.

Yanow argues that in addition to making our criticisms about racial categories plain, we need to begin to ask different questions. Instead of asking about a parents' country of origin (as an indicator of ethnicity) or race, we need to begin asking about behavioral practices and economic problems. It is past time for communications scholars to shift from simple polling surveys based on racist assumptions, and begin a more complex anthropological approach to better understand the different communities across our nation and why they make the communications choices they make.

Perhaps even more important than the kind of questions that are asked may be the way census takers or other social scientists gather information, and it may be more important to properly learn how to listen. More pointedly, perhaps it is time to demand that social scientists actually understand the rudimentary facts about the community they are engaging. Does the social scientist speak the language? Does the census taker understand the cultural practices of the community? Is the social scientist capable of determining what social conditions in the local neighborhood matter to the choices made by particular households and communities?

The great twenty-first-century advance in computer power combined with multidisciplinary research methods should be used to aggregate and sort through this more complex set of data gathered by competent researchers.

Journalists and social scientists must begin to write and conduct research that starts with acknowledging the damaging "lie" that is race, even while investigating inequality based on continuing racist, sexist, and discriminatory ideas, and even while exploring and celebrating difference.

CHALLENGE AND OPPORTUNITY

For policymakers, this analysis challenges the notion that succeeding in serving the critical information needs of *all* Americans communications can be achieved by holding on to the old notions of "race." We must openly and consistently acknowledge the lie at the heart of the concept of race, but address the enduring problem of racism. And we must let go of the old notions that one media alone can address the complex critical communication needs of our diverse community. Retooling and rethinking our critical communications frameworks require significant, localized study of the needs of language minorities, the poor, religious, and culturally isolated communities too often marginalized in our policymaking. Policymakers will do well to recognize the value of diversity, and seek to understand what fully embracing that complex diversity means in our local and national media ecologies. Critical communication planning that takes into account our rich American diversity will require sensitivity to bad old habits and sober recognition of the role of both "old" and "new" media.

REFERENCES

American Anthropological Association, Statement on Race. 1998. Available at http://www.americananthro.org/ConnectWithAAA/Content.aspx.

Anderson, Monica, and Andrew Perrin. 2015. *15% of Americans don't use the internet. Who are they?* Pew Research Center, July 28. Available at http://www.pewresearch.org/fact-tank/2015/07/28/15-of-americans-dont-use-the-internet-who-are-they/.

Belinfante, Alexander. 1993. *Telephone subscribership in the United States.* Washington, DC: Federal Communications Commission.

Brooks, John. 1975. *Telephone: The first hundred years.* New York: Harper & Row.

Chesapeake and Potomac Telephone Company. 1993. *Telephone penetration project: Door-to-door survey,* Affordability of Telephone Service 1: Non-customer survey. Washington DC: Field Research Corporation.

Fothergill, A., E.G.M. Maestas, and J.D. Darlington. 1999. Race, ethnicity and disasters in the United States: A review of the literature. *Disasters* 23: 156–173.

Frederickson, George M. 2002. *Racism a short history.* Princeton: Princeton University Press.

Hausman, Jerry, Timothy Tardiff, and Alexander Belinfante. 1993. The effects of the breakup of AT&T on telephone penetration in the United States. *American Economic Review* 83(2): 178–184.

Hodgkinson, Harold L. 2001. *What Should We Call People?.* Race and Ethnicity: Debates and controversies 1.2 (2001): 19.

Horrigan, John B., and Lodis Rhodes. 1995. *The evolution of universal service in Texas.* Austin: Lyndon B. Johnson School of Public Affairs, University of Texas.

Hunter, Margaret. 2016. Colorism in the classroom: How skin tone stratifies African American and Latina/o students. *Theory Into Practice* 55(1): 54–61.

Jacobson, Matthew Frye. 1998. *"Whiteness of a different colour." European Immigrants and the Alchemy of Race.* Cambridge: Cambridge University Press.

Lee, Sook-Jung, Silvia Bartolic, and Elizabeth A. Vandewater. 2009. Predicting children's media use in the USA: Differences in cross-sectional and longitudinal analysis. *British Journal of Developmental Psychology* 27(1): 123–143.

Lenhart, A., L. Rainie, and O. Lewis. 2001. *Teenage life online: The rise of the instant-message generation and the internet's impact.* Washington, DC: Pew Internet & American Life Project.

Mueller, Milton L., and Jorge Reina Schement. 1995. *Universal service from the bottom up: A profile of telecommunications access in Camden, New Jersey.* New Brunswick: Rutgers University Project on Information Policy.

Mueller, Milton L., and Jorge Reina Schement. 1996. Universal service from the bottom up: A study of telephone penetration in Camden, New Jersey. *The Information Society* 12: 273–292.

National Telecommunications and Information Administration (NTIA). 1995. *Falling through the net: A survey of the "have nots" in rural and urban America.* Washington DC: Department of Commerce.

National Telecommunications and Information Administration (NTIA). 1998. *Falling through the net II: New data on the digital divide.* Washington DC: Department of Commerce.

Perl, L.J. 1983. *Residential demand for telephone service 1983. Prepared for Central Service Organisation of the Bell Operating Companies, Inc. BOCs, National Economic Research Associates, Inc.* New York: White Plains.

Rainie, Lee. 2015. *Digital divides 2015.* Pew Research Center, September 22. Retrieved December 10 from http://www.pewinternet.org/2015/09/22/digital-divides-2015/.

Rideout, V.J., U.G. Foehr, and D.F. Roberts. 2010. *Generation M2: Media in the lives of 8- to 18-year-olds.* Menlo Park: Henry J. Kaiser Family Foundation.

Schement, Jorge Reina. 1995. Beyond universal service: Characteristics of Americans without telephones, 1980–1993. *Telecommunications Policy* 19(6): 477–485.

Schement, Jorge Reina. 1998. Thorough Americans: Minorities and the new media. In *Investing in diversity: Advancing opportunities for minorities and the media,* ed. Amy Korzick Garmer. Washington, DC: Aspen Institute.

Schement, Jorge Reina. 2003. Three for society: Households and media in the creation of twenty-first century communities. In *The wired homestead,* ed. Joseph Turow and Andrea L. Kavanaugh. Cambridge, MA: MIT Press.

Schement, Jorge Reina, and Scott C. Forbes. 2000. Identifying temporary and permanent gaps in universal service. *The Information Society* 16: 117–126.

Schement, Jorge Reina, Alex Belinfante, and Paurance Povich. 1997. Trends in telephone penetration in the United States 1984–1994. In *Globalism and localism in telecommunications,* ed. Eli M. Noam and Alex J. Wolfson. Amsterdam: Elsevier.

Smith, Aaron. 2014. *Older adults and technology use: Usage and adoption.* Pew Research Center, April 3. Available at http://www.pewinternet.org/2014/04/03/usage-and-adoption/.

Snipp, C. Matthew. 2003. Racial measurement in the American census: Past practices and implications for the future. *Annual Review of Sociology* 29. Annual Reviews: 563–588. http://www.jstor.org/stable/30036980.

Sussman, Robert Wald. 2014. *The myth of race: The troubling persistence of an unscientific idea.* Cambridge, MA: Harvard University Press.

U.S. Census Bureau. 2004. U.S. interim projections by age, sex, race, and hispanic origin. Available at http://www.census.gov/ipc/www/usinterimproj/.

Vespa, Jonathan, Jamie M. Lewis, and Rose M. Kreider. 2013. America's families and living arrangements: 2012. *Current Population Reports*, 20–570.

Vittrup, Brigitte, et al. 2014. Parental perceptions of the role of media and technology in their young children's lives. *Journal of Early Childhood Research*: doi:10.1177/1476718X14523749.

Williams, Frederick, and Susan Hadden. 1991. *On the prospects for redefining universal service: From connectivity to content (Report of the Policy Research Project).* Austin: Lyndon B. Johnson School of Public Affairs, University of Texas.

Yanow, Dvora. 2015. *Constructing "race" and "ethnicity" in America: Category-making in public policy and administration.* Abingdon/Oxon/Oxfordshire/ New York: Routledge.

Zickuhr, Kathryn, and Aaron Smith. 2013. *Home broadband 2013.* Pew Research Center, August 26. Available at http://www.pewinternet.org/2013/08/26/ home-broadband-2013/.

CHAPTER 5

Feminist Perspectives on Critical Information Needs

Carolyn M. Byerly and Alisa Valentin

Introduction

Women's status and responsibilities are central to understanding women's critical information needs in the USA, whether in times of local or national crisis, or when facing personal challenges of daily life. In spite of advancements legally, educationally, and politically since the 1970s, women in the USA remain a less powerful and more vulnerable population than men. Women continue to lag behind by all available indicators—income levels, education, access to affordable housing, and representation in political office, among others. Add to these facts the matter of gendered roles within families and across the broader society, with women still the primary caretakers for children and the elderly. Women in the workforce still occupy the lowest-paid jobs—many of those traditionally thought of as "women's work," that is, serving, cleaning, and caretaking. Indeed, many women bear the traditional burden of the double-day, coming from their paid jobs to the tasks of motherhood, management of households, and caring for family members.

C.M. Byerly (✉) and A. Valentin
Howard University, Washington, DC, USA

© The Editor(s) (if applicable) and The Author(s) 2016
M.I. Lloyd, L.A. Friedland (eds.), *The Communication Crisis in America, And How to Fix It*, DOI 10.1057/978-1-349-94925-0_5

What do women need to know for their well-being and to take part in aspects of community and political life in order to represent their own self interests? This chapter attempts to answer these questions by considering women's status in relation to health and welfare, economic opportunities, civic participation, and political participation. These aspects of women's experience correspond to four of the eight categories of critical information needs central to this book's concerns, and together, they define a much under-examined area in both feminist and communication research. We review current data on women's status in order to hypothesize the kinds of information that would enable women to address their status and the everyday problems that come with it. We end with a set of principles for policy development that take women's lives and aspirations into consideration.

WOMEN AND THE POLITICS OF INFORMATION

The connection between information and women's status has long been known to women working for political change. Early American suffrage leaders founded their own newspapers in the mid-to-late nineteenth century as a way to build their movement to gain women the vote, and modern feminists, beginning in the 1970s, founded newsletters and book publishing houses to speak for growing numbers of women deprived of a voice through the mainstream newspapers, television, and radio outlets of the day (Rosen 2000). Feminist media of this latter era helped to break the silence on wife battering, incest, and workplace harassment and to advocate for women's self-determination in health care. Women's media also provided the space for feminists to grapple publicly with controversial topics like pornography, abortion rights, and a range of sexuality issues. In addition to establishing their own media, women's rights advocates had also long recognized the importance of obtaining the attention of mainstream news to expand their access to public discourse (Kielbowicz and Scherer 1986; Barker-Plummer 1995). And research indicates that the feminist movement had some impact on how the news covered women's experiences, particularly violence against women, with reporters adopting new feminist terminology like domestic violence, sexual assault, sexual harassment, and acquaintance rape (Byerly and Hill 2012).

Women of color, like Ida. B. Wells, used the media as a way to uncover racial injustices in the South through her anti-lynching campaign (Bay 2009), and Black newspaper publishers like Lucile Bluford, editor and publisher of the Kansas City Call, used their positions to advocate for gender equality and civil rights (Brooks 2015). This sparked other Black women, like Rosa Parks, to join in political movements. Parks, who is traditionally known for her participation in the Montgomery Bus Boycott, also had a record of activism prior to the boycott, in which she reported sexual assaults on Black women (McGuire 2011). After investigating the gang rape of Recy Taylor, a 24-year-old Black mother, "[Parks] and the city's most militant activists launched a campaign that the *Chicago Defender* called the strongest movement for justice to be seen in a decade", stated McGuire in a 2011 interview with (National Public Radio 2011). These investigations helped spark the Civil Rights Movement, which led to groundbreaking federal laws and policies that improved the lives of Black people in America.

However, history turned a corner in the 1980s with the emergence of neoliberalism in the USA, Europe, and Latin America. With it came a shift in women's relationship to media. Economic and political forces contribute to the dynamics of social exclusion (Mansell 2009, p. 35), and neoliberalism has been that force for women, causing them to lose ground in the media's attention to women's lives and perspectives. Neoliberalism is a conservative philosophy that can be seen clearly in public policy. It emphasizes free market capitalism, as well as reductions in public expenditures, tax reform to benefit the private (corporate) sector, privatization of public services and assets, and the marginalization of organized labor, among other things (Couldry 2010; Harvey 2005). Neoliberalism is also decidedly androcentric, with its proponents opposed to expanding legislation and political spaces that had only years earlier opened up through feminist activism. Faludi (1991) captured the ways that the emerging conservative political climate of the 1980s in the USA crept into news coverage of women through a systematic privileging of anti-feminist news sources and perspectives. More than two recent decades of feminist media research has demonstrated the enduring nature of women's marginalization as news subjects and sources.

Neoliberalism's effects can also be seen in women's structural relationship to the media. Women have been unable to gain greater control within newsrooms or in ownership or in policymaking within media industries during this era of neoliberalism. We will return to this notion later in the discussion, but for now, suffice it to say that structural forces have come into stronger play over the last 30 years to deprive women's access to mass communication at every level. Whether new technologies and other communication mechanisms can supply women's critical information needs is an empirical question yet to be addressed by media scholars.

WOMEN'S POLITICAL AND ECONOMIC STATUS

In the USA, which takes pride in its democratic tradition, women lag behind men in access to social, economic, and political rights. The World Gender Gap Report (2015), which ranks women's status by nation each year, places the USA 28 out of 145. The USA ranks the lowest of the major industrial nations in gender equality, also falling behind developing nations like Rwanda, Philippines, Nicaragua, Namibia, South Africa, and Mozambique. Women in the USA have a longer life expectancy than men (71 and 68 years, respectively), according to the report, yet they are likely to have a lower quality of life. Women earn only 60 percent of what men make on average, for example. Neither are women sufficient in number in policymaking realms to push for measures to improve women's equality. In fact, women account for only 27 percent of those in legislatures (congressional and state), and only 24 percent of those in national-level ministerial (i.e., cabinet and appointed) positions. The USA—unlike many other nations—has never had a female head of state (World Economic Forum 2015).

Under neoliberalism, women have also lost ground in terms of public policy to support their well-being. American studies scholar Lynn M. Adrien (2006) is among those who have pointed out the retrenchment in safety net features over the years, the most dramatic being when federal welfare for poor families was essentially ended with passage of what she says was "euphemistically named the 1996 'Personal Responsibility Act,'" a bipartisan bill that Democratic President Bill Clinton signed into law. The hardships brought on through the elimination of welfare have fallen disproportionately on poor women with children, with women now required to reenter the workforce and typically assume low-paying jobs in domestic or food service, or in the agricultural sector, to support their children.

To be sure, conditions for women vary by state and region, according to the Institute for Women's Policy Research (2015), which ranks women's employment highest in the eastern USA (Washington, D.C., Maryland, Massachusetts, New Jersey, and Connecticut) and lowest in the South (West Virginia, Louisiana, Mississippi, and Arkansas), as well as in the western state of Idaho. Still, within even the states with greater equality, there remain pockets of poverty and other forms of inequality. Demographically, women living below the poverty line are disproportionately African-American or Latino, though there is variation by state.

The Great Recession since 2007 has been a "poverty disaster," with harm being "substantial and long-lasting," particularly without the presence of safety nets to assist those who suffered the worst (Pathways 2015, 20). Instead of depicting the structural barriers impacting women who live in poverty, women are depicted as lazy individuals in volatile relationships who were in some way largely responsible for what led up to their lack of income (Bullock et al. 2001).

The problems of lower political status and income inequality for women represent significant forms of structural (i.e., institutionalized) discrimination against women and serve to subjugate women within the society. Reinforcing these forms of subjugation is interpersonal violence that is usually experienced as battering by a family member, or as sexual assault, often by someone known to the victim. The US Department of Justice's national victims' survey reveals that approximately 293,066 individuals are raped or sexually assaulted each year, with the great majority of the victims being female (U.S. Department of Justice 2014). Sexual harassment in the workplace is another common problem that women face, something that may compound their already lower occupational status. Such is the case for female restaurant workers, 66 percent of whom said they experience routine harassment by managers and 78 percent of whom they are harassed by customers (Stampler 2014).

WOMEN'S HEALTH AND WELFARE

Although access to health care has been established as a human right, the USA leaves individual families to rely on their own (private) resources for services, particularly in terms of health care, rather than on publicly financed services (Albelda and Coronado 2014). Historically, race and gender have both played a role in shaping social protection programs, and this is seen today in data showing that nearly twice as many Black and three times as many Hispanic women are likely not to have health care, compared to White women (Albelda and Coronado 2014, 12). Income is also a predictor, with families below the poverty line less likely to have health care coverage than those above it.

These facts, which have become part of the common wisdom in America, were factored into publicity plans to promote the Affordable Care Act (more commonly called "Obamacare"), the massive health care reform to make health insurance affordable to most Americans, when it launched in 2013 (Radnofsky 2013). Reaching out to the hardest-to-reach communities—those with the fewest resources and least access to information—was a goal from the beginning, according to the then Health and Human Services Secretary Kathleen Sebelius. For example, follow-up reports show that women who learned about the provisions of Obamacare and signed up benefited substantially. In relation to birth control alone, women's annual expenditures for birth control pill users dropped from $32.74 per month to $20.37 (Lachman 2015). Research indicates that women with computer access seek information about health care through the Internet, particularly when they are in need of reassurance in times of uncertainty (Hsieh and Brennan 2005).

A study by Correra and Harp (2011) demonstrates how female journalists in decision-making positions have the power to influence coverage related to women. This study specifically focused on how two newspapers covered the human papillomavirus (HPV) vaccine. The results found that the Virginia newspaper with a more gender-balanced staff published a higher count of stories related to the HPV vaccine, and those stories were also displayed in a more prominent location within the paper. One study in information seeking in predominantly non-White communities found that women identified their greatest daily challenges to be locating services for elderly parents, counseling for juveniles in trouble with the law, job training to improve their own employment, and trying to find out how gentrification was affecting their neighborhoods. Most of those surveyed said the local media did not provide information on these (Byerly et al. 2006).

Studies in risk assessment have shown that during floods, including Hurricane Katrina in 2004 and Hurricane Sandy in 2012, women assume the key roles of getting children and others to safety and caring for the injured. Women generally are at greater risk than men during disasters and afterward. More women than men were living in poverty in New Orleans at the time of Katrina, when approximately 30 percent of females were living below the poverty line, compared to 20 percent of men (IWPR 2010). Poverty limits the resources that would contribute to the means of getting out or getting to places of safety. Women in New Orleans public housing at the time of Katrina were unlikely to have a car, and, once the levees broke, they could not take a bus or get out on foot. Women with responsibilities for aged or disabled family members, or newborns had the least chances of all for escape.

Women with disabilities receive little attention in communication research or in the news, and yet they make up a substantial number of those living in the USA. There are 37.6 million people living with hearing, vision, cognitive, and/or ambulatory disabilities in the USA, according to the National Science Foundation (2015), more than half of those female. Many have difficulty living independently. Their access to information is likely to vary, depending on their disability, according to Ortoleva (2015), a human rights lawyer and international advocate for women with disabilities. Women with disabilities typically look for information they need from the news, from the Internet, and from health care providers, Ortoleva says, but:

> If health care providers don't have sign language interpreters, deaf women won't be able to communicate with them. Blind women cannot access print information unless they have computer technology to "read" electronic information. And, many websites are not designed to work with "screen reading" [voice] technology yet, even though the Americans with Disabilities Act requires it (Ortoleva 2015).

One study by Women Enabled International (2015) indicates in its preliminary findings that sexual and reproductive health is the most important concern among women with disabilities, followed by preventing and ending gender-based violence, employment rights and support, and education (WEI 2015). While these data are international in scope, they include participants from the USA in their sample.

Other factors worsen the situation for women in crisis situations. Women in most regions share a greater responsibility for childcare than men and more often than men have the home as their workplace, with residences often of less stable construction than commercial or public buildings. Women who are pregnant or recovering from childbirth have limited mobility and face additional difficulties during disasters. Women also make up a greater proportion of the elderly, typically one of the groups with the highest mortality rates during disasters—especially when, as in the case of New Orleans, hospitals are not evacuated (IWPR 2010). The population of New Orleans was overwhelmingly African-American at the time of the hurricane, and most lived below the poverty line, even if they were working full-time. Thus, the interaction of gender, race, and economics has serious implications for government policy in managing disasters (Adrian 2006), as well as ensuring that people receive the information they need to respond and survive.

WOMEN'S CIVIC AND POLITICAL ENGAGEMENT

Women have a long history of civic engagement. Historically, women in the USA established libraries and schools, and they formed women's clubs to initiate a wide range of cultural events and to address community needs. Both White and Black women were active in organizing clubs of various kinds and setting up a range of community services, with women's civic involvement reaching a "golden age" in the 1950s. However, the rise of the Civil Rights Movement in the 1950s, and the women's rights movement a decade later, brought a shift in the kinds of things women attended to, with many taking greater part in activities more closely aligned with political work. Mathews-Gardner (2003) found that the 1950s introduced a new way of "being civic" to women's associations—something that is important to understanding women's community-level engagement today.

Women also have had a substantial history of political activity in mainstream politics. They formed the League of Women Voters in 1920, the year the 19th Amendment guaranteeing women's suffrage passed, to educate women on exercising their political responsibilities. They formed the International League for Peace and Freedom and the Women's Peace Party in 1915 to advocate against US involvement in war. Since 1964, the number of female voters has exceeded the number of male voters in every presidential election. Moreover, according to the Center for American Women and Politics, women have gradually increased their political participation since 1964, with the ages between 25 and 64 being the most active (CAWP 2013). Black women have voted at slightly higher rates than White women since 2004, but both vote at higher rates than women of Hispanic and other non-White races. And women tend to vote Democrat (Copeland 2012). As it relates to media coverage, research demonstrates that newspapers with women editors who covered US senate races in 2006 were more likely to have balanced coverage of Democratic and Republican candidates (Fico and Freedman 2008).

WOMEN'S (LACK OF) ACCESS TO INFORMATION

In spite of women's continuous and robust presence in the civic and political realms, journalism does little to inform the public about the female half of the population. Most traditional news remains focused on men and omits women's experience, needs, and voices. Research indicates that women in the USA do not receive basic information from either the traditional (broadcast and cable radio and television, or newspapers) or new media (Internet-based) sources to help them understand issues related to basic survival. For example, after the financial collapse of 2007–2008, major agenda-setting newspapers like the *Washington Post* and *New York Times* carried almost no information about women and the economy, even though polls had shown that women across income, race, and educational levels identified the economy as their number one concern (Byerly 2009). The latest report from the Global Media Monitoring Project (Who Makes the News 2010), the longest running longitudinal research on news coverage of women, found that North American media placed women as the subjects of news in only 27 percent of the 173 stories examined in both traditional and new media platforms. Women reporters accounted for only 30 percent of the bylines on stories about economics, politics, social, or legal issues (Who Makes the News 2010, 4).

Questions also arise as to whether Internet-based sources can fill the gap of information for and about women. Little is known about how women seek information they need for survival and wellbeing in the challenging moments of daily life and times of crisis. We know that some online resources exist—for example, checklists and basic principles of a gendered response to a disaster now are available through several organizations, including the Gender and Disaster Network, at http://www. gdnonline.org/. However, does every woman have access to smartphone and computer technology to access these and similar websites?

According to a 2015 report by the Groupe Speciale Mobile Association, 1.7 billion women do not own mobile phones in low- and middle-income countries (GSMA 2015). And, do they have control over what kind of information is organized and posted? Women have little authority within traditional or online news and information sources, as noted earlier. Nor is the information they receive broadly representative culturally. In fact, according to one recent United Nations report, an estimated 5 percent of languages are present on the Internet—hardly representative globally or in the increasing cultural diversity within the USA (United Nations 2015). Women with disabilities may also not be able to access information they need, particularly blind women who rely on print news or Internet, or women with learning disabilities who may have difficulty knowing how and where to search for information (Ortoleva 2015).

There is a dearth of research on the extent to which women seek out and use such information in order to address a crisis or to engage in more routine things, such as job hunting, finding a doctor, locating a community service, understanding and/or addressing changes going on in their neighborhoods, or informing themselves about issues before the next election. Concerns also arise as to whose perspectives are found in the information that is available.

The paradox of the information revolution of the twenty-first century is the simultaneous abundance of information availability for some groups in the midst of information poverty for others. A feminist perspective on critical information needs to consider not only the paltry amount of relevant information to women's wellbeing and participation in society, but also the matter of who produces that information available to them. The problem of media ownership concentration is often pointed to as an explanation for the dearth of news and information about and by women. Women's ownership in broadcast media has declined since passage of the Telecommunications Act of 1996, the basis for media deregulation (Who Makes the News 2010, 3). The most recent ownership report issued by the Federal Communications Commission (FCC) shows women's radio and television ownership in the low single digits (Byerly 2014).

Women broadcast owners indicate that they operate their stations in a hostile regulatory environment that favors wealthy, male-owned corporations over individual owners or smaller companies—a claim borne out by the rates at which the largest telecommunication companies have bought out the smaller, less well-financed companies in the present era of deregulation (Byerly 2011, 2014). Neither do women have much control at the policymaking levels of traditional or new technology companies, where men dominate in top management positions as well as on boards of directors (Byerly 2013, 2014, 2016). Data on gender representation for telecommunications companies show that women comprise only 14 percent of those on the board of CBS, 17 percent on the board of General Electric, and 25 percent of those on the board of News Corp (which owns Fox News). Women who might use the Internet to seek information are likely to use the dominant search engine Google, whose board of eleven includes only three women (27 percent) (Byerly 2016).

Women's media ownership has been the subject of legal action in recent years. The US Third Circuit Court of Appeals criticized the FCC for not doing more to fulfill its mandate to promote greater ownership opportunities for women (and minorities) in its *Prometheus v. FCC* (2004, 2011) rulings. The Prometheus Radio Project, a Philadelphia-based nonprofit organization that helps community groups establish low-power radio stations, sued the FCC in 2003 when the commission was considering further loosening ownership limits, charging that further media consolidation would threaten smaller broadcast companies (Prometheus Radio Project 2011). The court agreed with the plaintiffs in Prometheus I, mandating that the FCC retain the previous ownership rules until commissioners could provide a rationale for changes. The ruling also required that the commission consider ways to address the low rates of broadcast ownership by women and minorities, which was in the low single digits for both. Seven years later, the FCC still had not complied with the 2004 ruling by undertaking studies or adopting mechanisms to address the situation. While the court thus created the legal space for gender- and race-conscious regulation and for remedies for low levels of ownership by women and minorities in broadcast, the FCC to date still has done nothing to respond (see Byerly et al. 2011; Byerly and Valentin 2016).

Byerly and Valentin (2016) call women's low representation at the top (macro-level) of media industries, as well as in positions of authority in employment (meso-level), a problem of media access and they frame this lack of access as a problem of sex discrimination that interferes with women's right to communicate. In the USA, the First Amendment protects free speech for both men and women; however, women have much less opportunity to exercise that free speech without the ability to own or otherwise access the channels of communication to express themselves. Gallagher has linked media policy to women's free expression, observing that the discourse on freedom of expression "in the gender equality domain gives rise to an inevitable question: Whose freedom, defined by whom?" (Gallagher 2011, 457).

DISCUSSION AND POLICY RECOMMENDATIONS

Structural problems require structural solutions. Women's lack of access to and control over communication processes require laws and policies that will enable women to be better represented at the ownership levels in media industries, as well as in positions of decision making in news organizations—both traditional media and online. Therefore, laws and regulations matter to women's right to communicate because they provide the framework within which women can make legitimate demands. Deregulation of media ownership has been harmful to women. Therefore, we would like to see legislation that imposes limits on the number and kind of companies a single corporation can own. This will, of necessity, begin to break up the oligopolies that presently dominate the US telecommunications landscape. In terms of regulation, the FCC still has the responsibility to explore and adopt mechanisms that will increase gender and race representation in media ownership. The place to start will be the commissioning of studies that build on the FCC's own required quadrennial reporting of ownership by gender and race, which continues to show a downward slide of females and racial minorities in broadcast ownership.

Federal and state agencies with the responsibility of providing support to US residents should be held accountable for providing information on health, welfare, and other services with women's varied needs in mind—for example, language, learning levels, physical and mental abilities, and access to technology.

We encourage feminist organizations to place greater priority on the structural issues related to gender and media. Leaders of feminist and women's professional organizations should refocus their concerns about women's rights on women's lack of access to media, information, and the legislative process. Women media professionals and feminist activists working in advocacy roles might renew their consideration of ways to use the complaint process made available by the FCC to challenge broadcast license renewals (as they did in the 1970s). With this tactic, women may file comments with the FCC complaining when television and radio stations do not serve women's informational needs in programming. Last, we encourage feminist scholars to undertake empirical research involving field work that more clearly establishes what women see their critical information needs to be and how they seek to fill those needs.

<h1 style="text-align:center">REFERENCES</h1>

Adrian, Lynne M. 2006. *Definitions and disasters: What Hurricane Katrina revealed about women's rights.* Urbana: Forum on Public Policy. Available at http://www.forumonpublicpolicy.com/archive07/adrian.pdf.

Albelda, Randy, and Diana Salas Coronado. 2014. *Expanding women's healthcare access in the United States: The patchwork "Universalism" of the Affordable Care Act (Working Paper 2014–02).* Boston: UN Women for Progress of the World's Women Report, University of Massachusetts Boston Department of Economics. Available at http://repec.umb.edu/RePEc/files/2014_02.pdf.

Barker-Plummer, Bernadette. 1995. News as a political resource: Media strategies and political identity in the U.S. women's movement, 1966–1975. *Critical Studies in Mass Communication* 12(3): 306–324.

Bay, Mia. 2009. *To tell the truth freely: The life of Ida B. Wells.* New York: Macmillan.

Brooks, Sheila. 2015. *Lucile Bluford: Civil rights activist and Black feminist: An advocate for change in the Kansas City Call, 1968–1983*. Dissertation. Howard University, Washington, DC.

Bullock, Heather E., Karen Fraser Wyche, and Wendy R. Williams. 2001. Media images of the poor. *Journal of Social Issues* 57(2): 229–246.

Byerly, Carolyn M. 2009. Women, the economy and news: Analysis of the 2008 U.S. primary coverage. *St. John's Journal of Legal Commentary* 24(2): 387–402.

Byerly, Carolyn M. 2011. Behind the scenes of women's broadcast ownership. *Howard Journal of Communications* 22(1): 24–42.

Byerly, Carolyn M. 2014. Women and media control: Feminist interrogations at the macro level. In *The Routledge companion to media and gender*, ed. Cynthia Carter, Linda Steiner, and Lisa McLaughlin, 105–115. New York/UK: Taylor & Francis/Routledge.

Byerly, Carolyn M. (Ed.). 2013. *The Palgrave international handbook of women and journalism*. Abingdon, UK: Palgrave Macmillan

Byerly, Carolyn M. 2016. Feminist activism and U.S. communications policy. In *Media activism*, ed. Barbie Zelizer. New York: Routledge, forthcoming.

Byerly, Carolyn M., and Marcus Hill. 2012. Reformulation theory: Gauging feminist impact on news of violence against women. *Journal of Women and Gender*. https://www.academia.edu/2247510/Reformulation_Theory_Gauging_Feminist_Impact_on_News_of_Violence_Against_Women.

Byerly, Carolyn M., and A. Valentin. 2016. Women's access to media: Legal dimension of ownership and employment in the United States. In *Race and gender in electronic media: Challenges and opportunities*, ed. Rebecca Ann Lind. New York: Routledge, forthcoming.

Byerly, Carolyn M., Kehbuma Langmia, and Jamila A. Cupid. 2006. Ownership matters: Localism, the ethnic minority news audience, and community participation. In *Does bigger media equal better media?* Social Science Research Council and Benton Foundation. http://www.ssrc.org/programs/media.

Byerly, Carolyn M., Yong Jin Park, and Reginald D. Miles. 2011. Race- and gender-conscious policies: Toward a more egalitarian communications future. *Journal of Information Policy* 1: 425–440.

Center for American Women and Politics. 2013. *Gender differences in voter turnout (Fact Sheet)*. New Brunswick: Center for American Women and Politics, Eagleton Institute of Politics, Rutgers University. Available at www.cawp.rutgers.edu.

Copeland, Libby. 2012. Why do women vote differently than men? *Slate*, January 4. Available at http://www.slate.com/articles/double_x/doublex/2012/01/the_gender_gap_in_politics_why_do_women_vote_differently_than_men_.html.

Correa, Teresa, and Dustin Harp. 2011. Women matter in newsrooms: How power and critical mass relate to the coverage of the HPV vaccine. *Journalism and Mass Communication Quarterly* 88(2): 301–319.

Couldry, Nick. 2010. *Why voice matters: Culture & politics after neoliberalism*. London: Sage.

Faludi, S. (2009). *Backlash: The undeclared war against American women*. New York: Crown

Fico, Frederick, and Eric Freedman. 2008. Biasing influences on balance in election news coverage: An assessment of newspaper coverage of the 2006 U.S. Senate elections. *Journalism and Mass Communication Quarterly* 85(3): 499–514.

Gallagher, Margaret. 2011. Gender and communication policy: Struggling for space. In *The handbook of global media and communication policy*, ed. Robin Mansell and Marc Raboy, 451–466. Malden: Wiley Blackwell.

Groupe Speciale Mobile Association. 2015. Bridging the gender gap: Mobile access and usage in low and middle-income countries. Available at http://www.gsma.com/connectedwomen/wp-content/uploads/2015/02/GSM0001_02252015_GSMAReport_FINAL-WEB-spreads.pdf.

Harvey, David. 2005. *A brief history of neoliberalism*. Oxford: Oxford University Press.

Hsieh, Yichuan, and Patricia Flatley Brennan. 2005. What are pregnant women's information needs and information seeking behaviors prior to their prenatal genetic counseling? In *AMIA Annual Symposium Proceedings*, 355–359. U.S. National Library of Medicine National Institutes of Health. http://www.ncbi.nlm.nih.gov/pmc/articles/PMC1560653/.

Institute for Women's Policy Research. 2010. *Women, disasters, and Hurricane Katrina (Fact Sheet, IWPR #D492)*. Washington, DC: Institute for Women's Policy Research.

Institute for Women's Policy Research. 2015. *Status of women in the states (IWPR Report #R466)*. www.statusofwomendatalorg.

Kielbowicz, Richard, and Clifford Wayne Scherer. 1986. The role of the press in the dynamics of social movements. *Research in Social Movements, Conflicts and Change* 9: 71–96.

Lachman, Samantha. 2015. Women are spending $1.4 billion less on birth control due to Obamacare: Report. *The Huffington Post*, July 7. Retrieved November 25, 2015, from http://www.huffingtonpost.com/2015/07/07/obamacare-birth-control-_n_7747332.html.

Mansell, Robin. 2011. *Introduction Foundations of the Theory and Practice of Global Media and Communication Policy*. In Robin Mansell & Marc Raboy (Eds.), The handbook of global media and communication policy (Vol. 6). JohnWiley & Sons.

Mansell, Robin, and Marc Raboy (Eds.). 2014. *The handbook of global media and communication policy*. Malden: Wiley Blackwell.

Mathews-Gardner, A. Lanathea. 2003. *From woman's club to NGO: The Terrain of women's civil engagement in the mid-twentieth century United States*. (Doctoral dissertation). Syracuse University.

McGuire, Danielle L. 2011. *At the dark end of street: Black women, rape, and resistance — A new history of the civil rights Movement from Rosa Parks to the rise of Black power*. New York: Vintage.

McGuire, Danielle & Taylor, Recey. 2011, February 28. *Hidden pattern of rape helped stir Civil Righs Movement*. [Interview by Michel Martin, Transcript]. National Public Radio. Retrieved November 29, 2015, from http://npr.org/temgetplates/story/story.php?storyId=13413169

National Science Foundation. 2015. Women, minorities, and persons with disabilities in science and engineering (report). Available at http://www.nsf.gov/statistics/2015/nsf15311/tables/pdf/tab1-3.pdf.

Ortoleva, Stephanie. 2015. Personal communication.

Pathways. 2015. *State of the States: The poverty and inequality report*. Stanford Center on Poverty and Inequality. Retrieved November 25, 2015, from https://web.stanford.edu/group/scspi/sotu/SOTU_2015.pdf.

Prometheus Radio Project. 2011. *Federal court rejects media consolidation in Prometheus vs.FCC*. Retrieved October 31, 2015, from http://www.prometheusradio.org/content/federal-court-rejects-media-consolidation-prometheus-vs-fcc

Radnofsky, Louise. 2013. "Obamacare" insurance publicity campaign steps up. *The Wall Street Journal*, June 24. Retrieved November 25, 2015, from http://blogs.wsj.com/washwire/2013/06/24/obamacare-insurance-publicity-campaign-ramps-up/.

Rosen, Ruth. 2000. *The world split open: How the modern women's movement changed America*. New York: Penguin.

Stampler, Laura. 2014. 66% of female restaurant workers report being sexually harassed by managers. *Time*, October 7. Available at http://time.com/3478041/restaurant-sexual-harassment-survey/.

U.S. Department of Justice. 2014. *National crime victimization survey, 2009–2013*. Retrieved November 26, 2015, from http://www.bjs.gov/content/pub/press/cv13pr.cfm.

United Nations Educational, Scientific and Cultural Organization. 2015. *The state of broadband 2015*. Available at http://www.broadbandcommission.org/Documents/reports/bb-annualreport2015.pdf.

Who Makes the News. 2010. *United States of America (national report)*. Global Media Monitoring Project. Available at http://cdn.agilitycms.com/who-makes-the-news/Imported/reports_2010/national/USA.pdf.

Women Enabled International. 2015. *WEI survey & mapping project of advocates & organizations for the human rights of women & girls with disabilities worldwide (preliminary report)*. Available at http://womenenabled.org/mapping.html.

World Economic *Forum*. (2015). The Global Gender Gap Report. Retrieved from, http://www3.weforum.org/docs/GGGR2015/cover.pdf

CHAPTER 6

Ethnic Media and the Social Incorporation of New Americans

Matthew D. Matsaganis and Vikki S. Katz

Ethnic media, which we define as media created for (and generally by) immigrants, ethnic and language minority groups, and indigenous populations, are growing in size, audience, and visibility worldwide, as well as in the USA. In 2014, the National Directory of Ethnic Media contained information on over 3000 ethnic media organizations in the USA. Additionally, Allen's 2009 study indicated that nearly 60 million Americans regularly get their news and other information from ethnically targeted television, radio, newspapers, and websites; that figure was 16 percent lower just four years earlier. These data suggest that increased demographic diversity in the USA is correlated with increased diversity in the media landscape.[1]

Research documents the multiple roles that ethnic media serve for their audiences. They help immigrant populations, in particular, to *stay connected* to their country of origin (e.g., by keeping them informed about breaking and developing news). They also perform a *symbolic role*

M.D. Matsaganis (✉)
University at Albany, State University of New York Albany, NY, USA

V.S. Katz
Rutgers University, New Brunswick, NJ, USA

© The Editor(s) (if applicable) and The Author(s) 2016   81
M.I. Lloyd, L.A. Friedland (eds.), *The Communication Crisis in America, And How to Fix It*, DOI 10.1057/978-1-349-94925-0_6

by building knowledge of what it means to embody a particular ethnic identity, supporting performance of related behaviors, and instilling a sense of belonging to a particular community. Ethnic media produced in the local communities where immigrants and their families settle can also contribute to the creation of what Anderson called "imagined community," thereby building social cohesion at the local, community level. In addition, ethnic media have historically supported, and still facilitate, the integration of immigrant and ethnic populations into the social fabric of US society by serving the critical information needs (CINs) of these populations across the USA. Because mainstream media are interested in appealing to the broadest possible audience, they tend to overlook CINs specific to these vulnerable populations. As a result, ethnic media are a crucial feature of the media landscape for many Americans.

The audiences of ethnic media include both immigrant and ethnic minority communities; in the USA, these include media targeted to African-Americans, Native Americans, immigrants, and the descendants of immigrants. Since these audiences are social groups that have historically been socially marginalized and disenfranchised, they frequently face greater challenges in meeting CINs than members of the ethnic majority (i.e., English-speaking, European-origin individuals) and more privileged social groups (e.g., with higher levels of income and education). They may battle to afford new technologies and access to broadband Internet, the latter increasingly becoming a crucial resource for information to avoid threats (e.g., the spread of a disease, a possible natural disaster) but also for accessing a range of opportunities (e.g., jobs, scholarships, healthcare, and business-development programs).

Additionally, immigrant and minority populations often live in underserved communities where they cannot count on broadband access being freely available to them if they cannot afford it. These constraints disproportionately affect African Americans and Latinos, who are now collectively the majority population in seven of the ten largest urban centers in the USA. And for minorities who move outside of larger cities, they often encounter even fewer resources for addressing CINs, as smaller cities and suburbs are frequently not as well-equipped to serve non-English speakers. For example, in Hudson, New York (120 miles north of New York City), Matsaganis and Golden found that residents had virtually no local broadcast media, expensive options for accessing the Internet (relative to residents' incomes), and only one local newspaper, which few residents identified as a source they could depend on for health information.

As Noam has shown in his work on media concentration and ownership in the USA, the media landscape of Hudson is similar to that of many smaller cities that represent small media markets. In the case of Hudson, this media environment made it difficult for residents (especially for African-American residents with low incomes) and local health providers to reach each other, thereby contributing to the underutilization of available reproductive healthcare services by African-American women in the community and the generation of related health disparities.

In addition, immigrant and ethnic minority populations may be less able to "afford" to go without resources to address CINs than more affluent or longer-settled populations. This is clearly evident in the case of new immigrants who, as newcomers, often live in survival mode. Helping immigrant individuals, families, and groups to overcome barriers that lead to social inequalities, become integrated into the American mainstream, and thrive, requires enabling them to easily address their CINs.

THE AUDIENCES OF ETHNIC MEDIA AND THE CRITICAL INFORMATION NEEDS THESE MEDIA HELP ADDRESS

Low-income immigrants and minorities face a range of challenges in addressing their CINs, and resulting knowledge gaps which contribute to persistent social disparities related to education, health, and overall well-being. A growing body of research has moved away from a deficit-oriented approach to documenting their challenges, by instead focusing on uncovering how individuals and families develop innovative strategies to address their CINs. Connections to ethnic media are often an important feature of the strategies that individuals and families develop to do so.

Katz has found that families often pursue collective strategies by drawing on their relative strengths and fluencies in different languages, and with different media and technology platforms, to locate and understand resources that address their CINs. For example, immigrant parents' fluency in their native languages can open their children to an entire set of ethnic media information resources and help to encourage the second generation's maintenance of their mother tongue. And conversely, children in many immigrant families *broker* parents' connections to English-language media as well as to Spanish-language content available through online platforms, both of which are often less familiar to parents.

While there are no nationally representative data to document how many children broker media and technology for their parents, 2010 US

Census data indicate that 61 percent of children of immigrants in the USA had at least one parent who reported difficulty speaking English, up from 55 percent in 2000, and 49 percent in 1990.[2] These findings suggest that for children of immigrants, having a parent who needs help navigating English-language resources is more likely to be the norm than the exception. Furthermore, Louie reports findings from a representative survey of US adolescents with Central American, Mexican, Dominican, and Chinese parentage, which indicated that only 20 percent of respondents watched television "mainly alone," and that most co-viewing occurred with family members. By contrast, a representative survey that Rideout and colleagues conducted of all US teens during the same time period found that more than one-third watched TV "mainly alone," and that co-viewing with friends was common. Taken together, these findings indicate that immigrant families' media connections span ethnic and mainstream media, across both online and offline platforms—and that variations in language and media literacy capabilities within families contribute to shared sense-making activities. Katz documents how these collective, family activities enable immigrant families to address CINs related to health care, education, and civic information.

In our own work, we have documented how ethnic media address a range of goals related to CINs. We take an ecological approach to understanding the relationships between ethnic media and their audiences. An ecological approach emphasizes: (a) the importance of local context when assessing what resources residents have available to address their CINs; (b) individual choice, by focusing on differences in residents' strategies for addressing their CINs; and (c) the relevance of local constraints that residents encounter as they try to address their needs.

Wilkin, Ball-Rokeach, Matsaganis, and Cheong provide a relevant example of this approach. Their analyses focused on the media connections residents make to address their health-related CINs. They found, for instance, that residents who were not connected to the Internet depended primarily on ethnic media—including newspapers, television, and radio—for finding health information and resources. Residents in those same communities with an Internet connection indicated that going online was one of the top two ways they located health-related information.

Building on this earlier work, Matsaganis conducted a study of Latino populations living in Chicago, Charlotte (North Carolina), Los Angeles, and New York. He found variations in the communication ecologies that residents constructed to decide what technological services and devices to purchase. Latinos with a broadband connection in the home had appreciably different communication ecologies from those of mobile-only broadband users, nomadic Internet users (e.g., individuals who connected at a local library or the home of a relative), dial-up users, and individuals with no Internet connection (non-connectors). For example, ethnically targeted television was especially important to Latino Internet users who did not have broadband at home; 77 percent of those who identified television as their top communication resource relied on Spanish-language channels. While Latinos who had broadband at home relied on the Internet more frequently, one-quarter (23 percent) still relied primarily on television, and two-thirds of those specified Spanish-language channels.

Online communication resources are, of course, not distinctive from ethnic media, especially in today's rapidly transforming media environment. Like other news organizations, ethnic media are increasingly likely to be online. In a 2015 study, Matsaganis reported that over 90 percent of surveyed New York City-based ethnic media organizations had a website, more than 80 percent had a social media account, and 30 percent had their own mobile application (i.e., an app).

Collectively, the findings from these studies underscore the importance of ethnic media in the lives of diverse populations. They also stress the importance of these media evolving to online formats that can facilitate audiences' quick and easy connections to online resources that are becoming increasingly important for addressing CINs.

As further evidence of how ethnic media enable their audiences to address relevant threats and opportunities in their environments, we discuss three categories of CINs among those Friedland and colleagues identified in their review of scholarship on CINs for the Federal Communications Commission (FCC).

Emergencies and Public Safety
Ethnic media are trusted resources for disaster preparedness. Mathew and Kelly reported that by not providing information resources in accessible languages, the City of Los Angeles was not adequately prepared to provide immigrant communities with information immediately following disasters, such as earthquakes and wildfires. However, they found that Chinese, Spanish, and Vietnamese speakers all indicated that ethnic radio is the first place they turn for information during an emergency, followed by ethnic television, community organizations, and local schools.

These findings suggest that immigrants activate the limited, local options available to address their CINs during emergencies, and that ethnic media compensate for the city's failure to make information directly accessible to local residents. Mathew and Kelly concluded that the City of Los Angeles needs to pursue meaningful partnerships with ethnic radio stations to provide listeners with information in the aftermath of a disaster, so that they can mobilize accordingly.

Health Information
Ethnic media are crucial connections for addressing health concerns—especially, it appears, for individuals who were not early Internet adopters. Individuals who are slower to adopt new technologies often also face more personal constraints than their neighbors; in an immigrant community, these may include limited education, English-language capability, income, and unfavorable residency status, all of which Katz, Ang, and Suro reported are associated with less access to a broad range of communication resources for addressing health-related CINs.

Political Life
Ethnic media are also key resources for political information about candidates and public policy initiatives, and often strongly encourage constituents to become citizens and to register to vote. Prior to the 2012 US presidential election, Matsaganis and Katz conducted focus groups with ethnic media producers in Boston, New York, and Los Angeles, to identify what political issues they were covering for their audiences, and how. The manager of a television station serving Brazilian immigrants in New England illustrated how ethnic media address audiences' political CINs while increasing newcomers' familiarity with American civic history:

> The producers of that show felt that it would be very good for them, for the community, to understand the workings of the State House. So, I mean nobody does a show on the State House, right? (*Laughs*) But they decided to produce a program on the State House, and it was great! [The audience] *loved* it! I mean, even I learned things about the State House that I probably should have known.

The Pew Center has also reported that ethnic media keep a close eye on potential irregularities at voting booths by explaining what people should do if turned away from a polling station if they have been registered to vote.

ETHNIC MEDIA'S CONSTRAINTS ON MEETING AUDIENCES' CRITICAL INFORMATION NEEDS

The evidence clearly demonstrates that ethnic media are essential elements of residents' communication ecologies in many ethnic and immigrant communities. Overlooking ethnic media in any academic—and, most importantly, in any policy-related—discussions about how to best address the CINs of an increasingly diverse US population is likely to lead to less informed, and less effective, public policy choices. We consider three different levels of constraints that hamper ethnic media's capabilities to help ethnic communities address a broad array of CINs

Organizational-Level Constraints
Ethnic media can produce and disseminate critical information in part because they have a special relationship with their communities. These relationships are rooted in media producers coming from, and frequently living in, the communities they serve, in addition to speaking their audience's language. Ethnic media are often trusted sources of information that are treated as authentic "voices" of their communities, and these bonds of trust facilitate ethnic media acting as important connections between individuals and families, local services, and businesses. Ethnic media can also be key players in the diffusion of new communication and information technologies. We have argued elsewhere (with Ball-Rokeach) that ethnic media can be "anchor institutions" (akin to local libraries and community technology centers) to facilitate broadband diffusion in underserved minority and immigrant communities.

Performing all of these roles is not easy for ethnic media producers, whose organizations vary in size from mom-and-pop type of operations to global media enterprises. Most ethnic media are small organizations. In his 2015 survey of ethnic media organizations in New York City, Matsaganis reported that 47 percent of the 103 producers who participated had a staff of four or fewer people. Another 27 percent said their staff comprised five to nine individuals. Small ethnic media outlets often cover and produce fewer stories for their audiences due to limited human and financial resources. In the aforementioned survey, ethnic media organizations reported annual operating budgets ranging between less than $150,000 and over $1.5 million, but 44 percent of these organizations reported a budget of under $150,000 and another 28 percent between $150,000 and $349,000. With constrained budgets, ethnic media producers may update hardware less regularly and have less support for staff in using new communication technologies to stay connected with their audiences.

Media Market-Level Constraints
Ethnic media producers' limited financial resources are, at least in some cases, related to the size of their intended audiences. Media serving small ethnic communities face an inherent disadvantage. A more limited audience base means lower circulation figures or ratings (compared with larger ethnic media organizations, and especially, with larger mainstream media), which translates into a smaller potential advertising base. In addition, many ethnic media producers have access to fewer financial resources because reliable data on ethnic media audiences (e.g., their sizes, composition, and media consumption behaviors) is sorely lacking. One consequence of these missing data is that advertising professionals and their clients do not have information that they customarily need to make their ad-buying choices. This ultimately translates into less advertising revenue for ethnic media.

Nielsen and Arbitron, two of the most prominent agencies rating the size of media audiences, have both been challenged in recent years with regard to sampling methodologies that systematically underrepresented minority audiences. In the case of Arbitron, collective efforts of ethnic communities, journalism advocacy groups, and the Attorneys General of New York and New Jersey ultimately compelled Arbitron to improve its methodology. Accurate audience ratings help provide ethnic media the opportunity to attract advertising revenue commensurate with their market share.

There are also insufficient data on ethnic media at the federal government level. The FCC tracks and reports on the number of broadcast media licenses that are awarded to organizations owned by individuals of minority backgrounds. According to Eggerton, just 3 percent of all full-power television stations and 7 percent of radio stations were owned by all racial minorities combined in 2014. However, minority ownership does not necessarily make those holdings ethnic media, nor does it guarantee that they serve information needs of ethnic communities. The lack of data on ownership across media (mainstream and ethnic), media content, and of course, media audiences makes it difficult to accurately assess whether local media markets serve the CINs of an increasingly diverse US population.

Macro or Policy-Level Constraints
While national-level provisions are important, policy constraints on ethnic media are more clearly evident at the local level, where media market boundaries generally overlap with the administrative boundaries of cities, counties, or large metropolitan areas. In New York City, for example, there are over 270 ethnic publications published in 36 languages. The circulations of some ethnic newspapers is astounding; according to a recent report by the New York Press Association (NYPA), the combined circulation of 95 ethnic newspapers in New York City is 2.94 million—approximately 30 percent of the city's population. For the sake of comparison, the approximate circulation of *The New York Times*, which is based in New York City but enjoys wide national distribution, is 1.6 million.

Despite their broad circulation, ethnic publications secure less than 18 percent of total monies that the City of New York spends on advertising.[3] Because such ads frequently promote critical city resources and programs, this discrepancy in ad placement effectively means that the city does not support ethnic media at a level commensurate to the population that they serve. Even more importantly, this discrepancy means limited dissemination of critical information to the communities that often need it most.

While progress has certainly been uneven, there is growing recognition that increased population diversity requires shifts in how powerful individuals and institutions relate to their constituencies—and the media that serve them. For instance, Barack Obama, as President-elect in 2008, put legacy media like *The New York Times* on hold and gave his first interviews to ethnic media, starting with *Ebony* and *Black Enterprise* magazines, and then went on the air with radio talk show hosts "El Pistolero" and "El Piolin" of Radio La Que Buena 105.1 FM and Radio La Nueva 101.9 FM, respectively. His first television interview was on the Arab language channel al-Arabiya. At a more local level, some governors and mayors have also begun to pay more attention to ethnic media. For example, in 2009, Governor Deval Patrick of Massachusetts held his first press conference in Boston for ethnic media serving the state's Armenian, African-American, Haitian, Hispanic, Portuguese, Brazilian, Irish, Japanese, Chinese, Korean, and Indian communities.

When it comes to serving historically marginalized communities' CINs, awareness of ethnic media will not suffice. Evidence is mounting that awareness is translating into action beyond the offices of elected officials. For example, before the 2010 Census, the US Census Bureau launched a significant effort to engage ethnic media across the country as partners to promote participation. The Census Bureau reached out to ethnic media because it recognized them as trusted, credible sources of critical information for populations that the Census has historically had the most trouble reaching; namely, immigrants and ethnic minorities.

CONCLUSIONS

Ethnic media play crucial roles in the communication ecologies of immigrant and ethnic communities across the USA, in part because they are integral to serving these populations' CINs. However, for these media to continue to play these roles—and to perform them even more effectively—policy changes should address impediments that ethnic media face at the organizational, media market, and local, state, and national policymaking levels. Looking forward, policies should be designed and implemented to achieve three interrelated goals.

First of all, *stability*. Regardless of how small or big ethnic media organizations are, most rely not only on sales of copies or subscriptions but also on advertising revenue. Basic media economics research indicates that audience size drives advertising revenue because advertisers want to expose their products to as many eyeballs as possible. This relationship between audience size and advertising is the reason that many mainstream publications, broadcast, and now online media, too, rely on audience metrics (e.g., circulation, ratings, and, unique website visitors). It is also the reason that organizations that credibly collect and report these data (e.g., Circulation Verification Council, Nielsen, and Arbitron) exist. In many cases, ethnic media cannot afford services to produce audience metrics, even if they are larger operations.

Economic and political marginalizations are frequently entwined and negatively affect the sustainability prospects of ethnic media organizations. If ethnic broadcast media cannot have their audience's size accurately measured and reported alongside those of their mainstream media competitors, they face limited prospects for attracting advertising revenue. Since ethnic media serve the CINs of populations that are often socially vulnerable, inequalities that affect ethnic media organizations at the market level have a direct, negative impact on individuals' and communities' abilities to address their CINs.

The resolution of the legal cases brought against Nielsen by Spanish-language media giant Univisión in 2004 and against Arbitron by the Attorneys General of New York State and New Jersey in 2008 have shown a way forward, though. As a result of both cases, the two ratings agencies were forced to improve their methodology for assessing ethnic media audiences. But these cases also educated ethnic media, ethnic and immigrant communities, as well as their advocates in civil society, government, and the private sector on what must be done to address the lack of reliable audience data that disadvantages ethnic media producers. Doing so will require continued vigilance, as well as building and nurturing alliances between ethnic media organizations, the communities they serve, and advocates in government.

In addition to efforts to stabilize the ethnic media sector by recognizing them as legitimate players in media markets across the country, efforts to *directly support ethnic media operations* are necessary. At a basic level, this means granting them equal treatment to their mainstream media counterparts. The New York City case, discussed above, is an excellent example of this. The combined circulation of print ethnic media in NYC is nearly three million—over one-third of the city's population. Yet, ethnic media receive less than one-fifth of the city's advertising dollars. Thus, a first step toward supporting ethnic media would be to allocate them advertising revenues commensurate with the proportion of the population that they serve.

Ethnic media can also be supported through an array of local, state, and federal programs, in which they are treated as genuinely valuable partners for addressing the CINs of "hard-to-reach" immigrant and ethnic minority populations. The U.S. Census Bureau is a model for such efforts. And in order for ethnic media to play their roles effectively, policy accommodations like access to E-rate, would be helpful. As we have argued elsewhere, E-rate could boost ethnic media's capacities to serve as "anchor institutions" to promote broadband Internet adoption and use in their communities.

Finally, a review of research to date reveals significant gaps in what we know about ethnic media in the USA today. Unresolved questions include: *What are the unintended consequences, at the local level, of national-level decisions around media ownership and concentration?* Related to these concerns, even though the net neutrality debate may be settled (for now) by the February 26, 2015, FCC decision, *what are the impacts of net neutrality on ethnic media development and sustainability?* And, *how do these and other digital equity policies impact ethnic media's capabilities to address their audiences' CINs?* Digital equity issues are increasingly recognized as integral to addressing the broader social inequalities that disproportionately affect immigrant and ethnic minority communities. Supporting ethnic media as they work to address these communities' CINs, through traditional and digital outlets, is a crucial step toward ensuring that the increasingly diverse USA is increasingly equitable, as well.

NOTES

1. According to the US Census Bureau, between 2000 and 2014 alone, the number of new immigrants that arrived in the country was estimated at 14 million.
2. According to the 2010 US Census and a 2009 Urban Institute report, the proportion of children with a parent who has difficulty speaking English rises to 68 percent among children with a parent from Central America, and for children with a Mexican-born parent, to 82 percent.
3. According to Center for Community and Ethnic Media in 2013, ethnic *and* community publications combined secure approximately 18 percent of the advertising dollars spent by New York City. No precise figure is reported for ethnic publications alone.

REFERENCES AND FURTHER READINGS

Allen, Jeffrey. 2009. Ethnic media reaching record numbers in U.S. *New America Media*. http://news.newamericamedia.org/news/view_article.html?article_id=8bb0c256d866e8e99e74fc734d5cef67.

Anderson, Benedict. 1991. *Imagined communities: Reflections on the origins and spread of nationalism*. New York: Verso.

Center for Community & Ethnic Media. 2013. *Getting the word out (or not): How and where New York City advertises*. http://ccem.journalism.cuny.edu/research/.

Eggerton, John. 2014. FCC releases ownership diversity report. *Broadcasting & Cable*, June 27. http://www.broadcastingcable.com/news/washington/fcc-corrects-minority-ownership-figure/134256.

Friedland, Lewis, Philip Napoli, Katherine Ognyanova, Carola Weil, Ernest J. Wilson, and III. 2012. *Review of the literature regarding critical information needs of the American public*. Washington, DC: Federal Communications Commission.

James, Meg. 2004. Univisión sues Nielsen over ratings system. *The Los Angeles Times*, June 10. http://articles.latimes.com/2004/jun/10/business/fi-nielsen10.

James, Meg. 2005. Nielsen bows to Latino viewers. *The Los Angeles Times*, December 20. http://articles.latimes.com/2005/dec/20/business/fi-nielsen20.

Katz, Vikki S. 2014. *Kids in the middle: How children of immigrants negotiate community interactions for their families.* New Brunswick: Rutgers University Press.

Katz, Vikki S., Alfonso Ang, and Roberto Suro. 2012a. An ecological perspective on U.S. Latinos' health communication behaviors, access, and outcomes. *Hispanic Journal of Behavioral Sciences* 34(3):437–456. doi:10.1177/0739986312445566.

Katz, Vikki S., Matthew D. Matsaganis, and Sandra J. Ball-Rokeach. 2012b. Ethnic media as partners for increasing broadband adoption and social inclusion. *Journal of Information Policy* 2: 79–102.

Louie, Josephine. 2003. Media in the lives of immigrant youth. *New Directions for Youth Development* 100: 111–130. doi:10.1002/yd.66.

Mathew, Ann Bessie, and Kimiko Kelly. 2008. *Disaster preparedness in urban immigrant communities: Lessons learned from recent catastrophic events and their relevance to Latino and Asian communities in Southern California.* Los Angeles: Tomás Rivera Policy Institute and Asian Pacific American Legal Center.

Matsaganis, Matthew D. 2011. *Broadband adoption and Internet use among U.S. Latinos.* Los Angeles/Washington, DC: Tomás Rivera Policy Institute and Time Warner Cable Research Program on Digital Communications.

Matsaganis, Matthew D. 2015. *Broadband internet adoption & ethnic media organizations in New York City: How producers address challenges and leverage opportunities associated with new communication technologies.* Preliminary research report. University at Albany, State University of New York.

Matsaganis, Matthew D., Vikki S. Katz, and Sandra J. Ball-Rokeach. 2010. *Understanding ethnic media: Producers, consumers, and societies.* Thousand Oaks: Sage.

Matsaganis, Matthew D., and Annis G. Golden. 2015. The communicative construction of a field of health action: Interventions to address reproductive health disparities among African American women in a smaller urban community. *Journal of Applied Communication Research.* Advance online publication. doi:10.1080/00909882.2015.1019546.

New America Media. 2014. *About NAM.* http://newamericamedia.org/about/.

Noam, Eli M. 2009. *Media ownership and concentration in America.* New York: Oxford University Press.

Pew Project for Excellence in Journalism. 2009. *The state of the news media: An annual report on American journalism.* http://www.stateofthemedia. org/2009/narrative_overview_intro.php?media=1.

Rideout, Victoria, Ulla G. Foehr, Donald F. Roberts, and Mollyann Brodie. 1999. *Kids and media @ the new millennium.* Menlo Park: Henry J. Kaiser Foundation.

Stelter, Brian. 2008. Cuomo to sue ratings company, claiming minorities are underrepresented. *The New York Times,* October 6. http://www.nytimes. com/2008/10/07/nyregion/07arbitron.html.

Stelter, Brian. 2009. Arbitron settles suit alleging bias in radio ratings system. *The New York Times*, January 7. http://www.nytimes.com/2009/01/08/nyregion/08arbitron.html.

Telles, Edward, Mark Sawyer, and Gaspar Rivera-Salgado (eds.). 2011. *Just neighbors? Research on African American and Latino relations in the United States.* New York: Russell Sage.

Urban Institute. 2009. *Children of immigrants.* http://datatool.urban.org/charts/datatool/pages.cfm.

U.S. Census Bureau. 2010. Retrieved from http://www.census.gov.

Wilkin, Holley A., Sandra J. Ball-Rokeach, Matthew D. Matsaganis, and Pauline Hope Cheong. 2007. Comparing the communication ecologies of geo-ethnic communities: How people stay on top of their community. *Electronic Journal of Communication* 17: 1–2.

CHAPTER 7

Do Spanish-Language Broadcast Media Serve a Changing America?

Federico Subervi

If the owners and managers of the Spanish-language broadcast media in the USA were asked the question that serves as the title of this chapter, their immediate answer would most certainly be "yes, of course those media serve the changing America." They would feel confident in that answer especially because all the content their stations offer is *oriented* to the broad and diverse range of people of Latino heritage currently residing in the USA.

However, a more accurate answer to that question requires additional details that can help assess exactly how those broadcast media serve that diverse and dynamic Latino population. For example, *who* is being served and *how*? In this essay, answers to such queries will focus on a particular type of content that many Spanish-language broadcast media scarcely or don't ever offer their audiences: *news and information*, especially for civic–political engagement and during emergency situations. This chapter is derived from the author's empirical research on this topic, first in California (see Subervi-Vélez et al. 1992; Subervi-Vélez 1999), and most recently, in Texas (see Subervi 2010). The latter study was most telling

F. Subervi (✉)
President, Association for Latino Media, Markets & Communication Research Austin, USA

© The Editor(s) (if applicable) and The Author(s) 2016
M.I. Lloyd, L.A. Friedland (eds.), *The Communication Crisis in America, And How to Fix It*, DOI 10.1057/978-1-349-94925-0_7

of the challenges that non-English-speaking populations face in times of emergencies. Findings of that research experience, personal observations of more current emergency events, and other readings serve as basis for the views presented in the following pages. (For additional background, see Aldrich and Meyer 2014; Allen and Subervi 2014; Chourey 2015; Jaramillo López 2011; Liu 2007; Lindell and Perry 1992; Meyers 2007; Perry et al. 1981; Tierney and Perry 2001; Subervi and Correa 2008; Wang 2014; Wilkin et al. 2015).

Before delving into that subject, it is important to acknowledge that Spanish-language broadcast media provide on a daily basis a variety of entertainment content for thousands and even millions of Latinos who regularly tune in for fun, relaxation, joviality, and cultural connections. In addition to entertainment, some Spanish-language broadcast media occasionally offer—on air and/or via their websites—content that can be considered educational or civic-oriented.[1] This type of offering extends to sponsorships of community-based cultural activities and even fund-raising for important health-related and/or recreational causes. Taken together, such content and activities can be considered service to Latinos in a changing America, which then fuels the stations' ratings—that is, eyeballs and ears—that by extension attract commercial advertisers, and during elections, even more so, political candidates and parties, too.

It could therefore be acknowledged that Spanish-language broadcast media also serve well the commercial and political entities that advertise in those media. Otherwise, they would not spend the thousands and millions of dollars that they do in their on-air paid promotions and on the stations' corresponding websites.

By extension, it can be surmised that Spanish-language broadcast media must be serving quite well the owners and stockholders of those media, thanks to the profits generated from the advertisements and political promotions (especially during elections). If the stations weren't generating profits, they would have closed operations long ago.

The question still remains as to whether Spanish-language broadcast media serve a changing America with respect to *news and information*, especially for civic/political engagement and during emergency situations. In this respect, the answer is definitely no, or certainly not as well as it should be. The main exceptions are some of the Latino-oriented *public* radio stations.

SCARCITY OF CIVIC–POLITICAL NEWS AND INFORMATION

The evidence for this negative assessment lies in the fact that very few Spanish-language radio stations have local news staff—even part-time stringers—who can provide their audiences news segments about the daily occurrences that affect the Latino communities from which they rely on to make their sales profits. Regularly scheduled, up-to-date news or at least brief *factual commentary* about what takes place in the meetings of city councils, school boards, or county or state government offices—especially with respect to policy and budgetary matters that affect Latinos—are absent from practically every Spanish-language radio station in the USA. Even in cities such as Miami, New York, Chicago, and Los Angeles, where some Spanish-language radio stations have their own news staff, the coverage of policymaking entities can be scarce or nonexistent.

Also absent or hardly featured are *news stories* about the civic, advocacy, or cultural activities of the community's Latino organizations. For sure, many, but not all, radio stations will air public service-type announcements (PSAs) about some of the events that could be of interest to their audiences. However, *news* about such events and pre or follow-up interviews with the organizers and attendees is less common, if available at all. The exceptions will be regarding the events that the stations themselves sponsor. Otherwise, the productions of a local Latino theater troupe or advocacy issues being raised by a community group, for example, might not get any notice on those stations unless they pay for spots or buy on-air time to get the word out about their activities and perspectives.

Almost, but not exactly the same scenario is evident at the local Spanish-language television stations. A difference is that most have news staff—even if just a "skeleton crew"—that covers major news stories about Latino-related civic, advocacy issues, and cultural happenings. Such stories get their occasional or possibly regular airtime within the morning, evening, or nightly local news segments. However, aside from the top stories, which tend to focus on crime, transportation accidents, residential fires, or some other event selected to attract audience attention, and some local PSAs, there is a scarcity of airtime dedicate to *news and information* about civic/political engagement. Of course, some television stations have weekly Saturday or Sunday morning special programs during which Latino leaders of local civic, political, religious, cultural, and health organizations are interviewed about issues of central value to the community.

Important and valuable as the Spanish-language radio and television promotions, PSAs, interview programs, or occasional mentions of local civic/political events are for citizens' democratic engagement in society, they are very poor substitutes for regular news stories that purposely connect the dots between actions (or lack thereof) of government and civic leaders with the diverse and growing Latino communities.

Missing even in the civic and political news stories are answers to three critical questions: (1) Who is making decisions on policies and budgets that directly or indirectly affect one or more subgroups of Latino populations in a community? This refers to the identification of individuals, groups, committees, and/or agencies responsible for making decisions. (2) By what means are those decisions being made? In other words, how inclusive are the processes by which input from diverse Latino constituents is sought and then significantly considered in the decision-making process. (3) Who benefits, and who does not, from those decisions? Answers to this latter question would not only identify the individual or group beneficiaries/losers but also the particulars of their gains/losses, be these short-term or long-term.

Providing audiences with the answers to these questions, be it with news or factual commentary, on a daily (or at least more regular) basis would undoubtedly better serve Latinos in a changing America. It is such type of content that when contextualized to be most relevant to the diverse sub-segments of the Latino populations can more effectively contribute to incentivize and mobilize audiences to enhance their reliable and verifiable knowledge and thus engage in civic–political affairs of their local, state, and national life in the USA.

It can thus be summarized that with respect to civic/political news and information, Spanish-language stations are not serving well particular segments of the Latino community. Here it is important to add that even with respect to the entertainment content that Spanish-language media so amply provide, more often than not, there is a lack of service to local musical groups that are not given airtime unless they are part of a large record label and have promotional contracts that can be considered profit-generating by the stations.

THE SCARCITY OF NEWS AND INFORMATION DURING EMERGENCY SITUATIONS

The assessment with respect to Spanish-language broadcast media's service pertaining to emergency situations is even bleaker. Stations that lack any news staff to gather and then offer up-to-the-minute or on-the-scene accounts of developing situations due to crises caused by nature or humans are dependent on other sources of information to be shared with their audiences. Some sources can be reliable, such as is the case of official weather forecasters or law enforcement authorities. That retransmission of reliable news and information is based on the assumption that the station receives that content in Spanish, or has staff at hand to promptly and accurately translate what is received. As discussed below, such in not always the case.

Others sources that stations without news staff are dependent on are not as reliable. For example, text messages, tweets, or calls from audience members who contact the station with what can turn out to be false, misleading, or alarmist accounts of an emerging crisis. Lacking personnel trained to gather and transmit reliable, verifiable, and independent news accounts leaves Latino audiences more vulnerable to whatever crisis is at hand.

Worse yet is the absence of any news and information when a crisis is unfolding. That scenario of silence emerges in different ways. For example, a station may receive alerts or information in English but has no qualified bilingual staff person at hand to accurately and promptly translate and air it. News and information about crises also go un-aired when station managers are not able, or are not allowed, to interrupt network programming, either due to technical reasons or due to contractual "justifications," meaning loss of advertising revenues because spots would be preempted for emergency news coverage. Moreover, the absence of any news and information about a developing crisis happens when the emergency unfolds during "after-hours," such as weekdays after 5:00 p.m., before 8:00 a.m., or during weekends. Given that most stations, especially those that are part of a network, have during those times automatic computerized pre-scheduled programming of their own or of the satellite-fed network, there would be no staff at hand to offer urgent news or warnings. In each of these scenarios, the audience in a station's broadcast area could be threatened by a major flood, fire, tornado, or toxic spill. Yet the station would not air a single word of warning—unless the management has established and tested protocols to intercept the pre-recorded or network programming and offer either from the station or remotely the breaking news and information.

Sadly, each of the shortcomings summarized above—including the emergency news and information blackouts—has happened more than once across the country. For a recent example, during the major storms that afflicted Central Texas in late October 2015, on the local Spanish-language broadcast stations, there was very limited news and information about of the gravity of the torrential rains and impending flash floods.

That left hundreds, if not thousands, of Spanish-dependent Latinos without constant and up to date broadcast warnings, in their dominant language, for preparing for the looming crises, how to mitigate the challenges they faced, and then on, how to recover from losses caused by the floods.

This section would be incomplete without mentioning the Spanish-language broadcast stations that best serve their communities: Latino public radio stations. In the 13 states, plus Puerto Rico, where they operate, the majority of these stations serve Latinos not only with entertainment, but also with a variety of civic, political, cultural, educational, and social content that is relevant and valuable to those particular communities.[2] Because they are public stations, not commercial enterprises, they are locally owned and operated. Even the Radio Bilingüe and Radio Campesina network stations have local ownership and staff that works to offer content to serve their respective diverse Latino audiences. However, even some of these stations have shortcomings with respect to news staff and thus not only local news offerings, but by extension, in their capacities to serve their audiences with prompt and reliable news and information during emergency situations.

WHAT HELPS EXPLAIN THE SHORTCOMINGS?

First and foremost, commercial stations in any language are established to provide revenues for their owners—be they individuals, small businesses, or corporations. Whatever programming content the owners and their operators select for each station or the entire network is geared to attract as large an audience as possible in order to "sell" that audience to advertisers. Moreover, the programming is developed at the lowest possible cost that can generate the highest possible profits. Programming that does not generate the largest audiences is minimized or excluded altogether. What is kept is primarily programming that is most attractive to advertisers, and by extension, contributes to increasingly higher profit margins. The hiring and training of news staff; the equipment required for them to engage in quality news gathering; and the additional infrastructure needed for editing, producing, and disseminating news and information fall into this latter category.

This pattern of content decision-making has been most prevalent since station ownership changed from local families and small businesses and became part of larger corporations or conglomerates at which decisions about content is made by "corporate suites," that is, accountants and business managers that have little or no connection to the local communities in which the stations are located.

The value that those corporate decision-makers who are not part of the local community where the station operates is diminished even more in the face of increasingly competitive mass media as well as social media outlets and options. Content that will generate potentially small audiences, even if it is crucial and service-oriented, is certain to fall by the wayside.

Also, high-profit-oriented content overrides the service content that broadcast license holders are required to offer because Federal Communications Commission (FCC) regulations are too vague in establishing what constitutes "public service" and because that government agency is even weaker in enforcing challenges to stations' lack of service. This lackluster approach by the FCC is the modus operandi regarding general market broadcast stations and is not much different—or maybe even less attentive—to the lack of service of Spanish-language stations.

At the core of the aforementioned realities lies the deregulation of broadcast operations, which led to the corporatization of broadcast ownership. This made it much easier for station owners to renew the operating licenses while placing much more cumbersome processes for community groups that would challenge the renewals when they considered the stations that where out of compliance with the service requirement.

Taken together, the aforementioned changes in the broadcast industry paved the way for service content, especially that geared to civic–political news and information, to practically fade as a prime directive of general market as well as Spanish-language radio stations.

WHAT CAN AND SHOULD BE DONE TO BETTER SERVE THE CHANGING AND DYNAMIC LATINO AUDIENCES?

In an extensive research-based report, titled *An Achilles Heel in Emergency Communications: The Deplorable Policies and Practices Pertaining to Non English Speaking Populations*,[3] this author lists numerous recommendations that could ameliorate some of the service shortcomings discussed in this current chapter.[4] From this author's point of view, ideally there would be enforceable regulations that would require or become incentives for stations to provide more and better news and information, especially during emergency situations.

However, even lacking such regulations, there are many action items that should be considered for the sake of not only a well-informed American citizenry, but also during emergencies for the safety of all potential victims of any major crisis.

To begin, stations that cannot or will not invest in news staff and operations could and should partner with local journalism professors and students who could engage in (preferably paid) internships to gather and disseminate local civic–political news. That content could easily be placed on the station's website, and at a minimum, briefly promoted on air as a source for the community to be aware of the availability of Latino-relevant factual local news and information.

The professor and his/her students who engage in basic local news gathering and dissemination for Spanish-language broadcast stations could also be trained to be the eyes and ears for verifiable, independent, and accurate news and information for the prevention, mitigation, and recovery from emergency crisis situations. Local or national grants could be requested for this training and partnership.

Collaborative agreements should be established with stations that have news staff who are Spanish speakers so that these could potentially provide valuable news and information to the Spanish-speaking audiences. Such freelance-type collaborations would not be free of cost to the contracting station. However, both the partnerships with professors and students and/or with professional news gatherers of other media outlets would overcome the "excuse" of lack of having in-house staff for providing crucial news and information—at least during emergencies.

Another low-cost remedy is for each and every Spanish-language station to develop and implement policies on how *local management,* using signals generated from their smartphones, could interrupt pre-recorded or network feeds when they receive from government or other reliable sources bulletins about unfolding potentially life-threatening crises. Technology already exists for translation of emergency alerts. If not at hand, it should be obtained and used. Pre-recorded messages could thus be set up to broadcast something like "impending [tornado, flood, hail, etc.] weather situation. For further information, go to [a designated] website, or call this number [number to call]." There would thus be no excuse for leaving audiences who depend on Spanish-language broadcast media without life-saving information when crises take place outside of a station's normal operating hours or when some capable personnel is unavailable at the premises in order to promptly alert listeners on what is happening and what to do for safekeeping.

Unless required to do so by the FCC, commercial broadcast media will remain resistant to expenditures related to providing immediate emergency communication news and information. Therefore, public radio stations, including and especially Latino Public Radio Consortium affiliates, are a more feasible set of channels for such content. Greater support for these stations, many of which, as mentioned above, have local news operations and staff dedicated to public service, could prepare them to be the first news and information outlets in times of crisis. That support could come in the form of funds for training staff to gather and present emergency-related news and information and also equipment for personnel to go to hot spots for live coverage of developing events. With properly trained staff and action plans, these stations could then become the "go to" sources for current and reliable guidance for preparedness, mitigation, and recovery during emergency situations in their respective communities.

To conclude, it is important to keep in mind a fundamental proposition and also justification for this chapter and its recommendations: Even in the age of Internet-based communications and social media flows, traditional broadcast radio and television stations are crucial outlets for a well-informed citizenry. For primarily Spanish-speaking populations, media broadcasting in that language should not only serve as vehicles for audience entertainment, advertiser sales, and owner profits. These media are indispensable for promoting the engagement and active participation of the active, dynamic, and ever-growing Latino citizenry in their communities, government affairs, and democracy as a whole.

NOTES

1. An example of a very valuable educational service is Univision's *Clave al Éxito* (Key to Success) website. See https://exito.univision.com/en/.
2. For a list of the stations that are part of the Latino Public Radio Consortium, see http://latinopublicradioconsortium.org/station-services/latino-public-radio-stations/.
3. The report was based on a multifaceted research project that took place in the Central Texas region between 2008 and 2010 that assessed the emergency communication policies and procedures of local and state government agencies, as well as of the Spanish-language radio and television stations operating from north Austin to San Antonio. That study was made possible thanks to a grant from the McCormick Foundation. The report is available upon request from this author.
4. That report lists crisis communication recommendations for government agencies that deal with emergencies, the FCC, and other regulatory agencies, the broadcast media, academic units, and also business and community leaders.

REFERENCES

Aldrich, Daniel P., and Michelle A. Meyer. 2014. Social capital and community resilience. *American Behavioral Scientist* 1–16. doi: 10.1177/000276421 4550299.

Allen, Koya, and Federico Subervi. 2014. Prevention of post-disaster sequelae through efficient communication planning: Analysis of communication-seeking behavior in Alabama and Montana. Paper presented at the American Political Health Association Conference. New Orleans, Louisiana.

Chourey, Sarita. 2015. Spanish-only residents left out of alerts during S.C. flood. *Savannah Morning News*, November 5. http://savannahnow.com/news/2015-11-05/spanish-only-residents-left-out-alerts-during-sc-flood.

Jaramillo López, Juan C. 2011. Análisis de riesgos e identificación de vulnerabilidades de comunicación, en la gestión de crisis originadas en desastres naturales en empresas de acueducto y saneamiento. II Encuentro latinoamericano de comunicadores de las empresas de acueducto y saneamiento. Medellín, Colombia.

Lindell, Michael K., and Ronald W. Perry. 1992. *Behavioral foundations of community emergency planning*. Washington, DC: Hemisphere Publishing.

Liu, Brooke Fisher. 2007. Communicating with Hispanics about crises: How counties produce and provide Spanish-language disaster information. *Public Relations Review* 33: 330–333.

Myers, Harry K. 2007. *Delivering fire and life safety education to the Hispanic community. Leading community risk reduction*. National Fire Academy, Executive Fire Officer Program.

Perry, Ronald W., Michael K. Lindell, and M.R. Greene. 1981. *Evacuation planning in emergency management*. Lexington, Mass: Lexington Books.

Subervi, Federico A. 2010. *An Achilles heel in emergency communications: The deplorable policies and practices pertaining to non-English speaking populations*. Final report of the Emergency Communications Project, funded by the McCormick Foundation.

Subervi-Vélez, Federico A. 1999. The mass media and Latinos: Policy and research agendas for the next century. *Aztlán* 24(2): 131–147.

Subervi, Federico, and Teresa Correa. 2008. *Assessing the diversity of news voices in the Latino-Oriented broadcast media in central Texas*. Report presented to the Necessary Knowledge for a Democratic Public Sphere Program of the Social Science Research Council, New York.

Subervi-Vélez, Federico A., Maria Denney, Anthony Ozuna, Clara Quintero, and Juan-Vicente Palerm. 1992. *Communicating with California's Spanish-speaking populations: Assessing the role of the Spanish-language broadcast media and selected agencies in providing emergency services*. Berkeley, California: University of California, Berkeley, California Policy Seminar.

Tierney, Kathleen J., Michael K. Lindell, and Ronald W. Perry. 2001. *Facing the unexpected: Disaster preparedness and response in the United States.* Washington, DC: Joseph Henry Press.

Wang, Hansi Lo. 2014. Oklahoma's Latino community prepares for the next Tornado. NPR, May 20. http://www.npr.org/blogs/codeswitch/2014/05/20/314094632/oklahomas-latino-community-prepares-for-the-next-tornado.

Wilkin, Holley, Carmen González, and Michael Tannebaum. 2015. Evaluating health storytelling in Spanish-language television from a communication infrastructure theory perspective. *Howard Journal of Communications* 26(4): 403–421.

CHAPTER 8

The Whole Community Communication Infrastructure: The Case of Los Angeles

Minhee Son and Sandra Ball-Rokeach

A well-known foible in the anthropology of old was the assumption that an understanding of a community could be gained solely through the eyes of the researcher. We follow in the tradition of urban anthropologists and sociologists who came to the conclusion that grounded research strategies that give voice to community members are more likely to produce accurate understandings. In this mode of research, the researcher brings her or his knowledge, but leaves it open to correction by listening to community members and taking seriously their knowledge of themselves and their community.

Note: In the initial phase and under the inspirational leadership of Dean Geoffrey Cowan, the project received generous funding from the Annenberg Foundation and the Annenberg School for Communication and Journalism, funding that continues to date under the supportive leadership of Dean Ernest Wilson, III. Funding has also been received from First 5LA, the Pew Charitable Trusts, the California Endowment, the California Humanities, and the National Institutes of Health.

M. Son (✉) • S. Ball-Rokeach
University of Southern California, Los Angeles, CA, USA

© The Editor(s) (if applicable) and The Author(s) 2016   107
M.I. Lloyd, L.A. Friedland (eds.), *The Communication Crisis in America, And How to Fix It*, DOI 10.1057/978-1-349-94925-0_8

In order to identify the indigenous communication infrastructure of everyday life in the multitude of communities that constitute the metropolis of Los Angeles, you need a grounded plan of observation and data collection that allows you to gain access into those communities. Los Angeles has its own unique geographic characteristics, but it also serves as a prototype of a twenty-first-century urban city in terms of its socio-demographic complexity and the challenges of meeting the information needs of old-timers and newcomers.

The shared challenge of this volume is to understand the information needs of diverse communities in such a way that informs communication policy. Toward that end, we start with a description of The Metamorphosis Project—its origin, goals, study areas, and what we mean by "the whole community communication infrastructure." Next, we identify unmet information needs that have been unmasked from our research and analysis of diverse communities in Los Angeles, followed by details of the Metamorphosis Project grounded research strategy, through which we identified these needs. We conclude the chapter with our communication policy recommendation.

THE METAMORPHOSIS PROJECT

The Metamorphosis Project (Metamorph.org) was launched in 1998 as an in-depth inquiry into the transformation of urban community under the forces of globalization, population diversity, and new communication technologies. The project was developed by Sandra J. Ball-Rokeach. She became deeply motivated after the 1992 uprising that shook Los Angeles and felt communication research should have something to contribute to social changes that enable residents and community organizations to strengthen the ties that bind while respecting difference. Since its official launch at the Annenberg School at the University of Southern California in 1998, the project has served as a social laboratory in which generations of communication researchers continue to move back and forth between the theoretical drawing board and the multitude of ethnic communities of both new and settled immigrants. The goal has been to not only identify the whole community communication infrastructure of Los Angeles communities, but make it accessible as a communication utility for residents, practitioners, and policymakers seeking to improve civic engagement, access to health care, intergroup relations, and urban planning.

LOS ANGELES: THE PROTOTYPICAL TWENTY-FIRST-CENTURY URBAN COMMUNITY

Los Angeles has its own unique geographic characteristics, but it also serves as a prototype of a twenty-first-century metropolitan area in terms of its socio-demographic complexity and the challenges of meeting the information needs of diverse residents.

Initially, we selected study areas where the major racial/ethnic groups in Los Angeles County resided in the largest concentrations. Thus, in the early study areas, we only studied the race or ethnic group that set the tone and character of an area. Over time, it became increasingly clear that many areas were becoming more diverse. With all of the challenges that such demographic change suggests, we came to study the two or three major racial/ethnic groups in an area.

The Metamorphosis Project study areas are described below. Despite the general trend toward increased population diversity, some of the areas remain fairly homogeneous with respect to race/ethnicity, country of origin, and immigration generations (e.g., South East Los Angeles, Boyle Heights, and Pico Union). In one case—the city of Alhambra—the area was selected because Michael Parks, a professor in the School of Journalism at Annenberg, approached the Metamorphosis team with a proposal to design and implement a community news site (AlhambraSource.org) in a collaborative effort to increase the low level of civic engagement (Kim and Ball-Rokeach 2006) established in prior Metamorphosis research. With the exception of the incorporated cities of Alhambra, Glendale, and South Pasadena, study areas are composed of a number of residential communities, identifiable either by real estate labels and/or by common insider and outsider referents. The areas and race/ethnicities we have studied, in rough chronological order, include:

- Greater Crenshaw (African American): This large area in South LA includes five to six known communities. Residents vary from upper-middle class to working and underclass.
- Boyle Heights (First- to fourth-generation Mexican origin): This East LA area includes Boyle Heights and View Terrace. Residents vary from working to middle class.
- South Pasadena (Anglo and largely Protestant): This area east of downtown LA is an incorporated city with largely middle- and upper-middle-class residents.

- The Westside (Anglo with a large representation of Jewish residents): This area includes four to five known communities. Residents fall largely within the upper-middle class.
- Koreatown (first- and second-generation Korean origin): This Central City area serves as a commercial and service center for Korean-origin people in Southern California. Residents are largely working and lower-middle class.
- Pico Union (first- and second-generation Central American origin): Residents of this Central City area are generally poor and have relatively low levels of education.
- Central San Gabriel Valley (First- to fourth-generation ethnic Chinese): This area includes the incorporated city of Monterey Park and portions of three other incorporated cities. Residents vary from middle to upper-middle class.
- Southeast Los Angeles (largely first- and second-generation Mexican origin): The area includes three incorporated cities. Residents, on average, have low socioeconomic status.
- South Figueroa Corridor (Latinos from multiple national origins and African Americans): The population of this Central City area is largely working and lower-middle class.
- Crenshaw (second-generation Latino from multiple national origins and African American): Since our initial inquiry (see: Greater Crenshaw, above), this South LA area has experienced rapid demographic change with increased Latino population. Socioeconomic status varies from low to high for African-Americans and is generally lower for Latinos.
- Glendale (Armenian, Latino, and Anglo): This area north of downtown LA, once dominated by Anglo residents, has the second-largest Armenian population in the USA. Socioeconomic status varies from lower to middle levels.
- Alhambra (first- and second-generation ethnic Chinese, second- and third-generation Latinos, and long-term Anglos): This incorporated city in the Northeast has been studied in two waves to assess the impact of the Alhambra Source community news site. Residents vary from working to upper middle class.
- Northeast Los Angeles (first- and second-generation Latino, Asian, and Anglo): This area includes five known communities. Residents of these communities are largely working and lower-middle class.

COMMUNICATION ECOLOGIES FOR STAYING ON TOP
OF COMMUNITY NEWS

We define communication ecology as a network of communication resources constructed by an agent in pursuit of a goal and in context of their communication environment. A key challenge of increased diversity is to assess the extent to which there are overlapping or distinct communication ecologies exhibited by different racial/ethnic groups and new and settled immigrant populations. The answer to that question has direct implications for meeting community information needs; that is, how do we reach differnt groups to keep them on top of what is happening in their communities and beyond? To what extend to differnt communication resources need to be deployed to reach those groups?

To address this major policy question, much of the Metamorphosis Project work has been directed to the challenge of unmasking the complex and diverse communication ecologies that people rely upon to understand their communities. A key feature of these ecologies is the mix of interpersonal sources and traditional, new, and ethnic media that people put together in their efforts to stay on top of their communities—to meet their community information needs. Our research has demonstrated remarkable variation in these ecologies—variations by ethnic group, and immigrant generation, among other factors. These findings pose a huge challenge to media and civic policymakers: How can we increase the level of "met information needs" when there is so much variation in how people seek information?

Communication ecology maps (as shown in figures 8.1 and 8.2) illustrate the different ways that people stay on top of what is going on in their community. In Glendale, each ethnic group, though living in the same community, stays informed about local news and events in different ways. Anglos in Glendale most often turn to mainstream newspapers or interpersonal sources, while Latinos and Armenians rely on a combination of mainstream and geo-ethnic television designed specifically for Latino or Armenian consumers, respectively (Fig. 8.1). Similarly, people of the same ethnicity living in different communities may have surprisingly different patterns of how they stay on top of what is happening in their community. For example, compared to Latinos in Glendale, Latinos in Pico Union turn to mainstream television much less and rely more on geo-ethnic television or interpersonal sources (Fig. 8.2).

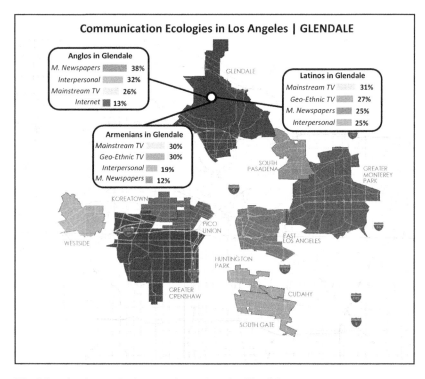

Fig 8.1   Anglos vs. Latinos vs. Armenians in Glendale

From Communication Ecologies to Communication Infrastructures

Communication ecologies are set within a larger communication infrastructure that includes key community storytellers. In addition to residents talking to each other about their community and local media reporting on the community, community organizations play an important part. In the Metamorphosis Project, we put all of this together in what we call "the storytelling network." The network concept connotes the ideal situation for meeting community information needs, as it suggests discursive connections between residents, local media, and community organizations. For example, when local media cover the activities of a community-building organization, this prompts residents to learn and talk about these activities, and we have a high-functioning case of a storytelling network.

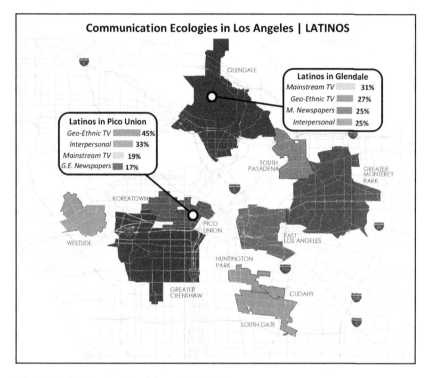

Fig. 8.2 Latinos in Glendale vs. Pico Union

The capacity for such storytelling networks to emerge and be sustained, however, is fundamentally affected by other features of the environment that either enhance or undermine community storytelling. Such features include demographic changes that bring diverse groups together, who may or may not speak the same language, have different ways of living, and different quantities and qualities of physical resources—e.g., parks, libraries, grocery stories—where people can safely meet and greet. The quality of the transportation system and the health of the local political economy may also vary. We call these features "the communication action context."

The community communication infrastructure is thus defined as the community storytelling network set in its communication action context. In all of the Metamorphosis Project study areas, we identify the strength of the communication infrastructure. If the infrastructure is strong, there is a much higher chance of meeting residents' information needs.

In the next section, we identify unmet information needs that are present to one extent or another in the many communities we have studied. Following on this discussion, we detail the Metamorphosis Project's grounded research strategy.

COMMUNICATION CHALLENGES THAT CREATE UNMET INFORMATION NEEDS

While there is remarkable variation in both communication ecologies and communication infrastructures, there are also identifiable reasons for unmet information needs, some of which apply across areas, and some of which apply to a type of area:

1. Insufficient local news media
   Across areas that vary widely in class, race/ethnicity, and immigration generation, we find little, if any, credible local news media that report daily on the happenings in our study areas. There may be advertising venues that include spotty reporting on community events or there may be a Chamber of Commerce publication that highlights the "positive" activities of local officials and businesses. In some communities, churches, community organizations, local governments, and others produce print newsletters, websites, or digital publications, but these tend to be focused upon the specific interests of the organization, which may or may not align with those of residents.
   In the previously mentioned case of the city of Alhambra, for example, focus group participants, interviewees, and survey respondents could only identify the monthly, English-language Chamber of Commerce publication as a regular source of local news—accessible only to English-literate readers. Ethnic Chinese are the majority population of Alhambra (53 percent), and two-thirds of them report that they cannot speak English very well. Our efforts to construct and sustain an online trilingual (English, Mandarin, and Spanish) community news site was motivated by this finding—and by our conviction that regular access to local media news is an essential condition for meeting community information needs.
   It should be noted that when Parks was editor of the *Los Angeles Times* in the 1990s, the newspaper created local-area sections of the paper in an attempt to better meet community information needs and to increase circulation. Unfortunately, these sections did not survive

the changes in the newspaper publishing business. In more recent attempts to fill the local news information void, many individuals, groups, and businesses (e.g., Patch.com) have created online community news sites. Their failure rate is high, and a glaring policy issue is how to enable the financial sustainability of such sites.

With rare exceptions, social media do not have the carrying capacity to operate as local media. Their news agendas tend to reflect those of traditional media. Their primary capacity has more to do with dissemination and protest mobilization than with news construction.

2. Mainstream media stigmatization of communities and areas

When the only localized news about a community or a geographic area, such as South Los Angeles, is about "bad happenings," it can anger residents and, in some cases, undermine their community pride. It is difficult to see how mainstream media mores will change in a way that counters such stigmatization.

In an unpublished content analysis of *The Los Angeles Times* circa 2005, we found that coverage of the largely Anglo and relatively wealthy Westside was made throughout the various sections of the paper. In contrast, coverage of the largely African American and Latino South was notably concentrated in what used to be the "Metro" section of the paper, where the most common stories were about crime and social problems. (The fact that the "Metro" section was discontinued in favor of what is now the "California" section speaks volumes about the de-localization of news in mainstream media.)

Stigmatization matters. In a socio-spatial analysis of Los Angeles County, focus group participants mapped how they felt about different areas; specifically, their level of comfort and fear. Our analyses revealed that fear and comfort are uncorrelated with the likelihood of crime victimization. They were also color coded, meaning that areas with concentrations of black and brown people were areas that people feared. We found the greatest distortions of fear and of comfort came from participants who relied primarily on television (as opposed to newspapers) for their "local" news. Of course, movies, rap music, and other media play a part in this process. But the bottom line for many of our research participants living in stigmatized areas was that such stigmatization undermined the political economy of the area by discouraging investment. One policy recommendation would be for city governments to sponsor events that bring "outsiders" into an area to see it for themselves. The car-free biking event, CicLAvia, is one example where a festive event allows people to bike through areas where many of them have never been.

3. Recognizing the roles of ethnic media

When dealing with new immigrants, ethnic media are paramount (see Matsaganis, Katz, and Ball-Rokeach 2011). However, they are usually left off research and policy agendas. Ethnic media often do not or cannot allocate resources to cover local host country communities. Content analyses reveal that the "gaze" or geographic focus of many ethnic media is on the home country with "local" host country news constituting only a small percent of the stories.

The most common information needs that are met by these media are news about the home country and, in many cases, troubleshooting guidance about how to negotiate legal and governmental issues in the host country. While troubleshooting information is helpful, it is not the kind of information that increases knowledge of the residential community.

Often, linguistic and cultural barriers make it difficult for multiethnic community members to meaningfully interact outside of their own ethnic groups. This leads to what we have identified as *ethnically bounded storytelling networks*. Ethnically bounded storytelling networks can be an added challenge to the free-flowing exchange of knowledge that is crucial to building a collective identity, recognizing the most pressing issues, and working toward a common vision for the community. Cross-cultural communication also becomes critical during times of emergencies and crises. Such communication is inhibited when storytelling networks are ethnically bounded.

4. Connecting the storytelling network

Another communication problem that we observe is the weak or missing connections between the components of the storytelling network. Over and beyond the strength of one storyteller, we discover both statistically and through our field observations that it is the *integration* of the three community storytellers that makes a difference in community-level outcomes such as civic engagement, health, and intergroup relations. However, often times, it is the case that the storytelling network is fragmented—the links between the residents, community organizations, and local media are missing. A particular challenge for community organizations that serve diverse communities is to have their outreach efforts bridge across race/ethnicities.

All too often, we find that community organizational membership tends to be ethnically specific in diverse areas. There are important exceptions where community organizations self-consciously seek to bridge ethnicity. This is especially the case with community building organizations and less so with religious organizations. Even when one church facility is shared by multiple ethnic groups, we may find ethnic separation or a lack of communication across church leaderships and congregations.

A critical feature of meeting community information needs is to remember that everyday conversations among residents are very important sources of knowledge, particularly when enough residents are connected to community organizations and to local media that address the needs and interests of residents. Meeting critical information needs, then, requires the circulation of stories that can improve the quality of family and community life. That circulation is best when there are bridges between ethnically bounded storytelling networks and residents learn about the "others" that coexist in their neighborhood and stay on top of what is going on at the community level.

We have found that a storytelling network is most effective when community organizations and local media work together to prompt everyday conversations among residents about pressing issues, community events, projects underway, and available resources that may affect their family's welfare. However, this storytelling network is endangered due to the decline of media that tell community stories other than the periodic crime story. It is also endangered by a lack of familiarity, exchange, and trust building between community practitioners and media reporters.

This situation has led us to take up the challenge of creating a program that invited community organizations and media to network and collaboratively brainstorm story ideas. During a series of workshops, community organizations learned how to pitch stories in media-savvy form and become comfortable talking to local media reporters—many of whom work for ethnic media organizations. Community practitioners, in turn, point local reporters to grassroots initiatives that are underway to address community issues, as well as connect reporters to residents who can serve as sources. In the process, knowledge is shared both ways and relationships are formed. The end product is the multimedia dissemination of solutions-oriented journalism that can inform policymakers and practitioners seeking to address community problems.

Having identified the major communication problems that underlie unmet community information needs in Los Angeles, we now turn to the research orientation and strategies behind the Metamorphosis Project, which allowed us to uncover these problems.

A Grounded Research Strategy: The Communication Infrastructure of Everyday Life

While the concept of communication infrastructure is a theoretical framework, it is also a method for systematically collecting data that can be analyzed to understand the nature of the storytelling network and the communication action context—and how improvements can be made to address the information needs of the communities being studied. This grounded research strategy is a method of urban communication research that can be utilized by (and speaks to) researchers, practitioners, and policymakers.

Research Orientation: Questioning (or Dropping) Assumptions

Established databases are often constructed from unrepresentative populations. All too often, data are collected only in English, thus excluding many new immigrant populations, and the racial and ethnic makeup of the data are often limited to whites/non-whites or whites/blacks, thus excluding the fastest-growing population groups in the US, Asians and Latinos, as well as other important population groups.

Do not assume that the findings you have from one study of an ethnic group living in one community generalize to all members of that group living in other communities. Similarly, do not assume that different ethnic groups living in the same community have the same communication patterns. We demonstrated this earlier in our discussion of communication ecologies.

Do not assume that all disadvantaged communities are alike or that they all have weak communication infrastructures. We have found weak or fragmented communication infrastructures in relatively rich communities and relatively strong communication infrastructures in relatively poor communities.

Do not assume that there is a single "magic bullet" mode of observation. Keep in mind that each research method is an entry point into the community's indigenous communication infrastructure and is an opportunity to listen to community members and take seriously their knowledge of themselves and their community. Select the set of methods that best suits your inquiry.

Gearing up to Learn About a Community

(1) Some members of your team must be linguistically and culturally competent to relate to residents and to avoid misinterpretations of your observations.

(2) From the American Community Survey, learn what you can about demographic composition and trends. However, many community boundaries, whether defined by residents or by real estate names, do not conform to census tract markers. Our community boundaries accord with the naming conventions of residents and knowledgeable others.

(3) Walk around the community. Go into the public spaces (parks, libraries, streets), private spaces (businesses, restaurants, grocery stores), and institutional spaces with permission (churches and schools). Pick up all media, including micro media (e.g., newsletters). Ideally, this would entail systematic field observation as well, but this is labor intensive and costly, so the more informal walking around method may be all that you can afford.

Conducting a Baseline Metamorphosis Project Survey

Over the course of 15 years, the Metamorphosis Project has developed and refined survey measures that are designed to uncover the three components of indigenous storytelling networks: (1) residents in their interpersonal neighborhood networks, (2) community organizations that residents affiliate with, and (3) media that residents consume in their everyday lives—legacy/mainstream, ethnic, and new media.

The survey includes measures that assess two critical aspects of the communication action context or the communication environment in which the storytelling network is set: (1) communication hotspots where residents gather with friends or neighbors and are most likely to have conversations about their shared neighborhood spaces, and (2) public, private, and institutional "comfort zones" where residents go and feel comfortable.

The survey also includes established measures of key outcome variables: neighborhood belonging, collective efficacy, civic participation, the nature of intergroup relations, and a range of health-related variables.

Ideally, the survey sample would be representative of the community population but this is expensive. We administer the survey by telephone (random digit dialing [RDD]) to take advantage of techniques that have been developed to overcome low response rates and the high prevalence of cell phones. Internet surveys are less expensive, but they often exclude groups that are of particular interest when trying to understand the information needs of diverse and underserved populations. Internet surveys may disproportionately include groups/households with higher levels of internet technology integration, and/or more confortable dealing with on-line content on a daily basis. When we have a lot of volunteers available, we conduct door-to-door resident surveys. Whatever you do, conduct the survey in the language preferred by respondents.

However, surveys alone do not give you the kind of in-depth or textured knowledge that you need to draw conclusions about the community's information needs. In our work, the next step is to hold focus groups.

Focus Groups

We systematically select focus group participants from the pool of survey respondents on the basis of representativeness and our particular substantive interest at the time (e.g., their unmet information needs). We gain respondent permission for possible focus group participation at the time of survey administration. A key advantage to this way of proceeding is that we have all of the survey-based information we need to select appropriate participants.

Our focus groups are conducted in the language preferred by participants and are led by a linguistically and culturally appropriate person. They are also held in the community in a neutral place, such as a library or recreation center.

Focus group discussions can bring out the stories behind the everyday challenges that residents face as they try to stay informed of what is going on in their community and access community resources. Focus group discussions can also be used to validate survey findings or to delve deeper into findings that are puzzling or surprising.

Socio-Spatial Mapping

One of the benefits of conducting focus groups is that we can include interactive activities to help participants better recall and communicate how they feel about their own (and other) communities. Earlier in this chapter, for example, we discussed fear and comfort mapping (see Matei et al. 2001). Another example is spontaneous word association, where we ask participants what words they associate with each of our other study areas.

Communication Asset Mapping

A recent trend in urban research is to go beyond the identification of community deficits to identify spaces and places that serve as assets for residents, including cultural, psychological, and health assets, among others. Our particular contribution has been to draw attention to "communication" assets.

Communication assets are the specific sites and spaces in the community that facilitate positive social interaction among residents. They may include parks, retail establishments, community associations, churches, schools, recreation centers, and clinics. However, these spaces and places may or may not be communication assets. In order to be a communication asset, we must make on-site observations of actual hotspots and comfort zones. That is, residents must gather there, feel comfortable (comfort zones), and talk with one another (hotspots). In our survey, we ask respondents to identify such spaces, and their responses offer a good start to the observation process.

Interviews with Community Organizations Important to Residents

From resident surveys and focus group discussions, we generate a list of community organizations that residents (or their family members) say they participate with and trust. Based on this list, researchers get in touch with the organizations and schedule either a phone or face-to-face interview with a staff member. Before the actual interview, the researcher browses through the organization's website for an overview of the types of programs, services, campaigns currently underway, as well as its overall mission. The organization's social media activity, if any, can also inform us of its most recent activities. Two key features of the interviews are: (1) the degree of inter-organizational collaboration and coalition building, and (2) the ethnic composition of the organization's clientele or membership; is it a bridging organization?

Interviews with Media Producers Important to Residents

The survey baseline data points us to the media outlets that are most important to residents. Interviews with media producers can reveal the extent to which they are (or are not) connected to key resources, such as community organizations, other media, community leaders, and residents. A key feature of our interviews is the identification of structural barriers present within the media organization that may prevent or discourage reporting on local news, and, thus, present an inability to serve community information needs.

Monitoring Media Coverage of the Local Community

Geo-ethnic media are media targeted either to a geographic area and/or to a specific ethnicity. As we have noted previously, these media are often overlooked in social research and policymaker discourse. Local media that produce stories in the appropriate language in ways that are culturally sensitive can be crucial for reaching out to recent immigrant groups. Monitoring the media content and conducting thematic analyses of the stories can help us to assess both quantitative and qualitative aspects of local media storytelling: (1) the extent to which the local community is covered in the media, (2) which specific media outlets are most actively producing stories about the community, and (3) *how* the local community is discussed in the media; for example, what issues are brought up and are those issues portrayed in a positive/negative light? We monitor both online and offline media.

Communicating Your Findings to the Right Audience

Thus far, we have discussed grounded research methods for how to give voice to community members. In order to make sure that the voice *gets heard*, it is important to communicate the findings and insights gained from academic research to the right audience, in ways that *relate to* that audience.

The Metamorphosis Project developed a translational community website called MetaConnects (MetaConnects.org), an online space for knowledge sharing between researchers and community-based social-change organizations across the Southern California region and beyond. In addition to translating many years of Metamorphosis research into actionable change strategies that are easy to digest and available online, Metamorphosis team members have attended community events and organized community workshops.

CONCLUSION: COMMUNICATION POLICY RECOMMENDATION

It requires considerable humility to make policy recommendations in light of the unstable media and communication environments that we experience today (Firmstone and Coleman 2014; Napoli 2015; Roderick 2015). We have made various specific recommendations throughout this chapter, so we close with the one most important recommendation to policymakers concerned about addressing the unmet information needs of communities:

> *Do whatever you can to increase the production of local news that serves increasingly diverse communities.*

We emphasize this recommendation in the conviction that democratic societies require a media system that informs the citizenry about the issues, opportunities, and resources in the places where they lead their lives. Regional, national, and international news, as important as they are, are no substitute for local news.

REFERENCES

Firmstone, Julie, and Stephen Coleman. 2014. The changing role of the local news media in enabling citizens to engage in local democracies. *Journalism Practice* 8(5): 596–606. doi:10.1080/17512786.2014.895516.

Kim, Yong-Chan, and Sandra J. Ball-Rokeach. 2006. Community storytelling network, neighborhood context, and civic engagement: A multilevel approach. *Human Communication Research* 32(4):411–439.doi:10.1111/j.1468-2958.2006.00282.x.

Matei, Sorin, Sandra Ball-Rokeach, and Jack Linchuan Qiu. 2001. Fear and misperception of Los Angeles urban space: A spatial statistical study of communication-shaped mental maps. *Communication Research* 28(4): 429–463.

Matsaganis, Matthew D., Vikki S. Katz, and Sandra J. Ball-Rokeach. 2011. *Understanding ethnic media: Producers, consumers, and societies.* Thousand Oaks: Sage.

Napoli, Philip M. 2015. Understanding what audiences want from local news. *Columbia Journalism Review*, September 22. Retrieved from http://www.cjr.org/united_states_project/understanding_the_local_news_audience.php

Roderick, Kevin. 2015. In the midst of a crisis in journalism, the new *LA Times* buyout names on farewell day for many. *LA Observed*, November 26. Available at http://www.laobserved.com/archive/2015/11/new_la_times_buyout_names.php

Preface: Government Capture and Market Failure

Section 3 addresses two issues that are necessary to understand the communication crisis in America today. First, our government (local, state, and federal) has failed to establish policy or provide a meaningful public interest oversight of the communications industry; some would argue that public servants have been captured by the industries they are supposed to regulate on behalf of the public. And second, the goal of the US communications industry to first and foremost make profit has profound implications on the degree to which critical information needs are addressed. Investors do not invest to serve the public interest. Our communications markets are spectacular successes at their mission, but the market fails miserably to serve the critical information needs of the public.

In this section, Victor Pickard provides a historical perspective on regulatory failure resulting from long-term capture by communication corporations. Al Hammond takes on the argument from the left and right regarding what some regard as ineffective overlapping government oversight of consolidation in the media and telecom industries. Danilo Yanich shows how local television consolidation and "shared services agreements" lead to the under production of news addressing critical information needs. James Hamilton and Fiona Morgan show how and why the needs of low-income Americans go systematically unmet by cycles of market failure built into the local communication ecology. Michelle Ferrier illustrates how these failures result in "news deserts"—areas of local American communities that are uncovered by local journalism. Finally, Eszter Hargittai and Kaitlin Jennrich demonstrate that racial and gender inequalities are not limited to legacy media, but affect how individuals produce digital content.

The section as a whole demonstrates that common assumptions about market efficacy and government oversight need to be rigorously re-examined if our communication ecology is to ever address the challenge of meeting the critical information needs of all Americans. Policymakers are not taking market behavior into account; thus, what is too often called market failure is really policy failure.

Confronting Market Failure: Past Lessons Toward Public Policy Interventions

Victor Pickard

INTRODUCTION

In the early decades of the twenty-first century, old problems afflict new media.[1] Once again, America anguishes over the diminished democratic promise of a new medium. Like broadcasting in the 1940s, digital communications have become dominated by oligopolies driven by a corporate libertarian logic that is antagonistic toward public interest principles. These ownership structures contribute to various shortcomings with American broadband, including disparities among communities and socioeconomic groups in terms of speeds and access, higher costs for service, and impediments to free-flowing information and content. Just as radio's full democratic potential was thwarted by commercial capture in the 1930s and 1940s, a similar fate faces the Internet today. This crisis in digital media coincides with a structural crisis in journalism as the newspaper industry continues its irreparable decline.

Earlier media policy debates are instructive to policymakers as they confront these crises. Although ultimately unsuccessful, policy battles in the 1940s that defined the social contract between media institutions, publics, and the regulatory state attempted to buffer media's public service

V. Pickard (✉)
University of Pennsylvania, Philadelphia, PA, USA

© The Editor(s) (if applicable) and The Author(s) 2016   127
M.I. Lloyd, L.A. Friedland (eds.), *The Communication Crisis in America,
And How to Fix It*, DOI 10.1057/978-1-349-94925-0_9

mission from undue market pressures. Nearly all of them were resolved in ways that aligned with a "corporate libertarian" logic that benefited commercial broadcasters and publishers over the public (see Pickard 2013). This "postwar settlement for American media" enshrined self-regulation, a "negative" First Amendment, and industry-defined social responsibility. Similar parameters are at work in today's political discourse, which presents policy problems in two broad, overlapping areas: digital media and journalism. The time has arrived for a renegotiated social contract. Instead of being constrained by past policy failures, we must learn from them and move forward with bold new models.

This chapter provides an overview of both the hindrances facing a public interest agenda as well as the promises for policy reform. Before I examine potential policy interventions for supporting public service media, I briefly discuss three key conceptual areas that are implicit in today's policy debates but rarely explicitly addressed: public goods, market failure, and policy failure. Understanding these political economic relationships is the first step toward challenging the corporate libertarian paradigm that constrains what otherwise could be a golden era for progressive media reform. Integrating these ideas into our political discourses, practices, and institutions might help transform our media system into that which our democracy requires.

Public Goods

A growing number of scholars have argued in recent years that the information produced by news media should be treated as a public good (Hamilton 2006, 8–9; Pickard et al. 2009; McChesney and Nichols 2010, 101–3; Starr 2011; Baker 2001; Pickard 2015). Because public goods are non-rivalrous (one person's consumption does not detract from another's) and non-excludable (difficult to exclude from free riders), they do not operate as other commodities do, such as shoes or cars, within a capitalistic economy (Samuelson 1954). They are, in the words of one economist, "both unique and fascinating because it is virtually impossible to allocate a pure public good through market mechanisms" (Trogen 2005). Journalism is not only a public good in an economic sense (especially in its digital form), it also serves "the public good" in a socially beneficial sense. Put differently, journalism produces *positive externalities* (benefits that accrue to parties outside of the direct economic transaction), such as increased knowledge and an informed populace that are vital for a democratic society. Goods that produce such tremendous positive externalities are sometimes referred to as "merit goods," which society requires, but that individuals typically undervalue (are unable or unwilling to pay for), and thus the market under-produces.[2] As an essential public service with social benefits that transcend its revenue stream, journalism is such a good. In its ideal form, it serves as a rich information source for important social issues, an adversarial watchdog over the powerful, and a forum for diverse voices and viewpoints.

Like many public goods exhibiting positive externalities, journalism has never been fully supported by direct market transactions; it always has been subsidized to some degree. Since the late nineteenth century, this has largely taken the form of advertisers paying for access to newspaper audiences, which produced news almost as a kind of by-product, a positive externality from the primary exchange. Today, this business model is increasingly unsustainable, as audiences and advertisers migrate to the Internet, where ads sell for a mere fraction of their paper-based counterparts. Despite their growth, digital ad revenues have not offset the enormous losses from traditional advertising. A 2012 Pew study found that declines in print ad revenues, which had fallen more than 50 percent since 2003, exceeded the gain in online digital revenue by a ratio of greater than ten to one (Edmonds et al. 2012). The 2013 report found some stabilization, but the growth in digital advertising "does not come close to covering print ad losses" (Edmonds et al. 2013).[3] These and other data suggest that as a support system for journalism, ad revenue-dependent models appear to be increasingly unviable. And other commercial models such as digital paywalls (online subscription models) are not filling the vacuum (Pickard and Williams 2014). The inadequacy of commercial support indicates what should be obvious by now: The market's systematic underproduction of journalistic media qualifies as a clear case of market failure.

Market Failure
Deriving from neoclassical economics, "market failure" is an analytical framework that typically refers to a scenario in which the market is unable to efficiently produce and allocate resources, especially public goods (see, e.g., Bator 1958; Stiglitz 1989; Medema 2007, and Taylor 2007; also, Brown 1996). This often occurs when private enterprise withholds investments in critical social services because it cannot extract the returns that would justify the necessary expenditures, or when consumers fail to pay for such services' full societal benefit. This scenario legitimates state

intervention in the provision of public education, a standing military, a national highway system, and other essential services and infrastructures not supported by market transactions.

In addition to the lack of support for externalities and public goods, other market failures that frequently occur in the American media system are associated with structural flaws, such as oligopolistic concentration and profit maximization. The leading consumer advocate and researcher Mark Cooper has made a convincing argument that various kinds of "pervasive market failures" specifically affect the media industry. Uncompetitive markets may lead to perverse incentives and the abuse of market power, which can result in a media system's degradation, including a failure to provide adequate interconnection between communication networks, communication services to all of society, and quality journalism (Cooper 2011). In the 1940s, market failure was evidenced by the rise of one-newspaper towns and a loss of local journalism. Signs of market failure in today's American media system are increasingly visible in the ongoing disinvestment in news production, exemplified by the reduction of home deliveries of leading metro dailies.

Whether discussing the lack of support for local journalism or deficiencies in providing universal access to affordable and reliable Internet service, a focus on market failure deserves more prominence in American media policy discourse. Indeed, that media policy even requires a "public interest" category is arguably an implicit acknowledgment of endemic market failure in commercial media. Yet an explicit discussion of this subject, especially its role in the journalism crisis, has been noticeably absent among policymakers, a condition that leads us to policy failure.

Confronting Policy Failure
The concept of policy failure is under-theorized in the scholarly literature; here it refers to existing policy mechanisms' insufficiency in dealing with significant social problems, including market failure. Beyond policymakers' lack of political will or incentive to act, a number of complications inherent to media policy debates combine to encourage such failure by masking the policy roots of media-related problems.

First, there is the invisibility of media policy. Because so many policymaking processes remain hidden, citizens' relationship to government and the connections between policy and politics in general are obscured. The political scientist Suzanne Mettler highlights aspects of this phenomenon with her useful formulation of what she calls a "submerged state," in which the state is involved in people's daily lives in profound ways that are rarely recognized (Mettler 2011). Whereas Mettler is drawing attention specifically to policies impacting households' economic security such as retirement benefits, the influence of the invisible state extends to countless rules and infrastructures including subsidized mortgages, road maintenance, and safety standards. Further, when state intervention is acknowledged, it is often stigmatized for providing "handouts" to disadvantaged (and presumably undeserving) groups. Even expenditures benefiting the general public (public education, public media, public arts) are held suspect, while the more prevalent policy interventions that aid corporations (tax breaks, relaxation of antitrust laws, intellectual property protections) often remain invisible and under-scrutinized, or even applauded. Misunderstandings about these largely hidden policy relationships lead to a distorted view of government's regulatory role in society.

In particular, much confusion exists around how government regulates media, which is often elided by celebrations of new digital technologies and other forms of technological determinism. A widespread assumption is that if society simply allows inventors and entrepreneurs to develop new technologies, the communication system is self-correcting. This ignores market constraints and the state's ever-present role. The Internet's genesis is a classic case. Its early development was largely dependent on state subsidies via military and research institutions, but many see the Internet as a wild, unregulated terrain that emerged naturally from new technologies, market forces, and individual genius. To the contrary, government is *always* involved, from enforcing copyright laws (often seen by corporations as "good regulation") to applying antitrust laws (or lack thereof). The real question should be *how* the government gets involved. This general confusion about government's regulatory role in everyday communication, combined with policymakers' lack of motivation to raise awareness, discourages public involvement in critical policy debates.

This leads us to the problem of policy inaction—what the political scientists Jacob Hacker and Paul Pierson referred to as "drift" (Hacker and Pierson 2010). Drift emphasizes policy failure's effect on society over time and how problems often worsen when regulatory agencies do nothing. For example, in the 1940s, as negative externalities such as excessive commercialism in the American media system increased, government could have intervened by applying structural measures like antitrust legislation to break up conglomerates or, with broadcast media, mandated stringent public interest obligations in return for using the public spectrum.

But such systemic interventions rarely occur—as a result of both institutional inertia and calculated neglect. Moreover, given what might be called a "submerged state syndrome," the public is unlikely to call for affirmative regulatory intervention. This perceived absence of the state has concrete policy outcomes by limiting the range of possible trajectories in the public imagination. Consequently, vacuums emerge within policy discourses that allow imbalances to continue unabated, particularly given the assumption that a media system has developed according to the natural laws of the market and technological progress.

A third major factor that distorts policy discourse and practice is what I referred to earlier as "regulatory capture." This process is often subtle, involving not only media corporations' significant donations to politicians and their campaigns but also the sheer boots-on-the-ground power of having legions of lobbyists crowding the halls of Congress and key regulatory agencies. Free Press, a leading media reform advocacy group, calculated that in 2009, amid net neutrality and other key telecom policy debates, six leading telecom and cable companies and their lobbying firms employed more than 550 lobbyists—working out to more than one lobbyist per member of Congress—and spent more than $70 million on telecom lobbying in Washington, D.C., alone (see Free Press 2015; Brodkin 2014).

Perhaps even more significant than direct payoffs to politicians is the much-lamented revolving-door phenomenon. Indeed, shuffling of personnel between the Federal Communications Commission (FCC) and the communication industries it is meant to regulate remains a common practice. One analysis found that of the 26 commissioners and chairs who have served on the FCC since 1980, at least 20 have gone to work for the industries they previously regulated.[4] Some cases have been quite blatant, as when the former commissioner Meredith Atwell Baker left the FCC to become a Comcast–NBC lobbyist not long after voting to approve those companies' mega-merger. She is now president of the leading trade group for the wireless telecommunications industry, CTIA-The Wireless Association. Similarly, former FCC chairman Michael Powell now heads the cable industry's top trade association, the National Cable and Telecommunications Association (NCTA). This regulatory capture contributes to a "discursive capture," yielding master narratives that systematically write off alternative policy options such as subsidizing public media and breaking up oligopolies.

Much of this ideological framework began to congeal in the 1940s and remains operative today, which leads to a fourth major constraint on media policy discourse, that of ideology. America's corporate libertarian ideology fails to recognize public goods and downplays the existence of market failure. This, in turn, encourages seemingly commonsensical notions about self-regulation, which, upon reaching the level of ideology, are difficult to dislodge. C. Edwin Baker observed two arguments that have long been used to discredit state intervention in cultivating a vibrant media system: that the government has no legitimate role in markets and that the First Amendment specifically forbids government intervention in media markets (see Baker 2006). It took decades of ideological work to turn these arguments into truisms—and they continue to require constant maintenance and repair—but thinking outside their confines today is exceedingly difficult. Des Freedman dubbed these phenomena "media policy silences," which he defined as the "ideological processes of exclusion and marginalization that distort media policymaking and undermine the emergence of alternative paradigms and policy outcomes" (Freedman 2010). Taken together, these discursive impediments obscure the policy roots of social problems, mask market inefficiencies in providing for society's communication needs, and narrow the possibilities for alternative policy trajectories—all leading to policy inaction and, ultimately, policy failure.

The antidote to this impasse requires a new policy vision based on positive liberties (e.g., freedom to access a diverse media system) that do not succumb to market fundamentalism or First Amendment absolutism.[5] We can draw from our past to reinvigorate our imagination of what policies are possible today. Indeed, a long-standing, if largely forgotten, tradition exists in which the American government affirmatively mandated that media systems serve public needs, from the birth of the postal system (John 1995) to key Supreme Court decisions that called for "diverse and antagonistic sources" in our media system.[6] Affirmative media policy based on positive liberties is entirely consistent with American history and democratic ideals, and this tradition informs the policy recommendations I discuss in the following sections.

POLICY REFORMS FOR DIGITAL MEDIA

The future of media is a digital one, yet as a society, we are still grappling with the implications of this transformation. It would be comforting if concerns about media ownership and public interest obligations no longer mattered in the age of the Internet. For many, caring about the future of news media might seem quaint and anachronistic given the ubiquity of digital communications. But despite dramatic technological changes, similar policy quandaries remain, especially as we witness a new wave of digital media monopolies, oligopolies, and cartels.[7] The commercial Internet faces a norm-defining moment not unlike that of commercial radio in the 1940s. Such moments require normative questions: What is the Internet's role in a democratic society? How can the public interest be protected in this digital media system? What is government's role in regulating that relationship? Thus far, we have failed to address these questions adequately.

Actualizing this new digital media system's democratic potential requires a paradigm shift. It requires moving away from corporate libertarianism toward a framework that recognizes the public-good qualities of media and embraces government's affirmative role in providing for society's communication needs—especially as systemic media market failure becomes increasingly evident. Nearly a fifth of all US households still lack broadband Internet (Federal Communications Commission 2015). Even for those with access, services are subpar and costly relative to the rest of the developed world. Among leading democracies, American broadband is the 7th most expensive and 19th in terms of speed. In terms of Internet penetration, the USA ranks 15th internationally, having dropped sharply over the past decade (Organization for Economic Co-operation and Development 2012). In terms of cost, the USA ranked 30th out of 33 countries, with an average price of $90 per month for higher speeds of 45 megabits per second (Mbps) and over (Geoghegan 2013). The average of $40 per month for 27 Mbps, while an average South Korean pays a fraction of that price for 70 Mbps (Organization for Economic Co-operation and Development 2011). A more recent report exposes the degree to which American cities lag in broadband speeds and prices behind other cities around the world. For example, the same broadband speed that fetches $21.75 in Riga, Latvia, costs $112.50 in Washington, D.C. (Hussain et al. 2013; see also Wyatt 2013). Given that duopolies presently dominate both the wired (Comcast, Time Warner) and wireless (Verizon, AT&T) US markets, it is reasonable to assume that a lack of competition plays an important role in this predicament.[8]

According to the FCC, 96 percent of American housing units have two or fewer choices for wireline Internet access (Federal Communications Commission 2010). In a 2010 report, Yochai Benkler determined that the relative decline of American broadband stems from policy differences with other democracies (Benkler 2010), suggesting that this American exceptionalism is primarily political, with telecom corporations exerting disproportionate control over the policy process. Susan Crawford makes a compelling argument that these digital communications industries wield such influence over the political process that aggressive structural intervention in the form of breaking up monopolies and oligopolies is highly unlikely for the immediate future. However, she sees hope in a smattering of community-owned Internet networks that provide cheap and reliable broadband services to their residents.

Indeed, building out community broadband capacity should be a primary objective. Because monopolistic Internet service providers (ISPs) have little incentive to make the necessary investments to address the digital divide, one first step toward increasing capacity is to subsidize the build-out of new networks that can compete with the incumbents.[9] Therefore, one arrow in the quiver against telecom monopolies should include community broadband initiatives—at least in the 30 states that have not yet passed laws making it extremely difficult or impossible for municipalities to offer these services, essentially ensuring a captive market for companies such as Comcast (Crawford 2013, 256). Locally owned and controlled wireless or municipal fiber Internet networks could be operated through community media centers supported by local and national tax revenues. Leveraging already-existing public infrastructure, these centers could be housed in post offices or public libraries to serve as hubs for community media production,[10] including local news content. This latter function is especially important since open digital infrastructures do not specifically address the journalism crisis, which I turn to next.

Taking the Profit Motive Out of News

With nearly all signs suggesting a slow but sure demise for advertising-supported journalism, traditional news organizations continue to flounder for a last-minute rescue, whether through digital paywall models or some other technological fix. The Internet, paradoxically, is seen as both journalism's destroyer and its potential savior. The latter view assumes that new digital media will somehow combine with market forces and organically produce new models for citizen journalism. Thus far, little evidence suggests that this will manifest at sufficient levels. Saving commercial journalism from itself—or rather, extricating its good parts—must happen quickly before its slide toward ruin leaves behind hundreds of hollowed-out newsrooms. For while its business model has collapsed, journalism's public service mission is as vital today as any point in history. Salvaging it, however, will require public policy interventions. Even modest policy changes could bolster public service journalism.

Lessening market failure within the digital realm would greatly benefit news media, but policy reforms aimed specifically at journalistic institutions are also necessary. A three-pronged approach to reinventing journalism would involve new tax laws, subsidies for a new public media system, and research and development efforts for new digital models. Together, these initiatives would remove or lessen profit pressures and help restore journalism's public service mission. An immediate stopgap measure like tweaking tax laws would help struggling news outlets transition to new low- and nonprofit business models while also eliminating barriers to new ventures.[11] A number of promising initiatives have been waiting for months and years to be granted nonprofit status, and the Internal Revenue Service's (IRS) inexplicable delays have caused unnecessary hardship for these news organizations (Stearns 2012; see also Council on Foundations 2013). Other worthwhile tax reform proposals have been floated in recent years but have yet to receive a full public hearing.[12]

Strengthening the already existing public media system would be another strong first step toward funding an alternative media infrastructure insulated from the commercial pressures that accelerated our journalism crisis. Right now, the USA is a global outlier among democracies in how little it funds public broadcasting (Benson and Powers 2011). The current crisis presents a rare opportunity to revitalize and repurpose this public media infrastructure by dedicating it to local news gathering as well as international and state-level news. Existing community and public radio stations could transition into multimedia centers (as many already are) that create digital media across multiple platforms and support investigative reporters in local communities, replacing the news media production often vacated by commercial newspapers.

Funding for public media should be guaranteed over the long term and carefully shielded from political pressures, a process that would require removing it from the congressional appropriation process. A permanent trust could be supported by spectrum fees paid by commercial operators, a small consumer tax on electronics, or something equivalent to the universal service fund added to monthly phone bills. In the meantime, the USA could allocate targeted subsidies toward increasing public media's capacity, reach, diversity, and relevance. These subsidies could help broaden public media to include not just the Public Broadcasting Service and National Public Radio but also low-power FM stations, public access cable channels, and independent community websites, as well as the aforementioned community media centers.

All of these efforts would benefit from R&D investments in new digital start-ups (discussed in Pickard et al. 2009). Similar to private initiatives like the Knight News Challenge,[13] this federal R&D program could nurture promising journalistic experiments to help them become self-sustaining. Recent years have witnessed numerous creative proposals to jump-start innovative forms of multi-platform public media, including federal support for a journalism jobs program based on the AmeriCorps model (Pickard et al. 2009), instituting $200 tax vouchers to put toward taxpayers' choice of media (McChesney and Nichols 2011, 201–206), repurposing funds currently used for international broadcasting (Powers 2011), charging commercial broadcasters for their use of the public spectrum (Lennett et al. 2012), and having journalism schools take over news operations abandoned by professional organizations (Downie and Schudson 2011). Given corporate libertarianism's control over American political discourse, such a policy reorientation may seem like a nonstarter. At a time when the need for public media should be most self-evident, conservative politicians routinely target public broadcasting for proposed budget cuts. At the same time, market pressures are further weakening public media, as dramatically exemplified when it was announced that the next five seasons of *Sesame Street,* one of public television's most celebrated shows, would air first on HBO (Vaidhyanathan 2015).[14] Nonetheless, survey data consistently show high levels of support for public broadcasting, suggesting that the American people might accept arguments for increased subsidies (Public Broadcasting System 2013). But implementing new reforms and expanding public media are possible only if we create a counter-narrative to corporate libertarianism.

Beyond Corporate Libertarianism

How we think about journalism is largely determined by how much we buy into a corporate libertarian paradigm that sees news and information primarily as commodities whose existence is dictated by profitability. If we see journalism first and foremost as a public service or public good, then it must be sustained, regardless of market support. Thus, an argument for subsidizing public media can be condensed to the following points:

first, despite its continued commercial devaluation, journalism produces a public good that is essential to democracy; second, the advertising model that has subsidized this public good for the past 125 years is no longer sustainable; third, no new commercial models are emerging that offset the loss of journalism within legacy media; and fourth, once society acknowledges this market failure, the need for policy interventions to promote and protect public service journalism becomes paramount.

This reframing of the journalism crisis allows for commercial and noncommercial models to coexist by restoring balance between profit-making and democratic imperatives and creating a mixed, structurally diverse media system that is not overly dependent on market relationships. The historical record as well as recent events would suggest that a wholly commercial news system focused on profit maximization cannot withstand market fluctuations and is inadequate in supporting a democratic society's communication requirements. Swaying a critical mass of Americans toward accepting a public policy approach to our media crises poses a difficult political struggle, but it is one that we retreat from at democracy's peril. History shows that democratization can occur when government, pushed by social movements, enters the fray on the public's behalf.

NOTES

1. This chapter draws from the conclusion of Pickard 2015.
2. For an excellent discussion of merit goods, see Ali 2013. Freedman 2008 similarly argues that media products, like preventive health care services, are merit goods, since individual consumers are likely to underinvest in them. See also Musgrave 1959, 13–15.
3. The 2014 Pew Report found that while other revenue streams are growing like capital investment and philanthropy, they account for a meager 1 percent of current financial support for news.
4. Personal correspondence with Timothy Karr of Free Press on May 2, 2013.
5. Unfortunately, given what some have called the "Lochnerization of the Frist Amendment," recent jurisprudence has equated First Amendment freedoms with corporate privilege. See 2016.
6. Associated Press v. United States 1945. For a comprehensive history of American policy battles and media reform, see Lloyd 2007.
7. McChesney 2015 offers a provocative argument for dismantling Internet cartels and monopolies.

8. For an international comparison of mobile Internet services, see Hussain and Kehl 2013.
9. For example, the governments of Japan, South Korea, and Sweden have made significant investments in building out broadband infrastructure. See Hansell 2009. President Obama's "broadband stimulus," which viewed the Internet as crucial infrastructure, was arguably a first tiny step in this direction, but insufficient.
10. The Independent Media Center (IMC or Indymedia) experiment of the early 2000s could serve as a model, though reliable funding is required instead of all-volunteer labor. See Pickard 2006. An important exemplar is the Urbana IMC, which purchased the downtown post office building. In addition to community wireless services, this space produces a wide range of media, including a monthly print publication, an LPFM station, and a community website.
11. For a discussion of these tax models, as well as historical models like municipal-owned newspapers, see Pickard 2011.
12. See, for example, Senator Ben Cardin's proposed bill, the "Newspaper Revitalization Act of 2009," to help struggling newspapers become non-profits. See also his op-ed, Cardin 2009.
13. The Knight News Challenge is an annual contest offering rewards of between $1,000 and $1,000,000 to promote innovative ideas in "news and information."
14. New episodes of *Sesame Street* will be available for free on Public Broadcasting Service stations nine months after HBO viewers receive them.

REFERENCES

Ali, Chris. 2013. Where is here? An analysis of localism in media policy in three western democracies. Ph.D. dissertation, University of Pennsylvania.
Baker, C. Edwin. 2001. *Media, markets, and democracy*. Cambridge: University Press.
Baker, C. Edwin. 2006. *Media concentration and democracy: Why ownership matters*. Cambridge: University Press.
Bator, Francis. 1958. The anatomy of market failure. *Quarterly Journal of Economics* 72(3): 351–379.
Benkler, Yochai. 2010. *Next generation connectivity: A review of broadband internet transitions and policy from around the world*. Cambridge, MA: Berkman Center for Internet & Society at Harvard University.
Benson, Rodney, and Matthew Powers. 2011. *Public media and political independence: Lessons for the future of journalism from around the world*. Washington, D.C.: Free Press.

Brodkin, Jon. 2014. ISP lobby has already won limits on public broadband in 20 states. *Ars Technica*, February 12.

Brown, Allan. 1996. Economics, public service broadcasting, and social values. *Journal of Media Economics* 9(1): 3–15.

Cardin, Ben. 2009. A plan to save our free press. *Washington Post*, April 3.

Cooper, Mark. 2011. The future of journalism: Addressing pervasive market failure with public policy. In *Will the last reporter please turn out the lights? The collapse of journalism and what can be done to fix it*, ed. Robert McChesney and Victor Pickard, 320–339. New York: New Press.

Council on Foundations. 2013. The IRS and nonprofit media: Toward creating a more informed public. Available at http://www.cof.org/nonprofitmedia?Item Number=18708#sthash

Crawford, Susan P. 2013. *Captive audience: The telecom industry and monopoly power in the new gilded age*. New Haven: Yale University Press.

Downie, Leonard, and Michael Schudson. 2011. The reconstruction of American journalism. In *Will the last reporter please turn out the lights? The collapse of journalism and what can be done to fix it*, ed. Robert McChesney and Victor Pickard, 55–90. New York: New Press.

Edmonds, Rick, Emily Guskin, Tom Rosenstiel, and Amy Mitchell. 2012. Newspapers: By the numbers. *The Pew Research Center's Project for Excellence in Journalism: The State of the News Media 2012.* Available at http://stateofthemedia.org

Edmonds, Rick, Emily Guskin, Amy Mitchell, and Mark Jurkowitz. 2013. Newspapers: Stabilizing, but still threatened. *The State of the News Media 2013.* http://www.stateofthemedia.org/2013/newspapers-stabilizing-but-still -threatened/

Federal Communications Commission. 2010. *Connecting America: The national broadband plan, 2010.* Accessed October 11, 2013. Available at http://download.broadband.gov/plan/national-broadband-plan.pdf

Federal Communications Commission. 2015. 2015 broadband progress report. Available at https://www.fcc.gov/reports/2015-broadband-progress-report

Free Press. 2015. Telecom lobbying. Available at http://www.freepress.net/ lobbying

Freedman, Des. 2008. *The politics of media policy.* Cambridge, MA: Polity Press.

Freedman, Des. 2010. Media policy silences: The hidden face of communications decision making. *International Journal of Press/Politics* 15(3): 344–361.

Geoghegan, Tom. 2013. Why is broadband more expensive in the U.S.? *BBC News Magazine*, October 27. http://www.bbc.co.uk/news/magazine-24528383

Hacker, Jacob, and Paul Pierson. 2010. *Winner take all politics.* New York: Simon and Schuster.

Hamilton, James. 2006. *All the news that's fit to sell.* Princeton: Princeton University Press.

Hansell, Saul. 2009. The broadband gap: Why do they have more fiber? *New York Times*, March 12.

Hussain, Hibah, and Danielle Kehl. 2013. Americans pay six times more for mobile internet data than the French. *Slate*, October 11. http://www.slate. com/blogs/future_tense/2013/10/11/itu_report_shows_americans_pay_ high_price_for_mobile_internet_data.html

Hussain, Hibah, Danielle Kehl, Patrick Lucey, and Nick Russo. 2013. *The cost of connectivity 2013: Data release, a comparison of high-speed internet prices in 24 cities around the world*. https://www.newamerica.org/oti/the-cost-of-connectivity-2013/

John, Richard. 1995. *Spreading the news: The American postal system from Franklin to Morse*. Cambridge, MA: Harvard University Press.

Lennett, Benjamin, Tom Glaisyer, and Sascha Meinrath. 2012. *Public media, spectrum policy, and rethinking public interest obligations for the 21st century*. Washington, D.C.: New America Foundation.

Lloyd, Mark. 2007. *Prologue to a farce: Communication and democracy in America*. Champaign: University of Illinois Press.

McChesney, Robert. 2015. Be realistic, demand the impossible: Three radically democratic internet policies. In *Future of internet policy*, ed. Peter Decherney and Victor Pickard. London: Routledge.

McChesney, Robert, and John Nichols. 2010. *The death and life of American journalism: The media revolution that will begin the world again*. New York: Nation Books.

McChesney, Robert, and John Nichols. 2011. *The death and life of American journalism: The media revolution that will begin the world again*. New York: Nation Books.

Medema, Steven. 2007. The hesitant hand: Mill, Sidgwick, and the evolution of the theory of market failure. *History of Political Economy* 39(3): 331–358.

Mettler, Suzanne. 2011. *The submerged state: How invisible government policies undermine American democracy*. Chicago: University of Chicago Press.

Musgrave, Richard. 1959. *The theory of public finance: A study in public economy*. New York: McGraw-Hill.

Organization for Economic Co-operation and Development. 2011. *Average advertised download speeds by country, annual report*. Available at http://www. oecd.org/sti/broadband/BBPortal_5a_13July_Final.xls

Organization for Economic Co-operation and Development. 2012. *Fixed and wireless broadband subscriptions per 100 Inhabitants, annual report*. Available at http:// www.oecd.org/sti/broadband/1d-OECD-WiredWirelessBB-2012-12_v2.xls

Pickard, Victor. 2006. Assessing the radical democracy of indymedia: Discursive, technical and institutional constructions. *Critical Studies in Media Communication* 23(1): 19–38.

Pickard, Victor. 2011. Can government support the press? Historicizing and internationalizing a policy approach to the journalism crisis. *Communication Review* 14(2): 73–95.

Pickard, Victor. 2013. Social democracy or corporate libertarianism? Conflicting media policy narratives in the wake of market failure. *Communication Theory* 23(4): 336–355.

Pickard, Victor. 2015. *America's battle for media democracy: The triumph of corporate libertarianism and the future of media reform.* New York: Cambridge University Press.

Pickard, Victor. 2016. Toward a people's internet: The fight for positive freedoms in an age of corporate libertarianism. Gothenburg: Nordicom.

Pickard, Victor, and Alex Williams. 2014. Salvation or folly? The promises and perils of digital paywalls. *Digital Journalism* 2(2): 195–213.

Pickard, Victor, Josh Stearns, and Craig Aaron. 2009. Saving the news: Toward a national journalism strategy. In *Changing media: Public interest policies for the digital age*, ed. Craig Aaron. Washington, D.C.: Free Press.

Powers, Shawn. 2011. U.S. International broadcasting: An untapped resource for ethnic and domestic news organizations. In *Will the last reporter please turn out the lights? The collapse of journalism and what can be done to fix it*, ed. Robert McChesney and Victor Pickard, 128–150. New York: New Press.

Public Broadcasting System. 2013. Today's PBS: Trusted, valued, essential. Available at http://pbs.bento.storage.s3.amazonaws.com/hostedbento-prod/filer_public/PBS_About/Files%20and%20Thumbnails/Release%20Files/2013_Trust%20Brochure.pdf

Samuelson, Paul. 1954. The pure theory of public expenditure. *Review of Economics and Statistics* 36: 387–389.

Starr, Paul. 2011. Goodbye to the age of newspapers (Hello to a New Era of Corruption). In *Will the last reporter please turn out the lights? The collapse of journalism and what can be done to fix it*, ed. Robert McChesney and Victor Pickard, 31. New York: New Press.

Stearns, Josh. 2012. No News Is Bad News for Nonprofit Journalism. *Yes Magazine*, May 3. http://www.yesmagazine.org/people-power/no-news-is-bad-news-for-nonprofit-journalism

Stiglitz, Joseph. 1989. Markets, market failures, and development. *American Economic Review* 79(2): 197–203.

Taylor, John. 2007. *Economics*, 5th ed, 15. New York: Houghton Mifflin.

Trogen, Paul. 2005. Public goods. In *Handbook of public sector economics*, ed. Donijo Robbins, 169–207. New York: Taylor & Francis.

Vaidhyanathan, Siva. 2015. Big bird and big media: What sesame street on HBO means. *Time*, August 21. http://time.com/4005048/problem-with-sesame-street-moving-to-hbo/

Wyatt, Edward. 2013. U.S. struggles to keep pace in delivering broadband service. *New York Times*, December 29.

CHAPTER 10

Tripartite Regulation in the Public's Interest: The Overlapping Roles of the DOJ, FCC, and FTC in Consolidation of the Communications Industry

Allen S. Hammond IV

INTRODUCTION

Media consolidation is perceived by many to be a growing problem endangering the American democracy. Concern about the continuing media consolidation[1] has led to questions about the regulatory process by which media[2] consolidation is policed—and the roles of the government agencies responsible for policing. Concerns about phalanxes of well-heeled, "revolving door" lobbyists speak to a perceived lack of regulatory transparency and fears of skewed regulatory policies augured by inequitable access to government decision-makers. Simultaneously, those favoring "limited government" have expressed sincere misgivings about the efficiency and efficacy of a regulatory process that may slow and/or stifle marketplace decision-making.

A.S. Hammond IV (✉)
Santa Clara University, Stanford, CA, USA

© The Editor(s) (if applicable) and The Author(s) 2016   143
M.I. Lloyd, L.A. Friedland (eds.), *The Communication Crisis in America,
And How to Fix It*, DOI 10.1057/978-1-349-94925-0_10

In the USA, the Federal Communications Commission (FCC), the Federal Trade Commission (FTC), and the Antitrust Division of the US Department of Justice (DOJ) are the trio of federal agencies that conduct the merger review processes by which proposed consolidation is approved or denied.[3] Their jurisdiction and corresponding authority and standards of review create regulatory overlap. This overlap is viewed by some as anti-democratic, by others as inefficient, and by still others as inequitable.

The process is deemed anti-democratic because it can be exploited by lobbyists who enjoy better access to decision-makers, often to the disadvantage of the public and the advocates representing the public. The process is deemed by some to be inefficient because the reviewing agencies have redundant but not coextensive authority often exercised in tandem which allegedly slows the review process for time-sensitive business transactions. Finally, the process is alleged to be inequitable because the government can extract concessions in one proceeding (the FCC public-interest review) that it would be unable to extract in the other (the DOJ/FTC antitrust review).

This chapter explores the overlapping regulatory process through an analysis of the successful merger of Comcast with NBC/Universal and the unsuccessful attempted merger of AT&T with T-Mobile. The exploration begins with a comparison of the reviewing agencies' statutory grants of jurisdiction and authority over complex media merger transactions. The exploration continues with a general analysis of the manner in which the agencies have allocated merger review responsibility among themselves. The chapter then briefly summarizes critiques of the agency review process. After establishing the general context in which the agencies share authority and critiques of the regulatory process, the chapter reviews the Comcast/NBC/Universal and AT&T/T-Mobile merger transactions.

Analysis of the joint-agency review process generally—and as it played out in the two mergers—suggests that any inefficiency caused by the overlapping DOJ antitrust and FCC public-interest review standards is more than offset by the benefits of transparency. Public-interest critics of the overlapping processes should instead focus more attention on the problems posed by lobbying and the "revolving door."

The Agencies

The DOJ is the executive-branch agency charged with the enforcement of the nation's laws. The attorney general, the head of the DOJ, serves at the pleasure of the president and is a member of the president's cabinet.

The DOJ derives its antitrust authority from the Sherman Antitrust Act of 1890 and the Clayton Antitrust Act of 1914. The Sherman Act outlaws "every contract, combination, or conspiracy in restraint of trade," and any "monopolization, attempted monopolization, or conspiracy or combination to monopolize" (15 U.S.C. §§ 1–7). The Clayton Act "addresses specific practices that the Sherman Act does not clearly prohibit, such as mergers." Section 7 of the Clayton Act prohibits mergers and acquisitions where the effect "may be substantially to lessen competition, or to tend to create a monopoly" (15 U.S.C. § 12–27).

The FTC is an independent administrative agency charged with the enforcement of several of the nation's antitrust laws. The FTC is headed by five commissioners nominated by the president and confirmed by the US Senate. The president selects the chairman but cannot remove the chairman without cause. A disagreement over policy is not grounds for removal. The FTC derives its antitrust authority from the Federal Trade Commission Act (FTCA) and the Clayton Act. The FTCA bans "unfair methods of competition" and "unfair or deceptive acts or practices."[4] As mentioned above, the Clayton Act prohibits mergers and acquisitions that may substantially lessen competition or tend to create a monopoly.

The FCC is an independent administrative agency charged with the regulation of communication by wire or radio (spectrum). Like the FTC, the FCC is headed by five commissioners nominated by the president and confirmed by the US Senate. The president selects the chairperson but cannot remove the chairperson without cause. A disagreement over policy is not grounds for removal. The FCC derives its antitrust authority from the Communications Act of 1934 (CA34), as amended by the Telecommunications Act of 1996 (TA96); although the FCC also may act pursuant to the Clayton Act, it has declined to do so.[5]

AREAS OF REGULATORY OVERLAP

The Sherman, Clayton, and FTC Acts are the three core antitrust laws still in effect (Federal Trade Commission 2015b). The three agencies—DOJ, FTC, and FCC—derive shared antitrust authority from the Clayton Act. The FCC has eschewed the exercise of its antitrust authority under the Clayton Act in favor of the measure of antitrust authority it enjoys via the Communications Act's public-interest standard which subsumes antitrust considerations.[6] The agencies avoid duplicated effort by coordinating their activities pursuant to interagency agreements.

DOJ/FTC
The DOJ and the FTC share authority in reviewing mergers for antitrust issues and apportion the work load through a clearance process based upon expertise in dealing with particular industries (Federal Trade Commission 2015, "Antitrust Laws"). Both agencies have reviewed mergers in the media and entertainment industry. For instance, the DOJ reviewed the News Corp/Direct TV merger in 2003, and the FTC reviewed the Adelphia Communications Corporation sale to Comcast and Time Warner in 2006 (Viswanatha 2009). However, pursuant to the 2002 DOJ/FTC clearance agreement, the review of mergers in the media and entertainment and telecommunications services and equipment markets is allocated to the DOJ (Federal Trade Commission 2002). The agreement provides that the allocation is subject to change.

FCC/FTC
The FCC and the FTC have an interagency agreement addressing the division of responsibility to regulate radio and television broadcasting.[7] The FCC and FTC have also exercised concurrent jurisdiction over business practices regarding the use, disclosure, or provision of access to mobile phone customers' personally identifiable information (Brodkin 2015). The agencies have engaged in other coordinated efforts in the telecommunications arena, as well.[8] Finally, the agencies have, until recently,[9] cooperatively asserted jurisdiction over the Internet.[10]

Moreover, from the vantage point of the interagency clearance agreement between the DOJ and the FTC, the DOJ has the responsibility for conducting antitrust merger reviews in the media, entertainment, and telecommunication industries. Hence, for purposes of analysis in this chapter, the primary focus will be on DOJ and the FCC.[11]

THE MERGER REVIEW PROCESS

DOJ (and FTC)
For most merger transactions requiring a filing, the merger parties submit data about the industry and their own businesses. Once the filing is complete, the parties must wait 30 days or until the agencies grant early termination of the waiting period before the parties can consummate the merger. Once the filing is substantially complete, the FTC and DOJ consult to determine which agency will conduct the merger review.

The matter is "cleared" to one agency for review. After a preliminary review of the premerger filing, the reviewing agency can terminate the waiting period, allow the initial waiting period to expire, or request additional materials. If the waiting period expires or is terminated, the parties are free to consummate the merger. If the agency requests more information, the request acts as an extension of the waiting period and prevents the companies from completing their merger until they have "substantially complied" with the second request and observed a second waiting period (Federal Trade Commission 2015a).

Once the parties have substantially complied with the second request, the agency has an additional 30 days to review the materials and take action, if necessary. A further extension of the review may occur if agreed to by the parties and the government in an effort to resolve any remaining issues without litigation.

Barring a mutually agreed further extension, if the waiting period following the second request expires, the agency may terminate the investigation and the parties are free to merge. Alternatively, the agency could elect to enter into a negotiated consent agreement or challenge the proposed merger in court. Once the parties have substantially complied with the agency's request, the agency has 30 days to make a decision to block or approve the merger (U.S. Department of Justice 2015). If the DOJ elects to challenge the merger, it must take the parties to court and has the burden of proving its case before the judge upon petitioning for a preliminary injunction against the merger.

FCC

The FCC's review is triggered by the filing of an application by the current license holder and the party seeking to acquire the license(s) (the applicants). The applications will describe the proposed transaction, the benefits expected to be achieved, and the potential harms. In addition, the application will explain why the harms will not occur or how they will be offset or remedied (U.S. Department of Justice 2015).

Once the application is accepted for filing, the FCC invites public comment on the application and petitions to deny the application. All comments and petitions are due within 30 days. The applicants are required to respond to the comments and petitions within ten to fifteen days, and the commenters' responses are usually due approximately seven days later (U.S. Department of Justice 2015). The Commission seeks to complete its review of all transactions and issue an order within 180 days of accepting the application for filing.

The merging parties have the burden of convincing the FCC that the merger is in the public interest or the license transfers will not be approved.[12] Pursuant to the CA34, the FCC is responsible for the initial assignment and subsequent review for approval of the transfer of all broadcast radio and television licenses, wireless licenses, satellite authorizations, and authorizations to provide landline telephone service licenses. Whether making the initial assignment or reviewing the transfer of any license, the FCC must determine whether "the public interest, convenience, and necessity" would be served by granting the application (Federal Communications Commission 2014).

The FCC's public interest review is broad. It encompasses more than an assessment of whether competition would be harmed by virtue of the license transfer. Unlike the inquiries of the DOJ and the FTC, the FCC does more than assess likely competitive harm. Under the public interest standard, the FCC also examines whether competition would be enhanced by the license transfer and what effect the transfer is likely to have on private sector deployment of advanced services, the diversity of license holders, and the diversity of information sources and services available to the public. Based on its review and of the record and taking into account public comments, the FCC issues its decision. The FCC can approve the application outright, or it can approve the transaction with conditions, or it can decide to not approve the transaction. In the event the commission cannot approve the transaction, it will refer application to an administrative law judge for a hearing (Federal Communications Commission 2014).

CRITIQUE OF THE TRIPARTITE AGENCY DUAL REVIEW PROCESS

The "tripartite" agency dual merger review process has been criticized by those favoring less concentration of ownership, as well as those favoring less regulation of mergers. Public interest advocates favoring less media concentration cite the failure of regulators operating within the merger review process to stem the growing tide of media and telecommunications industry consolidation. Their critique is supported by the data (Mirani 2014).

Losses in media ownership diversity and responsive public service and news programming continue as ownership concentration increases and the number of corporations controlling a majority of US media decreases. For instance, from 1983 to 2011, the number of corporations controlling the majority of US newspaper, radio, and television media dropped from fifty to five (Media Reform Information Center 2015). Consequently, it is no surprise that many public interest advocates question the extent to which the merger review process can be a viable and effective tool and cast a wary eye toward the suspected influence manifest in the parallel growth of revolving-door lobbying and campaign contributions.

By comparison, free-market advocates offer a litany of alleged shortcomings of the operation of the merger review process. Their critiques focus on the allegedly adverse impact of the FCC on efficiency and transparency of the merger review process. The commission is criticized for duplicating the merger review process conducted by the DOJ and the FTC (Weiser 2008).

In fact, as was mentioned earlier, the FCC operates under a public interest standard that takes into account but is not limited to antitrust considerations. The FCC's merger review assesses the advisability of the proposed license transfer(s) based on the merger's likely impact on the public interest. The public interest has been defined elsewhere as:

The welfare of the general public (in contrast to the selfish interest of a person, group, or firm) in which the whole society has a stake and which warrants recognition, promotion, and protection by the government and its agencies ... It is approximated by comparing expected gains and potential costs or losses associated with a decision, policy, program, or project. (Business Dictionary 2015b)

The FCC's use of the public interest standard has been criticized for allegedly precluding the development of a clear competition policy standard, thereby fostering uncertainty in the market. Free-market critics take special exception to the FCC's use of "negotiated voluntary conditions" to accomplish policy goals "unrelated" to the merger.

Some critics assert that the absence of a statutory time limit for conducting a review delay ultimate merger approval (Weiser 2008) and "drain mergers of their economic benefits" (Rinner 2009). Other critics raised procedural concerns asserting that the FCC's involvement allows the DOJ to eschew its burden of filing a preliminary injunction to stop the merger. As long as the FCC's parallel license transfer review is ongoing, the parties are stopped from merging. Thus, the DOJ may never have to meet its burden of proof by showing a likelihood of success on the merits (Kaplan 2012).

Reduced to their central premise, many critics of the FCC merger process argue that the FCC's public interest concerns should be accorded less weight than the DOJ's antitrust concerns. Critics assert that a finite time period should be established to limit the government's negotiating leverage on "voluntary conditions." And, voluntary commitments should not be allowed if they bear no relationship to the antitrust concerns. They argue the requirement that the applicants meet the burden of proof under the public interest standard "moots" the burden of proof extant under the requirements of the Hart–Scott–Rodino Antitrust Improvements Act of 1976. Therefore, it should be changed. They argue that if the public interest standard cannot be cabined to comport with the DOJ's competition standard, then it should be replaced. Of course, if it does mirror the DOJ competition standard, others argue, it is duplicative and should be jettisoned.

This line of reasoning ignores Congress' intent in establishing the Communications Act's public interest standard for governing licensing decisions. It ignores the fact that the FCC is entrusted with managing the allocation of a scare, essential public resource of immense importance to national welfare. Moreover, it conveniently ignores the fact that despite many opportunities to revise the standard, Congress has not done so. While the proposed merger is the event that triggers the bifurcated review, the DOJ is necessarily focused on market impact and competitive implications. However, the FCC is necessarily tasked with taking into account the broader public interests:

> [T]he "public interest" standard is not limited to purely economic outcomes. It necessarily encompasses the "broad aims of the Communications Act," which include, among other things, a deeply rooted preference for preserving and enhancing competition in relevant markets, accelerating private-sector deployment of advanced services, ensuring a diversity of information sources and services to the public, and generally managing spectrum in the public interest. Our public interest analysis may also entail assessing whether the transaction will affect the quality of communications services or will result in the provision of new or additional services to consumers. (Sallet 2014)

The Mergers: Comcast/NBCU

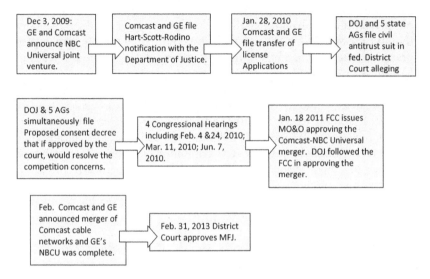

Fig. 10.1 Comcast/NBCU timeline

The Comcast/NBCU Merger Review Process

On December 3, 2009, Comcast and General Electric (GE) announced a joint venture worth a combined $37.25 billion (Goldman and Pepiton 2009) that would be 51 percent owned by Comcast, 49 percent owned by GE, and managed by Comcast. The joint venture would consist of the NBC Universal (NBCU) businesses and Comcast's cable networks, regional sports networks, and certain digital properties (Comcast 2009; Arango 2009). Comcast would later buy the remaining 49 percent from GE to acquire sole control of NBCU (Cozick and Stelter 2013). As part of their joint venture, Comcast and GE sought the FCC's approval for GE to assign and transfer the control of its broadcast, satellite earth station, wireless, and other licenses to the joint venture.

The proposed assignment and transfer of control would facilitate the aggregation of NBCU's two broadcast television networks (NBC and Telemundo), its 26 locally owned and operated broadcast television stations, its national cable programming networks, a motion picture studio, international theme park businesses, and online content businesses with Comcast's regional sports networks, other programming networks, and online businesses (Federal Communications Commission 2011a).

Despite significant opposition from the public, members of Congress, and industry, the merger was approved by the DOJ and FCC on January 18, 2011, subject to conditions (Federal Communications Commission 2011a; Stelter and Arango 2011). Among the conditions specifically cited by the FCC were: Comcast–NBCU commitments to increase local news coverage to viewers; expand children's programming; enhance the diversity of programming available to Spanish-speaking viewers; offer broadband services to low-income Americans at reduced monthly prices; and provision of high-speed broadband to schools, libraries, and underserved communities.[13]

Public interest opponents challenged the decision. The FCC's Comcast/NBCU merger decision was criticized for failing to advance the public interest. Opponents argued that the merger was not necessary to preserve, enhance, or extend the reach of critical infrastructure or extend or improve the provision of services. Given the aftermath of prior mergers, the merger might net Comcast and GE economic benefits but was likely to provide very little to the public at large. Moreover, the DOJ's and the FCC's insistence upon Comcast adhering to conditions on the merger was deemed deficient if not delusional (Hiltzik 2011).

Public-interest critics' assertions were confirmed to some extent when it was published that FCC officials were gamed into believing they had successfully negotiated for Comcast's "Internet Essentials" initiative when Comcast had postponed its introduction in order to use it as a bargaining chip to secure FCC approval of the merger (Bode 2012). Further confirmation came in the form of a judicial rebuff to the DOJ. The federal judge reviewing the consent decree between the DOJ, Comcast, and NBCU threatened to withhold court approval of the merger, criticizing the arbitration terms available to online-content companies that disagree with Comcast about program licensing, "noting that the arbitration agreements can't be appealed" (Gleason and Catan 2011). Public interest critics' predictions that Comcast and GE would be the immediate beneficiaries of the merger were also confirmed.[14]

Meanwhile, free-market advocates questioned the FCC and DOJ's use of "voluntary conditions," arguing that some of the conditions had little if any relevance to the issue of market competition. Members of Congress complained about the delay in coming to a decision (Romm 2010). According to the FCC's official "timeline clock" (Federal Communications Commission 2010; see below), the Comcast NBCU merger took a total of 234 days to complete, taking into account stoppages of 19 and 24 days caused by the need for more information from Comcast. According to at least one Comcast executive, the time spent proved very beneficial (Barthold 2011).

Lobbying During the Comcast NBCU Merger

The lobbying effort that undergirded the Comcast NBCU merger effort was strategic and substantial. Comcast is reported to have hired ex-government officials to help win approval of the proposed merger with NBCU Inc., "including former congressmen and congressional staff members, ex-government antitrust lawyers and former aides to two FCC commissioners" (Dunbar 2010). Cognizant that the merger would require the approval of the DOJ's Antitrust Division and the FCC, Comcast made certain to hire staff from both agencies as members of its lobbying team (Dunbar 2010). GE beefed up its lobbying staff, as well.[15]

Hiring ex-government officials was a prerequisite to generating a deluge of pro-merger letters from Congress to the FCC. A total of 97 letters of Congressional support were received. Of those letters, 88 were reported to be from lawmakers who had received money from Comcast's political action committee.[16] Congress and the agencies were not the only source of lobbying recruits. Non-profit groups to whom Comcast had donated funds were tapped, as well (Lipton 2014). Comcast defended its hiring, stating: "Comcast faces a competitive, complex legislative and regulatory environment, and we hire those with the best expertise and experience to help us navigate Washington. Having representation in Washington is important for our customers, our 107,000 employees, and our shareholders" (Dunbar 2010).

THE MERGERS: AT&T/T-MOBILE

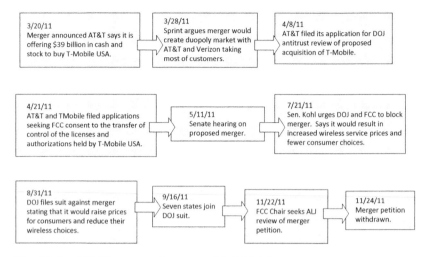

Fig. 10.2   AT&T's proposed merger with T-Mobile

The AT&T/T-Mobile Merger Review Process

On March 20, 2011, AT&T and Deutsche Telekom (DT) announced that they had entered into an agreement under which AT&T would acquire T-Mobile from DT for approximately $39 billion (AT&T 2011). AT&T and DT justified the merger by asserting that the acquisition would provide an optimal combination of network assets to expand network capacity to improve network quality for both companies' customers. In addition, the acquisition was portrayed as an efficient solution to the "impending shortage of wireless spectrum, which threatened to limit both companies' ability to meet the 'explosive' demand for mobile broadband." AT&T also committed to expanding its fourth-generation LTE wireless network to 95 percent of the US population and to reaching an additional 46.5 million Americans beyond its then current plans, including rural communities and small towns, thereby helping to achieve the national goal of increasing broadband access (AT&T 2011).

The proposed acquisition's likelihood of saving consumers money was greeted with significant skepticism. Concerned consumer advocates argued that "a merger of the two companies ... would create a duopoly of

AT&T and Verizon Wireless with more than three-quarters of the market between them" (Sorkin et al. 2011). The DOJ filed a complaint arguing that the combination of the country's second and fourth largest wireless carriers would violate antitrust law and substantially lessen competition. Ultimately, the DOJ concluded that: "Had AT&T acquired T-Mobile, consumers in the wireless marketplace would have faced higher prices and reduced innovation" (De La Merced 2011). The FCC concluded that the acquisition, if approved, would be anticompetitive and would result in the largest single concentration in the US mobile market in history (Gross 2011). Within eight months, AT&T, faced with opposition from both DOJ and the FCC, withdrew its bid (International Business Times 2011; Isaac 2011). The FCC timeline clock was stopped on the 178th day, when AT&T withdrew its application for transfer of control of T-Mobile (Federal Communications Commission 2011).

According to the DOJ, the behavior of market competitors since the withdrawal of the acquisition proposal confirms that the decision to oppose the merger was the right one. Since the planned AT&T/T-Mobile merger came to an abrupt end in 2011, "competition in the wireless sector has flourished and consumers have benefitted" (Morran 2014).

Lobbying During the AT&T T-Mobile Merger Review

In contrast to Comcast's lobbying strategy, AT&T and T-Mobile made similar expenditures with a far less desirable outcome. This was a surprising result, given AT&T's history as a lobbying juggernaut (Kang and Yang 2011). It is reported that "[s]ince 1998, AT&T had given more money in campaign contributions than any other firm in corporate America" (Kang and Yang 2011). In addition, it was ranked among the top ten corporate spenders on lobbying, according to the Center for Responsive Politics. In the 15 years leading up to its attempt to acquire T-Mobile, AT&T is reported to have successfully "acquired a dozen firms" and regularly won regulatory battles on Capitol Hill and at the FCC (Kang and Yang 2011). Given its track record, and following on the heels of the successful Comcast NBCU merger approval, the company officials were reported to be confident about the prospects of acquiring T-Mobile.

As part of the launch of a massive lobbying campaign, AT&T hired seven former congressional lawmakers to help lobby for the merger. It also spent $6.8 million in the first three months of 2011 to hire lobbying firms and lawyers to argue AT&T's case to federal officials to approve the deal. The company also hired economists, PR firms, pollsters, and others and called in favors from among the charities to whom they had donated.

AT&T spent more than $40 million on political advertising and counted among its assets the support of lawmakers whose campaigns it had funded and the third-party groups it supported financially. AT&T's political action committee gave $616,500 to lawmakers and political parties in the first three months of 2011, according to an analysis by the Sunlight Foundation. The corporation had 31 lobbying firms registered with it (Blumenthal 2011).

AT&T asserted that the merger would result in public access to wireless high-speed Internet service sooner than would be the case without the merger and that the merger would create new jobs. The assertions were backed by dozens of community, civic and minority organizations, 14 governors, multiple labor unions, and elected officials.

However, the letters from third-party groups with no real ties to broadband policy reportedly backfired at the government agencies and on the Hill. Subsequent news reports exposing the groups' financial ties to AT&T engendered skepticism (Signorile 2011). Meanwhile, AT&T's argument that the merger would generate jobs was deemed directly contrary to the history of big firm post-merger behavior (Kang and Yang 2011). And, in this case, it was unsubstantiated by the facts.

Ultimately, regulators concluded that T-Mobile was an innovative and low-cost competitor in the national cellular market, and consumers would suffer if it was acquired (Brodsky 2011). AT&T's proposed merger with T-Mobile was a move to "take out one of its three national wireless competitors, a company which had 33 million customers and employed about 40,000 people" (Brodsky 2011).

PROCESS OR ACCESS?

When people come and go in the industry, they have all these contacts and better access than other people have and more opportunity for their voices to be heard and their influence to be deployed ... I think that only enhances the power of the special interest at the expense of the public interest.—Jon Brodkin

Process

It is reasonable to view the growing media concentration as indicative of problems with the bifurcated merger review process. However, the importance of the review process is evident. It is essential to assuring the public an opportunity to be a participant in the merger review process, at least before the FCC, where issues of standing to participate are not as constraining as in the federal courts.[17] Moreover, the FCC review process affords the opportunity for a broader array of public concerns, including, but not limited to, competition policy to be considered. The FCC review is necessarily broader in scope, because the commission is charged with the responsibility to assure that the allocation and use of scarce public resources are made in the public interest.

But access to the administrative or to the judicial process for that matter does not provide assurance of an equitable opportunity for input or an outcome that meets with approval.

Access

Perhaps the problem is not with the process per se, but with the gross disparity in the quality and extent of access to the process. What seems evident from a brief analysis of the Comcast/NBCU and AT&T/T-Mobile merger processes is that parallel, multi-million-dollar lobbying campaigns targeting the regulators and congress were orchestrated and conducted to accompany the merger applications. Former FCC and DOJ regulatory staff, as well as former members of Congress, were recruited to serve as lobbyists financed by corporate interests and deployed as part of a sophisticated strategy. The strategy included soliciting letters of support from legislators, many of whom had accepted past political campaign contributions and from grassroots organizations that had received past charitable contributions from a merging party.

According to a recent study of federal-level revolving-door lobbying, "[h]aving greater aggregated material resources such as campaign donations, lobbying expenditures, corporate financial resources, or organizational size is not associated with successful policy outcomes. *But having a greater number of well-connected lobbyists on your side can be decisive*" (LaPira and Thomas 2014, emphasis added).

This conclusion both qualifies and gives credence to concerns about the impact of revolving-door lobbying. Massive expenditures of money alone may not be effective in achieving one's legislative objective, but having well-connected lobbyists is essential to success. And, while there is skepticism about the consistent efficacy of lobbying congress to influence regulatory decisions, there is also acknowledgement that congressional hearings or letters from legislators can be effective in affecting the timing of regulatory decisions and sometimes the outcome (McConnell 2012).

These conclusions are qualified by the fact that the number of revolving-door lobbyists is significantly underreported (LaPira and Thomas 2014), leading some researchers to conclude that "the revolving door problem … is much bigger than the existing lobbying disclosure regime reveals and—most importantly—significantly distorts the representation of interests before government" (LaPira and Thomas 2014).

It's not the process, it's the access.

NOTES

1. For additional background, see Free Press 2015; ePluribus Media 2008; Anderson 2002; and The Leadership Conference 2015.
2. Media are defined as communication channels through which news, entertainment, education, data, or promotional messages are disseminated. Media include every broadcasting and narrowcasting medium, including newspapers, magazines, television, radio, billboards, direct mail, telephone, fax, and the Internet. See Business Dictionary 2015a.
3. This chapter does not address state and, in some cases, local assertion of jurisdiction and authority over particular types of media transactions.
4. The US Supreme Court has held that all violations of the Sherman Act also violate the FTCA. Thus, although the FTC does not technically enforce the Sherman Act, it can bring cases under the FTCA against the same kinds of activities that violate the Sherman Act. See Federal Trade Commission 2015b.
5. While the FCC also has the authority under the Clayton Act to review mergers, the FCC does not generally exercise its Clayton Act authority. See England-Joseph 1999.
6. Sections 7 and 11 of the Clayton Act provide the FCC with the authority to oppose the acquisition or wire or wireless (radio) where the effect of the acquisition may be the lessening of competition or tend to create a monopoly.

See 15 U.S.C.A. §21 (a), 18 (1994). It has been suggested that the FCC's reluctance to assert authority under the Clayton Act may be due in significant part to its recognition that its public-interest standard affords it greater regulatory flexibility. See, generally, Weiss and Stern 1998.

7. Under the agreement, the FTC has primary jurisdiction over regulation of unfair or deceptive advertising in all media, including the broadcast media. However, the FCC will take into account findings of unfair and deceptive advertising when considering a broadcast licensee's application for a license or renewal of a license. See Ward 2014.

8. In 2003, in an effort to increase consumer protection, the FCC helped establish the national Do-Not-Call list with the FTC. See Federal Communications Commission 2015.

9. The FCC's recent reclassification of ISPs (Internet service providers) as common carriers may preclude FTC regulation of ISPs due to the FTC Act's express exclusion of FTC jurisdiction over telecommunications.

10. The FTC uses its law-enforcement powers to protect the privacy of Americans online, while the FCC sets policies to hasten the deployment of Internet services nationwide and to keep the Internet itself open and competitive for companies. See Barbagallo and Baschuk 2013.

11. The DOJ and FTC merger review process is governed by the same statute and essentially operates in the same manner.

12. However, the FCC review is subject to more public pressure from filed comments and "lobbying," while the investigation process at the DOJ is a confidential and staff-driven investigation. See Viswanatha 2009.

13. Comcast created most of the NBC merger conditions itself, knowing full well it would meet them during the ordinary course of doing business. Still, in many cases, even those conditions proved to be too much for the company. See Bode 2014; Stelter and Arango 2011, and Federal Communications Commission 2011.

14. Comcast's acquisition of the remaining 49 percent of NBCU was viewed as benefiting both Comcast and GE as shares of both companies rose to new five-year highs. See Forbes 2013.

15. GE hired former House Majority Leader Richard Gephardt, D-Mo., along with 18 other ex-government officials, to lobby for the merger. See Dunbar 2010.

16. Another source reported that 91 of the 97 members of Congress who signed a letter in 2011 supporting the Comcast NBC merger received contributions during that same election cycle from the company's political action committee or executives. See Queally 2014.

17. The FCC establishes a pleading cycle that includes the opportunity for comments and petitions to deny to be timely filed and answered.

REFERENCES

Anderson, Byron. 2002. Media consolidation. In *Alternative voices: Essential books and media that most libraries don't carry, but should.* http://libr.org/amtf/bibliographies/bib.1.pdf

Arango, Tim. 2009. G.E. Makes it official: NBC will go to Comcast. *New York Times*, December 3. http://www.nytimes.com/2009/12/04/business/media/04nbc.html?_r=0.

AT&T. 2011. AT&T to acquire T-Mobile USA from Deutsche Telekom. http://www.att.com/gen/press-room?pid=19358&cdvn=news&newsarticleid=31703&mapcode

Barbagallo, Paul, and Bryce Baschuk. 2013. Can the FTC really regulate broadband?. *Bloomberg BNA*, November 12. http://www.bna.com/ftc-really-regulate-n17179880064/

Barthold, Jim. 2011. Regulatory delays gave Comcast time to understand NBC Universal. *FierceCable*, February 17. http://www.fiercecable.com/story/regulatory-delays-gave-comcast-time-understand-nbc-universal/2011-02-17

Blumenthal, Paul. 2011. Massive lobbying operation for telecom merger. Sunlight Foundation, May 11. https://sunlightfoundation.com/blog/2011/05/11/massive-lobbying-operation-for-telecom-merger/

Bode, Karl. 2012. Comcast lobbyist delayed $10 broadband to grease NBC deal while FCC took credit for program that actually did little. *DSLReports*, November2.http://www.dslreports.com/shownews/Comcast-Lobbyist-Delayed-10-Broadband-to-Grease-NBC-Deal-121883

Bode, Karl. 2014. Comcast applauds itself for barely adhering to NBC merger conditions, most of which Comcast created. Techdirt, March 6. https://www.techdirt.com/articles/20140304/08195726426/comcast-applauds-self-barely-adhering-to-nbc-merger-conditions-most-which-they-themselves-created.shtml

Brodkin, Jon. 2015. Judge rejects AT&T claim that FTC can't stop unlimited data throttling. *ArsTechnica*, April 1. http://arstechnica.com/tech-policy/2015/04/judge-rejects-att-claim-that-ftc-cant-stop-unlimited-data-throttling/

Brodsky, Art. 2011. How AT&T's takeover of T-Mobile went wrong (or didn't). *Huffington Post*, December 2. http://www.huffingtonpost.com/art-brodsky/how-atts-takeover-of-t-mo_b_1125505.html

Business Dictionary. 2015a. Media. http://www.businessdictionary.com/definition/media.html#ixzz3hhDmJrll

Business Dictionary. 2015b. Public interest. http://www.businessdictionary.com/definition/public-interest.html#ixzz3hgbuObCE

Chozick, Amy, and Brian Stelter. 2013. Comcast buys rest of NBC in early sale. *New York Times*, February 12. http://mediadecoder.blogs.nytimes.com/2013/02/12/comcast-buying-g-e-s-stake-in-nbcuniversal-for-16-7-billion/

Comcast. 2009. Comcast and GE to create leading entertainment company. http://corporate.comcast.com/news-information/news-feed/comcast-and-ge-to-create-leading-entertainment-company

De La Merced, Michael J. 2011. AT&T ends $39 million bid for T-Mobile. *New York Times,* December 19. http://dealbook.nytimes.com/2011/03/20/att-to-buy-t-mobile-usa-for-39-billion/

Dunbar, John. 2010. Ex-Reps. To aid Comcast takeover bid. *Politico,* May 26. http://www.politico.com/story/2010/05/ex-reps-to-aid-comcast-takeover-bid-037772

England-Joseph, Judy. 1999. *Telecommunications: Process by which mergers of local telephone companies are reviewed.* Washington, D.C.: U.S. Government Accountability Office. Available at http://www.gao.gov/assets/230/228048.pdf

ePluribus Media. 2008. Media consolidation, a historical perspective. Available at http://discuss.epluribusmedia.net/node/548

Federal Communications Commission. 2010. Timeclock history for Comcast corporation and NBC universal. https://www.fcc.gov/transaction/comcast-nbcu-clockhis

Federal Communications Commission. 2011a. AT&T and T-Mobile clock history. https://transition.fcc.gov/transaction/att-tmobile-clockhis.html

Federal Communications Commission. 2011b. Comcast corporation and NBC universal, MB Docket 10–56. https://www.fcc.gov/transaction/comcast-nbcu

Federal Communications Commission. 2014. Overview of the FCC's review of significant transactions. https://www.fcc.gov/guides/review-of-significant-transactions

Federal Communications Commission. 2015. Unwanted telephone marketing calls. https://www.fcc.gov/consumers/guides/unwanted-telephone-marketing-calls

Federal Trade Commission. 2002. FTC and DOJ announce new clearance procedures for antitrust matters. https://www.ftc.gov/news-events/press-releases/2002/03/ftc-and-doj-announce-new-clearance-procedures-antitrust-matters

Federal Trade Commission. 2015a. Premerger notification and the merger review process. https://www.ftc.gov/tips-advice/competition-guidance/guide-antitrust-laws/mergers/premerger-notification-and-merger

Federal Trade Commission. 2015b. The antitrust laws. http://www.ftc.gov/tips-advice/competition-guidance/guide-antitrust-laws/antitrust-laws

Forbes. 2013. How Comcast 'stole' NBCUniversal from general electric. February 13. http://www.forbes.com/sites/thestreet/2013/02/13/how-comcast-stole-nbcuniversal-from-general-electric/

Free Press. 2015. Who owns the media? http://www.freepress.net/ownership/chart

Gleason, Stephanie, and Thomas Catan. 2011. Judge threatens Comcast, NBCU merger delay. *Wall Street Journal,* July 28. http://www.wsj.com/articles/SB10001424053111904888304576472652219116660

Goldman, David, and Julianne Pepitone. 2009. GE, Comcast announce joint NBC deal. CNNMoney.com, December 3. http://money.cnn.com/2009/12/03/news/companies/comcast_nbc/

Gross, Grant. 2011. FCC finds AT&T's purchase of T-Mobile not in the public interest. *Macworld.* http://www.macworld.com/article/1163809/fcc_finds_atandts_purchase_of_t_mobile_not_in_the_public_interest.html

Hiltzik, Michael. 2011. Comcast-NBC merger does nothing to enhance the public interest. *Los Angeles Times,* January 1. http://articles.latimes.com/2011/jan/01/business/la-fi-hiltzik-20110101

International Business Times. 2011. AT&T, T-Mobile merger: A timeline of events in the wireless debate, November 26. http://www.ibtimes.com/att-t-mobile-merger-timeline-events-wireless-debate-374994

Isaac, Mike. 2011. AT&T drops its T-Mobile merger big in $4B fail. *Wired,* December 19. http://www.wired.com/2011/12/att-tmobile-merger-ends/

Kang, Cecilia, and Jia Lynn Yang. 2011. How AT&T fumbled $39 billion bid to acquire T-Mobile. *The Washington Post,* December 10. http://www.washingtonpost.com/business/technology/how-atandt-lost-its-39-million-bid-to-acquire-t-mobile/2011/12/01/gIQAkTQ6hO_story.html

Kaplan, Laura. 2012. One merger, two agencies: Dual review in the breakdown of the AT&T/T-mobile merger and a proposal for reform. *Boston College Law Review* 53(4). http://lawdigitalcommons.bc.edu/cgi/viewcontent.cgi?article=3258&context=bclr

LaPira, Timothy M., and Herschel F. Thomas III. 2014. Revolving door lobbyists and interest representation. *Interest Groups & Advocacy* 3: 4–29. doi:10.1057/iga.2013.16; published online 21 January 2014.

Lipton, Eric. 2014. Comcast's web of lobbying and philanthropy. *New York Times,* February 20. http://www.nytimes.com/2014/02/21/business/media/comcasts-web-of-lobbying-and-philanthropy.html?_r=0

McConnell, Bill. 2012. Lobbying AT&T-T-Mobile, express Scripts-Medco. *The Deal Pipeline,* March 30. http://www.bhfs.com/Templates/media/files/news/TheDeal_LobbyingATTTMobile_033012.pdf

Media Reform Information Center. 2015. http://www.corporations.org/media/

Mirani, Leo. 2014. What's really going on with all those crazy tech deals, in charts. *Quartz,* August 4. http://qz.com/244435/whats-really-going-on-with-all-those-crazy-tech-deals-in-charts/

Morran, Chris. 2014. DOJ's antitrust chief: Decision to block AT&T/T-Mobile deal has helped consumers. *Consumerist,* January 31. http://consumerist.com/2014/01/31/dojs-antitrust-chief-decision-to-block-attt-mobile-deal-has-helped-consumers/

Queally, Jon. 2014. Before Comcast's mega-merger: Mega-bucks and mega-lobbying. *Common Dreams,* February 21. http://www.commondreams.org/news/2014/02/21/comcasts-mega-merger-mega-bucks-and-mega-lobbying

Rinner III, William J. 2009. Optimizing dual agency review of telecommunications mergers. *Yale Law Journal* 118: 1571–1583.

Romm, Rony. 2010. Lawmakers rebuff calls to delay Comcast-NBC merger timeline. *The Hill*, May 19. http://thehill.com/business-a-lobbying/98815-lawmakers-rebuff-calls-to-delay-comcast-nbc-merger-timeline

Sallet, Jon. 2014. FCC transaction review: Competition and the public interest. *FCCBlog*, August 12. https://www.fcc.gov/blog/fcc-transaction-review-competition-and-public-interest

Signorile, Michelangelo. 2011. How gay media helped sink the AT&T/T-Mobile merger. *Huffington Post*, December 20. http://www.huffingtonpost.com/michelangelo-signorile/how-gay-media-helped-sink_b_1160449.html

Sorkin, Andres R., Michael J. De La Merced, and Jenna Wortham. 2011. AT&T to buy T-Mobile USA for $39 million. *New York Times*, March 20. http://dealbook.nytimes.com/2011/03/20/att-to-buy-t-mobile-usa-for-39-billion/

Stelter, Brian, and Tim Arango. 2011. Comcast-NBC deal wins federal approval. *New York Times*, January 18. http://mediadecoder.blogs.nytimes.com/2011/01/18/f-c-c-approves-comcast-nbc-deal/

The Leadership Conference. 2015. Why you should care about media diversity. http://www.civilrights.org/media/ownership/care.html?referrer=http://nortonsafe.search.ask.com/web?o=APN10504&geo=en_US&prt=&ctype=&ver=&chn=&tpr=10&q=recent%20history%20of%20media%20consolidation&page=2&ots=1438545259322

U.S. Department of Justice. 2015. The relationship between antitrust agencies and sectoral regulators. http://www.justice.gov/atr/annex-3-b

Viswanatha, Aruna. 2009. Justice of FTC: Which agency will review Comcast-NBC deal? *Main Justice*, December 9. http://www.mainjustice.com/2009/12/09/justice-or-ftc-which-agency-will-review-comcast-deal/

Ward, Peter C. 2014. *Federal trade commission: Law, practice and procedure*. Law Journal Press: New York, NY.

Weiser, Philip. 2008. Reexamining the legacy of dual regulation: Reforming dual merger review by the DOJ and the FCC. *Federal Communications Law Journal* 61(1): 168–197.

Weiss, James R., and Martin L. Stern. 1998. Serving two masters: The dual jurisdiction of the FCC and the justice department over telecommunications transactions. *CommLaw Conspectus* 6: 195–212.

CHAPTER 11

Same ol', Same ol': Consolidation and Local Television News

Danilo Yanich

INTRODUCTION

The consolidation of local television stations in the USA has reached epic proportions. However, the general public does not even know it, though the actions are being played out, literally, in their backyard.

One justification for consolidation is that broadcasters must get bigger and more efficient in order to compete successfully against cable and the Internet. Some broadcasters also argue that consolidation helps relieve many of the economic burdens shouldered by local stations to produce and present news content. However, consolidation, whether it involves sharing news-gathering resources or station management, has wide-ranging implications for the critical information needs of local communities across the USA—and directly affects the content that ultimately streams into American homes Yanich (2014).

Note: Some of the findings in this chapter were originally published in an article in *Journalism & Mass Communication Quarterly*, Vol. 91 (1), 2014.

D. Yanich (✉)
University of Delaware, Newark, DE, USA

© The Editor(s) (if applicable) and The Author(s) 2016   165
M.I. Lloyd, L.A. Friedland (eds.), *The Communication Crisis in America, And How to Fix It*, DOI 10.1057/978-1-349-94925-0_11

Television broadcast consolidation has taken two forms. The first has been the outright purchase of stations in the same market by one owner. And that activity has increased exponentially since 2012, when only 95 stations were sold for a total of $1.9 billion. In 2013, that number increased over 300 percent (290 stations) at over four times the dollar value ($8.8 billion). According to the Federal Communications Commission (FCC), between 1996 and 2010, there was a 15 percent *increase* in the number of commercial television stations in the USA and a 33 percent *decrease* in the number of owners of those stations (Federal Communications Commission 2010).

The other form of consolidation is the implementation of service agreements (SAs) among stations within the same market. Of the 210 television markets in the USA, 175 include station duopolies, whose owners have entered into "attributable local marketing agreements" (FCC 2010). These agreements are arrangements among stations in the same market to share news-gathering resources, video/graphics, and/or marketing and management activities. They take several forms. Local News Sharing (LNS) Agreements involve multiple stations which pool and share journalists, editors, equipment, and content. In Joint Sales Agreements (JSA), a licensed station sells some or all of its advertising time to another station in return for a fee or a percentage of the revenues. A Local Marketing Agreement (LMA) occurs when the owners of one station take over the operation of another station, including programming and advertising. In a Shared Services Agreement (SSA), the stations combine newsrooms assets and personnel and share facilities and administrative functions (Federal Communications Commission 2011). As of June 2015, 28 percent of local television stations in the USA reported being involved in a SA (Papper 2015).

This consolidation is acute among the affiliates of the four networks (ABC, CBS, NBC, and Fox). These are the stations on which the overwhelming majority of local news is presented. In the top 100 television markets, which contain 86 percent of all US television households, 18 companies control over three-quarters of these stations (Turner 2013). Put more starkly, five companies own almost one-third of the 1400 local television stations in the USA (Matsa 2014). Further, one in three local stations does not produce the news content that it presents, a drop of 8 percent since 2005 (Papper 2016). The pace of consolidation led Nextar Broadcast Group President Perry Sook to predict the landscape of future of local television ownership in bold terms:

I would think that within two to five years, you'll see the emergence of what I call three or four super-groups. Those companies will continue to drive the business, while those that are sub-scale will choose [to sell and] not to be a house by the side of the road as the parade passes by. (Malone 2013)

Sook has helped significantly in the endeavor. In February 2016, the FCC approved a merger between his company and Media General in which Nextar would assume a $4.6 billion debt. As a result, Nextar now controls 171 full-power TV stations in 100 markets and reaches 39 percent (the limit set by the FCC) of US households. Since 2011, Sinclair Broadcasting Group, Inc. (SBG) has spent nearly $2 billion to acquire stations across the country, and it now controls 134 stations in 69 markets and reaches one-third of the television households in the USA. But, this may be only the tip of the merger and acquisitions iceberg. The era of station "super-groups" may be approaching. However, the only way for these super-groups to emerge is the assumption of significant debt, which will put even more pressure on the stations to achieve economies of scale.

Although SSAs date as far back as 2000, in the midst of national economic instability, increasing numbers of local television news stations signed these agreements. As of 2015, SSAs are operative in 94 of the 210 television markets in the USA, an increase from 55 in 2011 (Potter and Matsa 2014).

The SAs among stations have been subject to relatively little oversight by the FCC—partly because the agency has not had an accurate accounting of where they are operating. The media industry's position regarding these agreements is that they do not violate the ownership restrictions, because there is no transfer of license from the brokered station to the brokering station. The FCC tacitly agreed with that position until March 31, 2014. In some respects, the FCC's about-face was a response to an ex parte brief the US Department of Justice (DOJ) filed with the FCC, making its position clear that "sharing" agreements "often confer influence or control of one broadcast competitor over another. FCC Chairman Tom Wheeler called the agreements "legal fiction." Failure to account for the effects of such arrangements can create opportunities to circumvent FCC ownership limits and the goals those limits were intended to advance (U.S. Department of Justice 2014).

This research is directed at answering the crucial questions that the FCC and the DOJ have raised regarding these service arrangements. Specifically, we examined the impact that SAs had on the content of local news in eight markets where such agreements exist. In so doing, we provide a prism through which the FCC can determine the extent to which these arrangements comply with serving the public interest. Do the stations in these arrangements function as separate entities? What effect, if any, do these agreements have on the content of news? Do the stations achieve economies of scale? If so, how? What might this mean for the public interest?

The Importance of Local Television News

Television news remains the critical news source of information for the American public about their localities. Even in the age of the Internet, almost eight of ten Americans get their news from a local television station (Federal Communications Commission 2011). The Pew Research Journalism Project found that almost three-fourths (71 percent) of US adults view local television news over the course of a month (Olmstead et al. 2013). That's compared to 65 percent and 38 percent for network news and cable news, respectively. To be sure, Pew also found that cable news viewers spent about twice as much time as local television news viewers consuming news (25.3 vs. 12.3 minutes per day, respectively). However, they made a distinction between heavy, medium, and light news viewers. Heavy news viewers regularly consume news across all three platforms (Olmstead et al. 2013). Moreover, even as engagement with news media is in decline (except for digital/mobile), almost half of the public (48 percent) indicated they regularly watched local television news, more than all other media (Kohut et al. 2012). Even across different types of television markets, local news matters to local residents as nine out of ten follow local news closely. Further, residents are involved in the local news process in varying ways, but to those who are most politically active, local news is vital (Pew Research Center 2015).

Beyond simple viewing, local television news is a starting point for citizen conversations regarding news. Research by TVB Local Media Marketing Solutions found that, "across all demographics, there was no comparison between local Broadcast News and Cable News. Local television news maintains *the* prominent place in the political information calculus of citizens across the ideological spectrum" (TVB 2013). Almost half (49 percent) of those surveyed used the medium as a source of news about politics and government in the previous week (see Table 11.1). Moreover,

Table 11.1   % who got news about politics and government in the previous week from...

Total	Consistently liberal	Mostly liberal	Mixed	Mostly conservative	Consistently conservative
Local TV 49	NPR 53	Local TV 50	Local TV 51	Fox News 61	Fox News 84
CNN 44	CNN 52	CNN 48	CNN 49	Local TV 50	Local TV 50
Fox News 39	Local TV 39	NBC News 39	ABC News 44	ABC News 42	Hannity (radio) 45
NBC News 37	MSNBC 38	ABC News 38	NBC News 38	CNN 40	Limbaugh 43
ABC News 37	NBC News 37	MSNBC 37	Fox News 32	NBC News 39	Beck (radio) 34

Source: http://www.journalism.org/2014/10/21/section~1~media~sources~distinct~favorites~eme rge-on-the~left-and-right/#the~long-tail

local television news retains its prominence within each of the ideological groups identified by the Pew Research Center. It is either the primary or secondary source (capturing at least half of the audience) for four out of the five groups. Only for the group identified as "consistently liberal" does it place third, reaching 39 percent.

The availability of information about public concerns has significant consequences in localities. There was a strong relationship between local civic literacy and engagement and local media such that the "use of local news in newspapers was a somewhat better predictor of community knowledge and participation, but local television news had a decided edge in local political interest" (McLeod et al. 1996).

As media organizations have increasingly been subsumed into larger corporate entities that have no experience with news, the tension between news as a public service and as a product has been exacerbated. News divisions are increasingly viewed by investors and media executives as just another profit/loss node, rather than as a federal license obligation (see Pickard 2011, 175–184; and McChesney 2008). As a result, the production of news is subject to a calculus that treats information as a commodity (Hamilton 2004), and that treatment has an effect on the nature of news and public affairs programming in local places (Yan and Napoli 2004).

RESEARCH QUESTION AND METHODOLOGY

This research examines the content of the local television newscasts in eight television markets in which SSAs and/or LMAs were implemented. There were two research questions, and they addressed the economies of scale that the managers of the SSAs cite to justify the arrangements. First, the SSA managers point out that the arrangements provide the opportunity to disseminate the same content across various "platforms," thereby reducing the cost of production relative to the number of opportunities to broadcast that content. Therefore, the first research question was: How were the stories that were presented on the newscasts distributed across the stations in each market?

The economies of scale extend beyond the use of platforms. They also are reflected in the use of production resources that affect the bottom line of the cost of presenting news, specifically the use of anchors, reporters, scripts, and video. Therefore, the second research question was: What is the distribution of anchors, reporters, story scripts, and video/graphics in the stories that were presented on the broadcasts of the SSA/LMA stations?

The methodology for this research was content analysis (Riffe et al. 2005, 23–39). This method produces a systematic and objective description of information content. The analytical method used in this research was the Chi-square measure of association.

The Television Markets

This research focused on SSAs and/or LMAs in which the stations shared the news function because, by definition, they affected the production of the newscasts. At the time that the sample was drawn, the universe of television markets in which SSAs were operative was 55. The existence of these agreements was confirmed by the author's research using various data sources, including phone calls to the stations. The randomly drawn sample included eight television markets in which thirty-seven stations regularly produced local newscasts. The markets ranged in size (as measured by the number of television households in the market) from number 17 (Denver, Colorado) to number 146 (Wichita Falls, Texas), and collectively comprised over four million television households.

The markets represented a variety of ownership and management profiles. For example, Denver, Colorado; Des Moines, Iowa; Burlington,

Vermont; and Columbus, Georgia, each had only one consolidated management structure in the market, and there were at least two stations in each of the markets that were not a party to a services agreement (a condition called independent in this research). However, the remaining four television markets in the sample each had some combination of two SSAs or LMAs or duopoly. In Jacksonville, Florida, there was an SSA (two stations) and a duopoly (two stations), leaving only one independent station in the market. In Dayton, Ohio, two separate LMAs involving two stations each left only one independent station in the market. The phenomenon was most pronounced in Peoria, Illinois, and Wichita Falls, Texas, where there was no station in either market that was independent of an SSA or LMA arrangement.

The Stations in the Sample
The stations in the sample consisted of every station in the television market that regularly delivered a daily local newscast. For purposes of clarity and simplicity, the stations involved in an SSA or LMA will be identified as SA stations and those not involved in such an arrangement will be identified as non-SA stations.

The Sample of Broadcasts
The sample of broadcasts for this research consisted of a constructed week of broadcasts during which the SSAs were operative in the television market. A constructed week consisted of the newscasts of a particular day gathered over an extended period of time. For example, the Monday of the first week and the Tuesday of the second week were in the sample, and so on, until the broadcast week was constructed. The broadcast week was limited to the five weekdays, Monday through Friday, to eliminate the possibility of weekend sporting events that might have preempted newscasts. Therefore, the constructed week covered five weeks of time.

The broadcast content for this research was acquired from DirecTV. Due to the technical nature of the capture and archival process that DirecTV used, the exact same constructed week could not be used for all eight markets. The capture of broadcasts had to occur in a sequence to accommodate that technical process. However, the date to begin capture was randomly determined. That day was Wednesday, May 4, 2011. The first market in which broadcasts were captured was Dayton, Ohio. The Dayton broadcasts were those on Wednesday, May 4; Thursday, May 12; Friday, May 20; Monday, May 30; and Tuesday, June 7. That same approach was applied to the other markets. Because DirecTV could only capture the broadcasts of six markets at one time, the constructed weeks for the two remaining markets began immediately after the first six were completed. The broadcasts of Wichita Falls, Texas, and Jacksonville, Florida, began on June 5 and June 6, respectively. The fact that different constructed weeks were used in the analysis was consistent with the research questions because the comparisons across stations only occurred *within* the television markets.

Unit of Observation

The unit of observation for this research was the individual story that appeared on the broadcasts. Initially, the stories were distilled from the 25 broadcast units that were coded. These units included 21 story types and 4 other broadcast categories that were not included in the analysis—promos for the station/network, the weather segment, the sports segment, and commercials. The professional literature regarding the construction of a newscast recognizes that the sports and weather segments are structural features of the broadcast (Donald and Spann 2000; Jones 2005). They are always included in the newscast, and, as a result, they are not subject to the news selection calculus that is applied to all other stories. They are always "in" the broadcast. And, even within the segments, the "in-or-out" decision model is less stark than that used for the general news outside of the segments. In general, the sports segments on local television news deal with the day's scores or activities of whatever sport is in season and not with in-depth sports reporting. The coding revealed a total of 2555[1] separate stories that were broadcast across the stations. The stories were distilled from the 4725 broadcast units that were presented. In addition to the stories (n = 2555), the distribution across the other broadcast units was: station promotions (n = 895), commercials (n = 746), weather segments (n = 338), and sports segments (n = 191).

FINDINGS

The analysis revealed that the implementation of SSAs and LMAs had a profound effect on the local newscasts in the markets (referred to jointly here as SA stations). The effect was evident in the distribution of stories across the stations and in the use of shared resources, such as the anchor, the reporter, the script, and video/graphics for the story.

Sharing Platforms

By definition, the duplications did not occur on the non-joint operating agreement (non-SA) stations in the markets. However, there may have been stories that, on their merits, would have been broadcast on all of the stations in the market and that proportion would temper the duplicated distribution across the SA stations. The analysis showed that only 7 percent of the stories were broadcast on all of the stations in the market. Therefore, story duplication was an SA/duopoly phenomenon. There was a statistically significant difference across the television market in that distribution ($p \leq .05$).

The proportion of duplicated stories on the SA/duopoly stations was above 50 percent in six out of the eight markets (see Fig. 11.1). However, there was also an overall pattern to the duplication rate. In general, the duplication rate among SA stations was less prominent in the markets in which there were non-SA stations. For example, the highest proportion of duplicated stories occurred in Dayton, where there were two LMAs and only one independent station. The LMA between WRGT and WKEF resulted in a 98 percent duplication rate, and the rate for the second LMA between WDTN and WBDT was 35 percent. In Peoria, where there were no non-SA stations, the SSA proportion of combination stories was 78

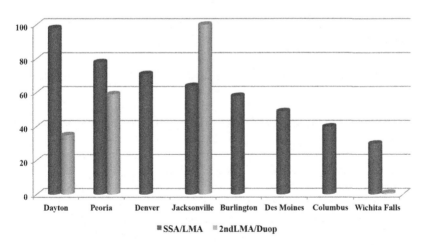

Fig. 11.1   Percentage of duplicated stories on the SA/LMA/duopoly stations

percent; the LMA's proportion was 59 percent. In Jacksonville, with one independent station, the SSA proportion of combination stories was 64 percent, but the duopoly in the market produced a simulcast so the proportion of combination stories for that arrangement was 100 percent. That said, the market that did not follow that trend was Wichita Falls. There were no non-SA stations in the market; however, the duplication rate for the SSA between KFDX and KJTL was only 30 percent. The second SSA between KSWO and KAUZ duplicated very few stories. In the opposite direction was Denver, Colorado; with three non-SA stations, it also did not follow the trend where its one LMA had a duplication rate of 71 percent.

On the other side of that equation, the markets with at least two SA stations saw, in general, lower story duplication rates among its SA partners. For example, Des Moines, Burlington, and Columbus (smaller markets in the sample) had substantially lower rates. The SSA in Burlington between WFFF and WVNY duplicated 58 percent of their stories, and the SSAs in Des Moines and Columbus had duplication rates below 50 percent.

These findings show that, for the most part, the SA stations took advantage of the arrangement to present similar or the same stories on a combination of their stations. Given the nature of the agreements, these results could be expected.

Sharing Scripts and Video/Graphics

The use of various "platforms" to present stories is one aspect to consider in examining the implementation of the SAs. However, perhaps the most important factor to gauge the economies of scale achieved through SAs is the use of particular resources that affect the bottom line—the personnel used to convey the content of the story (anchors and reporters) and the content used to describe the story (script and video/graphics). The use of resources was operationalized in this study as the proportion of stories that used the same anchor, same reporter, same script, and/or same video/graphics on the newscasts of the stations that were parties to the SAs. The effect of these characteristics was varied across the markets. The SA stations took full advantage of the access to their partner resources, particularly scripts and video/graphics. Across all of the SA stations, the duplicated stories, on average, shared the same script almost three-quarters of the time (73 percent) and the same video/graphics eight times out of ten (80 percent). There was a statistically significant difference across the DMAs in the distributions (see Fig. 11.2, $p \le .05$).

In Dayton, with one independent station, the LMA between WRGT and WKEF used the same script and the same video/graphics in almost all of the duplicated stories (97 percent for each). As a result, the audiences for both of those newscasts saw the exact same story presented in the exact same way. The second LMA in the market (between WDTN and WBDT) shared the same script over half of the time (52 percent) and shared the same video/graphics 80 percent of the time. In Peoria, where there is no independent station, the stations in the SSA used the same script and the same video/graphics almost all of the time (95 percent and 91 percent, respectively). In addition, the LMA in the market (between WYZZ and WMBD) used the same script and same video/graphics almost as much (92 percent and 89 percent, respectively).

At the lower end of the spectrum for the use of these resources was the SSA (WAWS and WTEV) in Jacksonville at 21 percent (script) and 47 percent (video/graphics). However, that was tempered by the activity of the duopoly (WLTV and WJXX) in the market that presented the same news as a simulcast on both stations. By definition, the result was a use of the same script and same video/graphics 100 percent of the time.

In Columbus and Wichita Falls, the proportion of combination stories in both markets was well below 50 percent, but when the stories were broadcast on the combination of stations, they used the same script most

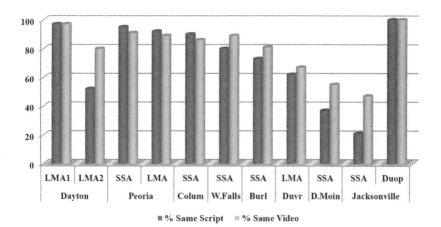

Fig. 11.2 Distribution of the use of same script/video on the SA/LMA/duopoly stations

of the time (90 percent and 80 percent for Columbus and Wichita Falls, respectively) and the same video/graphics (86 percent and 89 percent, respectively).

In Burlington, about three-fourths of the combination stories used the same script and four out of five stories used the same video/graphics. In Des Moines, the SSA had the least effect on the use of these resources, with just over one-third of combination stories sharing the same script and over half sharing the same video/graphics.

Sharing Anchors and Reporters

Scripts and video/graphics are two areas in which the effects of the services agreements are played out. As in most labor-intensive enterprises, personnel represent a critical factor in the cost calculus. For television stations, part of that cost that translates into the cost of anchors and reporters. Of course, there are other personnel costs for stations, including producers, directors, news writers, graphic artists, and camera operators, but for this research, the use of anchors and reporters was the most visible representation of those costs. For the stations that are parties to the SAs, this cost also offers another possibility to achieve economies of scale—using the same anchors and reporters to present the stories across several stations' newscasts. The stations did so for both anchors (on average, 42 percent of stories) and reporters (on average, 37 percent of stories). However, there was wide variation across the television markets (see Fig. 11.3).

In Dayton, the LMA between WRGT and WKEF shared the same anchor for almost all of the stories (97 percent) and shared the same reporter for just over one-third (37 percent) of the stories. However, we must keep in mind that the LMA also shared script and video/graphics well over 90 percent of the time. Therefore, for two-thirds of the stories, the LMA stations just used another reporter to deliver the exact same script and video/graphics. The second LMA in Dayton (between WDTN and WBDT) used the same anchor and same reporter much less often (31 percent and 14 percent, respectively).

In Jacksonville, the SSA duplicated the anchor for almost two-thirds of the stories (64 percent), but it only used the same reporter for a small proportion of stories (14 percent). However, the duopoly in the market, with its simulcast of the news, used the same anchor and reporter for 100 percent of its stories. Columbus was the only other market in which the same reporter was used for well over half (61 percent) of the stories.

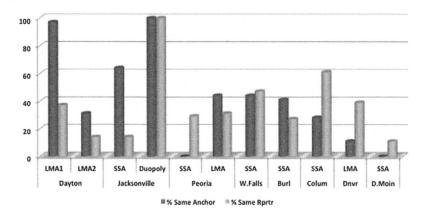

Fig. 11.3 Distribution of the use of the same anchor/reporter on the SA/LMA/duopoly stations

By these measures, we see that the SSAs and LMAs had their intended effects regarding the achievement of economies of scale. These measures focus on the specific aspects of the agreements that their managers said would underpin the combined news operations—the use of multiple platforms and the shared use of resources. These findings confirm that the SSAs and LMAs functioned as planned; they used multiple platforms and shared the resources necessary to convey news stories. One could expect those actions; otherwise, the stated economic purposes of entering into the agreements would be moot. The obvious and unambiguous result was a reduction in the number of separate news voices in the markets.

CONCLUSION

The movement toward SAs will undoubtedly continue. There are economic incentives for such endeavors. In fact, the Coalition of Smaller-Market Television Stations filed an ex parte comment with the FCC and met with FCC staffers in December 2011 to press the case for the need for SSAs (Eggerton 2011). The record shows that these arrangements have invariably resulted in a loss of jobs. In addition to the losses in Honolulu, the SSA in Idaho Falls, Idaho, resulted in the loss of 27 jobs (Ariens 2011). In Providence, Rhode Island, 15 jobs were lost when Citadel Communications implemented an LMA with ABC affiliate (Derderian 2011). Such is the nature of mergers.

These arrangements can also result in conditions that turn the notion of a competitive market on its head. One such situation occurs in upstate New York. In Syracuse, the CBS (WTVH) and NBC (WSTM) affiliates are parties to an SSA. In Utica, 57 miles east of Syracuse, there is no CBS affiliate. Therefore, the Syracuse station, WTVH, is granted a spot on the cable in Utica to operate in that market. The NBC affiliate in Utica is WKTV, and it is called upon several times a month by the NBC affiliate in Syracuse (WSTM) to supply video and materials, generally for a local lead story. However, due to the SSA between the two Syracuse stations, WSTM shares the material with the CBS affiliate (WTVH), which then broadcasts back in Utica. In effect, then, the NBC affiliate in Utica is supplying content directly to its competition in its own market.[2]

There has been some suggestion that the development of services agreements, whether Shared Services, Joint Services, Local Marketing or Local News, has, on the whole, added news content to the market in which they were implemented. That is an empirical question, not a philosophical one. Empirically, we can look at the news operations of the stations that were parties to the SAs and determine whether or not they provided a newscast before entering into the agreement. For the eleven SSA/LMA combinations examined in this research, eight of them involved stations that each produced their own newscasts before the agreement was implemented. In addition, the stations in the duopoly (in Jacksonville) that were also part of this research each produced separate newscasts before joining. Therefore, the result is that three-fourths (nine of twelve) of the agreements included stations that produced separate newscasts before the implementation of the arrangement.

Those who suggest that the arrangements add news to the market by broadcasting the same newscast on a station that had not previously presented news stretch the logic of the claim. Simply showing the same news on another station is not a qualitative addition of information to the public. It is not *more* news.

Local television stations are private firms, and they have a fiduciary responsibility to provide a return on investment for their owners. However, they conduct their business using a public good—the electromagnetic spectrum. And that imposes public interest responsibilities on the stations as well.

This research has revealed that, to this point, the SAs have a significant effect on local broadcast news content for those stations that are parties to the arrangement. Economies of scale dictate that production costs and cross-platform marketability limit the diversity and the availability to the public of news stories.

As noted earlier, the FCC expressed concern about the impact of SSAs on local news diversity in March 2014 and sent a warning to the broadcasters regarding future and existing SSAs:

> We reject arguments that we should automatically grandfather all television JSAs permanently or indefinitely. In these circumstances, we find that such grandfathering would allow arbitrary and inconsistent changes to the level of permissible common ownership on a market-by-market basis based not necessarily on where the public interest lies…Moreover…[current] licensees may seek a waiver of our rules if they believe strict application of the rules would not serve the public interest. (Federal Communications Commission 2014)

In the face of increased debt resulting from the wave of consolidation, and a panic in the face of increased competition from cable and other media, station licensees and the National Association of Broadcasters (NAB) were able to convince members of the Senate to sponsor legislation (S. 1182) in May 2015 that would "grandfather in" the SAs that were in effect prior to the FCC March 2014 ruling. The Senate sponsors were bipartisan, including Republicans Blunt, Scott, and Johnson along with Democrats Mikulski, Schumer, and Durbin. The intention of the Senate bill was inserted as a rider into the Financial Services and Government Appropriations bills that were passed by the respective committees in the House and Senate. The purpose was expressed starkly—it would prohibit the FCC from carrying out two of its most recent signature decisions: the implementation of the net neutrality rules and the imposition of limitations on existing joint services agreements. In December 2015, Congress passed a massive spending package that contained a rider that "grandfathers in" existing JSAs for ten years. The final House vote was 316–113; in the Senate, it was 65–33. The NAB was extremely happy with the result.

There is no doubt that the information landscape of the USA has changed in the last 20 years. There are many sources of information. But local television news still holds a preeminent position as a news source for the public. The managers of SA stations recognize that fact, most often through the prism of quarterly profit. That is understandable—media firms are businesses, first and foremost. The SAs were implemented to increase the bottom line—to create economies of scale in which the costs of the production and the dissemination of news are structured to increase profit.

However, policymakers and the general public must understand that there is nothing new or innovative about recycling infotainment news packages and stretching them thin across several hours and multiple stations purporting to serve the same local community. That veneer masks the fact that we are getting less news, not more—and it creates the illusion that we are being informed, when we are not.

NOTES

1. The distribution of the stories across the eight television markets was: Denver = 412; Dayton = 366; Jacksonville = 336; Des Moines = 329; Peoria = 272; Wichita Falls = 243; Burlington = 374 and Columbus = 223.
2. Personal communication with knowledgeable source regarding station news practices who requested that his/her identity be kept confidential. October 30, 2012.

REFERENCES

Ariens, Chris. 2011. New year brings change to Idaho Falls. *Adweek TVSpy*, January 3. http://www.adweek.com/tvspy/new-year-brings-change-to-idaho-falls/5741.

Derderian, Jeff. 2011. Exclusive: Layoffs at channel 6 start. *GoLocal*, April 15. http://www.golocalprov.com/business/exclusive-layoffs-at-channel-6-start/.

Donald, Ralph, and Thomas Spann. 2000. *The fundamentals of television production*. Hoboken: Wiley-Blackwell.

Eggerton, John. 2011. Small TV stations to FCC: We need shared services agreements. *Broadcasting & Cable*, December 21. http://www.broadcastingcable.com/news/local-tv/small-tv-stations-fcc-we-need-shared-services-agreements/43236.

Federal Communications Commission. 2010. *Quadrennial regulatory review (FCC 10-92)*. Washington, DC: GPO.

Federal Communications Commission. 2011. *The information needs of communities: The changing media landscape in a broadband age*. Report by Steven Waldman and the Working Group on Information Needs of Communities. Washington, DC: Federal Communications Commission.

Federal Communications Commission. 2014. *Further notice of proposed rule making and report and order (FCC 14-28)*. Washington, D.C.: GPO.

Hamilton, James. 2004. *All the news that's fit to sell: How the market transforms information into news*. Princeton: Princeton University Press.

Jones, Clarence. 2005. *Winning with the news media: A self defense manual when you're the story*, 8th ed. Anna Maria: Winning News Media, Inc.

Kohut, Andrew, Carroll Doherty, Michael Dimock, and Scott Keeter. 2012. *Cable leads the pack as campaign news source: Twitter, Facebook play very modest roles.* Pew Research Center for the People and the Press, February 7. http://www.people-press.org/2012/02/07/cable-leads-the-pack-as-campaign-news-source/.

Malone, Michael. 2013. The rise of station super-groups. *Broadcasting & Cable* 143(5): 12–13.

Matsa, Katerina E. 2014. *The acquisition binge on local TV.* Pew Research Center, May 12. http://www.pewresearch.org/fact-tank/2014/05/12/the-acquisition-binge-in-local-tv/.

McChesney, Robert W. 2008. The commercial tidal wave. In *The political economy of media*, 265–281. New York: Monthly Review Press.

McLeod, Jack M., Katie Daily, Zhongshi Guo, William P. Eveland, Jan Bayer, Seungchan Yang, and Hsu Wang. 1996. Community integration, local media use and democratic processes. *Communication Research* 23(2): 179–209.

Olmstead, Kenneth, Mark Jurkowitz, Amy Mitchell, and Jodi Enda. 2013. *How Americans get their news at home.* Pew Research Center, October 11. http://www.journalism.org/2013/10/11/how-americans-get-tv-news-at-home/.

Papper, Bob. 2015. *The business of news: Newsroom profitability, budgets and partnerships.* RTNDA/Hofstra University Survey, June 1.

Papper, Bob. 2016. Local news by the numbers. RTNDA/Hofstra University. http://www.rtdna.org/article/rtdna_research_local_news_by_the_numbers.

Pew Research Center. 2015. *Local news in the digital age.* Pew Research Center, March 5. http://www.journalism.org/2015/03/05/local-news-in-a-digital-age/.

Pickard, Victor. 2011. Revisiting the road not taken: A social democratic vision of the press. In *Will the last reporter please turn out the lights: The collapse of journalism and what can be done about it,* ed. Robert W. McChesney and Victor Pickard. New York: The New Press.

Potter, Deborah, and Katerina E. Matsa. 2014. *A boom in acquisitions and content sharing shapes local TV news in 2013.* Pew Research Center, March 26. http://www.journalism.org/2014/03/26/a-boom-in-acquisitions-and-content-sharing-shapes-local-tv-news-in-2013/.

Riffe, Daniel, Stephen Lacy, and Frederick G. Fico. 2005. *Analyzing media messages*, 2nd ed. Mahwah: Lawrence Erlbaum Associates, Inc.

Turner, S. Derek. 2013. *Cease to resist: How the FCC's failure to enforce its rules created a new wave of media consolidation.* Washington, DC: Free Press.

TVB Local MediaMarketing Solutions. 2013. *The American conversation study: How local TV news drives consumer engagement.* Retrieved October 21 from http://www.tvb.org/measurement/American_Conversation_Study.

United States Department of Justice. 2014. In the matter of 2010 quadrennial regulatory review – Review of the Commission's broadcast ownership rules and other rules adopted pursuant to section 202 of the Telecommunications Act of 1996. *Ex parte submission of the United States Department of Justice*, February. http://www.justice.gov/sites/default/files/atr/legacy/2014/02/24/303880.pdf.

Yan, Michael, and Philip Napoli. 2004. *Market structure, station ownership, and local public affairs programming on local broadcast television.* Paper presented at the Telecommunications Policy Research Conference, Arlington, Virginia, October.

Yanich, Danilo. 2014. Duopoly light? Service agreements and local TV. *Journalism and Mass Communication Quarterly* 91(1): 159–176.

CHAPTER 12

Bridging the Content Gap in Low-Income Communities

James T. Hamilton and Fiona Morgan

Information is generally produced in order to influence people's decisions, such as what to buy or whom to vote for. If the consequences of your decisions matter little to those who produce information, what type of information gets produced for you? The answers to that question explain how income inequality translates into information inequality in America. Each individual has four information demands—as a consumer, producer, audience member, and voter. Individuals with less income are likely to have lower demands expressed in each of these roles. They are less likely to be sought after as consumers of a product, voters in an election, subscribers or viewers to be sold entertainment and news, or workers to be hired or investors to be informed. As a result, both the market and the political arena produce less information to meet their needs.

The income disparity in access to communication technologies, termed the digital divide, reflects the contending priorities of people who struggle to pay for food, rent, and basic utilities. Related to the problem of Internet

J.T. Hamilton (✉)
Stanford University, Stanford, CA, USA

F. Morgan
Free Press, Durham, NC, USA

© The Editor(s) (if applicable) and The Author(s) 2016   183
M.I. Lloyd, L.A. Friedland (eds.), *The Communication Crisis in America,
And How to Fix It*, DOI 10.1057/978-1-349-94925-0_12

access is the problem of what sort of content the Internet permits access to. Those who struggle financially have lower buying power and voting power, which means that less and lower quality content is produced to sway their choices. This gives rise to content gaps in low-income communities. One is a content gap between the ideal amount of information for an informed decision and the reality of what's available for individuals in poverty. The other is the relative content gap between the type of information generated for wealthier individuals and that produced for those with less disposable income and fewer resources. In addition to the gap, there is also a problem of bad information online targeted to people who are financially vulnerable. Those with lower incomes may have lower levels of literacy and less experience with computers. In markets, this can translate into targeting meant to sway choices through deceptive, inaccurate, or incomplete information.

Even when people with low incomes would seem to be the ideal target demographic, as in the case of public programs offering aid, the incentive structures within firms and bureaucracies can lead to a disincentive to provide low-income consumers or beneficiaries with information. In programs where revenues and services flow to those in need, more people participating in these programs costs governments money and leads to budget pressures. This can skew incentives away from providing effective information to ensure full participation. In cases where government benefits or services that flow to low-income beneficiaries go through a third party, there is incentive to produce information that will generate take-up, but that information may not be complete or accurate. Private tax preparers spend considerable amounts on advertising to target taxpayers who are eligible for the Earned Income Tax Credit (EITC) because the preparers make large sums on refund-anticipation loans and similar financial products; meanwhile, EITC filers are often unaware that they are also eligible for free tax preparation from nonprofit agencies. Mobile phone companies advertise their services to low-income consumers eligible for the Lifeline program, meant to subsidize phone access by relatively poor consumers. Some of those firms have engaged in fraud by misrepresenting enrollments and gaining millions in government payments.

Three concepts from the study of information markets—bundling, behavioral economics, and big data—help explain the dearth of high-quality content tailored for consumption in low-income communities.

Newspapers have historically bundled stories about multiple topics and stories about many areas within a locality into a physical paper to be tossed onto your doorstep each morning. This bundling economized on delivery costs (e.g., no need for a separate sports paper and political paper to be transported around town) and allowed media outlets to gain more revenue than if topics and tales were sold separately. The Internet broke the bundle, allowing readers to find high-quality news from specialized sites that aggregated attention across wide geographies—while diverting the attention of a given geographic community away from local affairs. The drop in advertising and subscription revenue caused papers to constrict their distribution areas and the focus of their coverage, with remaining boots on the ground less likely to be stationed in neighborhoods with lower subscription rates and fewer advertisers. Given that the geography of poverty means individuals with low incomes cluster in communities with lower rents and higher incidence of many social problems, the type of journalism that holds institutions accountable is less likely to exist in poor communities, because residents there lack the subscription and advertising revenue to cover the costs of content creation.

Behavioral economics has shed light on the ways in which people's decisions systematically diverge from a model of a rational consumer with full information. Empirical research has shown that people who are experiencing financial scarcity or cognitive stress are more susceptible to making irrational choices. Companies that target consumers with less education and lower incomes have, over time, developed sales scripts and business practices that heighten the stress to capitalize on imperfect reasoning and limited options. The financial decisions that result often center on trade-offs involving gains today and costs tomorrow. These include payday loans, subprime mortgages, rent-to-own furniture, and student debt incurred at for-profit colleges. In each of these areas, firms use framing, simple default options, and sometimes deception to entice low-income consumers into transactions that they may end up regretting.

Increasingly sophisticated uses of data, culled from multiple sources such as financial transactions, online activity, and demographic profiling, have allowed firms to target their messages to the desired audience. While use of big data has broad implications across the media landscape, its use in politics raises concerns about how low-income Americans may be marginalized in public life. Political campaigns once viewed television advertising as the most cost-effective option to reach targeted demographics and get them to turn out at the polls. Political ads bought on local television news programs reached politically engaged and likely voters, and also were viewed by those with lower incomes and less likelihood of voting.

In the era of big data, campaigns can now use Facebook and Google ads to reach narrowly defined sets of individuals with precisely phrased appeals and calls to action. The refinement in targeting avoids the "wasted" exposure of less likely voters, which ultimately means less incidental exposure of low-income voters to information meant to prompt political actions.

In the examples above, the concepts of bundling, behavioral economics, and big data contribute to information inequality, yet they also have the potential to address the problem. While economic theory explains how lower incomes translate into lower quantities and qualities of information in poor communities, the magnitudes of the resulting content gaps are often unknown. Smaller returns in the market or in politics for changing the minds of individuals with low incomes mean that less data are generated about their information environments. This chapter does not attempt to summarize empirical research on the extent of content gaps or point out where additional research is needed to map the information needs of communities, topics covered by other essays in this volume. Instead, we provide evidence on how bundling, behavioral economics, and big data (which we call the 3Bs) can aid decisions made by individuals with low incomes in the USA. Policymakers who wish to address the real-world effects of content gaps should consider how to use these concepts in the design and execution of policies aimed at alleviating poverty.

BUNDLING

A bundle is a combination that economizes on costs. For low-income people, those costs can include time and cognitive effort, resources that those who struggle financially must constantly substitute for money. Allowing people to apply for and obtain benefits and services from many different government programs at one location reduces travel and search costs. Combining application forms with a person to guide you through the process cuts the cognitive load required to make decisions. Sometimes, bundling can occur as a byproduct, reaching people who have sought out one experience with an unrelated message. For instance, people attending a church service may be given access to a health screening. At other times, bundling is a signal, using information as an indicator that can economize on time or effort. For instance, a person who meets the requirements for a utility subsidy may be advised that they are likely to be eligible for food assistance. Bundling in government programs has not been extensively tested in random-assignment field experiments with full benefit–cost analyses. But the use of bundling as a way to reduce costs of finding and utilizing government or NGO services has shown that this approach can increase participation in programs by low-income individuals.

Though we often think of information as flowing from government institutions to low-income individuals, citizens can express their preferences back to the government through voting. One way to facilitate voting is to use bundling to increase voter registration. The National Voter Registration Act of 1993 (NVRA) requires states to provide people with the opportunity to register to vote at places where they can apply for a driver's license, receive public assistance benefits, or obtain state-funded disability services. In the first two years of operation of this "Motor Voter" law, more than 18 million people registered to vote at locations they had visited for other purposes. These registrations did translate into eventual votes in the 1996 election, though people who took advantage of low-cost registration at NVRA sites turned out at lower rates to cast their ballots (Wolfinger and Hoffman 2001).

NGOs increasingly use bundling of multiple services at one location to increase program uptake and effectiveness. The Benefit Bank program offers individuals the ability to explore online their eligibility for several federal programs, including food stamps (i.e., Federal Supplemental Nutrition Assistance Program), medical assistance (e.g., Medicaid), and tax credits (e.g., Earned Income Tax Credit, dependent care, education). Sites such as food banks and community centers can affiliate with Benefit Bank and offer low-income residents advice on registering for these programs. An evaluation of use of Benefit Bank in Ohio between 2007 and 2010 found that bundling programs likely helped residents gain $77.8 million in benefits via Supplemental Nutrition Assistance Program (SNAP), $36.6 million in federal medical assistance, and almost $25 million through tax credits such as EITC and education, dependent care, or elderly tax credits (Voinovich School 2011). The Local Initiatives Support Corporation (LISC) saw similar success in combining job training and placement services with financial coaching and income support counseling at their Financial Opportunity Centers. LISC determined that:

> [Those] who spent the most time on all three bundled services offered by the FOCs (employment, coaching, and public benefits) had the highest job placement rates and the highest job retention rates – a 74 percent placement rate and a 78 percent six-month retention rate. Clients who received

both financial counseling and employment services had net income increases that were 89 percent higher than those receiving only financial or income support counseling (Rankin 2015, i).

While some bundling studies offer evidence of correlations rather than direct causation, Bettinger and his coauthors (2012) used a randomized field experiment to measure the real gains possible when tax preparation services are combined with a person offering onsite help in filling out the Free Application for Federal Student Aid (FAFSA). At a set of 156 H&R Block tax assistance sites, low-income individuals were randomly assigned to one of three treatments: no intervention (i.e., the control group); provision of information about likely federal and state aid for college education based on their tax information and data about local college costs; or the aid and cost information, supplemented by personal help from an H&R Block professional in filling out the college aid form. The study demonstrated the great gains from providing onsite help in filling out forms, noting:

> The combined assistance and information treatment substantially increased FAFSA submissions and ultimately the likelihood of college attendance, persistence, and aid receipt. In particular, high school seniors whose parents received the treatment were 8 percentage points more likely to have completed two years of college, going from 28 percent to 36 percent, during the first three years following the experiment. Families who received aid information but no assistance with the FAFSA did not experience improved outcomes (Bettinger et al. 2012, 1205).

Bundling as a byproduct involves focusing on people coming to a specific location for one reason and then targeting them with information and services for something completely different. Public health researchers have used barbershops and hair salons to target the provision of health information, often in African-American communities. A review of ten intervention studies with statistically significant results at these locations found "five changed behavior such as mammography adherence, hypertension control, and fruit and vegetable consumption, and four increased intentions or knowledge related to mammography, stroke, and cancer" (Linnan et al. 2014, 81). An analysis of the use of African-American churches as avenues to provide information on diabetes self-management education determined that "the faith-based studies reviewed ($n = 18$) reported significant health outcomes, such as reductions in weight, blood pressure, glycemic, and lipid levels and increases in disease-related knowledge, physical activity, and intake of fruit and vegetables" (Newlin et al. 2012, 1092). The separate impacts of factors such as how and by whom the information was conveyed were harder to establish.

Bundling as a signal involves using the knowledge that a person meets one set of requirements to target them for information about a program or service with similar requirements. Though the EITC lifts millions out of poverty each year by providing a cash benefit, the Internal Revenue Service (IRS) estimates that roughly 20 percent of households that are eligible for the program do not claim the benefits. Virginia's state legislature passed a law that required the state Department of Social Services to contact all those receiving public assistance through Temporary Assistance for Needy Families (TANF), SNAP, or a medical assistance program who appeared to be eligible for EITC but were not claiming the benefit based on evidence from the Virginia Department of Taxation. The Department of Social Services sent a low-cost mailing (35 cents per postcard) to let households know they were likely eligible, the potential for a refund, and instructions on how to claim the EITC. Some households also received an automated call (at 16 cents per completed call) (Beecroft 2012). This resulted in an estimated increase in EITC claims of two percentage points, and given the low cost of the mailings and calls, the ratio of new EITC benefits claimed in the state to costs for this information intervention was more than fifty to one.

Behavioral Economics

Behavioral economics studies how people actually behave when they have to economize on something. When things are scarce, like time, effort, money, or attention, people make tradeoffs that often reveal biases or flaws in decision-making. Rich and poor alike exhibit patterns in choices that show a great aversion to losses relative to the happiness associated with a similar gain, which results in a preference for the status quo (Bertrand et al. 2004). People may overestimate the likelihood of events with small probabilities or reason more heavily from incidents that recently happened. While these biases may cause members of the middle class to miss out on ideal investments, the margin for error for the poor is much smaller and can carry greater consequences. Missed bills can result in utilities being turned off, and missed opportunities can result in ruinous borrowing. One lesson from behavioral economics is that mistakes that plague most people have a greater impact on the lives of the poor because they live on thin margins.

Recent research shows that people who are poor face additional challenges because scarcity can cause you to focus deeply on a problem at hand and neglect to think about impacts farther in the future. Those lacking the money to pay rent or a utility bill this week, for example, may focus on getting a short-term loan that solves the current problem. The interest rate at a pay-day loan center may come at exorbitant rates, but that impact is felt down the road (Shah et al. 2012). In addition, poverty can actually impede choices, because the pressing concerns about finances crowd out the ability to think about other topics. The distractions of worrying about money demands make it harder to complete cognitive tasks accurately (Mani et al. 2013).

Fortunately, theories and experiments from behavioral economics offer suggestions on how to help low-income individuals take actions that result in greater satisfaction. To encourage better financial management among the poor, options include setting up default mechanisms for direct deposit of benefits or salaries, improving decision channels so that people get information directly from a person knowledgeable about a program who can help complete a form, making prices transparent and fees simpler to understand, prompting identities in interactions that promote saving, and encouraging planning (Bertrand et al. 2006; Thaler and Sunstein 2008; Mani et al. 2013; Chetty 2015).

Several researchers have explored how these concepts might improve uptake of the EITC by low-income individuals. Each year, more than six million eligible taxpayers forego claiming the benefit, with the average non-claimant failing to collect more than $1000 (Bhargava and Manoli 2015). Failure to file for the EITC refund stems, in part, from ignorance about how the program operates. Chetty, Friedman, and Saez found that being around neighbors who know about the EITC affected use of the program. They concluded that "individuals in high-knowledge areas change wage earnings sharply to obtain larger EITC refunds relative to low-knowledge areas" (Chetty et al. 2013, 2683). Yet simply providing information about the EITC does not guarantee long-term learning about the policy. In a field experiment involving more than 40,000 EITC recipients getting tax help at H&R Block, Chetty and Saez (2013) determined that providing these low-income individuals with information on how their earnings affected the size of their EITC payment did not, on average, have an effect on their earnings in the following year.

Manoli and Turner (2014) found that information provision about a short-term gain can nudge a person to file for the EITC (a decision perhaps easier to influence than altering labor decisions over the course of a year to influence the size of the EITC payment). The IRS now sends a notice and information on filing to those taxpayers who are apparently eligible but have not filed a letter, which can lead them to get a payment numbering in the thousands of dollars. In 2005, a computer problem meant that some eligible taxpayers did not receive the notice, thereby creating a natural control group to compare with those who did get the notice. Manoli and Turner found that:

> [The] IRS notices have a meaningful nudge effect, increasing EITC take-up by 30 percentage points for taxpayers with kids and by 60 percentage points for taxpayers without kids in 2005. For taxpayers who respond to the notice and claim the EITC in 2005, the credit represents on average roughly 4 percent of labor earnings. Despite this relatively large benefit, learning effects from the notices are much smaller than the nudge effect and quickly attenuate over time (Manoli and Turner 2014, 3).

However, while the IRS letter led people to claim the EITC that year, there was no significant long-term learning, and the impact of the letter eventually declined to zero over several years.

In a field test with the IRS, Bhargava and Manoli (2015) experimented by sending a second notice from the IRS to those presumed eligible based on tax information who had not claimed their EITC tax credit. They posited that psychological frictions, including lack of awareness of the program, confusion about its requirements, and reluctance to fill out potentially complex forms, accounted for part of the failure of low-income individuals to claim the EITC when eligible. They found that nudges did increase uptake. Mailing a second notice, using simplification through visuals or shorter worksheets, and highlighting potential benefits through headlines all increased filing for the EITC. They estimate that if their most effective interventions were scaled nationally, disbursements under EITC to low-income individuals would increase each year by more than $500 million.

Big Data

Though we are living in the era of "big data," there is no readily accepted definition of what amount of data merits this term. In this chapter, we use the term as a shorthand for truly big data (e.g., information generated by interactions on the web, information available via the market for consumer data, the growing array of data generated by sensors), for smaller data that government agencies or nonprofits might collect, for open government data released to the public (which can include information that governments release to build businesses—the "D.C. to VC" connection), and information generated by the process of governing (e.g., contracts) that can be liberated through the Freedom of Information Act and used to hold government accountable.

Big data come with obvious policy concerns: targeting of low-income consumers for deception by some companies, the potential for privacy violations by public and private sector actors, and disadvantages in data-driven policies or plans when decision-makers lack data on low-income communities (Castro 2014). Yet big data can provide many advantages, such as identifying likely information gaps and targeting individuals for interventions. Big data can also make behaviorally informed interventions more effective by helping to personalize information depending on the contexts of decisions and helping to simplify the architecture of choices.

Consider the case of high-achieving high school students from low-income families. Hoxby and Avery (2013) note that most of these students do not apply to selective colleges, even though the actual costs of attending these schools would be lower than the less selective two- or four-year schools they choose to apply to. Part of this likely stems from information gaps among low-income students about the net price of college, factoring in financial aid, schools' student body characteristics (such as test scores and GPAs), and graduation rates. The Expanding College Opportunities (ECO) project tested the impact of information provision in an experiment made possible by data on students and families. ECO sent materials to 18,000 high school seniors in 2011–2012 who had scored in the top 10 percent in the SAT or ACT and came from families whose estimated income was in the bottom third of families with a senior in high school. ECO not only used data to target these high-achieving students from low-income households. Data were also used to personalize the mailings so that the information provided related to a student's household circumstances and location. The mailings offered information on likely financial aid, net prices, and graduation rates for schools salient in the area, other schools in the state, and a randomized set of out-of-state peer institutions (defined as those where "the median student's college assessment score is within 5 percentiles of the student's own") (Hoxby and Turner 2015, 515). The mailings also included information about the application process and "no paperwork" fee waivers to use in applying.

Hoxby and Turner (2015, 514–515) find that the provision of information targeted and tailored through data analysis had significant effects on the college choices of low-income students. They note that:

> Relative to the controls, treated students submitted 48 percent more applications and were 56 percent more likely to apply to a peer college (or better). They applied to colleges with 17 percent higher graduation rates and 55 percent higher instructional spending. Treated students were admitted to 31 percent more colleges and were 78 percent more likely to be admitted by a peer college. They were admitted at colleges with 24 percent higher graduation rates and 34 percent higher instructional spending. Treated students enrolled in colleges that were 46 percent more likely to be peer institutions, whose graduation rates were 15 percent higher, and whose instructional spending was 22 percent higher.

Hoxby and Turner show what types of information changed student decisions. Relative to students in the control group that did not get the mailing, students provided with the information said they were "much more likely to apply" to schools if they could tell from the college materials if they would get sufficient financial aid and if the college had a high graduation rate.

The struggle to enroll students from low-income families does not end with admission. Castleman and Page (2015, 146) point out that in the summer before college starts, "low-income high school graduates face many competing pressures—work, family responsibilities including childcare and translating for parents, spending time with friends—which diminish their attention to completing required prematriculation tasks." This all unfolds when these students are no longer in the high school structures that provide guidance on the process. The result is "summer melt," the description of what happens when high school graduates who intended to go to college fail to matriculate in the following year. Castleman and Page designed an experiment with two interventions to reduce the melt among low-income students. One was a set of ten automated text messages sent to students (and, when possible, parents) to provide reminders about college matriculation dates and prompts with offers of help. A second approach was to connect students during the summer with peer mentors enrolled in college who could provide prompts about topics such as completing FAFSA forms and making registration deadlines.

The text intervention was relatively low cost, totaling $7 per student, including the cost of hiring counselors to answer questions when students had questions in response to the information. In terms of content sent via text to low-income high school graduates who intended to go to college:

> The messages reminded students to: log on to their intended college's web portal to access important paperwork; register for orientation and placement tests; complete housing forms; and sign up for or waive health insurance, if relevant. The messages also offered students help completing the FAFSA if they had not already, and interpreting their financial aid award letter and tuition bill from their intended college (Castleman and Page 2015, 149).

In areas where there were not high levels of support for college planning during senior year and the following summer, Castleman and Page found that those students who got the text messages were "over 7 percentage points more likely to enroll in college than their control group counterparts." The peer mentor program increased enrollment by 4.5 percentage points relative to the control group. The availability of data on students and families from school districts, educational nonprofits, and the US Department of Education makes it possible to target students from low-income families aiming for college. The data thereby bolster behavioral interventions, such as automated texts that can be personalized around specific college deadlines to provide information that gets more students ultimately to enroll in college.

PUBLIC POLICIES AND THE 3Bs

Information generates value by changing individual choices. Content gaps exist in the lives of low-income individuals because fewer institutions seek to change their decisions. Public or private sector actors trying to reach poor communities should consider how bundling, behavioral economics, and big data could make their efforts more effective. Insights based on the 3Bs are now making their way into the design and implementation of public policies. Bundling, targeting with big data, and a focus on how people actually come to decisions animate work in multiple agencies: the Consumer Financial Protection Bureau's focus on mortgages, prepaid cards, payday loans, and debt collection; the Federal Trade Commission's fight against fraud and deceptive advertising; and the federal Social and Behavioral Sciences Team's cross-agency work on improving access to government programs and increasing the efficiency of public policies.

The Federal Communications Commission's recent proposal to expand the Lifeline program to support broadband access illustrates how technology subsidies may help bridge the digital divide. The actual success of the program in closing content gaps may depend on adoption of the 3Bs. Proposed Lifeline reforms include bundling signups and outreach for Lifeline with other government assistance programs such as SNAP, using data from state and federal databases to reduce the chance of improper signups, and transferring Lifeline benefits to electronic benefit transfer (EBT) cards to make it easier to register and use the benefit (FCC 2015). Newly connected households would certainly have greater opportunities to complete homework and apply for jobs. Bringing more low-income individuals online may also help to fill content gaps by raising the returns to creating content to educate, entertain, and inform people living in low-income communities. What people are able to watch, read, do, and publish online is central to their sense of the Internet's value to their lives, which makes filling content gaps central to the issue of Internet adoption.

If Lifeline and affordability questions grapple with the problem of "last mile" connectivity, the 3Bs grapple with the problem of the "last minute"—where, when, and how information is provided, how choices are structured, and how to present information in a way that serves people's immediate needs. Paying attention to these concepts raises the chances that good content can reach and improve the lives of people who need it.

Policy opportunities to close content gaps exist in arenas far beyond telecommunications. Every single government entity at the federal, state, and local levels that grapples with poverty also deals with information, as does every NGO and nonprofit organization working with low-income individuals. These organizations struggle to target their messages effectively to populations that can be hard to reach, and their messages must compete with those produced by profit-seeking firms that may have more to spend on advertising precisely because the incentives behind their messaging have little to do with helping fight poverty. The scarcity of time and cognition among financially struggling people is exactly why the concepts of bundling, behavioral economics, and big data are so important and so potentially powerful.

REFERENCES

Beecroft, Erik. 2012. *EITC take-up by recipients of public assistance in Virginia and results of a low-cost experiment to increase EITC claims.* Working paper. Richmond: Virginia Department of Social Services.

Bertrand, Marianne, Sendhil Mullainathan, and Eldar Shafir. 2004. A behavioral-economics view of poverty. *American Economic Review* 94(2): 419–423.

Bertrand, Marianne, Sendhil Mullainathan, and Eldar Shafir. 2006. Behavioral economics and marketing in aid of decision making among the poor. *Journal of Public Policy and Marketing* 25(1): 8–23.

Bettinger, Eric P., Bridget Terry Long, Philip Oreopoulos, and Lisa Sanbonmatsu. 2012. The role of application assistance and information in college decisions: Results from the H&R Block FAFSA experiment. *The Quarterly Journal of Economics* 127(3): 1205–1242.

Bhargava, Saurabh, and Dayanand Manoli. 2015. Psychological frictions and the incomplete take-up of social benefits: Evidence from an IRS field experiment. *American Economic Review* 105(11): 3489–3529.

Castleman, Benjamin L., and Lindsay C. Page. 2015. Summer nudging: Can personalized text messages and peer mentor outreach increase college going among low-income high school graduates? *Journal of Economic Behavior and Organization* 115: 144–160.

Castro, Daniel. 2014. *The rise of data poverty in America.* Washington, DC: Center for Data Innovation.

Chetty, Raj. 2015. Behavioral economics and public policy: A pragmatic perspective. *American Economic Review* 105(5): 1–33.

Chetty, Raj, and Emmanuel Saez. 2013. Teaching the tax code: Earnings responses to an experiment with EITC recipients. *American Economic Journal: Applied Economics* 5(1): 1–31.

Chetty, Raj, John N. Friedman, and Emmanuel Saez. 2013. Using differences in knowledge across neighborhoods to uncover the impacts of the EITC on earnings. *American Economic Review* 103(7): 2683–2721.

Federal Communications Commission. 2015. *Second further notice of proposed rulemaking, order on reconsideration, second report and order, and memorandum opinion and order (FCC 15–71).* Washington, DC: Federal Communications Commission.

Hoxby, Caroline, and Christopher Avery. 2013. The missing "one-offs": The hidden supply of high-achieving, low-income students. *Brookings Papers on Economic Activity* 2013(1): 1–65.

Hoxby, Caroline M., and Sarah Turner. 2015. What high-achieving low-income students know about college. *American Economic Review* 105(5): 514–517.

Linnan, Laura A., Heather D'Angelo, and Cherise B. Harrington. 2014. A literature synthesis of health promotion research in salons and barbershops. *American Journal of Preventive Medicine* 47(1): 77–85.

Mani, Anandi, Sendhil Mullainathan, Eldar Shafir, and Jiaying Zhao. 2013. Poverty impedes cognitive function. *Science* 341(6149): 976–980.

Manoli, Dayanand S., and Nicholas Turner. 2014. *Nudges and learning: Evidence from informational interventions for low-income taxpayers.* Working paper. Austin: University of Texas-Austin.

Newlin, Kelley, Susan MacLeod Dyess, Emily Allard, Susan Chase, and Gail D'Eramo Melkus. 2012. A methodological review of faith-based health promotion literature: Advancing the science to expand delivery of diabetes education to Black Americans. *Journal of Religion and Health* 51(4): 1075–1097.

Rankin, Sarah. 2015. *Building sustainable communities: Integrated services and improved financial outcomes for low-income households.* New York: Local Initiatives Support Corporation.

Shah, Anuj K., Sendhil Mullainathan, and Eldar Shafir. 2012. Some consequences of having too little. *Science* 338(6107): 682–685.

Thaler, Richard H., and Cass R. Sunstein. 2008. *Nudge.* New Haven: Yale University Press.

Voinovich School of Leadership and Public Affairs. 2011. *Economic impact of the Ohio Benefit Bank: Technical report.* Working paper. Athens: Ohio University Voinovich School of Leadership and Public Affairs.

Wolfinger, Raymond E., and Jonathan Hoffman. 2001. Registering and voting with motor voter. *Political Science and Politics* 34(1): 85–92.

CHAPTER 13

The Online Participation Divide

Eszter Hargittai and Kaitlin Jennrich

Every day, hundreds of millions of Internet users consume online content, many of them also contributing their own opinions in the form of posts on social media, photo and video uploads, comments on news articles, edits to collaborative sites, and more. But who exactly is participating in such ways online? While the Internet certainly lowers the barriers to putting one's contributions out there (Hargittai 2000), with the potential to level the playing field when it comes to whose voices are available to and heard by others (Benkler 2006), evidence we present in this chapter suggests that it has not met this potential. We examine to what extent participatory activities are equally distributed across different types of people. We look at what types of people are most likely to contribute, and in converse, we reveal whose voices are least likely to be represented online, often on the most trafficked websites.

When the Internet first became popular, fears surfaced about a "digital divide," understood as the difference between those who have access to the Internet and those who do not (Hoffman and Novak 1998). However, as Internet use spread widely, it was accompanied by dwindling concerns about the disconnected (Compaine 2001). Recognizing that mere access

E. Hargittai (✉) • K. Jennrich
Northwestern University, Evanston, IL, USA

© The Editor(s) (if applicable) and The Author(s) 2016
M.I. Lloyd, L.A. Friedland (eds.), *The Communication Crisis in America, And How to Fix It*, DOI 10.1057/978-1-349-94925-0_13

to technology was not the only potential source of inequality regarding digital media, some scholarship started calling attention to a "second-level digital divide" (Hargittai 2002) or "digital inequality" to highlight differences in effective and efficient usage even once people gained Internet access (DiMaggio and Hargittai 2001; van Dijk 2005; Warschauer 2003; Mossberger et al. 2003). This work noted the importance of variations in types of access, including the quality of Internet connectivity, the frequency of one's use (Bonfadelli 2002), and one's autonomy in going online (Hassani 2006; Robinson 2009; Barron et al. 2010). Having found such differentiated usage contexts, the literature then also explored how these variations might influence what people do online in a multitude of areas such as information seeking (Hargittai 2002; Van Deursen 2012), privacy management (Litt 2013; Park 2013), accessing various types of content (Hargittai and Hinnant 2008; Howard et al. 2001), and sharing materials such as one's opinions and creative output (Schradie 2011, 2015; Correa 2010; Hargittai and Walejko 2008; Blank 2013; Hoffmann et al. 2015). It is this latter type of activity that is of central concern in this chapter. From blogs to wikis, from photo sharing to video uploads, who is most likely to put their contributions out there for their friends—or potentially the entire world—to see? Conversely, whose opinions are not represented in online dialogues? As material from sites mainly made up of user-generated content (e.g., Facebook, Twitter, Wikipedia) is increasingly used as the basis for analyses about social behavior writ large, it is crucial to know whose voices are underrepresented or not at all present on such platforms (Hargittai 2015).

Categorizing Online Participation

One of the great challenges of reviewing the literature on online content sharing, understood broadly, is the lack of consistency in how researchers categorize such participation and engagement. Of course, given the multitude of online opportunities for sharing one's perspectives and creative output, it is perhaps not surprising that this scholarly area is a bit untidy and constantly shifting (Jenkins et al. 2015). After all, activities as diverse as penning a blog post about a health matter, sharing a cute turtle video, reminiscing about one's favorite childhood recipe, engaging in the comments section of a political article, and fixing a mistake on a Wikipedia page are all types—albeit very different ones—of online content sharing.

For the purposes of this piece, we consider online participation any type of online engagement whereby the user contributes content that others can access (see also Hoffman et al. 2015, 696). People's online content sharing can be analyzed on several dimensions including: (a) the platform on which they are sharing material (e.g., social network sites, video sites, news sites, personal blogs, wikis); (b) their forms of expression (e.g., posts, images, comments, links, up-votes); (c) content topic (e.g., art, politics, sports, social causes, health); (d) the level of public-ness and distribution (e.g., a private mailing list, a closed group on a social platform, a forum that requires registration, a blog where anyone can comment, a wiki open to editing and viewing by all); and (e) the type of community and main audience (e.g., family, friends who share a hobby, colleagues, fans of a particular topic, the world). Most studies tend to focus on one or two of these dimensions. We do not claim this review to be comprehensive, but we believe it gives a good idea of the types of patterns that exist when it comes to differentiated online engagement.

While looking for work to include here, we were agnostic to the content of the material studied, as well as the extent to which the material was being shared privately or publicly (as long as it is viewable potentially by *someone*). We also did not impose limits on format (e.g., whether it is a comment on a Facebook post, an upload of a short video, or an edit to a shared online document). Given that the goal of this chapter is to identify trends across population groups, we mainly focus on studies that have sufficient diversity on key variables of interest (such as gender, race/ethnicity, and socioeconomic status) to allow for drawing conjectures about how the activity of interest may differ by user background. Important work exists about online participation in other ways that we do not discuss here (e.g., Jenkins et al. 2009).

DIVIDES IN ONLINE PARTICIPATION

First, it is important to establish that 15 percent of American adults are not online (Pew Research Center 2015). Adults in this group tend to be older, of a lower socioeconomic status, and reside in rural areas. Therefore, it is important to note that any study of Internet use and online content creation in particular will include a lower proportion of such people than their prevalence in the US population at large.

As noted above, the literature relevant to our focus is not organized in any tidy fashion. This is likely due in part to the fact that it is a new area with an ever-changing landscape as its focus of inquiry. We have organized the sections below based on the focus of groups of papers that we identified as dealing with various aspects of online participation by different population segments.

Use of Social Network Sites

Social network sites (SNSs), such as Facebook, Twitter, Instagram, Pinterest, Tumblr, and LinkedIn, are some of the most visited websites (comScore 2015). All such sites rely largely on users sharing content. To contribute to these sites, one must have an account on them, which is why looking at site adoption is an important way to assess the likelihood of whose voices are most likely to show up on these platforms. Additionally, given that data from such sites are often publicly available and can be amassed in large quantities, content on such sites has increasingly come to form the basis of research on various social behavioral questions (Hargittai 2015). To understand the extent to which the results of such studies are generalizable, it is important to know whether users who participate on such sites represent the diversity of perspectives in the larger population.

Adults living in urban or suburban areas use SNSs at a consistently higher rate than adults living in rural areas (Duggan et al. 2015). Research on SNS users has found that people of different backgrounds adopt the sites at varying rates. The literature has identified that socioeconomic status relates to likelihood of being on various platforms among both adults (Duggan et al. 2015; Hargittai 2015) and teens (Lenhart 2015). Studies have also found racial and ethnic differences in adoption rates. For example, young African-Americans are more likely to be on Twitter than other groups of the same age (Smith 2014), although after controlling for an interest in celebrities, this relationship was no longer significant in a study of young adults (Hargittai and Litt 2011). While the particular platform that those from various socioeconomic status favor may change over time—Instagram, for example, is more popular with the more privileged in 2015 (Lenhart 2015), as Facebook was in 2009 (Hargittai 2011)—adoption of SNSs by socioeconomic status has been found consistently across studies since the popular spread of social media (Hargittai 2007b; boyd 2011).

Even among SNS users, research has found divergences in how people use particular sites. For example, one study found that on Facebook, college students of a lower socioeconomic status were less likely to send private messages, post videos, tag photos, or create events (Junco 2013). Several studies have identified gender differences in how people use SNSs. Female adults post updates on Facebook more frequently than men, according to a nationally representative study (Hampton et al. 2012). Young adult women are more likely to engage in stronger-tie activities, such as communicating with friends, than young adult men, whereas the latter are more likely to engage in weaker-tie activities, such as communicating with people they have only met online through SNSs (Hargittai and Hsieh 2010). An implication of these differences is that women are more likely to share content with more private groups that are restricted to those in their trusted networks, as compared to men, whose behaviors on SNSs are more likely to be more public, and thus reach a potentially wider group (Litt and Hargittai 2014). Another line of work that speaks to this point concerns privacy management on SNSs. Research has found that women are more likely to have changed the privacy settings of their profile and to have done so more often than men (boyd and Hargittai 2010; Hargittai and Litt 2013).

Blogging

Blogs tend to be written by one individual or a small group of writers, often focusing on a particular type of content or community. They resemble traditional opinion pages in that they are more often about expressing people's individual perspectives than objective reporting. In newspaper op-ed pages, men have tended to dominate the conversation by a considerable margin (Yaeger 2012). Blogs offer a potential to sidestep the gatekeeping role of mainstream media editors allowing writers to reach audiences directly.

According to the popular blogging platform WordPress, over 409 million people view more than 20.4 billion blog pages each month (WordPress 2015). Blogs exist on every imaginable topic from politics to fashion, from parenting to travel, from personal finance to religion. While men and women blog in relatively even numbers, there are considerable divides in who engages with what type of content. Women focus on family updates more frequently than male bloggers (Lopez 2009) and have created a powerful genre of blogging, called "mommy blogging," which garners considerable traffic. Racial divides do exist in this highly popular blogging area; in a 2011 list of the top mommy bloggers, white women were, by far, the most represented (Barcelos 2012).

Women may dominate the blogosphere when it comes to family and parenting topics, but men outnumber women in other blog domains. In 2006, researchers found that only 10 percent of the top political bloggers were women (Harp and Tremayne 2006). In another study, analyzing 89 influential political blogs—that is, blogs read by special interest groups, political national committees, and so on—researchers found that the vast majority were authored by white males and the highly educated (Tomaszeski 2006). Other work on influential political blogs has also tended to highlight male authors (Hargittai et al. 2008; Benkler and Shaw 2012; Farrell and Drezner 2008).

User-generated content such as blogs has the potential to challenge mainstream stereotypes about a group. While men are generally more likely to engage with sports content online (Fallows 2005), a study focused specifically on women's sports blogs found that their authors tended to discuss women's sports participation in a way that defied stereotypical assumptions about women's role in sports (Antunovic and Hardin 2013). So while men may outnumber women in a domain, the underrepresented group still has the potential to make important contributions to existing dialogue on a topic. This is precisely why more representation of diverse voices is important.

Overall, the findings about research on bloggers suggest that demographic divides exist in multiple subject areas; women dominate conversations about parenthood, while men garner the lion's share of attention when it comes to political topics. Regarding race and ethnicity, whites tend to blog in greater numbers and with higher levels of readership than members of other groups.

Wikipedia and Other Collaborative Sites

Wikis are collaborative platforms that can be edited and modified by any Internet user. One of the most well-known wikis is Wikipedia, the massive online free encyclopedia, which any Internet user can edit. Despite accessibility to all, research has found dramatic gender divides among Wikipedia contributors. Men are much more likely than women to have edited a Wikipedia article. A study of young adults found that a significantly smaller portion of women had edited Wikipedia than men (Hargittai and Shaw 2015). Generally, work on Wikipedia editing tends to estimate female editors in the high teens or low 20s, percent-wise, both in the USA and globally (Antin et al. 2011; Hill and Shaw 2013).

Beyond the gender divide, Wikipedia editors also tend to be more educated than the general population (Brake 2014). Additionally, the culture of Wikipedia has long been reported as complicated, bureaucratic, and oftentimes hostile, which creates even more potential barriers to participation (Hern 2015; Auerbach 2014; Paling 2015; Collier and Bear 2012).

One of the reasons for concern about such divides is that the gender imbalance in authorship may create biases in the content coverage of Wikipedia. An analysis of Wikipedia articles on notable people discovered that articles about notable women tended to use words like "woman" and "female," while articles about men rarely referenced the men's gender (Wagner et al. 2016). Additionally, words relating to people's private lives, such as "married," "children," "family," and "divorced," are used more frequently in articles about women than articles about men. Other gender-related content controversies have sprung up over the years, such as moving female American novelist names away from the "American Novelists" section into an "American Women Novelists" section, resulting in the former section being restricted mainly to men (Filipacchi 2013; Gleick 2013). Generally speaking, topics with a more female orientation are often shorter than topics that are more of interest to male audiences.

Digital divides in content creation also have an effect on volunteered geographic information, which includes user-generated geo-tagged posts and user-generated cartographic information. User-generated cartographic information, such as OpenStreetMap (OSM), allows a community of users to generate a map of the world, much like Wikipedia allows users to create an encyclopedia. Users of OSM tend to be highly educated. Gender differences exist in this domain as well: One study found that 20 percent of women who were aware of OSM had ever added data to the site, compared to 40 percent of men (Stephens 2013).

Gaps also exist between urban and rural areas. Extremely urban counties in the USA have significantly more Twitter users than extremely rural counties (Hecht and Stephens 2014). This leads to a significantly higher percentage of geo-tagged posts in urban areas than rural areas. A similar divide exists on the photo-sharing site Flickr, where considerably more photos per capita are posted in urban areas versus rural ones. These findings indicate that studies that rely on user-generated geo-tagged posts to study human mobility and behavior may be presenting an urban-biased view due to such content disproportionately originating from urban users.

Creative Work (Photos, Videos, Creative Writing)

The ability to share creative content, such as photos and creative writing, is especially significant for groups that have been marginalized traditionally in creative culture, including, for example, women, who are often underrepresented in various types of content creation, ranging from ads to magazines (Bosman 2005; Lauzen 2007). Divides in creative content sharing online can be found even among highly wired groups, such as college students. One study found that men were generally more likely to post content, a gender difference especially notable for sharing music and videos (Hargittai and Walejko 2008). A study of a different college population found similar gender differences in video sharing (Vedantham 2011). Highlighting another important variation in sharing by gender, research has found that young women are much more likely than young men to share their photos with restricted access only instead of posting the material publicly (Litt and Hargittai 2014).

Among teens, those who create artistic content, such as remixed music, tend to live in urban areas and have reliable broadband access at home (Lenhart and Madden 2005). Analyzing data from a nationally representative sample, Schradie (2011) found that college-educated Internet users were twice as likely to post photos and videos online, as compared to a user with only a high-school education.

THE ROLE OF INTERNET SKILLS IN ONLINE PARTICIPATION

As the literature reviewed above clearly shows, online participation varies by user background, such as gender and socioeconomic status. While it is important to be cognizant of this fact, it does not in and of itself address how inequalities in participation could be reduced. There is a promising line of inquiry to help with potential interventions, however. Some research has looked at how Internet skills relate to online participation, suggesting that those who are more skilled are more likely to be engaged online (see references below). Accordingly, offering opportunities for people to acquaint themselves better with digital media may be the key to reducing the participation divide.

Internet skills concern effective and efficient uses of digital media. The dimensions of skill range from awareness of what is possible to knowing how to search for information and being able to assess the credibility of the found content. It also encompasses the ability to perform tasks such as joining communities, sharing content, and managing one's privacy (Hargittai 2007a; van Dijk 2005). Differences in Internet skills have been documented in several countries for a range of adult populations, highlighting that it is an important aspect of varied Internet experiences (Hargittai and Hinnant 2008; Wasserman and Richmond-Abbott 2005; Bonfadelli 2002; Van Deursen and van Dijk 2011; Hargittai and Shafer 2006; Hargittai 2010; Gui and Argentin 2011). Research on youth in the UK has also found that young children's online engagement is tied to their skill level (Livingstone and Helsper 2007). Findings from these studies tend to be consistent in that those from lower socioeconomic status have lower-level skills compared to those from more privileged backgrounds.

Theoretically, it makes sense to expect that skills would relate to online participation. Users must know about the possibility of sharing content, know how to join platforms, and know enough about how they function to contribute. Young adults with more Internet skills and higher socioeconomic status are more likely to be Twitter users (Hargittai and Litt 2011), as well as LinkedIn and Tumblr users (Hargittai 2015). Such young adults are also more likely to share content online, such as photos and videos (Hargittai and Walejko 2008; Correa 2010), a finding that emerged from data about UK adults' skills and online contributions, as well (Blank 2013). Skilled young adults are also more likely to have edited Wikipedia than their less-skilled counterparts, even when controlling for numerous other factors (Hargittai and Shaw 2015).

Although men and women do not necessarily differ in their actual Internet skills (Hargittai and Shafer 2006), women tend to rate their skills lower than men rate theirs (Hargittai 2010; Correa 2010). Of concern here is that lower self-assessed skills—even if these may not reflect actual skills precisely—have been linked to lower levels of content sharing, whereby women who assess their skills as lower share less (Hargittai and Walejko 2008; Correa 2010).

IMPLICATIONS

There is no doubt that the Internet has made the potential for the dissemination of content easier and within the reach of a significantly larger group than was previously possible. Nonetheless, as the review of related literature shows, mere technical availability of such opportunities is not enough to put it within equal reach of everyone. Women, members of underrepresented racial and ethnic groups, and those of lower socioeconomic status tend to contribute to online conversations at lower levels. Such unequal participation then results in the underrepresentation of certain perspectives on the many user-generated content platforms that hundreds of millions of people peruse on a daily basis. Also, as more and more studies rely on automatically generated log data, or so-called "big data," from such sites to study social behavior, the perspectives of people not participating on sites are also less likely to show up in an increasing number of scientific studies that may then form the basis of policy interventions (Hargittai 2015).

What can be done to level the playing field in online engagement? As the review above highlights, existing work has identified Internet skills as an important factor explaining differential rates of participation. Controlling for other factors, those with higher Internet skills tend to be more actively engaged online, that is, by contributing their own content. So while tackling digital inequality requires the necessary first step of ensuring technical access to the Internet (e.g., public access points at libraries or affordable high-speed connectivity in people's homes), it is not a sufficient step to reduce barriers to more universal online participation. Rather, resources must also be put toward educational support, whether that be through formal training at schools, workplaces, and libraries; informal training at workshops; or peer mentoring. Users from diverse backgrounds must have access to opportunities to learn how to use the technology if they are to become actively engaged online citizens and have their perspectives represented in the vast amount of content that makes up the Internet.

REFERENCES

Antin, Judd, Raymond Yee, Coye Cheshire, and Oded Nov. 2011. Gender differences in Wikipedia editing. In *Proceedings of the 7th international symposium on Wikis and open collaboration*. Mountain View.

Antunovic, Dunja, and Marie Hardin. 2013. Women bloggers: Identity and the conceptualization of sports. *New Media and Society* 15(8): 1374–1392. doi:10.1177/1461444812472323.

Auerbach, David. 2014. Encyclopedia Frown. *Slate*, December 11. Available at http://www.slate.com/articles/technology/bitwise/2014/12/wikipedia_editing_disputes_the_crowdsourced_encyclopedia_has_become_a_rancorous.html.

Barcelos, Christie. 2012. *Social privilege and mom blogging.* http://thesocietypages.org/socimages/2012/02/23/social-privilege-and-mom-blogging/.

Barron, Brigid, Sarah E. Walter, Caitlin Kennedy Martin, and Colin Schatz. 2010. Predictors of creative computing participation and profiles of experience in two Silicon Valley middle schools. *Computers and Education* 54(1): 178–189. doi:10.1016/j.compedu.2009.07.017.

Benkler, Y. (2006). The Wealth of Networks: How Social Production Transforms Markets and Freedom. Yale University Press.

Benkler, Yochai, and Aaron Shaw. 2012. A tale of two blogospheres: Discursive practices on left and right. *American Behavioral Scientist* 56(4): 459–487.

Blank, Grant. 2013. Who creates content? Stratification and content creation on the Internet. *Information, Communication and Society* 16(4): 590–612. doi:10.1080/1369118x.2013.777758.

Bonfadelli, Heinz. 2002. The internet and knowledge gaps. A theoretical and empirical investigation. *European Journal of Communication* 17(1): 65–84.

Bosman, Julie. 2005. Stuck at the edges of the ad game. *The New York Times*, November 22. http://query.nytimes.com/gst/fullpage.html?res=9807E4D8 1F3EF931A15752C1A9639C8B63&pagewanted=all.

boyd, danah. 2011. White flight in networked publics? How race and class shaped American teen engagement with MySpace and Facebook. In *Race after the internet*, ed. P. Chow-White and L. Nakamura, 203–222. New York: Routledge.

boyd, danah., and Eszter Hargittai. 2010. Facebook privacy settings. Who cares? *First Monday* 15(8).

Brake, David R. 2014. Are we all online content creators now? Web 2.0 and digital divides. *Journal of Computer-Mediated Communication* 19(3): 591–609.

Collier, Benjamin, and Julia Bear. 2012. Conflict, criticism, or confidence: An empirical examination of the gender gap in Wikipedia contributions. In *Proceedings of the ACM 2012 conference on Computer Supported Cooperative Work*. Seattle.

Compaine, Benjamin M. 2001. Declare the war won. In *The digital divide: Facing a crisis or creating a myth?* ed. Benjamin M. Compaine, 315–335. Cambridge, MA: MIT Press.

comScore. 2015. *comScore ranks the top 50 U.S. Digital media properties for September 2015.* Available at https://www.comscore.com/Insights/Market-Rankings/comScore-Ranks-the-Top-50-US-Digital-Media-Properties-for-August-2015.

Correa, Teresa. 2010. The participation divide among 'online experts': Experience, skills and psychological factors as predictors of college students' web content creation. *Journal of Computer-Mediated Communication* 16(1): 71–92. doi:10.1111/j.1083-6101.2010.01532.x.

DiMaggio, Paul, and Eszter Hargittai. 2001. *From the 'digital divide' to 'digital inequality': Studying internet use as penetration increases.* Princeton: Center for Arts and Cultural Policy Studies at Princeton University.

Duggan, Maeve, Nicole B. Ellison, Cliff Lampe, Amanda Lenhart, and Mary Madden. 2015. Social media update 2014. *Pew Research Center*.

Fallows, Deborah. 2005. *How women and men use the Internet.* Washington, DC: Pew Research Center. Available at http://www.pewinternet.org/2005/12/28/how-women-and-men-use-the-internet/.

Farrell, Henry, and Daniel W. Drezner. 2008. The power and politics of blogs. *Public Choice* 134: 15–30.

Filipacchi, Amanda. 2013. Wikipedia's sexism toward female novelists. *The New York Times*, April 28. http://www.nytimes.com/2013/04/28/opinion/sunday/wikipedias-sexism-toward-female-novelists.html?_r=1.

Gleick, James. 2013. Wikipedia's women problem. *The New York Review of Books*, April 29.http://www.nybooks.com/daily/2013/04/29/wikipedia-women-problem/.

Gui, Marco, and Gianluca Argentin. 2011. Digital skills of internet natives: Different forms of digital literacy in a random sample of northern Italian high school students. *New Media and Society* 13(6): 963–980. doi:10.1177/1461444810389751.

Hampton, Keith N., Lauren Sessions Goulet, Cameron Marlow, and Lee Rainie. 2012. Why most Facebook users get more than they give. *Pew Internet & American Life Project*.

Hargittai, Eszter. 2000. Open portals or closed gates? Channeling content on the World Wide Web. *Poetics* 27: 233–253.

Hargittai, Eszter. 2002. Second-level digital divide: Differences in people's online skills. *First Monday* 7(4).

Hargittai, Eszter. 2007a. A framework for studying differences in people's digital media uses. In *Cyberworld Unlimited?* ed. Nadia Kutscher and Hans-Use Otto, 121–137. Wiesbaden: VS Verlag für Sozialwissenschaften/GWV Fachverlage GmbH.

Hargittai, Eszter. 2007b. Whose space? Differences among users and non-users of social network sites. *Journal of Computer-Mediated Communication* 13(1): 276–297.

Hargittai, Eszter. 2010. Digital na(t)ives? Variation in internet skills and uses among members of the 'net generation'. *Sociological Inquiry* 80(1): 92–113.

Hargittai, Eszter. 2011. Open doors, closed spaces? Differentiated adoption of social network sites by user background. In *Race after the internet*, ed. Peter Chow-White and Lisa Nakamura, 223–245. New York: Routledge.

Hargittai, Eszter. 2015. Is bigger always better? Potential biases of big data derived from social network sites. *The ANNALS of the American Academy of Political and Social Science* 659: 63–76.

Hargittai, Eszter, and Amanda Hinnant. 2008. Digital inequality: Differences in young adults' use of the internet. *Communication Research* 35(5): 602–621.

Hargittai, Eszter, and Yu-li Patrick Hsieh. 2010. Predictors and consequences of differentiated social network site uses. *Information, Communication and Society* 13(4): 515–536.

Hargittai, Eszter, and Eden Litt. 2011. The tweet smell of celebrity success: Explaining variation in Twitter adoption among a diverse group of young adults. *New Media and Society*. doi:10.1177/1461444811405805.

Hargittai, Eszter, and E. Litt. 2013. New strategies for employment? Internet skills and online privacy practices during people's job search. *IEEE Security and Privacy* 11(3): 38–45.

Hargittai, Eszter, and Steven Shafer. 2006. Differences in actual and perceived online skills: The role of gender. *Social Science Quarterly* 87(2): 432–448.

Hargittai, Eszter, and Aaron Shaw. 2015. Mind the skills gap: The role of Internet know-how and gender in differentiated contributions to Wikipedia. *Information, Communication and Society* 18(4): 424–442. doi:10.1080/1369 118x.2014.957711.

Hargittai, Eszter, and Gina Walejko. 2008. The participation divide: Content creation and sharing in the digital age. *Information, Communication and Society* 11(2): 239–256.

Hargittai, Eszter, Jason Gallo, and Matthew Yale Kane. 2008. Cross-ideological discussions among conservative and liberal bloggers. *Public Choice* 134: 67–86.

Harp, Dustin, and Mark Tremayne. 2006. The gendered blogosphere: Examining inequality using network and feminist theory. *Journalism and Mass Communication Quarterly* 83(2): 247–264. doi:10.1177/107769900608300202.

Hassani, Sara Nephew. 2006. Locating digital divides at home, work, and everywhere else. *Poetics* 34: 250–272.

Hecht, Brent, and Monica Stephens. 2014. A tale of cities: Urban biases in volunteered geographic information. *Proceedings of ICWSM*.

Hern, Alex. 2015. Wikipedia votes to ban some editors from gender-related articles. *The Guardian*, January 23. http://www.theguardian.com/technology/2015/jan/23/wikipedia-bans-editors-from-gender-related-articles-amid-gamergate-controversy.

Hill, Benjamin Mako, and Aaron Shaw. 2013. The Wikipedia gender gap revisited: Characterizing survey response bias with propensity score estimation. *PLoS ONE* 8(6): e65782.

Hoffman, Donna L., and Thomas P. Novak. 1998. Bridging the racial divide on the internet. *Science* 280: 390–391.

Hoffmann, Christian P., Christoph Lutz, and Miriam Meckel. 2015. Content creation on the internet: A social cognitive perspective on the participation divide. *Information, Communication and Society* 18(6): 696–716.

Howard, Philip N., Rainie Lee, and Steve Jones. 2001. Days and nights on the internet: The impact of a diffusing technology. *American Behavioral Scientist* 45(3): 383–404.

Jenkins, Henry, Ravi Purushotma, Margaret Weigel, Katie Clinton, and Alice J. Robison. 2009. *Confronting the challenges of participatory culture: Media education for the 21st century*. Cambridge, MA: MIT Press.

Jenkins, Henry, Mizuko Ito, and danah boyd. 2015. *Participatory culture in a networked era: A conversation on youth, learning, commerce, and politics*. Malden: Polity.

Junco, Reynol. 2013. Inequalities in Facebook use. *Computers in Human Behavior* 29(6): 2328–2336. doi:10.1016/j.chb.2013.05.005.

Lauzen, Martha M. 2007. *Boxed in: Women on screen and behind the scenes in the 2006–07 prime-time season.* San Diego: San Diego State University.

Lenhart, Amanda. 2015. Teens, social media and technology overview 2015. *Pew Research Center.*

Lenhart, Amanda, and Mary Madden. 2005. Teen content creators and consumers. In *Pew Internet & American Life Project.* Washington, DC: Pew Research Center.

Litt, Eden. 2013. Understanding social network site users' privacy tool use. *Computers in Human Behavior* 29(4): 1649–1656. doi:10.1016/j.chb.2013.01.049.

Litt, Eden, and Eszter Hargittai. 2014. Smile, snap and share? A nuanced approach to privacy and online photosharing. *Poetics* 42(1): 1–21.

Livingstone, Sonia, and Ellen Helsper. 2007. Gradations in digital inclusion: Children, young people, and the digital divide. *New Media and Society* 9: 671–696.

Lopez, Lori Kido. 2009. The radical act of 'mommy blogging': Redefining motherhood through the blogosphere. *New Media and Society* 11(5): 729–747. doi:10.1177/1461444809105349.

Mossberger, Karen, Caroline J. Tolbert, and Mary Stansbury. 2003. *Virtual inequality: Beyond the digital divide.* Washington, DC: Georgetown University Press.

Paling, Emma. 2015. Wikipedia's hostility to women. *The Atlantic,* October 21. Available at http://www.theatlantic.com/technology/archive/2015/10/how-wikipedia-is-hostile-to-women/411619/.

Park, Yong Jin. 2013. Digital literacy and privacy behavior online. *Communication Research* 40: 215–236. doi:10.1177/0093650211418338.

Pew Research Center. 2015. Offline population has declined substantially since 2000. Available at http://www.pewresearch.org/fact-tank/2015/07/28/15-of-americans-dont-use-the-internet-who-are-they/ft_15-07-23_notonline_310px/.

Robinson, Laura. 2009. A taste for the necessary. *Information, Communication and Society* 12(4): 488–507. doi:10.1080/13691180902857678.

Schradie, Jen. 2011. The digital production gap: The digital divide and Web 2.0 collide. *Poetics* 39: 145–168.

Schradie, Jen. 2015. The gendered digital production gap: Inequalities of affluence. *Communication and Information Technologies Annual* 9: 185–213. doi:10.1108/S2050-206020150000009008.

Smith, Aaron. 2014. *African Americans and technology use: A demographic portrait.* Washington, DC: Pew Research Center. Available at http://www.pewinternet.org/2014/01/06/african-americans-and-technology-use/.

Stephens, Monica. 2013. Gender and the GeoWeb: Divisions in the production of user-generated cartographic information. *GeoJournal* 78(6): 981–996. doi:10.1007/s10708-013-9492-z.

Tomaszeski, Michael Steven. 2006. *A baseline examination of political bloggers, who they are, their views on the blogosphere, and their influence in agenda-setting via the two-step flow hypothesis.* Master of Arts thesis, Department of Communication, Florida State University (1282).

Van Deursen, Alexander J.A.M. 2012. Internet skill-related problems in accessing online health information and services. *International Journal of Medical Informatics* 81(1): 61–72.

Van Deursen, Alexander J.A.M., and Jan van Dijk. 2011. Internet skills and the digital divide. *New Media and Society* 13(6): 893–911.

van Dijk, Jan. 2005. *The deepening divide: Inequality in the information society.* Thousand Oaks: Sage Publications.

Vedantham, Anu. 2011. *Making YouTube and Facebook videos: Gender differences in online video creation among first-year undergraduate students attending a highly selective research university.* PhD dissertation, University of Pennsylvania.

Wagner, Claudia, Eduardo Graells-Garrido, David Garcia, & Filippo Menczer. 2016. Women through the glass ceiling: gender asymmetries in Wikipedia. EPJ Data Science, 5(1). http://doi.org/10.1140/epjds/s13688-016-0066-4

Warschauer, Mark. 2003. *Technology and social inclusion.* Cambridge, MA: MIT Press.

Wasserman, Ira M., and Marie Richmond-Abbott. 2005. Gender and the internet: Causes of variation in access, level, and scope of use. *Social Science Quarterly* 86(1): 252–270.

WordPress. 2015. *A live look at activity across wordpress.com.* https://wordpress.com/activity/.

Yaeger, Taryn. 2012. Who narrates the world? In *The OpEd Project Byline Report.* http://www.theopedproject.org/index.php?option=com_content&view=article&id=817&Itemid=149.

CHAPTER 14

Media Deserts: Monitoring the Changing Media Ecosystem

Michelle Ferrier, Gaurav Sinha, and Michael Outrich

INTRODUCTION

Michelle Ferrier worked as a night news editor and online community manager from 2002 to 2009 at the *Daytona Beach News-Journal,* a two-county, daily newspaper serving Volusia and Flagler counties in Florida. She survived four rounds of layoffs of reporters, photographers, designers, advertising salespeople, and many others before she left the newsroom to return to higher education. Ferrier watched as the two-county newspaper where she worked began closing bureaus and tightening its reach across the region. At one time, the newspaper management had aggressively competed with the *Orlando Sentinel* and other newspapers on their borders. However, by 2007, the newspaper had ceded that space to focus on the core geographic distribution area around Daytona Beach. The newspaper management experimented with technological solutions to bolster their shrinking readership base by creating a hyperlocal online community where user-generated content dominated. Ferrier became the managing editor of this online community hub.

M. Ferrier (✉) • G. Sinha • M. Outrich
Ohio University, Athens, OH, USA

© The Editor(s) (if applicable) and The Author(s) 2016   215
M.I. Lloyd, L.A. Friedland (eds.), *The Communication Crisis in America, And How to Fix It,* DOI 10.1057/978-1-349-94925-0_14

Ferrier visited the 12 communities now carved into the new hyperlocal online news platform. As trainer and evangelist for this online platform, she began to interact with communities that were no longer actively covered by the newspaper's reporting staff. She wondered about the effects of this change in coverage on residents and their ability to stay informed about local issues and engaged in local decision-making. Could user-generated content and the new online platform provide a way for residents to communicate with each other? And as she clung to her job at the newspaper, she watched as colleagues across the country were laid off from their journalism jobs. Newspapers across the country were experiencing an economic downturn and a technological disruption from the growth of digital native news sites and social media. The media landscape was changing and shifting and leaving some communities without access to local information.

According to Newspaperlayoffs.com, more than 160 newspapers have shut down since 2008. More than 33,000 American newspaper journalists have lost their jobs from newsrooms large and small, across every state in the nation in that same time. According to the American Society of News Editors' Newsroom Employment Census, overall newsroom employment was down 3 percent to 36,700 in 2013, the most recent year for which figures are available (Pew Research Center's Project for Excellence in Journalism 2015). Technological disruption has changed the business model and newspapers have laid off many journalists and staff in an effort to slow revenue decline. Newspapers shuttered bureaus and created online news sites, modeling the belt-tightening behavior Ferrier experienced at the *News-Journal*.

According to the Pew Research Center, the loss of jobs in the media industry resulted in a reduction in the quality and quantity of news and information gathered and circulating within a community (Pew Research Center's Project for Excellence in Journalism 2013). This "brain drain" has created growing voids in local news coverage. In addition, the industry is disproportionately shedding journalists of color. The American Society of News Editors reports that in 2004, minority journalists represented 14 percent of the newsroom. In 2012, newsroom diversity had fallen to 12 percent, while the US minority population grew to 28 percent.

This decline in news investment neglects stories that reflect the growing communities of color in the USA. In addition, too many issues that once came to the public's attention through newspapers are now fragmented across media and platforms—if covered at all. As a result, the ability of local citizens to be informed and engaged with their neighborhoods, schools, community organizations, and governments has become more difficult according to recent research (Knight Commission 2010; Friedland et al. 2012; Waldman 2011; Dolezal 2010; Gonzalez and Torres 2011).

The issue of community information needs and how communities access information has been addressed by several national reports. These key reports include "Informing Communities: Sustaining Democracy in a Digital Age," the report of The Knight Commission on the Information Needs of Communities in a Democracy published in 2009, and Steven Waldman's "The Information Needs of Communities: The Changing Media Landscape in a Broadband Age" published by the Federal Communications Commission in July 2011 (Knight Commission 2010; Waldman 2011). The reports as a whole point to a dynamic and troubling media ecosystem. News gathering, reporting, dissemination, and reader engagement have changed as a result of changing advertising revenue models, changing technological platforms, and behavioral changes of the people formerly known as readers and audiences (Fancher 2011; Marketing Charts 2012). Community-based reporting projects and other online media entrepreneurship endeavors have tried to fill some of these information gaps, but their effects, reach, and sustainability are in question (Ferrier 2013; Shane 2011).

Scholars such as de Tocqueville (1997) and Habermas Bohman (2004, 139) have argued that newspapers fill critical information needs for communities and that the media have supplanted the "public sphere" of community information exchange and dialogue around important local issues. Some have begun to wonder if democracy itself is at risk. Residents need not only to understand the issues at hand but also to talk with others about what should be done. The newspaper and local media have been key mediators in these democratic processes in many communities. But as the reach, penetration, and accessibility of the media landscape changes, who has been affected by these changes and are these declines a cause for concern?

The net impact of these changes is an unstable news and information environment where the depth, quality, and quantity of news and information sources have changed significantly or have been severely eroded in some cases (Pew Research Center's Project for Excellence in Journalism 2013). This erosion has a direct impact on the health of communities.

The Knight Commission sought to understand the complexities of the current and future media environment, and their report offers broad guidelines for strengthening the news and information needs of communities in this climate of sea change. In "Informing Communities: Sustaining Democracy in the Digital Age," the Knight Commission reports:

> Information is essential to community vitality. Informed communities can effectively coordinate activities, achieve public accountability, solve problems, and create connections. Local information systems should support widespread knowledge of and participation in the community's day-to-day life by all segments of the community. To achieve the promise of democracy, it is necessary that the creation, organization, analysis, and transmission of information include the whole community (Knight Commission 2009, XIV).

Many of the basic information needs have traditionally been performed by the local daily newspaper—through classified advertisements announcing jobs and housing, reports of city council meeting decisions regarding taxes, crime reports, shopping inserts for food and shopping, calendar items announcing recreation and entertainment, and other editorial and advertising content. With the contraction in the reach and penetration of media at the local level, newspapers may not be serving the local need for a robust news and information ecosystem.

Researchers continue to describe these changes using quantitative and qualitative methods. They seek to answer the question "How does this changing media ecosystem affect the ability of a community's residents to access fresh, local news and information?" However, researchers, policymakers, and funders need better tools to measure trends in access to news and information over time and whether critical news and information needs are being met (Fancher 2011). Some researchers have attempted to do so with the Community Information Needs Indicators, an assessment tool that attempts to quantify what is happening at the local level (Thorson and Newton 2008). None of the research to date has sought to visualize the geographic scope and patterns of changes in the media ecosystem. We need the scalable, visual tools to help identify where valuable human and capital resources might be deployed to establish or restore news and information coverage (Deifell 2009). Our mapping-based data visualization seeks to fill this gap in the literature and provide trend data for future research.

Geospatial Media Analytics

Existing Methodologies

Researchers examining changes to the media ecosystem have used both statistical and content analyses. Some researchers examine the decline in advertising/circulation, while content analyses focus on examining the media product. Marketers and newspaper staff have used maps to determine what media operate in specific markets and where competitors operate. Beyond these marketing uses, there has been limited use of mapping and geographic information systems (GIS) to visualize media changes for the public and local decision-makers (Herzog 2003).

Nor has there been extensive research on the effects of media changes on local communities. The case study approach has been used in several areas such as cities in New Jersey (Napoli et al. 2015), North Carolina (Morgan and Allie Perez 2010; Ferrier 2014), and reports in Chicago (Chicago Community Trust 2010a, b). In 2015, the Pew Research Center examined three local media ecosystems—in Denver, Colorado; Macon, Georgia; and Sioux City, Iowa. The results of these studies demonstrate that local news climates differ across US cities, in terms of the volume of media news providers and in terms of which providers residents choose to get their local news and information.

While these case studies provide us with an in-depth picture of specific regions, we lack the big-picture view of how the economic downturn has affected news and information distribution on a national level. These approaches lack the ability to discern geospatial patterns that can only be seen in a visual context. Nor do they help us understand the reach and penetration of media into communities in the USA and the ability to track these changes over time.

Why Geospatial Analysis?

Maps have been used as illustrative graphics in print and electronic communication for almost a century now in journalism, since words alone are not sufficient to capture the geographic elements (e.g., location, distance, size, shape, connection, spatial pattern, and temporal trends) that often need to be communicated for conveying the local, regional, or global contexts of news events (Monmonier 1989, 2009, 869–873). The widespread use of interactive mapping technologies, such as Google Earth satellite imagery maps, for television news reporting and the phenomenal popularity of web mapping and online cartography for electronic news communication (Miller 2014) are testament to the growing importance of both the geographic perspective and geospatial technologies in media communication.

A GIS is also a powerful computational environment that supports many types of tools for developing location intelligence, geospatial data processing and database management, spatial and spatiotemporal analysis, and planning and modeling of future geographic scenarios. Despite its wide-ranging application in many social science fields, surprisingly, the role of GIS expertise in news analysis and media is still quite limited. Herzog (2003) was one of the first to make a case for GIS in not just mapping, but in the creation of news. GIS can help investigative journalists and other media specialists analyze environmental, political, socioeconomic, health, and other types of geographic data to verify details about stories and, more importantly, to discover entirely new stories from computational data analysis.

The rapid democratization of geographic information resources and technologies easily allows non-experts to create, access, and visualize geographic information today (Sinha et al. 2015). When this geo-information revolution is juxtaposed with data journalism (Gray et al. 2012), data visualization (Barlow 2014), and geographic information retrieval techniques (Purves and Jones 2011), we envisage that GIS will play a foundational role in the emergence of what we term as geospatial media analytics.

GIS Application to Media

Circulation data of both subscriptions and newsstand sales can address the limitation of existing methodologies by yielding geographical data. By mapping circulation data onto geographies, our Media Deserts Project (http://www.mediadeserts.com) explicitly relies on a geographic framework and a GIS technology to assess and track the changes in the information health of communities across the USA.

A particularly inspiring interactive online mapping service was created by the U.S. Department of Agriculture (USDA) in its Food Access Research Atlas, released in 2011, which allowed users to enter a ZIP code to find if they were located in a food desert. This mapping service helped focus attention on access to local, fresh food and made local decision-making sensitive to transportation routes, vehicle accessibility, and the location of farmers' markets. The USDA tool has been valuable in engaging various community stakeholders around issues of access to food.

It was the success of the USDA mapping service that inspired our GIS-based mapping and analysis of the changing media ecosystem. Similar to the USDA's tool, the Media Deserts Project is working to create new mapping tools for researchers, policymakers, and local leaders to help them identify communities lacking access to local news and information, as well as measure trends in access to critical news and information needs. We also seek to provide the tools to help identify where valuable human and capital resources might be deployed to establish or restore news and information coverage.

THE MEDIA DESERTS PROJECT

The gaps in media coverage—both in reach and penetration—have created what we call "media deserts." A media desert is a geographic locale that lacks access to fresh, local news and information. Community is defined as geography, or a niche community, or a community of intention. Fresh is defined as daily, local news. Others have used "news desert" to describe the lack of news in a community news and information ecosystem. However, we use the term "media deserts" since it describes not just the content layer as Lawrence Lessig describes in his framework, but also the conduit layers and code layers (Lessig 2002, 23). For example, if at the content layer we are describing "news deserts," the conduit layer would address access issues through broadband or mobile devices and the code layer would address issues with Google algorithms for determining "news" to the effects on search engine results. The term "media desert" is, therefore, multidimensional and allows us to begin to see the larger complexity of the communication ecosystems in which we operate.

The Media Deserts Project was conceived to develop new concepts and tools to identify communities that lack access to fresh news and information. The project maps media deserts and oases through GIS-based mapping and geospatial analysis of the U.S. media ecosystem that includes daily newspaper circulation, hyperlocal (both independent and AOL Patch) and a growing weekly and alternative publication database. GIS allows not just mapping of media deserts, but also geographic and spatial analyses of the demographic and economic conditions in the media deserts. This is crucial for understanding the broader communication ecosystem as it evolves.

Mapping Media Deserts

The Media Deserts Project is currently still in its earlier phases, and we focus primarily on daily newspapers to examine how readership patterns have evolved in the last decade. We rely on data collected by the Alliance for Audited Media (AAM) to map and analyze daily newspaper circulation (see www.auditedmedia.com). The AAM conducts circulation audits to provide independent verification of publishers' paid, unpaid, or verified circulation. These audited data include AAM data along with the Certified Audit of Circulations, providing the largest dataset of daily newspapers in the USA. We purchased national datasets from AAM for 2007, 2011, and 2014 to map changes in the circulation footprint of newspapers for ZIP codes across the USA.

The AAM dataset we acquired is not comprehensive. It represents only daily newspapers and does not include weekly newspapers or newspapers that operate on a more limited schedule. Nor does the circulation data account for the migration of readers to online platforms and social media for news. In addition, some newspapers forgo auditing services because of the time and cost to prepare the audits. Therefore, areas that show "no data" in our maps should not be assumed to be media deserts. In addition, during the period from 2007 to 2014, the AAM not only changed their name (from their prior moniker Audit Bureau of Circulation) but also changed their audit reporting methods for their latest 2014 cycle. The data fields that remained consistent across audits included average weekly circulation, average weekday circulation, and average weekend circulation. We used these variables to estimate newspaper circulation in a ZIP code.

AAM reports its data aggregated to postal ZIP codes, which are generally used by media companies to report circulation and other subscriber data. Mapping ZIP codes, however, is not as simple because the United States Postal System (USPS) conceptualizes ZIP codes not as areal features but as a collection of mail delivery routes to facilitate sorting and delivering of mail using existing street networks. Despite this limitation, the ZIP code is an important "social tool for organizing and displaying demographic information, a support structure for entire industries such as insurance and real estate, and even a representation of social identities" (USPS 2013). In response to these problems, the US Census Bureau (USCB) created ZIP code tabulation areas (ZCTAs) as generalized areal representations of US Postal Service ZIP codes. The USCB also uses areal interpolation methods to provide estimates (and error margins) for the most widely used Census variables (e.g., population, education, income, and race/ethnicity). UCSB provides these estimates both for data collected for the decennial Census and annual American Community Survey.

The Media Deserts Project uses ZCTAs for mapping and spatial analysis of AAM datasets referenced to ZIP codes. It also depends on USCB's population estimates for ZCTA units to calculate Circulation Penetration for a ZIP code, which we define as the (percentage) ratio of newspaper circulation for the ZIP code (from AAM data) to the population above the age of 18 (from USCB estimates for the corresponding ZCTA). Raw circulation numbers are influenced by population changes and can mask changes in the proportion of people subscribing to newspapers, whereas circulation penetration accounts for population change and better estimates changes in proportion of adults in an area subscribing to newspapers.

Additionally, our project seeks to contextualize newspaper coverage and penetration data with ancillary data about population, education, income, and race/ethnicity characteristics. The use of demographic and socioeconomic characteristics of communities is critical for assessing if communities that grew or saw declines in the number of daily newspapers are similar on one or more socioeconomic dimensions and if communities across the nation could be compared to understand national and regional patterns of access to fresh news and information.

Analyzing Media Deserts

It is important to note that the Media Deserts Project was conceived in response to firsthand experience with the newspaper industry's troubles with maintaining coverage and readership. Many newspapers closed satellite bureaus during their belt-tightening phase from 2007 to 2012. Others changed or consolidated ownership. Even before mapping and analyzing our data, we expected to find overall declining numbers of newspapers and changes in circulation penetration across the nation. We also expected to detect, at least for some newspapers, a loss of coverage and circulation around the perimeter of a newspaper's coverage area. We surmise that newspaper subscribers living in those outlying areas noticed the decline in newspaper coverage and terminated their subscriptions.

To test these assumptions, we experimented with this methodology in North Carolina with 2007 and 2011 datasets. Starting in 2011, Ferrier worked with Ryan Kirk of Elon University to explore GIS use on the project (Ferrier 2014). They looked at the 12 newspapers operating in North

Carolina and created a heat map of ZIP codes that lost daily newspapers. Using "distribution by ZIP code receiving twenty-five or more copies" and "total paid circulation for morning distribution," they charted this number for each sample year. The Daily Circulation data were extracted from the AAM and Community Newspaper Audit reports for available years.

As the researchers looked more closely at metropolitan areas in North Carolina, Ferrier expected to see erosion around the perimeter of a newspaper's service area. However, Ferrier also documented circulation erosion in the core service areas of newspapers. This "donut effect" showed that newspapers lost significant subscribers in their newspaper offices' backyard. The Pew Research Center confirmed this loss in their State of the Media 2013 survey. They found that consumers lack knowledge of the financial difficulties of the newspaper industry and the impact on the breadth and depth of coverage. They state that nearly a third (31 percent) of US adults have deserted a news outlet because it no longer provides the news and information they have grown accustomed to receiving. Fully 61 percent said they noticed that stories were less complete compared with 24 percent who said they noticed fewer stories overall (Pew Research Center's Project for Excellence in Journalism 2013).

The Media Deserts Project continued after 2013 at Ohio University with these co-authors and an interdisciplinary team of geography, public policy, and journalism researchers. As mentioned earlier, we obtained AAM data for their 2007, 2011, and 2014 audit cycles and used standard GIS and spreadsheet functionalities to process multiple AAM national datasets covering daily newspapers. The project website (www.mediadeserts.com) is periodically updated with the latest datasets, including color maps with more detailed legends and more detailed state map profiles. In the rest of this section, we provide a synopsis of our main findings.

Figure 14.1 and Table 14.1 represent the growth and decline of the number of newspapers across the USA following the economic downturn of 2007. Between 2007 and 2014, we see that 24.5 percent of communities experienced a loss of a newspaper. While the category "no data" might suggest a media desert, we cannot assume that "no data" also means the absence of a newspaper. Some newspapers choose not to be audited and therefore might exist in these "no data" ZIP code areas. Some ZIP Codes did see growth in daily newspapers with 12 percent of all ZIP Codes growing by one or more newspapers.

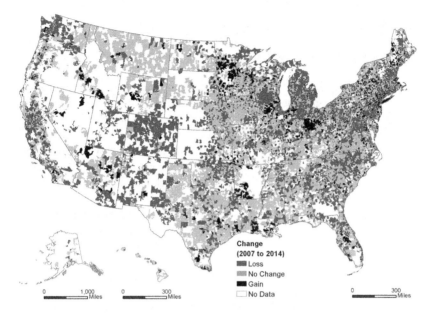

Fig. 14.1 Change in total number of daily newspapers serving a ZIP code between 2007 and 2014.

Table 14.1 Change in number of newspapers serving a ZIP code between 2007 and 2014

Change in number of newspapers (2007–2014)	Number of ZIP codes	Percent of total ZIP codes
Loss of 5 or more	46	0.1
Loss of 3 to 4	777	2.3
Loss of 1 to 2	7,301	22
No change	12,450	37.6
Gain of 1 to 2	2,656	8
Gain of 3 to 4	161	0.5
Gain of 5 or more	1	0
No data	9,728	29.4

The map in Fig. 14.1 reveals that much of the USA experienced a contraction in the marketplace. West Coast states, like Washington and California, experienced substantial loss. Central states, such as Colorado and New Mexico, were hard hit by the contraction. In the Midwest,

Michigan and areas bordering the Great Lakes experienced significant loss. On the East Coast, states such as New Hampshire, Pennsylvania, New Jersey, Virginia, North Carolina, and Georgia experienced significant loss.

When we examine these data using 2014 cycle audit data of the numbers of newspapers operating in a particular ZIP code, we find that 36 percent of the country now supports only one daily newspaper (see Table 14.2). Twenty-seven percent of the ZIP codes show "no data," which means areas with no newspapers or areas that may have a newspaper, but that newspaper is not audited. However, we see a more robust media ecosystem still exists around major metropolitan areas, such as Los Angeles, San Francisco, and Seattle in the West; Denver in the Central states; Chicago and Cincinnati in the Midwest; and in the coastal areas of the East Coast, extending up from Northern Virginia through Washington, D.C. and eastern Pennsylvania, New Jersey, eastern New York, Connecticut, Rhode Island, and eastern Massachusetts.

Figure 14.1, Tables 14.1 and 14.2 focus only on the number of newspapers serving ZIP codes, but that measure alone is not sufficient for understanding actual readership levels, for which one must examine circulation data. Therefore, in Table 14.3, we summarized circulation penetration in 2014, then map and describe changes in circulation penetration for ZIP codes between 2007 and 2014 in Fig. 14.2 and Table 14.4, respectively. As defined earlier, circulation penetration is circulation normalized by population over the age of 18. For this preliminary analysis, we used only the 2010 U.S. Census population for both years for simplicity, since 2010 is the central year and population changes in three years are generally negligibly small for areas as small as ZCTAs.

Table 14.2 Total number of newspapers serving a ZIP code in 2014

Number of newspapers (2014)	Number of ZIP codes	Percent of total ZIP codes
1	11,909	36
2	6,630	20
3	2,973	9
4 to 6	2,594	7.8
>6	154	0.5
No data	8,860	26.8

Table 14.3 Newspaper circulation penetration for a ZIP code in 2014

Newspaper circulation penetration (2014)	Number of ZIP codes	Percent of total ZIP codes
<10%	4,161	12.6
10%–25%	9,151	27.6
25%–50%	8,970	27.1
50%–75%	1,390	4.2
>75%	548	0.8
No data	8,900	26.9

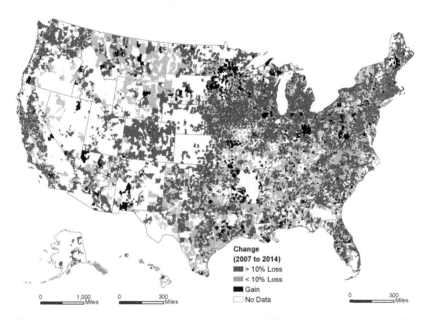

Fig. 14.2 Change in circulation penetration of daily newspapers serving a ZIP code between 2007 and 2014

Figure 14.2 shows losses and gains in circulation penetration normalized by population over the age of 18 between 2007 and 2014. Most of the US ZIP codes lost circulation, with gains highlighted in the few black areas scattered across the country. California, Oregon, and Washington saw greater than 10 percent loss in circulation penetration, as did Colorado and Midwestern states, including Iowa, Wisconsin, Illinois, Indiana, and

Table 14.4   Change in newspaper circulation penetration for a ZIP code between 2007 and 2014

Change in newspaper circulation penetration (2007–2014)	Number of ZIP codes	Percent of total ZIP codes
>50% loss	1,229	3.7
25%–50% loss	3,791	11.4
10%–25% loss	9,597	29
0%–10% loss	6,336	19.1
0%–10% gain	1,581	4.8
10%–25% gain	544	1.6
25%–50% gain	207	0.6
>50% gain	79	0.2
No data	9,756	29.5

Michigan. Eastern states, such as Rhode Island, New Jersey, Massachusetts, Maine, and Connecticut, also experienced greater than 10 percent loss.

When examining circulation penetration in 2014 (Table 14.3), we found that 41 percent of the ZIP codes achieve less than 25 percent newspaper penetration among adults aged 18 or older, while 68 percent of the ZIP codes have 50 percent or less newspaper penetration. When examining changes in circulation penetration between 2007 and 2014 (Table 14.4), we found that 63 percent of the total ZIP codes saw a loss in circulation penetration from 2007 to 2014. Compared to Fig. 14.1, what is strikingly obvious from the map in Fig. 14.2 is that an overwhelming majority of areas across the nation have experienced declines in circulation penetration implying decreasing levels of readership of daily newspapers. On the other hand, the gain in circulation penetration is limited to only a few areas (shown in black on the map in Fig. 14.2) that account for only approximately 7 percent of ZIP codes. Note that since about 29 percent of the ZIP codes remain unmapped either because they were not audited or the ZIP codes do not cover populated areas (implying lack of ZCTA coverage), both gains and loss statistics and spatial patterns could change somewhat. However, the current national pattern is unlikely to change appreciably from the current picture of readership losses across the nation.

Our map-based analysis of circulation and subscriber data to geographies confirms our belief in the importance of exploring the geographic dimension of local media ecosystems. In addition to our visual analysis, we then analyzed the areas with the greatest change against education and income using 2010 U.S. Census data to determine if correlations exist.

Statistical analysis shows a very weak correlation on income and education levels. We would surmise from prior work that newspapers continue to thrive best in communities that are able to support a robust marketplace of goods and services, that is, higher household income, or communities with residents who have achieved higher levels of education. Since 2007, however, the decline in newspaper coverage has crossed income and education level boundaries. And it demonstrates that daily print newspapers, as a medium, will continue to erode even within regions with growing populations that hold desirable education and income levels to support a commercial media model.

DISCUSSION

This research has focused on developing and applying a visual methodology to monitor the community news and information ecosystem at the local level. It is important to note that the presence of a daily newspaper is not a reflection of the quality or quantity of local news and information in a local ecosystem. Despite widespread talk of a shift to digital, the 2015 Pew State of the News Media report states most newspaper readership continues to be in print; 56 percent of those who consume a newspaper read it exclusively in print. Local news matters deeply to the lives of residents (Pew Research Center 2015). Our mapping shows that while a one-year drop in circulation may seem insignificant, over time we see significant changes to the geography of local news ecosystems.

The Media Deserts Project will allow us to monitor the health of these media ecosystems and will provide a valuable tool in policy and resource allocation. The project will become much richer as we add additional data layers such as community newspapers, weekly and alternative news publications, a network analysis of news sites including hyperlocal online news sites and other media distributors, such as broadband and broadcast technologies, that address the conduit level of our methodology. Additional research methods such as survey research would help us measure public perceptions and sentiment about changing media access. Ethnographic and content analysis work, such as Ferrier 2013, can help us understand what news and information is available at the local level. Finally, we also seek to relate the local news conditions we are mapping to other indicators of well-functioning democracies such as voting patterns or community engagement.

Our data from this type of analysis might match local conditions to successful potential interventions. It also might inform local decision-making between community residents, existing news, and information distributors, and community foundation partners on regional communication strategies. Communities might innovate with demonstration projects that explore different business models such as nonprofit investigative news or cooperative, community-owned media. We suggest monitoring these models, analyzing the community needs and measuring the success of interventions expressed through visualizations like ours. At a minimum, our model helps visually tell the story of the decline of the daily newspaper at the start of the twenty-first century and the communities most affected by this change.

REFERENCES

Barlow, Mike. 2014. *Data visualization: A new language for storytelling.* O'Reilly Media. Sebastopol, CA.

Bohman, James. 2004. Expanding dialogue: The Internet, the public sphere and prospects for transnational democracy. *The Sociological Review* 52: 131–155. doi:10.1111/j.1467-954X.2004.00477.x.

De Tocqueville, Alexis. 1835/1997. *Democracy in America,* vol. 1. The Library of America. Last modified February 8, 2013. http://Gutenberg.org/files/815/815-h/815-h.htm.

Deifell, Tony. 2009. The big thaw: Charting a new future for journalism. *The Media Consortium.* http://www.themediaconsortium.org/thebigthaw/download/.

Dolezal, Lauren (ed.). 2010. Brave news worlds: Navigating the new media landscape. International Press Institute Report.

Fancher, Michael R. 2011. *Re-imaginingjJournalism: Local news for a networked world, a white paper on recommendations 1 and 3 of the Knight Commission on the information needs of communities in a democracy.* The Aspen Institute.

Ferrier, Michelle. 2013. Hyperlocal online news: Are they meeting community news and information needs? *Wiki,* March 17. http://hyperlocalonlinenews.wikispaces.com.

Ferrier, Michelle. 2014. *The media deserts project: Monitoring community news and information needs using geographic information system technologies.* Paper presented at the AEJMC Midwinter Conference, University of Oklahoma, February 2014.

Friedland, Lewis, Philip Napoli, Katherine Ognyanova, Carola Weil, and Ernest J. Wilson III. 2012. *Review of the literature regarding critical information needs of the American public.* Washington, DC: Federal Communications Commission.

Gonzalez, Juan, and Joseph Torres. 2011. *News for all the people: The epic story of race and the American media.* New York: Verso.

Gray, Jonathan, Liliana Bounegru, and Lucy Chambers. 2012. *The data journalism handbook*. O'Reilly Media.
Herzog, David. 2003. *Mapping the news: Case studies in GIS and journalism*. Redlands: ESRI Press.
Knight Commission on the Information Needs of Communities in a Democracy. 2009. *Informing communities: Sustaining democracy in the digital age*. Last modified April 7, 2010. http://www.knightcomm.org/read-the-report-and-comment/.
Lessig, Lawrence. 2002. *The future of ideas: The fate of the commons in a connected world*. New York: Vintage Books.
Marketing Charts. 2012. *Newspaper Ad expenditures continued fall in '11*. Last modified March 16. http://www.marketingcharts.com/print/newspaper-ad-expenditures-continued-fall-in-11-21519/.
Miller, Greg. 2014. The speedy cartographers who map the news for the New York Times. *Wired*, October 23. Available at http://www.wired.com/2014/10/new-york-times-maps.
Monmonier, Mark. 1989. *Maps with the news: The development of American journalistic cartography*. Chicago: University of Chicago Press.
Monmonier, Mark. 2009. Maps in journalism. In *Encyclopedia of Journalism*. Thousand Oaks: Sage Publications, Inc.
Morgan, Fiona, and Allie Perez. 2010. *An information community case study: The research triangle, North Carolina*. New America Foundation, Release 1.2, September 16, 2010. Available at http://newamerica.net/publications/policy/the_research_triangle_north_carolina.
Napoli, Phillip, Sarah Stonbely, Kathleen McCollough, and Bryce Renninger. 2015. *Assessing the health of local journalism ecosystems: A comparative analysis of three New Jersey Communities*. A report prepared for the Democracy Fund, the Geraldine R. Dodge Foundation, and the John S. and James L. Knight Foundation, June 2015.
NewspaperLayoffs.com. 2008. *Paper cuts: Buyouts and layoffs in the newspaper industry*. Accessed October 24 at http://newspaperlayoffs.com.
Pew Research Center. 2015. *Local news in a digital age*. Created March 5, 2015. http://www.journalism.org/2015/03/05/local-news-in-a-digital-age/.
Pew Research Center's Project for Excellence in Journalism. 2013. *The state of the News Media: An annual report on American journalism 2013*. Available at http://www.stateofthemedia.org/2013/.
Pew Research Center's Project for Excellence in Journalism. 2015. *The state of the news media: An annual report on American journalism 2015*. Available at http://www.journalism.org/2015/04/29/state-of-the-news-media-2015/.
Purves, Ross, and Christopher Jones. 2011. Geographic information retrieval. *SIGSPATIAL Special* 3(2): 2–4.
Shane, Peter M. 2011. Finding information pathways to community inclusion. *Nieman Reports* 65(2): 19–21.

Sinha Gaurav, Kronenfeld, Barry J., and Brunskill Jeffrey C. 2015. Toward democratization of geographic information: GIS, remote sensing and GNSS applications in everyday life. In *Remote sensing handbook (Volume I): Data
characterization, classification, and accuracies: Advances of last 50 years and a
vision for the future*, ed. P.S. Thenkabail. Boca Raton: Taylor and Francis.

The Chicago Community Trust and The John S. and James L. Knight Foundation.
2010a. *Realizing potential: What Chicago's online innovators need*. September.

The Chicago Community Trust and The John S. and James L. Knight Foundation.
2010b. *The new news 2010: Mapping Chicago's online news scene*. September.

Thorson, Esther, and Eric Newton. 2008. *Indexing community information needs
in a democracy*. Available at http://www.docstoc.com/docs/164567409/
Checklist-for-Community-Information-Needs-in-a-Democracy.

United States Postal Service (USPS) Office of Inspector General. 2013. *The untold
story of the ZIP code*. Report Number: RARC-WP-13-0062013. Available at
http://permanent.access.gpo.gov/gpo47009/rarc-wp-13-006.pdf.

Waldman, Steven. 2011. *The information needs of communities: The changing
media landscape in a broadband age*. FCC Working Group on the Information
Needs of Communities, June 9.

Preface: Net Neutrality Is Not Enough

We have titled this section "Net neutrality is not enough" to bring the reader's attention to the hard limits of reliance upon one policy mechanism as a solution to our current and future communication problems. There have been few more positive examples of American democracy in action than when millions of Americans participated in the Federal Communication Commission's (FCC's) 2015 deliberation over whether to reverse itself and treat advanced telecommunication service (a.k.a. broadband) as a telecommunication service. A key argument by the opponents of this re-classification was that the FCC was violating the First Amendment rights of the telecommunication companies/internet service providers. Another argument is that Metcalfe's law (that the value of a telecommunications network is proportional to the square of the number of connected users of the system) has clearly been realized, and increased government oversight would only interfere with the naturally virtuous relationship between the market and digital technology.

Mark Lloyd and Michael Park demonstrate that the Constitution (and a clear-eyed examination of the First Amendment as practiced) actually compels government oversight of our media ecology. Ernest J. Wilson III, Sasha Constanza-Chock, and Michelle Forelle show that the exponential benefits claimed for network inclusion also work in reverse—when whole communities are excluded they can become even more isolated from the means to meet their basic needs, and the isolation of these communities erodes network benefits for all.

More than a few of our contributors have suggested that regulations requiring a net neutrality (what the FCC calls "open internet" rules) will not be sufficient to address the communication crisis facing all American communities, and more than a few of our contributors have turned to public media as a solution. Wick Rowland provides us with a hard look at the challenges the USA has yet to address in establishing a public media service that can realistically meet the communication crisis in America. And Dharma Daily and Kate Starbird bring us a real-world example of a rural community confronting a natural disaster—it is clear evidence of both policy failure and human resourcefulness.

The Constitutional Case for Addressing Critical Information Needs

Mark Lloyd and Michael Park

INTRODUCTION

The government has a duty to protect the public. Whether we are under attack by terrorists or our fellow Americans, our local, state, and federal representatives have a duty to keep us reasonably safe. This duty, in practice and in court decisions, overrides the simplistic notion some hold that the free speech clause of the First Amendment prohibits government interference with speech. If government action requires curtailing or promoting speech to keep the public safe, this duty supersedes limits on government abridgement of speech. Indeed, the core purpose of constitutional speech protection is to promote speech that keeps the public safe and keeps our democratic form of government sound.

All Americans must have reasonable access to information about a hurricane and how best to survive it. Even the poorest and most vulnerable citizen in a democracy should have access to information about the safety of their food and water. Information about a hurricane or tsunami

M. Lloyd (✉)
University of Southern California, Los Angeles, CA, USA

M. Park
Assistant Professor of Communication at the S.I. Newhouse, School of Public Communications, Syracuse University, Syracuse, NY, USA

© The Editor(s) (if applicable) and The Author(s) 2016   235
M.I. Lloyd, L.A. Friedland (eds.), *The Communication Crisis in America, And How to Fix It*, DOI 10.1057/978-1-349-94925-0_15

or nuclear meltdown are the easiest cases. But the case can also be made regarding the "forced speech" warnings about the less immediate potential dangers of tobacco or pesticides.

The government also has a duty to maintain a democratic form of government. In other words, a primary responsibility of a democratic republic is to maintain a democratic republic: a government where the ultimate decisions about policy and power belong to the sovereign citizen. Decision-making in our republic is not, and has never been, simply about voting, nor is it solely about the right to petition the government or to learn what our representatives are doing. What Richard John (2012) calls the "civic mandate of communication" was, at least for the founding generation, at its core about government facilitation of the democratic deliberation of citizens.

The founding generation established a postal service quite unlike any delivery service created before; the post offices and post roads were not built to promote commerce, or to issue edicts from the empire, or even to fund government operations. When they enacted the Postal Service Act of 1792, the founding generation subsidized the distribution of newspapers to protect the deliberative nature of the unique form of government they put in motion. This fundamental constitutional duty of government to advance civic discussion has not faded with time.

For purposes of public safety and civic discourse, the government has a duty to establish policy to protect the critical information needs of the public. The right to be informed is a constitutional right.

The Equal Protection Clause of the 14th Amendment provides additional support for the argument that the government must be involved in promoting the speech rights of *all* citizens. If the founders turned a blind eye to addressing the challenges of political inequality, the generation that preserved the nation after the Civil War amended the Constitution to begin to remedy this problem. The Fourteenth Amendment is the constitutional support for the proposition that the wealthy should not be the only citizens with the power to access information to keep them safe or to participate effectively as citizens who matter in our society.

The government has a constitutional duty to address the vestiges of the oppression of so-called minorities in America and the historically second-class citizenship status of women reflected in our communication ecology.

However, the troubled history of censorship in the USA teaches us that government action intended to protect the public, or to protect our form of government, may conflict with the legitimate speech rights of the public. Simply asserting a government duty to protect the public is insufficient. The Supreme Court has established a standard that government must meet when it creates law or regulation that may intrude on the speech rights of the public. It is the same standard the Court uses in determining whether policies to address inequality violate equal protection law. Known as strict scrutiny, the standard is seemingly straightforward: (1) the government must establish a compelling governmental interest, and (2) it must use a narrowly tailored means to advance that interest.

In this short chapter, we argue that addressing the critical information needs of the diverse American public is a compelling governmental interest, and that a fuller appreciation of the local media ecology provides regulators with the tools to narrowly tailor policy to meet the governmental duty to protect the public. Part I of this chapter will trace the historical underpinnings of the US Constitution's embrace of the duty to protect citizens and will show how that duty is advanced in the modern government in the area of speech. Part II will explain why strict scrutiny is not fatal to government policies focused on the provision of critical information needs to the diverse US public. This chapter will conclude with a suggestion of narrowly tailored policies.

Part I. Government's Duty to Preserve Our Republic and to Protect the Public

The free speech clause of the First Amendment is often understood as an individual right against government coercion or compelled speech, protecting the rights of a speaker when the government attempts to silence the speaker because of the content of what the speaker is saying. But we must remember that the objectives of the Constitution (and the Bill of Rights) are tied to the creation of a republic—a form of government in which citizens share sovereign authority and participate in the creation of public policy. The Constitution begins with "We the People," cementing the directive that the people of the USA shall be self-governed. That sovereignty, that revolutionary notion of self-governance, was what the founding generation called liberty.

Liberty is at risk when democratic deliberation is restricted by private interests. As Cass Sunstein (1993) notes, if people are unaware of the consequences of their choices, "they are, to that extent, less free" (655). U.S. Supreme Court Justice Stephen Breyer (2005) reminds us that "liberty" means not only freedom from government coercion or from a despotic government, but also freedom to participate in collective power, the sharing of sovereign authority among the nation's people. Justice Breyer contends that constitutional interpretation and application should take greater account of the Constitution's democratic nature (i.e. participatory self-government and democratic deliberation) when courts interpret the Constitution (2005, 5). Since sovereignty rests in citizens, information about public issues, proposed policies, social and personal risks, and information by, for, and about citizens, concerning the consequences of their choices is critical to a democratic republic (Sunstein 1985).

Moreover, the initial conception of liberty in American constitutional thought was not freedom from responsibility or freedom to consume, or the negative freedom from government interference—liberty was a freedom to participate, and it was also freedom from fear, the freedom that comes with the protection of individual rights under law (Heyman 1991).

The Framers of the Constitution shared the view that government was formed to protect the life, liberty, and property of its citizens ... and they understood that to mean protection not just against government, but protection against fellow citizens. As Stephen Heyman notes, in the Federalist papers, James Madison wrote the "protection" of "the faculties of men," and of "the rights of property" to which these faculties give rise, "is the first object of government." (Heyman 1991, 524). The Constitution is not "a charter of negative liberties" but a charter infused with the positive protection of rights by the community through the Privileges or Immunities, Due Process, and Equal Protection Clauses (Heyman 1991). Liberty is dependent on the public receiving information about public affairs in order to make informed decisions about the important issues of the day, who to vote for, but also how to protect themselves and their property if at risk. And, once again, the risk was not only government, but also foreign and domestic threats ... and, once again, this sometimes meant overriding private interests.

The establishment of the Postal Service with the Postal Act of 1792 was a clear realization of this duty to inform and protect liberty. The Postal Act provided huge subsidies for the transmission of newspapers, along with the creation of postal routes to expand the communications network to ensure that the people of the newly established republic would be informed about public affairs. Congress imposed higher postal rates for business and personal use in order to subsidize lower rates for newspapers. Congress created protections against mail surveillance, and, later, protection against fraudulent activity through the mail.

The American approach was rooted in the founders' belief that a republic, or what Madison called a "popular government," needed to both facilitate democratic deliberation and to protect the public. Subsidies for the press were predicated on a Madisonian vision of participatory self-government by an informed public. Privacy protections were premised upon an understanding that it is the government's affirmative responsibility to protect core freedoms from government and private interests.

If the founders postal subsidies (many still in effect) reflect a foundational approach to "free speech," then modern concerns with the inadequate dissemination of information about public affairs should prompt a government response to advance that "originalist" goal of access to critical civic information.

This goal was emphasized in the 1945 U.S. Supreme Court case Associated Press v. United States, 326 U.S. 1 (1945), where Justice Hugo Black wrote that the same core values of the First Amendment, which limited the government from stifling the dissemination of information, also gave the government the means to regulate private interests when those interests interfered with "the widest possible dissemination of information from diverse and antagonistic sources" (20). In Associated Press, the Court abridged the power of an influential corporation, which used its monopoly to limit access to information and created barriers of entry toward other news groups. The Associated Press asserted a right to limit access to its members on First Amendment grounds. The Supreme Court, however, disagreed, and held that the Associated Press was using its monopoly power to inhibit competition in the gathering and reporting of news. Justice Black's opinion emphasized that the government had a duty to restrain the speech activity of a private corporation if that activity interfered with the public's right to access the widest possible dissemination of information.

Black's emphasis of the public's speech rights as compared to the rights of corporations was repeated in the Supreme Court case upholding the Federal Communication Commission's enforcement of the Fairness Doctrine. In the words of a united Court:

> [T]he people as a whole retain their interest in free speech by radio and their collective right to have the medium function consistently with the ends and purposes of the First Amendment. It is the right of the viewers and listeners, not the right of the broadcasters, which is paramount. It is the purpose of the First Amendment to preserve an uninhibited marketplace

of ideas in which truth will ultimately prevail, rather than to countenance monopolization of that market, whether it be by the Government itself or a private licensee. It is the right of the public to receive suitable access to social, political, esthetic, moral, and other ideas and experiences which is crucial here Red Lion Broadcasting Co. (1969).

Despite the recent abandonment of the Fairness Doctrine, and the Robert's Court elevation of corporations to the status of citizens in the case Citizens United (2010), both the Federal Communications Commission (FCC) and the Federal Election Commission (FEC) continue to "abridge" speech to promote fair democratic deliberation. Both the equal time and reasonable access regulations continue to be enforced by the FCC (Fleming 2012 and 1934 Communications Act 2006). And a large majority of the current justices continue to support the FEC's regulation of campaign contributions and the extensive disclosure ("forced speech") requirements imposed on both candidates and contributors (Levitt 2010). The public's right to a fair campaign is more important than unabridged speech according to the ultimate authority on the meaning of the Constitution.

Protecting democratic deliberation is not the only area where constitutional support is found to abridge speech. The government has long abridged speech that harmed commercial activity. Fraud, including fraud via the mail, was generally considered a violation of common law and a state, rather than a federal, concern. However, the first federal mail fraud legislation was adopted in 1872 when Congress made it a crime to mail material intended to put into effect "any scheme or artifice to defraud." The Mail Fraud Act survived constitutional challenge in Badders v. United States, 240 U.S. 391 (1916). The Court held that Congress has the authority to regulate the act of mailing a letter, and to prohibit any act of mailing "done in furtherance of a scheme that [Congress] regards as contrary to public policy."

In addition to mail fraud and the anti-competition rules noted in the Hammond chapter (Chapter 10) regarding the Justice Department and the Federal Trade Commission, the U.S. Food and Drug Administration of the Department of Health and Human Services, the Occupational Safety and Health Administration (OSHA) of the Department of Labor, and other government agencies have long compelled speech and punished speech to protect consumers.

The regulation of speech regarding food and drugs in the USA has a long history, but a clear mark was set on June 30, 1906, with the original

Pure Food and Drug Act passed by Congress and signed by President Theodore Roosevelt. That act prohibited misbranded and adulterated foods, drinks, and drugs in interstate commerce. Since then, Congress has abridged the speech of the food and drug industry regarding thousands of products, including milk, meat, tea, sleeping pills, saccharin, contraceptives, dietary supplements, soda pop, and the list goes on.

In 1970, the US Congress and President Richard Nixon created OSHA. In addition to requiring employers to provide workers with a workplace that does not have serious hazards, Congress abridged the speech of employers by requiring that employers must: (1) prominently display the official OSHA Job Safety and Health "It's the Law" poster, which describes employee rights and employer responsibilities; (2) inform workers about chemical hazards through training, labels, alarms, color-coded systems, chemical information sheets, and other methods; and (3) post OSHA citations and injury and illness data where workers can see them.

In 1984, thousands died when a toxic chemical leaked from a Union Carbide plant in Bhopal, India. In 1985, another leak occurred, this time at a Union Carbide plant near Charleston, West Virginia (Franklin 1985). In response, Congress passed and President Ronald Reagan signed the Emergency Planning and Community Right-to-Know Act (EPCRA 1986). EPCRA abridges free speech by requiring reporting by private industry of information on the uses (and any release) of chemicals into the environment. Under OSHA regulations, all employers must keep a material safety data sheet (MSDS) regarding any hazardous chemicals stored or used in the workplace. Approximately half a million products used in the workplace require an MSDS.

To ensure that communities are prepared to respond to potential chemical accidents, each state is required to establish a State Emergency Response Commission (SERC). The SERC designates local emergency planning districts and appoints, supervises, and coordinates the work of a Local Emergency Planning Committee (LEPC). The LEPC must, in turn, develop an emergency response plan. The emergency response plan must: (1) identify affected facilities and transportation routes, (2) describe emergency notification and response procedures, (3) designate community and facility emergency coordinators, (4) describe methods to determine whether a chemical release occurred and its extent, (5) identify available personnel and equipment needed to respond, (6) provide evacuation plans, (7) describe training and practice programs and schedules, and (8) detail methods and schedules for executing the plan.

Only the most extreme "free speech" advocates argue that our government has no right to prevent or compel speech to protect the public or a functioning democracy.

PART II. PROTECTING THE PUBLIC AND PRESERVING OUR REPUBLIC PASS STRICT SCRUTINY

Government reluctance to address communication inequality is, at least in part, the result of a fear to confront strict judicial scrutiny. However, strict scrutiny is not fatal to either government abridgement of speech or to government efforts to protect the interests of those Americans who have been historically marginalized (Abrams 2015). Adam Winkler calls Gerald Gunther's memorable phrase (that strict scrutiny is "strict" in theory but fatal in fact) a "popular myth." In 2006, Winkler published an empirical analysis of all strict scrutiny cases in federal courts between 1990 and 2003 and found that government action survived strict scrutiny 30 percent of the time, with equal protection cases surviving at a rate of 27 percent and free speech cases surviving at a rate of 22 percent (Winkler 2006). While strict scrutiny is not fatal, government actors are wise to be cautious in establishing policy that may need to reach over such a high bar.

Frankly, the courts have been less than clear about what it takes to meet the first part of strict scrutiny (Bagshaw 2013; Sheppard 1994). What constitutes a compelling governmental interest? In Morse v. Frederick, 551 U.S. 393 (2007), the Court found that the protection of the school environment from even opaque student references to drugs (i.e. "Bong Hits for Jesus") was a compelling government interest. Creating incentives for prisoners was a compelling interest in Beard v. Banks, 548 U.S. 521 (2006) and avoiding the appearance of judicial impartiality was a compelling state interest in Williams-Yulee v. Florida Bar, No. 13-1499, (2015). Surely, if these examples meet the compelling state interest test, protecting the public's access to information about a tornado or information about their elected representative's actions constitute a compelling state interest.

The second prong of strict scrutiny—narrowly tailoring—is also the subject of considerable legal confusion. Although not uniformly applied, narrow tailoring analysis in strict scrutiny generally applies at least three elements: (1) Is the regulation over-inclusive, meaning it restricts more speech than necessary to achieve its goal? (2) Is the regulation under-inclusive; that is, does it fail to regulate speech that would be as harmful to the government's interest in the speech at issue? (3) Does the regulation use the "least restrictive means" possible to satisfy the state's interest?

But as Justice Harry Blackmun has noted, "a judge would be unimaginative indeed if he could not come up with something a little less 'drastic' or a little less 'restrictive' in almost any situation, and thereby enable himself to vote to strike legislation down Illinois State Bd. (1979)."

Perhaps the most serious problem with "narrow tailoring" in strict scrutiny analysis is that there seems to be no explicit criteria for the range of alternatives to contrast with the contested regulation (Bunker and Erickson 2001). The genesis of the contrast space notion is found in Alan Garfinkel's *Forms of Explanation: Rethinking the Questions in Social Theory* (1981). Other scholarly treatments of issues surrounding narrow tailoring include Ian Ayres (1996) and R. George Wright (1997). In general, courts have been more receptive to non-speech methods as less restrictive alternatives to direct speech regulation. For example, in Ashcroft v. ACLU, 535 U.S. 564 (2002), the Supreme Court found that Internet filtering software installed by parents was less restrictive than the Child Online Protection Act, which attempted to criminalize speech on the Internet deemed harmful to minors Morris et al. (2009). However, in Action for Children's Television v. FCC, 58 F.3d 654 (D.C. Cir. 1995), the court did not even consider non-speech alternatives, such as the V-Chip, as a contrast to the congressional mandate of a safe-harbor period for broadcast indecency United States v. Playboy (2000).

To be safe, policymakers should at least consider content neutral options rather than any direct regulation of speech. Structural policies, such as placing limits on media ownership and/or enabling other interests (such as historically marginalized groups or speakers not supported by advertising) to speak, are content neutral means to address the government obligation to promote the delivery of critical information to all Americans. In order to inform what content-neutral rules need to be established, the government must conduct smarter more inclusive research to identify where local media ecologies fail to provide critical information to all members of the local community.

Whether to protect and advance First Amendment (free speech) goals or Fourteenth Amendment (equal protection) goals, the judiciary has not been consistent (or in some cases comprehensible) in applying strict scrutiny. But then, even Supreme Court justices are only human. Epstein et al. (2013) examined all the Supreme Court cases touching on free speech from 1953 through 2010, and concluded that neither liberal nor conservative justices were particularly "attached to the First Amendment" and that "the justices' votes tend to reflect their preferences toward the expresser (or expression), and not solely an underlying taste for the First Amendment qua Amendment." And more than one student of the Supreme Court has concluded that the current majority of justices are simply not to be trusted regarding the application of equal protection law, and that those decisions that touch on the rights of women and "minorities" should be left to others (Sunstein 1996; Tushnet 2000).

And, yet, while fully aware of the challenges of the current Court, we do not offer here a mere critique. The communications crisis we face is too great to simply ignore the Court that we have. With a focus on the critical information needs of *all* Americans (not just women and minorities), and a goal of finding content neutral means to promote the diverse dissemination of such information, the federal government can meet any reasonable application of strict scrutiny.

The federal government has a duty to advance a communications ecology that promotes the accessibility of critical information to the diverse American public ... this is a compelling state interest. Meeting this compelling state interest can be done by promoting the active participation of a diverse American public in all media platforms, by promoting a more robust public broadcasting service responsible not to commercial interest but to community need, and by monitoring whether our local communications ecologies continue to serve the critical information needs of the public despite the rapid changes in technologies and market behavior. What is proposed is thus content neutral and cognizant of the need to advance more speech from more Americans, rather than curtailing speech from any group or class of society. This approach is in line with prior strict scrutiny review of both free speech and equal protection law ... even accepting the limits of a biased or blind judiciary.

CONCLUSION

The free speech and equal protection clauses of the Constitution suggest that protecting those most disadvantaged members of the public is of particular importance under the Constitution. At least one First Amendment jurist suggests that the very essence of the free speech in America conveys to the public a right to "the widest possible dissemination of information from diverse and antagonistic sources" (Associated Press).

In the face of arguments about government intrusion trampling the free speech rights of broadcasters, the FCC has abdicated its responsibility to properly protect the First Amendment rights of the public. The Commission has failed to meet the core legislative rationale for federal regulation of the electromagnetic spectrum: "to make available, so far as possible, to all the people of the United States, without discrimination on the basis of race, color, religion, national origin, or sex, a rapid, efficient, Nationwide, and world-wide wire and radio communication service with adequate facilities at reasonable charges, for the purpose of the national defense, for the purpose of promoting safety of life and property through the use of wire and radio communication 1934 Communications Act 2006."

But the FCC is not alone. The federal government as a whole has failed to protect the constitutional right of citizens to a democratic republic and has failed to establish a means to communicate with the American public in the event of an attack or an environmental disaster. The proliferation of new communication technologies, which are subject to limited government oversight in terms of content, is not an argument against clear, enforceable regulation or greater support for publicly funded media. The chaos of today's media ecology is actually an argument for smarter, narrowly tailored policies that promote information availability. This is not an argument against the value of promoting a competitive and innovative communications market, nor is it an argument against the legitimate free speech rights of even the most hateful broadcasters. Promoting the widest possible access to and participation in communication is a core constitutional goal; and that goal, combined with a compelling governmental interest to promote public safety and foster civic engagement, is paramount.

REFERENCES

Abrams, Floyd. 2015. Symposium: When strict scrutiny ceased to be strict. *SCOTUSblog*, April 30. http://www.scotusblog.com/2015/04/symposium-when-strict-scrutiny-ceased-to-be-strict/.

Action for Children's Television v. Federal Communications Commission, 58 F.3d 654 (D.C. Cir. 1995).

Ashcroft v. American Civil Liberties Union, 535 U.S. 564 (2002).

Associated Press v. United States, 326 U.S. 1 (1945).

Ayers, Ian. 1996. Narrow tailoring. *UCLA Law Review* 43: 1781–1829.

Bagshaw, Timothy M. 2013. Phantom standard: Compelling state interest analysis and political ideology in the affirmative action context. *Utah Law Review* 1: 409–435.

Beard v. Banks, 548 U.S. 521 (2006).

Breyer, Stephen. 2005. *Active liberty: Interpreting our democratic constitution*. New York: Vintage Books.

Bunker, Matthew D., and Emily Erickson. 2001. The jurisprudence of precision: Contrast space and narrow tailoring in First Amendment doctrine. *Communication Law and Policy* 6(2): 259–285.

Citizens United v. Federal Election Commission, 558 U.S. 310 (2010).

Communications Act of 1934 (as amended), 47 U.S.C. §§ 312(a)(7) and 315(a) (2006).

Emergency Planning and Community Right-to-Know Act. 42 U.S.C. §11001 et seq. (1986).

Epstein, Lee, Christoper M. Parker, and Jeffrey Segal. 2013. Do justices defend the speech they hate? In-group bias, opportunism, and the First Amendment. In *APSA 2013 annual meeting paper*. http://ssrn.com/abstract=2300572.

Fleming, John Stewart. 2012. Renewing the chase: The First Amendment, campaign advertisements, and the goal of an informed citizenry. *Indiana Law Journal* 87: 767.

Franklin, Ben. A. 1985. Toxic cloud leaks at Carbide plant in West Virginia. *The New York Times*, August 12. Accessed October 1, 2015: http://www.nytimes.com/1985/08/12/us/toxic-cloud-leaks-at-carbide-plant-in-west-virginia.html.

Garfinkel, Alan. 1981. Forms of explanation: Rethinking the questions in social theory. *Philosophical Review* 93(1): 116–118.

Heyman, Steven J. 1991. The first duty of government: Liberty and the Fourteenth Amendment. *Duke Law Journal* 41(3): 507–571.

Illinois State Bd. of Elections v. Socialist Workers Party, 440 U.S. 173, 188–89 (1979).

John, Richard R. 2012. From Franklin to Facebook: The civic mandate for communications. In *To promote the general welfare: The case for big government*, ed. Steven Conn, 156–172. New York: Oxford University Press.

Levitt, Justin. 2010. Confronting the impact of 'citizens United'. *Yale Law and Policy Review* 29(1): 217–234. http://www.jstor.org/stable/41308528.

Morris Jr., John B., and Cynthia M. Wong. 2009. Revisiting user control: The emergence and success of a First Amendment theory for the internet age. *First Amendment Law Review* 8: 109.

Morse v. Frederick, 551 U.S. 393 (2007).

Red Lion Broadcasting Co. v. Federal Communications Commission, 395 U.S. 367 (1969).

Sheppard, Stephen M. 1994. The state interest in the good citizen: Constitutional balance between the citizen and the perfectionist state. *Hastings Law Journal* 45: 969–1027.

Sunstein, Cass R. 1985. Interest groups in America public law. *Stanford Law Review 38* Stan. L. Rev. 29 3829–3887.

Sunstein, Cass R. 1993. Informing America: Risk, disclosure, and the First Amendment. *Florida State University Law Review* 20(3): 653–677.
Sunstein, Cass R. 1996. Public deliberation, affirmative action, and the Supreme Court. *California Law Review* 84(4): 1179–1199.
Tushnet, Mark. 2000. *Taking the constitution away from the courts,* 154–176. Princeton: Princeton University Press.
United States v. Playboy Entertainment Group, 529 U.S. 803 (2000).
Williams-Yulee v. Florida Bar, No. 13–1499 (2015).
Winkler, Adam. 2006. Fatal in theory and strict in fact: An empirical analysis of strict scrutiny in the federal courts. *Vanderbilt Law Review* 59: 793.
Wright, George R. 1997. The fourteen faces of narrowness: How courts legitimize what they do. *Loyola Law Review* 31: 167–212.

CHAPTER 16

A Provocation on Behalf of the Excluded

Ernest J. Wilson III, Sasha Costanza-Chock,
and Michelle C. Forelle

INTRODUCTION

"Black Lives Matter!" These three words, chanted at street protests and direct actions, printed on posters and t-shirts, and spread across platforms by activists from the #BlackLivesMatter movement, have reignited a broad, sustained, public conversation about race in the USA (Garza 2014). Activists with #BlackLivesMatter use every medium necessary, from the latest social media tools to stickers and banner drops, from podcasts and live streams to traditional documentaries and op-eds, to draw attention to the persistence of structural, institutional, organizational, and interpersonal racism. This form of highly mediated multiplatform activism has been described as *transmedia organizing*, and it is the emerging norm in our converged, networked media ecology (Costanza-Chock 2014). #BlackLivesMatter has emphatically demonstrated the political possibilities of sustained cross-platform intervention; however, in this chapter, we

E.J. Wilson III (✉) • M.C. Forelle
University of Southern California, Los Angeles, CA, USA

S. Costanza-Chock
Massachusetts Institute of Technology, Cambridge, MA, USA

249
M.I. Lloyd, L.A. Friedland (eds.), *The Communication Crisis in America,*
And How to Fix It, DOI 10.1057/978-1-349-94925-0_16

will describe the ways that systematic digital inequality structured by race and class continues to pose an acute problem for our polity.

In 2011, in a chapter in the edited volume *Race After the Internet*, Wilson and Costanza-Chock analyzed a shift in the early 2000s by scholars, policymakers, and the popular press away from the discourse of the "digital divide."[1] The Bush administration's reframing of "digital inclusion," combined with the dot-com boom and bust, largely eliminated the streams of funding, research, and policymaking that had been geared toward overcoming digital inequality in the USA. This shift also obfuscated the real costs of exclusion from networked communication, and prevented the research and implementation of policies that might attempt to address the needs of the most vulnerable members of our society.

In the five years since that chapter, the media ecology has become more complex, but the costs of exclusion remain dire. Research continues to show that People of Color (POC)[2] remain underrepresented in every media platform, according to nearly every available metric: ownership, employment, standing (frequency of quotation or position as a source of expert knowledge), representation, access to connectivity, and so on (Friedland et al. 2012; Sandoval 2009; American Society of News Editors 2014; Butler 2012). Platform-by-platform data about racial/ethnic inequality are not encouraging; additionally, this approach to understanding the dynamics of exclusion is limited by compartmentalization. In order to paint a full picture of the costs of exclusion borne by POC, we must understand our media as a converged system (Jenkins 2006), a broader media ecology made of networked nodes rather than distinct silos.

In the pages that follow, we argue that a media-ecology approach is more consistent with people's lived experiences, whether they are POC or otherwise. Using this approach, we can understand the media ecology as a network within which representation, ownership, employment, and access all play a role. We can also use the Wilson–Tongia formulation (Wilson and Costanza-Chock 2011) to illustrate the urgency of studying and addressing the costs of exclusion from the media ecology, not only the benefits of inclusion.

The U.S. Census reports that minorities, now 38 percent of the US population, are expected to become the majority in 2044, with the nation projected to be 56 percent minority in 2060 (Colby and Ortman 2015). Yet race-based inequality persists across all sectors of our society, including our media ecology, where white people continue to dominate ownership, employment, representation, and access. Racial inequality across the converged media ecology contributes to the reproduction of both explicit racial stereotypes and implicit racial bias, as well as limiting the diversity of information and viewpoints available to audiences. Both of these, in turn, make it difficult, or impossible, for the USA as a nation to openly discuss the legacy and continued persistence of structural, institutional, and inter-personal racism, and contribute to broken policies in areas such as mass incarceration and policing (Alexander 2012), education (the school-to-prison pipeline) (Kim et al. 2012), housing, employment, and beyond.

DIVERSITY IN MEDIA OWNERSHIP AND EMPLOYMENT ACROSS PLATFORMS

We hold media access, ownership, employment, and representation as equally important, parallel dynamics. In print and broadcast media, access is near universal, representation is deeply unequal but arguably is improv-ing (not everyone agrees; for example, Herman Gray (2013) describes a crisis of *over-* and *mis- representation* of black bodies in US mass media), and yet ownership and employment metrics are abysmal, and not improv-ing. The concern is not simply whether Americans can read, hear, or watch print or broadcast media, but whether what they are reading, hearing, or watching is representative of the diverse issues and viewpoints to which their communities need access in order to be fully informed citizens; whether they have the opportunity to produce, create, and narrate their own stories; and who owns, controls, and profits from those stories. (We also need to explore whether the relationship between ownership, person-nel, and content production in legacy media carries into the digital world.)

Measuring media diversity to the satisfaction of the courts and the legis-lature remains a struggle (Forelle 2015). There is a robust body of literature that indicates that where there are POC and/or women-owned stations, or where the employment rates of POC in a station are high, those stations are more likely to produce content that better represents the concerns of POC (Bachen et al. 1999; Turner 2007; Kim 2012; Sandoval 2009). This research demonstrates the need to maintain diversity data about the state of ownership and employment within different broadcast media. Nevertheless, although the Telecommunications Act of 1996 requires the Federal Communications Commission (FCC) to conduct reviews of diver-sity in American mass media every four years, the 2010 review has not, as of the writing of this essay, been completed, leaving media researchers with a dearth of data for analysis. In Tables 16.1 and 16.2 below, we have com-piled the most recent data available through the FCC and various media industry organizations. The lack of an up-to-date and centralized reposi-tory for this data is a major obstacle for researchers and policymakers, one which we address later in our policy recommendations.

MEDIA OWNERSHIP BY RACE/ETHNICITY

These tables (16.1 and 16.2) present a disturbing picture of the state of POC ownership and employment across the media ecology in 2015. What's more, as worrying as these tables are, they only represent a snapshot: When we examine the trends over time, the situation is even more alarming. In nearly all media sectors, ownership by and employment of POC has either plateaued or even begun to decrease. The Radio-Television News Directors Association (RTNDA) reports that, after increasing steadily through the late 1990s, from 17 percent in 1995 to 24 percent in 2008, the percentage of POC employed in the television workforce has plateaued at 21–22 percent; in the radio workforce, numbers have dropped, from 15 percent in 1995 to 10 percent in 2015 (Papper 2015). The American Society of News Editors' (ASNE) 2015 report reveals that, after peaking in 2006 and 2007, the employment of POC in American newsrooms

Table 16.1 Data gathered from: U.S. Census Bureau 2007; Federal Communications Commission 2014; Corporation for Public Broadcasting 2011[a]

	% POC	Year[a]
Print	7.83	2007
Commercial TV	3.5	2013
Commercial radio	4.2	2013
Public broadcasting	2.6	2013
Internet	9.67	2007

[a]Most recent year of available data

Table 16.2 Data gathered from: American Society of News Editors 2014; Papper 2015; and Corporation for Public Broadcasting 2011[b]

	% POC	Year[a]
Print	12.7	2015
Commercial TV	22.2	2015
Commercial radio	9.8	2015
Public TV	22	2012
Public radio	21.5	2012
Internet	20	2014

[a]Most recent year of available data

has since declined. Employment of African Americans dropped from 5.51 percent in 2006 to 4.74 percent in 2015, Asian Americans from 3.15 to 2.8 percent, Hispanics from 4.5 to 4.19 percent, and Native Americans from 0.57 to 0.36 percent (American Society of News Editors 2014). Even if this pattern is miraculously and immediately reversed, and media employment trends return to the slow, long-term improvement in hiring and retention of POC that began in the 1970s, that rate of improvement is so slow that the American mass media would not see racial parity in ownership or employment until 2040—if ever (American Society of News Editors 2014; Wilson and Costanza-Chock 2011).

DIGITAL DIVERSITY?

There exists a broad cultural optimism that the affordances of online media would provide for media equality and diversity that print and broadcast could not—after all, it costs nearly nothing to set up and share your thoughts on a blog, social media account, or YouTube channel. We take a more critical approach and hypothesize that, given the patterns of correlation that have been found between POC ownership/employment and POC-oriented content in print and broadcast media, such correlations may be found in online media as well. In order to begin examining this proposition, we must assess the state of diversity upstream: How diverse is ownership and employment at the websites that make up our online experiences?

Disappointingly, we find that media ownership and employment online remain deeply unequal. In October 2015, Leslie Miley, the only African American engineering manager at Twitter, made headlines with a blog post after leaving his position at the microblogging giant (Miley 2015). In his post, he details his reasons for leaving Twitter, centered on the company's lack of diversity in employment. Miley points out that, despite the fact that African Americans and Hispanics make up more than 30 percent of Twitter's monthly active users in the USA, they represent less than 5 percent of the company's engineering and product management positions.

The problem is not unique to Twitter. According to the *Washington Post*, at Yahoo, African Americans make up only 2 percent of the workforce, and Hispanics just 4 percent. At Facebook, in 2014, only 81 of the company's 5500 employees were African American (Kang and Frankel 2015). Harkinson analyzed 2012 employment data of the top ten Silicon Valley companies and discovered that Hispanics and African Americans comprised only 6 percent and 4 percent of the workforce, respectively (Harkinson 2014). Ownership data in the digital media sector are similarly disappointing: The 2007 Survey of Business Owners (U.S. Census Bureau 2007) reports that 78.56 percent of Internet broadcasting and web portal companies are owned by whites, while 2.7 percent are owned by Hispanics, 5.14 percent by Asians, and 0.19 percent by Native Americans.[3] Part of this problem stems from systematic biases in the venture capitalist groups that fund tech startups. In 2010, 87 percent of venture capital-backed company founders were white; fewer than 1 percent identified as black, and an even smaller proportion identified as Hispanic (CB Insights 2010). The relationships between POC employment and ownership, the production of online content, and the design of online services that specifically address the needs of communities of color are understudied. The experiences of industry insiders like Miley, as well as similar studies in the fields of broadcast and print media, indicate that such research is sorely needed.

Data on digital newsrooms, specifically, are similarly difficult to locate. This is partially due to characteristics of the Internet many consider strengths: its breadth and ease of entry. Simply put, organizations that regularly gather diversity data for print and broadcast journalism have a hard time developing a clear definition of online news, let alone identifying and maintaining online news diversity data (Gold 2013).[4] This dynamism is one of many major shake-ups the Internet has introduced to the world of journalism. The rise of "citizen journalism" has also provided a multitude of new avenues for information and forced the journalism industry, and the public, to reconsider the meaning of journalism (Allan 2009; Shirky 2009; Castells 2007; Schaffer 2007; Gillmor 2006). Again, this is another space that has been critically under-examined by scholars, and in which data, theory, and rigorous analysis are sorely needed.

If ownership and employment remain slippery stats to track online, content downstream is even more elusive. In print and broadcast media, "content" was a fairly narrow category, and largely determined by ownership and employment in those media industries. Online, "content" is a much broader category, including everything from websites, videos, and news articles to private posts on social media sites However, when considering the production of content meant for the digital public sphere (as opposed to content meant for consumption via private networks), research has found persistent class-based gaps, indicating that elite voices continue to dominate the digital commons (Schradie 2011).

Even prior to considerations of ownership, employment, or content diversity lies the question of which individuals or communities are even able to access these new media. Uniquely among the platforms discussed in this chapter, unequal access to the Internet remains an important concern. Although broadband access rates continue to improve, access remains far from universal. In the USA, broadband penetration has reached 70 percent (Pew Research Center 2013). Internet access, and specifically broadband connectivity in the home, has thus moved from a competitive advantage to a competitive necessity. However, a significant gap remains between non-Hispanic white households, 74 percent of which have broadband connectivity; black households, at 62 percent; and Hispanic households, where just over half (56 percent) have broadband (Pew Research Center 2015). There's also a troubling class-based gap: Ninety-one percent of households that make over $75,000 per year have broadband, compared to 52 percent of households that make less than $30,000 per year (Pew Research Center 2015).[5] Furthermore, research has found that Internet use (and non-use) is strongly correlated with age, educational attainment, and household income. The 19 percent of Americans who say they do not use the Internet cite financial obstacles (lack of computer or high cost of Internet access) as the main reason (Zickuhr 2013). These material obstacles, while affecting rates of online content consumption, have an even more significant impact on content production (Schradie 2011).

In sum, then, online media firms, just as print and broadcast media firms, also reflect structural access inequalities and are marked by systematic network exclusion, as well as participation gaps along race, class, and gender lines. We argue that, rather than focusing on the inequalities that exist in each media platform, effective change must embrace an approach that understands inequality as a multilayered, convergent concern.

MEDIA ECOLOGICAL APPROACH

Traditionally, most media scholarship has focused on a particular platform. While this approach has merits, it runs the risk of oversimplification. For one, media ownership structures are very complicated. Media consolidation is a critical concern, and cross-ownership rules are a perennial target of regulatory relaxation for the FCC. In 2007, attempts to loosen the 32-year-old restrictions on owning both a newspaper and a television or radio station in the same city, while passed by the FCC, were struck down by the courts; in 2013, a similar proposal was met with so much opposition, from both media companies and coalitions of grassroots activists, that the commission was forced to withdraw it (Nagesh 2013). In spite of these rules, the consolidation of major media companies and major market shifts (Napoli 2015) have resulted in a dwindling number of sources for print and broadcast media in America. In the 1980s, the majority of media consumed via these platforms in the USA was produced by 50 different companies; by 2012, that number was down to six (Lutz 2012; McChesney 2013). Although the number of media outlets has increased since the 1970s, ownership has become increasingly more concentrated (Gomery 2002).

Other research has shown that media platforms are also increasingly interconnected at the level of content. In 2010, the Pew Research Center's Project for Excellence in Journalism examined the news "ecosystem" of Baltimore and found that, "while the news landscape has rapidly expanded, most of what the public learns is still overwhelmingly driven by traditional media—particularly newspapers" (Pew Research Center 2010). Of the six news narratives they tracked, only 17 percent of the stories produced across media platforms contained new information, 95 percent of which came from traditional media, either in their legacy platforms or in new digital ones (Pew Research Center 2010). This information sharing across platforms indicates that inequalities in one media form may result in echoes of that inequality across others. Another question that then arises is whether those reverberating biases are further exacerbated by ownership or employment inequalities in the platforms they travel through—yet another topic to be taken up by future research.

There are clearly significant concerns across various media platforms regarding access and opportunity for POC. However, the full impact of these inequalities is more than the sum of its parts, since the lived reality of media use takes place in a networked, converged, ecology. While some communities and individuals may rely more on one form of media over another, we all draw information from a networked media ecology where exclusion at each node contributes to harmful exclusion from the network as a whole (Kim and Ball-Rokeach 2006).

In 2012, the University of Southern California, working with researchers from the University of Wisconsin-Madison, Fordham, and other institutions (collectively calling themselves the Communication Policy Research Network) submitted to the FCC an exhaustive literature review that synthesized a number of media ecology theories to argue for the implementation of a new approach to understand how local communication ecologies were serving diverse communities (Friedland et al. 2012; Friedland 2015). The research group concluded that, in order to develop more effective media policy, research must:

> [C]apture the increasingly complex functioning of local media systems in ways that fully account for the role played by *all* relevant stakeholders, the interconnections and interdependencies that exist among media platforms that embed the analysis of media systems within the analysis of the ways different kinds of communities actually function (xi).

As we can see, for many scholars, the future of progressive change in our communications systems must be rooted in an understanding of the full media ecology as a network, the inclusion in or exclusion from which significant consequences can stem. To understand the full implications of exclusion from the media network, we next build off the work of Wilson and Tongia to reframe the emphasis of discussions of access to the network in terms of the costs of network exclusion.

Wilson–Tongia Formulation[6]

The cost of excluding POC from the converged, networked media ecology can be evaluated by both inclusion- and exclusion-based models. Scholarly work on network structure and value tends to focus on the positive values associated with network inclusion. Perhaps the greatest, most-cited example of a model of network inclusion is Metcalfe's Law. In contemporary discourse on the value of communication networks, Metcalfe's Law has become synonymous with connectivity, stating that as more people join a network, the value they add to the network increases exponentially; that is, *the value of the network is proportional to the square number of users*. The underlying mathematics for Metcalfe's law is based on pairwise connections (e.g., telephony). If there are four people with telephones in a network, there are a total of 3 + 2 + 1 = 6 links. Metcalfe's reasoning involves the sum of all possible pairings between nodes, so the value of the network size n is $\dfrac{(n)(n-1)}{2}$, which is often simplified as approaching n^2. With this model, one can evaluate the per person value of inclusion in a network.

If we know the value of a network as per Metcalfe's Law assuming each member is equal (a simplification that is likely to be untrue, but that is a matter for another text), we can calculate the value of inclusion per person. But what of the excluded? Intuitively, as a network grows in size and value, those outside the network face growing disparities. How do we measure these disparities? Using an inclusion-based model, one might decide that the cost of exclusion is simply the difference between the outsiders' value (=0) and the per person value of those included. For example, if Metcalfe's Law has a value approximating n^2, the per person value of inclusion simply approaches $\frac{n^2}{n} = n$. Thus, exclusion would lead to a disparity of n based on the size of the network, which is the difference between the per person value of those inside (=n) and those outside (=0).

What inclusion-based models fail to capture, however, is that any network is of a finite size—if not in theory, then in practice. For example, if we state that our network size is 19, Metcalfe's Law finds a value proportional to $19^2 = 361$, and a per person included value of ~19. Thus, the cost of exclusion from our network with $n = 19$ is also 19 (the difference between 19 and 0, which is the value assigned to those not in the network).

This formulation for calculating the cost of exclusion indicates the same cost regardless of whether the applicable population universe is 20 people or 200 people. However, the cost of exclusion should certainly be different if we have only one excluded person or 181! Therefore, we posit that the cost of exclusion should depend on the number (and/or proportion) of people excluded as well as the size of the network.

And so, we refer to the Wilson–Tongia formulation, which makes the costs of exclusion endogenous by taking the number of people excluded into account in the formulation:

Table 16.3 Wilson–Tongia Formulation

Equation 1: Inclusion-based Framing	Existing Exclusion Cost (i.e., disparity) formulation = per person included value	$\frac{[Network\ Value\ as\ per\ any\ Law]}{Members\ in\ the\ Network\ (=n)}$
Equation 2: Exclusion-based Framing	Proposed Exclusion Cost formulation = total network value divided by number of people excluded	$\frac{[Network\ Value\ as\ per\ any\ Law]}{Members\ outside\ the\ Network\ (=N-n)}$ (Where N = total applicable population)

If we compare the inclusion-based framing to the exclusion-based framing, the ratio of these two formulations is the same for any network law and equal to $\dfrac{n}{N-n}$ where n is the people in the network, and N is the total applicable population size. We can recognize that this ratio is growing, and inclusion and exclusion formulations cross over (are equal) only at $n = (0.5)(N)$. This means that the costs as calculated by exclusion-based formulations become higher as a network (e.g., technology adoption) reaches half of the population (Tongia and Wilson 2011).

In other words, the greater the proportion of people in a population included within and enjoying the benefits of a network, the more quickly the costs of exclusion grow for those excluded from that network. The costs to those who are already in the network of excluding others from the network can also be calculated in this way. A critical issue before us is under what conditions, or in what sequence, do the costs of exclusion become most severe to the excluded (and how might we demonstrate the costs to the included)?

Wilson and Tongia have shown that the severity of exclusion costs shift depending, in part, on the proportion of the population included and excluded, on the differential quality of the "new" network, and on the availability and relative quality of other networks (Tongia and Wilson 2011). Inclusion- and exclusion-based framings are similar in value, up to a point: roughly half the population. *It is precisely when only a minority of the population is not in the network that the costs of exclusion rise dramatically.* When only a few people are members of a network, the exclusion is spread out among the majority of the population but the *advantage* is held by only a few. Once a network includes the majority of the population, the *disadvantage* is held only by a few. In logical terms, for $n < 0.5\,N$, the included have an advantage they share, while for $n > 0.5\,N$, the excluded have a disadvantage they share. In such a formulation, the lowest disparity between frameworks is when $n = 0.5\,N$. When only a small fraction of the population is in the network, the median person in the population is excluded. Hence, inclusion is the exception, and not the norm. When the majority of the population is in the network, exclusion is the exception, and not the norm (Tongia and Wilson 2011).

This has profound implications for how we understand diversity and race-based exclusion from the converged, networked media ecology.

According to all available data about print, broadcast, and online media, POC and low-income people continue to face exclusion from a networked media ecology; and according to the Wilson–Tongia formulation, the costs of that network exclusion—the disadvantages already faced by those excluded from the network—will not only continue to rise, but will increase at an exponential rate.

CONCLUSION AND POLICY RECOMMENDATIONS

Digital media platforms continue to proliferate, but as we have seen, the age-old problems of diversity in ownership, employment, participation, and content can still be found. While some encouraging progress has been made, more must be done before our increasingly multiracial and multicultural society will finally be reflected in the media we produce, circulate, and consume. The Wilson–Tongia formulation allows us to frame the issues of racial exclusion, diversity, and the digital divide in network terms. We maintain that, by considering media as a networked ecology, we gain analytic depth and introduce a set of concepts and theories not typically included in these discussions.

There are, of course, limitations to the network ecology approach. As Watson and Cavanagh point out, a robust network is not necessarily indicative of robust information—a question of quantity versus quality (Watson and Cavanah 2015). More nodes and linkages do not assure that the communities within these networks are getting the critical information they need. However, research indicates that the more POC occupy positions of ownership and employment in these communication nodes, the more likely we are to find content that addresses the particular needs of all of our communities. Furthermore, using the Wilson–Tongia formula, we contend that the quality of information might not matter if those communities are excluded from accessing and/or producing that information in the first place.

We recognize that many of the issues we have surfaced are deeply complex, and will require cooperation between the government, civic organizations, and communities themselves to tackle. This chapter has been an attempt to galvanize research at all levels that takes that cost of exclusion as a central concern, and explore in more detail how exclusion from the multilayered, complex media ecology of a community, city, or nation has exponentially dire consequences for the those who are excluded. Such research is sorely needed to provide activists, community leaders, and policymakers with the data they need to produce the changes we need at the legislative level. We suggest the following as critical first steps that can be taken to provide this information:

- Diversity in digital journalism.
- Critical assessments of POC-oriented content online.
- Silicon Valley diversity at multiple sites: executive, engineering, and community management.
- Funding agencies (National Science Foundation [NSF], National Research Council [NRC], Social Science Research Council [SSRC], and private foundations) should support more empirical investigation and conceptualization into such key issues, as whether the causal relationships between ownership, personnel, and content in the legacy media also obtain in the digital media, where barriers to entry are lower.

As we near the 2016 elections, it is also critical that these issues be brought to the fore, and that the candidates of all parties be made aware of their importance. We need to press for responsible progressive policies that will bring more people greater opportunities to create their own stories, and gain access to the information they need to lead fuller, more meaningful and productive lives as citizens of multiple communities. We offer the following as steps that begin to address this concern:

Media Equity Index

In a converged media ecology, we need better public data on media equity and diversity. Currently, there is no clear, well-maintained, up-to-date, public data on race, ethnicity, and gender in media investment, ownership, employment, and representation. In theory, this dataset should be developed, maintained, and made available and accessible to the public by the FCC, and should be a regular reference point for rulemaking.

Access to Capital for POC-Owned Media Startups Online

We know that most venture capitalists are white and Asian men, and they invest in startups led by people who look like them. We need federal-, state-, and city-level policies to foster innovation in media startups led by POC.

Universal Broadband Access

Given persistent inequality across the media ecology, including broadband access and use, we need renewed attention from policymakers to universal broadband access, with clear targets and implementation strategies based on the assumption that universal access is the goal, and a recognition that the market is not going to get us there on its own.

Additional policies that we believe will further a diverse networked media ecology include e-Rate reform, maintenance of network neutrality, vigilance against additional telco consolidation, and support for municipal broadband, among others.

The Communications Act of 1934 and its subsequent revisions have long upheld the goal of communications policy, through the mission of the FCC, to be the promotion of the public interest, which is fundamentally interpreted to include the pursuit and protection of a diversity of voices in our media to promote a vibrant and healthy democracy. The democratic ideals of our country demand that all individuals have access to the resources they need to become informed participants in American political life. As movements like Black Lives Matter, Occupy Wall Street, and others have shown, this exchange of information and ideas is at its strongest when the communities that have been pushed to the margins have the opportunity to participate. What we need now are communication policies that create and protect those opportunities.

NOTES

1. Attention to the digital divide continues to decline; for example, see steadily falling web search interest in the term from 2005 to 2015 at http://www.google.com/trends/explore#q=digital%20divide.
2. We recognize the complexities of categorizing individuals as "of color" or not, and the implications of that decision on research methodologies and findings. We use "People of Color" as shorthand throughout this piece to refer to racial and ethnic minorities, including Hispanics of any race. Statistics presented adhere, as much as possible, to this categorization.
3. Data for African-American employment numbers were withheld.
4. However, we note recent encouraging developments in the Online News Association's speaker lineup, see Corporation for Public Broadcasting 2011b. Also see http://diversify.journalismwith.me/about-this-project/.
5. Globally, digital inequality is also persistent. ITU data on Internet use in developed versus developing countries reveal that the Internet use gap has

remained constant, or even increased: whereas in 2005, the gap in Internet use rates between developed and developing countries was 43.1 percent, 2015 statistics place the gap even wider, at 46.9 percent.
6. This section is adapted from Wilson and Costanza-Chock 2011.

References

Alexander, Michelle. 2012. *The New Jim Crow: Mass incarceration in the age of colorblindness*. New York: The New Press.

Allan, Stuart. 2009. *Citizen journalism: Global perspectives*, First printingth ed. New York: Peter Lang Publishing Inc.

American Society of News Editors. 2014. 2014 census. Columbia: American Society of News Editors, July 29, 2014. http://asne.org/content.asp?pl=121 &sl=387&contentid=387

Bachen, Christine, Allen Hammond, Laurie Mason, and Stephanie Craft. 1999. Diversity of programming in the broadcast spectrum. Unpublished manuscript submitted to the Federal Communications Commission. Available at http:// transition.fcc.gov/opportunity/meb_study/content_ownership_study.pdf

Butler, Bob. 2012. 2012 NABJ diversity census: An examination of television newsroom management. National Association of Black Journalists. http://c. ymcdn.com/sites/www.nabj.org/resource/resmgr/onrmore.2012_nabj_ diversity_.pdf

Castells, Manuel. 2007. Communication, power and counter-power in the network society. *International Journal of Communication* 1(1): 29.

CB Insights. 2010. Venture capital demographics – 87% of VC-backed founders are white; All-Asian teams raise largest funding rounds. *CB Insights Blog*. Available at https://www.cbinsights.com/blog/venture-capital-demographics -87-percent-vc-backed-founders-white-asian-teams-raise-largest-funding/

Colby, Sandra L., and Jennifer M. Ortman. 2015. Projections of the size and composition of the U.S. Population: 2014 to 2060. In *Current population reports: Population estimates and projections*. Washington, D.C.: U.S. Census Bureau. https://www.census.gov/content/dam/Census/library/publica- tions/2015/demo/p25-1143.pdf

Corporation for Public Broadcasting. 2011a. Annual report. Available at http:// www.cpb.org/annualreports/2011/

Corporation for Public Broadcasting. 2011b. Public media's services to minority and diverse audiences. http://www.cpb.org/aboutcpb/reports/diversity/

Costanza-Chock, Sasha. 2014. *Out of the shadows, into the streets!: Transmedia organizing and the immigrant rights movement*. Cambridge, MA: The MIT Press.

Federal Communications Commission. 2014. *Report on ownership of commercial broadcast stations*. Washington, D.C.: Federal Communications Commission. https://apps.fcc.gov/edocs_public/attachmatch/DA-12-1667A1.pdf.

Forelle, Michelle C. 2015. The FCC and the problem of diversity. *International Journal of Communication* 9: 8.

Friedland, Lewis. 2015. Defining America's information needs. In *The communication crisis in America, and how to fix it*, ed. Lewis Friedland and Mark Lloyd. Basingstoke: Palgrave Macmillan.

Friedland, Lewis, Philip Napoli, Katherine Ognyanova, Carola Weil, and Ernest J. Wilson III. 2012. Review of the literature regarding critical information needs of the American public. Unpublished manuscript submitted to the Federal Communications Commission. http://transition.fcc.gov/bureaus/ocbo/Final_Literature_Review.pdf

Garza, Alicia. 2014. A Herstory of the #BlackLivesMatter movement. *The Feminist Wire*, October 7. http://www.thefeministwire.com/2014/10/blacklivesmatter-2/

Gillmor, Dan. 2006. *We the media: Grassroots journalism by the people, for the people*. Beijing/Sebastopol: O'Reilly Media.

Gold, Riva. 2013. Newsroom diversity: A casualty of journalism's financial crisis. *The Atlantic*, July 9. http://www.theatlantic.com/national/archive/2013/07/newsroom-diversity-a-casualty-of-journalisms-financial-crisis/277622/

Gomery, Douglas. 2002. *The FCC's newspaper-broadcast cross-ownership rule: An analysis*. Washington, D.C.: Economic Policy Institute. http://www.epi.org/files/page/-/old/books/cross-ownership.pdf.

Gray, Herman. 2013. Subject(ed) to recognition. *American Quarterly* 65(4): 771–798. doi:10.1353/aq.2013.0058.

Harkinson, Josh. 2014. Google just released its diversity numbers. Our exclusive data show it lags behind other tech firms. *Mother Jones*, May 29. http://www.motherjones.com/media/2014/05/google-diversity-labor-gender-race-gap-workers-silicon-valley

Jenkins, Henry. 2006. *Convergence culture: Where old and new media collide*. New York: ACLS Humanities E-Book/New York University Press.

Kang, Cecilia, and Todd C. Frankel. 2015. Silicon valley struggles to hack its diversity problem. *The Washington Post*, July 16. https://www.washingtonpost.com/business/economy/silicon-valley-struggles-to-hack-its-diversity-problem/2015/07/16/0b0144be-2053-11e5-84d5-eb37ee8eaa61_story.html

Kim, Yong-Chan, and Sandra J. Ball-Rokeach. 2006. Civic engagement from a communication infrastructure perspective. *Communication Theory* 16(2): 173–197. doi:10.1111/j.1468-2885.2006.00267.x.

Kim, Dam Hee. 2012. The triangle of minority ownership, employment and content: A review of studies of minority ownership and diversity. Paper presented at the annual meeting of the Association for Education in Journalism and Mass Communication, Chicago, 9–12 Aug 2012.

Kim, Catherine Y., Daniel J. Losen, and Damon T. Hewitt. 2012. *The school-to-prison pipeline: Structuring legal reform.* New York: New York University Press.

Lutz, Ashley. 2012. These 6 corporations control 90% of the media in America. *Business Insider,* June 14. http://www.businessinsider.com/these-6-corporations-control-90-of-the-media-in-america-2012-6

McChesney, Robert W. 2013. *Digital disconnect: How capitalism is turning the internet against democracy.* New York: The New Press.

Miley, Leslie. 2015. Thought on diversity part 2. Why diversity is difficult. *Medium,* November 3. https://medium.com/tech-diversity-files/thought-on-diversity-part-2-why-diversity-is-difficult-3dfd552fa1f7

Nagesh, Gautham. 2013. FCC withdraws proposal to relax media-ownership rules. *Wall Street Journal,* December 16. http://www.wsj.com/articles/SB10001424052702303949504579262803786617112

Napoli, Philip. 2015. Understanding our new communications economy. In *The communication crisis in America, and how to fix it,* ed. Lewis Friedland and Mark Lloyd. Basingstoke: Palgrave Macmillan.

Papper, Bob. 2015. Research: Minority numbers slide, women make gains. Radio Television Digital News Association, July 20. http://www.rtdna.org/article/research_minority_numbers_slide_women_make_gains

Pew Research Center. 2010. How news happens. *Pew Research Center's Journalism Project,* January 11. http://www.journalism.org/2010/01/11/how-news-happens/

Pew Research Center. 2013. Home internet access. Available at http://www.pewresearch.org/data-trend/media-and-technology/internet-penetration/

Pew Research Center. 2015. Broadband technology fact sheet. *Pew Research Center: Internet, Science & Technology.* Available at http://www.pewinternet.org/fact-sheets/broadband-technology-fact-sheet/

Sandoval, Catherine J. K. 2009. Minority commercial radio ownership in 2009: FCC licensing and consolidation policies, entry windows, and the nexus between ownership, diversity and service in the public interest. Unpublished manuscript submitted to the Federal Communications Commission. http://law.scu.edu/wp-content/uploads/faculty/Minority%20Commercial%20Radio%20Broadcasters%20Sandoval%20MMTC%202009%20final%20.pdf

Schaffer, Jan. 2007. Citizen media: Fad or the future of news? College Park, Maryland: J-Lab. The Institute for Interactive Journalism. http://www.j-lab.org/_uploads/publications/citizenmedia.pdf

Schradie, Jen. 2011. The digital production gap: The digital divide and web 2.0 collide. *Poetics* 39(2): 145–168. doi:10.1016/j.poetic.2011.02.003.

Shirky, Clay. 2009. *Here comes everybody: The power of organizing without organizations,* Reprintth ed. New York: Penguin.

Tongia, Rahul, and Ernest J. Wilson III. 2011. The flip side of Metcalfe's Law: Multiple and growing costs of network exclusion. *International Journal of Communication* 5: 17.

Turner, S. Derek. 2007. Out of the picture 2007: Minority & female TV station ownership in the United States. Free Press. http://www.freepress.net/sites/default/files/fp-legacy/out_of_the_picture.pdf

U.S. Census Bureau. 2007. Survey of business owners. American Fact Finder. Available at http://factfinder.census.gov/faces/tableservices/jsf/pages/productview.xhtml?pid=SBO_2007_00CSA01&prodType=table

Watson, Brendan R., and Sarah Cavanah. 2015. Community information needs: A theory and methodological framework. *Mass Communication and Society* 18(5): 651–673. doi:10.1080/15205436.2015.1059948.

Wilson III, Ernest J., and Sasha Costanza-Chock. 2011. New voices on the net? The digital journalism divide and the costs of network exclusion. In *Race after the internet*, ed. Lisa Nakamura and Peter A. Chow-White. New York: Routledge.

Zickuhr, Kathryn. 2013. Who's not online and why. *Pew Research Center: Internet, Science & Tech.* Available at http://www.pewinternet.org/2013/09/25/whos-not-online-and-why/

CHAPTER 17

A Public Trust Unrealized: The Unresolved Constraints on US Public Media

Willard D. "Wick" Rowland

INTRODUCTION

The term "a public trust" has long had strong resonance in character-izations of public service broadcasting. Its use in the title of this chapter derives from a particular rhetorical celebration that has been regularly deployed by public broadcasting leadership in recent years, but that also stretches back over a generation to one of the most comprehensive and visionary semi-official planning documents for US public media. I argue here that public broadcasting in the USA can and should become a place to which all Americans can turn to meet their critical information needs. However, for it to live up fully to the "public trust" standard, major federal policy and structural changes must be made.

Note: This chapter is drawn largely from the author's Ralph L. Crosman Lecture, "A Public Trust in Jeopardy: An Insider's Look at The Unresolved Constraints on U.S. Public Media," at the University of Colorado Boulder, April 23, 2013. The author wishes to acknowledge Mark Lloyd's considerable assistance in editing this abridged version.

W.D. Wick Rowland (✉)
University of Colorado, Denver, CO, USA

© The Editor(s) (if applicable) and The Author(s) 2016   267
M.I. Lloyd, L.A. Friedland (eds.), *The Communication Crisis in America,
And How to Fix It*, DOI 10.1057/978-1-349-94925-0_17

The seminal planning document for US public broadcasting was "Public Television: A Program for Action," the report of the Carnegie Commission on Educational Television (Carnegie I 1967). Within ten months of its publication, many of its recommendations were implemented in the Public Broadcasting Act of 1967 (PBA) (Public Law 1967) as a result of a unique confluence of relatively unified political commitment in the White House and Congress, widespread public disquiet about many social issues, and an unusual amount of internal public media cooperation and determination.

The 1967 law was the first major amendment to the Communications Act of 1934, laying out a new vision for the transition of the older structure of noncommercial educational (NCE) radio and television into a more general-service public broadcasting system. The report and the new act led to federal funding for programming and operations, a large increase in the number of noncommercial radio and television stations, and the development of national funding and programming entities, such as the Corporation for Public Broadcasting (CPB), the Public Broadcasting Service (PBS), and National Public Radio (NPR).

However, for all of their importance, both Carnegie I and the 1967 Act were seriously flawed, and over time, it became clear that they had failed to have as fully revolutionary an impact on US public media as initially anticipated. By as early as the mid-1970s, it was increasingly evident that there were shortcomings in the amounts and mechanisms of federal funding, major weaknesses in the new national agency structures, and no internal or external consensus on the necessary long-term numbers, resource needs, organizational patterns, and service profiles of the quickly growing cohorts of public stations around the country.

In that light, it soon became apparent that further policy re-visioning and system planning were necessary, and that imperative led, among other things, to a second Carnegie Commission report entitled, "A Public Trust" (Carnegie II 1979).

The new Commission chose its title for at least two reasons. First, it argued that in a relatively short time—only 12 years since the PBA—and despite its challenges, public broadcasting had "managed to establish itself as a national treasure." It had, the report said, "come into its own" and was "now firmly embedded in the national consciousness." The report argued that through a rich array of programming, the institution had clearly set itself apart from commercial broadcasting, thereby readily justifying the federal tax dollars that had begun to flow to it.

Second, however, the second Carnegie report was not at all dewy-eyed about the difficulties facing the enterprise. It identified a number of serious organizational and process flaws in the new system, and it called for a major restructuring, particularly at the national level. In a bold—and to many, heretical—move, it recommended the replacement of CPB by two new entities, one to be named the "Program Services Endowment" and the other the "Public Telecommunications Trust."

Hence a dual meaning for the word "trust"—the then emerging, highly laudatory brand for public media as a widely admired institution meriting even greater public support, plus a new structural arrangement embedding the fiduciary notion in its very name.

There is not space here to delve into the details of the full report. It merits rediscovery, however, because it was an acute articulation of most of the key problems already facing public broadcasting in the pre-broadband age—for example, vulnerability to political interference, insufficient funding, awkward national programming structures, and unclear local service plans—all of which persist today. Despite all the changes in technology and media in the decades since, the problems outlined by the report still ring true, and the public has not been well served by the failures of successive congresses and presidential administrations, and by public media themselves, to take seriously the report's recommendations (plus other contemporary and subsequent critiques) and to attempt to implement any of its key provisions.

The other aspect of the "public trust" imagery invoked in the chapter title is the more recent set of claims by public media leaders, centered around a series of annual national opinion surveys which over a dozen years have repeatedly reported that the public credits PBS as the most trusted institution in the USA and, further, that public broadcasting is one of the best investments of federal dollars made by the government. Those survey results have become a staple in the marketing and political lobbying plans of the national public media agencies and many stations (PBS 2015).

Yet all that positive imagery belies a seriously inconvenient and unexplained truth, namely that despite the plaudits, as well as countless major national and local programming awards, US public broadcasting remains profoundly under-resourced, much marginalized and struggling to find its way to the more prominent role envisioned for it by the two Carnegie Commissions. How is it, then, that the public can so revere an institution and yet fail to support it adequately?

The goal of this chapter is to try to answer that question by highlighting a series of external constraints in federal communications policy, along with parallel internal issues in the structure and processes of public media. In the end, the chapter will suggest a few of the many changes that might help public broadcasting better capitalize on the public's trust—to help it earn a better base of material support and thereby to find an even larger and more stable place for itself in serving the information needs of the nation.

EXTERNAL AND INTERNAL CHALLENGES

There are many challenges to public broadcasting that merit review. The focus here is on five: (1) the history of US communications policy and broadcasting prior to the PBA; (2) the funding, structural, and process contradictions in that law; (3) the challenges of new media technologies; (4) the continuing pattern of federal media policymaking indifference to public media; and (5) the difficulties public media themselves have in responding to that indifference and in shaping their own case for the future.

The Legacy of Early US Media Policy

The key defining characteristic of US broadcasting is that it is principally an instrument of commerce that, from the outset, has been largely shaped to serve privately held, for-profit interests. That model was quite different from the initial pattern for broadcasting in most other industrial democracies. Elsewhere, broadcasting was understood first and foremost as a cultural institution. It was seen as an extension of language, theater, and the arts, with a mission to help build and sustain national identity; so it was initially chartered to public-service entities.

The initial forms of broadcast radio in the USA were a mix of commercial and noncommercial entities. The latter included many educational, religious, government, and private interests less interested in profit than in experimentation and programming aimed at specific communities. But their numbers were soon to wither under the prevailing political economy of the day. The 1920s were a period of "ballyhoo" business boosterism (Allen 1931) in which the role of the federal government was seen to be predominantly one of dedicating the country to the core elements of corporate capitalism and the primacy of private ownership in all forms of production, including culture.

Major, government-sponsored communications equipment manu-facturers, telephone companies, and retail and advertising entities came to dominate the nascent commercial broadcast industry. But they were unable to manage their own transmission standards, and the existing law, dating from the earlier radiotelephony period, did not give the government adequate authority to regulate broadcasting, even in technical matters.

The result was a growing state of signal interference and chaos. The commercial industry, along with military support, petitioned Congress and the Coolidge and Hoover administrations to bring order to broadcasting by passing The Radio Act of 1927. That law established the Federal Radio Commission (FRC) and provided it with a discretionary fiduciary licens-ing standard known as the "public interest, convenience and necessity."

But little understood at the time, and under-appreciated even today, the terms of FRC operation and the public interest standard itself were inherited from a preceding generation of administrative law which in such areas as transportation, banking, and commerce had already proven to be highly favorable to the private industries being regulated. That pat-tern carried over into radio broadcasting and was most visibly manifest when, in the wake of the new law, the FRC effectively forced most of the noncommercial broadcasters off the air, giving their frequencies over to the commercial industry and leaving only a handful of school and univer-sity broadcasters struggling to survive throughout the 1930s and 1940s (Blakely 1979).

Many proponents of progressive social uses of broadcasting had assumed that the "public interest" meant that the FRC's oversight would lead to highly informative, educational, and culturally enlightening programming in the commercial industry. But in actual regulatory practice, the fidu-ciary standard guaranteed only technical competence among broadcasters, which in turn favored those with strong, steady streams of revenue, as in advertising (Rowland 1996).

Meanwhile, the rapidly growing commercial industry quickly estab-lished codes of conduct and other measures that had the effect of divert-ing Congress and the FRC (and later the Federal Communications Commission [FCC]) from writing any meaningful programming require-ments into the public interest standard. Those efforts also helped keep the government from giving serious consideration to any major noncommer-cial or publicly supported BBC-like competition.

Educational radio continued to be largely an afterthought in the American system, and even as television came into being in the mid-twentieth century, the noncommercial stations remained under-resourced and marginal. They were aided in an important respect by an FCC policy reserving some spectrum space for "noncommercial, educational" (NCE) stations, but there still was no federal commitment to creating a strong national general audience, public-service enterprise.

During the 1940s and 1950s, commercial broadcasters made significant contributions to popular entertainment, civic discussion, and national wartime efforts, and in the early days of television, they provided some educational and high cultural programming. Such efforts helped mute calls for a stronger noncommercial alternative. But the commercial system also soon became marked by quiz show, payola, and ratings system scandals, concerns about violence and social mores, and charges that it was "a vast wasteland." Critics also charged that the FCC was too readily continuing to grant licenses to under-performing and even racist stations.

The 1960s were largely defined by an increasing range and depth of social change, including the civil rights, feminist, environmental, and anti-war movements. In that context, there was a new emphasis on the possibility of some significant change in communications policy. President Lyndon Johnson's Great Society program seemed to be just the spur needed to boost the ambitions of reformers and educational broadcasters to develop a significant alternative to commercial broadcasting. It was this rich milieu that helped lead to Carnegie I and the 1967 Act.

The Mixed Results of the Public Broadcasting Act of 1967

The terms of the PBA were ambitious and promising. It stated that: "it furthers the general welfare" for the federal government to support "a national policy" that encourages NCE radio and television programming and services that "will be responsive to people [locally and nationally]," "constitute an expression of diversity and excellence," and "be available to all citizens" (PBA 1967).

In that light, it was not uncommon to hear hopeful claims that: "Finally in the United States, we are building our own version of the BBC." Indeed, in certain respects, the PBA appeared to be a major breakthrough. The law created a whole new superstructure at the national level, authorizing the formation of CPB, which in turn, led to the chartering of PBS and NPR. It also provided for the first time for the infusion of substantial federal funds into the operations and programming of what until then had been a relatively weak aggregation of educational radio and television stations. It mandated CPB to provide monies directly to the stations, to national programming, and to technical interconnection infrastructure.

But, perhaps not surprisingly, neither the broader social and political transformations that fostered them, nor the changes in public media were to be as thorough and definitive as many had imagined. The ink was hardly dry on the Great Society legislation when various conservative and libertarian agendas resurfaced with the explicit goal of unpacking many of the recent reforms, including the PBA.

Funding problems
One of the major flaws of the 1967 Act was that there was no "public dividend" funding plan. Against the firm warnings of the first Carnegie report and others, the law provided for no permanent federal funding source. There were no requirements for anything like the Carnegie I recommendation for a tax on the sale of television receivers, nor for spectrum use fees, taxes on the proceeds of commercial broadcasting, or the television receiver use taxes common in other countries (the "license fee"). Despite considerable knowledgeable commentary noting that public broadcasting's independence would be seriously compromised without such protected forms of revenue, a long-term, secure source of funding for public broadcasting would never materialize.

Instead, federal funding was, and has remained, embedded in the annual congressional appropriations process, just like any other government agency. As such, it has been vulnerable to constant legislative oversight and therefore made the subject of considerable political discord.

To add to the problem, not only was there no guarantee of funding, but what Congress allocated was kept small and in check. Nearly a half century later, federal tax support for public television and radio is less than $500 million a year, which is remarkably low by comparison with less wealthy countries abroad. While the national treasury support for public broadcasting in all other advanced democracies is in the range of $20–$100 per capita, the US amount is less than $1.50.

To be sure, there are other sources of funding for US public media. State governments, corporate underwriting, foundations, universities, and individual personal membership contributions all constitute important elements of the annual public broadcasting budget. Altogether they add roughly $2.5 billion a year, giving the system a total of about $3 billion. But seen comparatively, the amount is small. The total revenues of the BBC and NHK (Japan) exceed $6 billion—twice the size of the entire budget of all of US public radio and television, and for much smaller populations. Canada, Australia, France, Italy, Sweden, and many other countries likewise have smaller populations and yet public-service media tax support that is larger than that of the USA.

Not only does the lack of a reliable funding mechanism make it impossible for the public broadcasting system to meet all the goals set out in the PBA, the necessarily constant efforts to retain the small annual appropriations also seriously distract public broadcasting's leadership and stations from planning for growth and development.

The small amount of federal funding has two telling additional effects at the local level. First, it drives the stations into incessant fundraising appeals that in tone and volume approach commercial station advertising levels, especially in public radio. In turn, those imperatives lead the stations to seek ever more corporate support and thereby to think and behave more commercially and safely. Seen another way, limited public funding is every bit as much a censorship device as outright government interference in programming decisions.

National system structural complexity
Another troublesome legacy from 1967 has been the highly complex organizational structure of the system, particularly at the national level. By comparison with most other public or commercial broadcasting systems worldwide, American public broadcasting is highly decentralized. In the USA, there are three major, inside-the-Beltway public broadcasting organizations with national programming responsibilities (CPB, PBS, and NPR, which, along with Association of Public Television Stations (APTS), constitute the so-called G-4). There are several more programming entities elsewhere that are both redundant and competitive and that also contribute to a confusing welter of alphabet soup that the public, policymakers, and major funders often do not understand.

Despite its grand name, CPB is quite limited in its authority. It is largely a federal funding laundering agency, designed in part to shield the stations and other agencies from direct congressional and presidential interference in programming. It has none of the operational responsibilities in national-level production and programming common to most national broadcasters, public or private, and it has no real statutory mandate for system-wide leadership. Yet its funding programs do permit it to influence the behavior of the stations and the structure of the system in ways little known to the press or public. So, the "primary" US public broadcasting entity is at once quite restricted in its authority and yet more quietly determinative of various system policies than is widely understood.

PBS, too, is strictly limited in its mandate. Unlike all other national broadcasters in the world, including NPR, PBS is prevented from producing any programming. That right is reserved largely for a few of its member stations, reflecting longstanding, even pre-1967, station-based national production conflicts of interest. Meanwhile, both PBS and the producing stations are beholden to an often conflicting mix of sources for program funding: CPB, foundations, and corporate sponsors.

The number of players and the indistinct lines of authority lead to large inefficiencies and to tremendous confusion about who is in charge of national program decisions. Television producers in the independent community and among the stations report tremendous difficulties in seeking approval and funding for national program projects.

There are parallel confusions in policy development. The national agencies have no statutory or fiscal incentives for changing the status quo. While they are able to work together on short-term funding and regulatory matters, their independent institutional interests are such that they have little capacity to agree upon and cooperate sufficiently well to articulate and pursue markedly new and enhanced federal public media policy initiatives.

Moreover, they are not publicly accountable to any significant degree. Again, the case of CPB is telling.

There is nothing in the appointment and review of CPB board members that resembles the expectations and scrutiny associated with the governing boards of public-service broadcasting corporations in most other democracies. In the UK, for instance, the BBC is a Royal Charter corporation, the governors of which are widely understood (and without any populist embarrassment) to be from among "the great and the good." It is not as if every appointee fully meets the standard, or that political affinity with the government of the day doesn't come into play, but there is an understanding that in keeping with their name ("The BBC Trust"), the governors are to be leading citizens who have a strong commitment to the BBC itself and to the prior notion that public-service media should lie at the heart of the nation's identity, not on its margins.

By contrast, in the USA, little attention is given to the White House and congressional selections for the CPB board. CPB directors are little known to the public and rarely covered by the press. Additionally, while CPB appointees may become public media enthusiasts, they quickly learn not only that CPB is limited in its authority (and therefore in directors' influence), but also that, as with government agencies generally, they are restricted relative to representation and lobbying. This is yet another example of how CPB is not the independent, non-political leadership entity many had originally envisioned.

The member stations largely control the boards of the other G-4 organizations. The station representatives are a mixture of professional station CEOs and public lay members who usually have had roles on station boards. By definition, they are closer to the ground than CPB directors; yet, however highly committed to the cause of public media, their mandates are limited largely to matters of corporate policy, membership criteria, and budget and personnel review. As with CPB, their frames of reference are the status quo, giving them little incentive for macro-level national policy development.

The contradictions of localism

At the local and state levels, there are hundreds of radio and television stations that constitute the great base of US public media. The enterprise is a hyper-Jeffersonian system that regularly touts its local ownership and control as a fundamental American political value and a significantly distinguishing characteristic from the commercial system.

The stations are fiercely independent of one another and variously suspicious of and in league with the national entities. They come together in several ways for certain core programming, operational, and lobbying tasks by participating on the boards of PBS, NPR, APTS, and other program entities. They also work together in aggregates of "affinity groups"—associations of various licensee types—and other professional cohorts. But those organizations differ widely among themselves, and even internally, about system priorities. As with the national entities, those unstable tribal divisions among local public media are difficult to manage, and they prevent focus on the longer term, overarching policy challenges that would help address many of the problems the system faces.

Periodically the stations will cohere sufficiently to push back at one or more of the G-4, expressing concerns about particular national agency policies, budgets or projects. But generally the national organizations find it relatively easy to keep the stations in check. They are able to use a variety of funding, dues policies, board election, and advisory committee appointment carrots and sticks to prevent outright rebellion and depress any instincts for the stations to think and act outside of the given institutional parameters.

As a result of these complexities, pressures and restrictions, comprehensive public media system planning has proven nearly impossible. Over the decades there has been only one serious system-wide planning effort emerging from within public television (Gunn et al. 1980), the recommendations of which would have nicely complemented the Carnegie II plan. But the stations and national agencies could not reach consensus on its key provisions; so its major recommendations were rejected, and there has been no comparable effort since. Radio has had better internal planning debate mechanisms, but it too has not had a capacity for comprehensive review.

Similarly, there has been only one other major independent, national-level study since Carnegie II (Twentieth Century Fund 1993). But, apart from an insightful introductory consultant's essay, its report was little more than an uncoordinated collection of papers by individual task force members that led to no serious discussion with public broadcasting and no legislative proposals.

Given this history, it is difficult to avoid the conclusion that public media are deliberately, if not overtly, designed by federal law and policy to be highly decentralized and unorganized. However unspoken, the national policy legacy has been to leave public media with many internally competing interests, without well-defined leadership and lacking any coherent internal capacity to think through and make major reforms and advancement.

New Technology Innovations

Despite its structural and process constraints, public broadcasting has been creative in its response to new technology opportunities over the years. For instance, in the 1970s it helped lead the development of the national closed captioning system for the hearing impaired, and it was among the first broadcast entities to employ satellite distribution for its national programming. Subsequently, it regularly upgraded that capacity and more recently has been working toward more flexible and cost-effective Internet-based solutions. It also has experimented with the nation's new digital television capacity for multi-casting far more creatively than commercial broadcasting.

Nationally and locally, via vehicles such as PBS Kids, LearningMedia, TeacherLine, the Online Film Festival, program websites, and social media, there are steadily increasing numbers of inventive efforts to exploit online opportunities and to think beyond the legacy broadcast business.

In addition, public broadcasting has been working with a number of national and local stakeholders to address gaps in the US emergency alert system. In response to congressional and White House concerns about chronic communication failures during regional and national disasters, the Department of Commerce and CPB have funded public broadcasters to work with community partners to acquire digital wireless technology to assist first responders, emergency management agencies, and the public during disasters. As part of that initiative, the PBS Warning Alert and Response Network (WARN) is using the public television interconnection system to back up the government's Wireless Emergency Alert system for advising mobile phone subscribers about emergencies in their area.

But such contributions to critical public information needs and all the other public media technology innovations are expensive. It is a tremendous challenge to leverage them on top of the costly regular broadcasting operations and programming services that remain the core statutory and regulatory obligations of public media, and that also, of course, are the primary vehicles for raising local money.

Federal Indifference to Public Media Policy-Making Needs

It is important to recognize that the difficulties outlined here are not unknown to the policy-making establishment. The realities of funding shortfalls, how public media are being forced out into the commercial marketplace, the system's structural complexity, its lack of authoritative leadership, and the new media challenges are all well documented. Yet despite official awareness of these fundamental difficulties, as for instance in the FCC's major community information needs study (FCC 2010a), there has been no sustained attempt to address them by any Congress, President, FCC, or others with resources and authority. To the contrary, there has been an almost studied indifference about the core challenges.

Ignoring public media

At every juncture of major communications policy-making in the past 30 years, the government has regularly avoided addressing the important issues related to public media. The most recent example has been with the National Broadband Plan (FCC 2010b), which has been implemented with little thought about how it might best enhance public media.

The plan was undertaken on the premise of a major crisis in broadband capacity, and one of its key provisions was the arguable need to auction a large portion of the broadcast television spectrum for handover to the wireless industries. Such selling of frequencies is an extension of the longstanding pattern of government complicity in private entity trafficking of publicly owned spectrum, and public broadcasters have now come under pressure to join in the practice. The consequent likely reduction in diversity of services and the undermining of the previous reservations policy were little considered in federal thinking. Likewise, in its zeal to devote the auction proceeds only to deficit reduction, the government made no effort to consider how the vast bulk of the profits from those one-time-only spectrum license sales might have helped address the long-term public media funding challenges and enhance their service capacity.

In no other major democracy could there be any such sweeping national communications policy initiative without special attention to their impact on the public-service media. Because the public institutions are understood as being central to their national media cultures, most governments would not so simply and blithely ignore them. Nor would the public media themselves fail to inject themselves at the outset into the core of the policy debates.

No Collective Public Media Vision and Case Statement

The policymaking shortcomings are exacerbated by the structural contradictions discussed above. The variety of competing institutional interests throughout the system makes it exceedingly difficult for its entities to formulate a clear common vision and organize themselves to pursue it. The national agencies and the stations have little capacity to work collectively to do the macro-level work. They find it difficult to step back to consider their overall, collective sets of missions, structures, and challenges with an eye to reform, let alone significant growth and improvement. They can nibble around the edges of issues, such as ideas for improved operating efficiencies and local revenue opportunities. But they cannot come to any broad-based plan that really drives the system forward.

Nor do the foundation, think tank, and other non-profit policymaking communities seem interested in enhancing that process. Since the original Carnegie studies, and despite important continuing support for various aspects of public media operations and programming, there has been little philanthropic willingness to address the major policy and structural challenges.

This is not to say that public broadcasting is totally dysfunctional. Despite the difficulties, it works remarkably effectively to provide a great deal of valuable programming and community service all across the country. This again is testimony to the people in the system who work so hard with limited resources.

But what public broadcasting cannot do collectively, and what no other interested parties are encouraging it to do, is to imagine a much larger and more robust future for itself. It has consistently been unable to articulate a concise case statement that tells Congress, the White House, foundations, and the American public, about all that it would like to do differently and better in the future, nor how it intends to get there and what the costs would be.

RECOMMENDATIONS

While drawing a fairly gloomy picture of the public media policy situation, it is important not to dismiss the excellent work and successes throughout the system. So, for instance, one cannot observe the increasing improvements in public radio's news capacity, nationally and locally, without coming to the conclusion that a major shift has occurred in at least one aspect of public media vision. Meanwhile the public television services in such areas as science, history, cultural performance and children's programming all continue to be first rate. Daily and weekly local public affairs and music programming abound among the stations across the country. All that work garners countless awards and other recognition and is clear evidence of what is missing in the commercial world.

But, that said, it also is clear that in the face of all the digital media competition and its persistent structural and funding challenges, the public system is in need of substantial change. What follows is a summary of just a few representative proposals for reform. There are many others that could be elaborated with more space (and should be elicited in subsequent debates about the analysis in this chapter).

Become the primary, most reliable, and trusted source addressing the public's critical information needs
There are many ways to do this. Here are just two: In the area of traditional broadcasting public media should have the ambition of bringing themselves even further into the center of American journalism and raising its standards. The system should build on the public radio successes in

news, combining systematically with public television and other nonprofit news organizations to provide a set of co-produced, universally available, diverse, multi-platform, 24/7 national and local public news services.

The goal should be no less than to help redefine US journalism around public service principles and to help it transcend the current ratings-driven commercial mix of crime blotter, weather and sports news, and the short-comings of social media. This effort should be a concerted joint radio, television, and online news effort that goes far beyond and is much more comprehensive and flexible than the current handful of CPB-sponsored regional and local journalism centers, and that includes strong investiga-tive elements.

Among the many opportunities in newer technology realms, public media should build on the WARN system to take a leading role among broadcasters, the wireless industries, and government agencies in emer-gency communications services. This means establishing even more robust and redundant communication links with a wider range of local, state, and national agencies, emergency responders and the public. Beyond alerts, public media should assist communities in planning for, responding to, and recovering from weather, environmental and civil disasters. They should aspire to becoming the first and most trusted place to which the public turns when there is a threat to safety.

Overhaul the entire national public media organization, production and policy development capacities

It is difficult to review the public television structural and process issues outlined in this chapter and many other critiques and still seriously argue for the status quo. Despite considerable hard work by countless talented professionals and external true believers, the national system is inefficient, it is not growing, it is not taking full advantage of the existing diversity among the stations and their local digital platforms, and it has no plan for substantial enhancement of the system's services and revenues.

To improve the range and depth of national programming it is long past time to replace the complex CPB, PBS, and producing stations arrangement with a more integrated, efficient and cost-effective struc-ture and multiple services model. Even public radio would profit by a more deliberate, wider-ranging, multiple-services initiative. Similar reforms are likewise necessary among the G-4 and stations for more comprehensive, longer-term system visioning, planning, and federal policy development.

Develop and incentivize a model for clearer complementary collaboration and diversity among the stations throughout the country

Much of the discussion about public television spends considerable time and uninformed energy on decrying the existence of multiple stations in certain communities—the "overlap problem." But those critiques are based on inaccurate comparisons with the structure of commercial television. They demonstrate little awareness of the multi-service models abroad and they ignore the reality of considerably more overlap in public radio. Most seriously, they reflect regressive, protectionist thinking that directly violates the original Carnegie and statutory expectations for diversity and growth.

The discussions also seriously confuse the opportunities in some cities, where there are two or more well-differentiated stations, with the conditions in dozens of other communities with overlapping signals of essentially the same PBS content on two, three, or even four stations. The latter situation is wasteful; the former is not. As in radio, a differentiated services model should be encouraged nationwide.

Public media, nationally and locally, should constitute a much larger share of the US media complex. To that end, CPB funding policies aimed at station consolidation should be terminated; the relevant funds should be turned around instead to encourage station growth, new programming services, and differentiation nationwide.

Adopt a substantive federal "Public Dividend" policy for long-term, insulated public media funding by establishing an adequately endowed and increasing Public Media Trust Fund generated from both government and private sources

As has long been known, public media need a sustained means of adequate federal and other revenues divorced from the annual appropriations process and not subject to congressional and partisan political interference. The federal options include: a spectrum-use fee applied to every commercial spectrum licensee (including commercial broadcasters), a fee on broadcast and other spectrum license sales, a sales tax on every device that receives public media service, and the proceeds from spectrum auctions.

But unlike most prior proposals, it is important to develop the trust fund as a major public–private partnership. The foundation community and other private parties can do much more to help build the national-level and local station endowment capacity in public media. They should partner with the federal and state governments to generate sources and amounts of revenue sufficient to ensure that the original goals for a robust public media system are met and, that going forward, the public has access to a wider range of information and programming services—nationally, locally, and on multiple platforms.

CONCLUSIONS

In 1979, the second Carnegie Commission recognized that public broadcasting was a great, yet still under-performing public asset, and it encouraged the nation to invest much more in what it called "a public trust." It recommended that public broadcasting and public authorities work together to redesign the system to re-establish it on a whole new level.

In the intervening years, the public has regularly acknowledged the value of the enterprise and it has accorded it an extraordinarily high degree of such trust. Yet all that faith has not translated into political action commensurate with the promise and needs of a truly comprehensive public media system.

Clearly, the key political and private institutions—Congress, successive presidential administrations, the FCC, foundations and others—have all been complicit in that contradiction. It is as if there has been a quiet agreement to provide just enough support to keep public broadcasting alive, but not enough to foster its growth and a move into a more central place in US media culture.

But another major reason for the contradiction has been that public broadcasting itself has remained divided diffident and uncertain about its own sense of expanded purpose and importance. Despite all its solid work in various dimensions, it has not given the public, the government, or the private sector sufficient evidence of its own convictions about where it wants to go and how it intends to get there.

While partnerships in building the public media system are essential, the first step in establishing those relationships and in engendering the necessary support must come from within the public broadcasting community itself. No one else is going to take that lead on its behalf. While it is a great blessing to have warm public admiration, if public broadcasting is to realize its full potential, it must itself do much more to build on the public's trust that it has a clear vision for itself and is therefore worthy of considerably more support.

REFERENCES

Allen, Frederick L. 1931. *Only yesterday: An informal history of the nineteen-twenties.* New York: Blue Ribbon Books.

Blakely, Robert J. 1979. *To serve the public interest: Educational broadcasting in the United States.* Syracuse: Syracuse University Press.

Carnegie Commission on Educational Television. 1967. *Public television: A program for action [Carnegie I].* New York: Bantam Books.

Carnegie Commission on the Future of Public Broadcasting. 1979. *A public trust [Carnegie II].* New York: Bantam Books.

Federal Communications Commission. 2010a. *The future of the media and the information needs of communities in the digital age.* Public Notice DA 10-100, GN Docket No. 10-25. January 21.

Federal Communications Commission. 2010b. *Connecting America: The national broadband plan.* March 17.

Gunn Jr., Hartford N., G.G. Crotts, P.M. Fannon, M.E. Hobbs, M.B. Rice, W.D. Rowland Jr., and G.V. Schenkkan. 1980. In search of the formula: The system planning project papers. *Public Telecommunications Review* 8(3): 7–102.

Public Broadcasting Service. 2015. Today's PBS: Trusted, valued, essential. http://to.pbs.org/most_trusted_2015

Public Law 90–129, 90th Congress, November 7, 1967. As amended to April 26, 1968.

Rowland Jr., Willard D. 1996. The meaning of 'the public interest' in communications policy – Part I: Its origins in state and federal regulation. *Communications Law & Policy* 2(3): 309–328.

Twentieth Century Fund. 1993. *Quality time? The report of the twentieth century fund task force on public television.* New York: Twentieth Century Fund Press.

CHAPTER 18

Addressing the Information Needs of Crisis-Affected Communities: The Interplay of Legacy Media and Social Media in a Rural Disaster

Dharma Dailey and Kate Starbird

INTRODUCTION

To make informed decisions about the future of our communications infrastructure in the USA, it is important to have a clear, evidence-based understanding of how the information needs of crisis-affected communities are being addressed. For this chapter, we examine the interplay between traditional "legacy" media and network-enabled information and communication technologies (ICTs), such as "social media," to explore how they together, and separately, meet the information needs of disaster-affected communities.

Note: We thank interviewees and community members who participated in this research. Initial research took place through WGXC Hands-On Radio. Thanks to Amirah Najid and Ying-Yu Chen for early reviews of this chapter.

D. Dailey (✉) • K. Starbird
University of Washington, Seattle, WA, USA

© The Editor(s) (if applicable) and The Author(s) 2016
M.I. Lloyd, L.A. Friedland (eds.), *The Communication Crisis in America, And How to Fix It*, DOI 10.1057/978-1-349-94925-0_18

Our analyses are based upon our empirical research looking at how information was created, shaped, and shared in several recent disasters. We give an extended example of how a specific information need was addressed in 2011 in rural upstate New York, when Hurricane Irene devastated several local communities. In the last week of August 2011, Hurricane Irene struck New York State, followed a week later by Tropical Storm Lee. The combined damage of the two storms became the state's largest natural disaster and the second most costly. Of 62 New York counties, 38 were declared disaster areas (NY Office of the Governor 2012). We describe several key resources that were important to surfacing and sharing useful, actionable information in the New York's Catskills region, an area hard hit by these storms. We find that the interplay between traditional legacy media organizations and a crowd empowered to act through social media is not a simple one. Rather, useful, actionable information comes to light through the complex and not entirely new interplay between these media and the public. Likewise, while the trend among organizations (including regional legacy media) appears to be an increasing reliance on ICTs, evidence suggests that legacy technologies continue to play an important role in the diffusion of information. Further, different communities addressed the same information needs in somewhat different ways, highlighting the importance of fostering infrastructures that enable dynamic and flexible information-sharing structures in disaster-affected communities.

This empirical account of how people get actionable information during a disaster illustrates how networked ICTs enable people to produce and share critical information. It highlights the diversity of approaches to meeting an information need that are extant even within the same disaster. This example of successful, yet diverse, problem-solving in rural areas affected by Hurricane Irene raises the question of how policy can support the plurality of approaches enacted by those working within a disaster-affected region. The increasing reliance of networked ICTs also raises some questions. As information work within disaster-affected communities becomes increasingly reliant on third-party networked services, the role that those services have in shaping information, as well as practical matters such as remuneration for increased network traffic and the quality of networked infrastructures, becomes increasingly an important consideration.

Before we walk through our example of how a specific information need was met in a recent disaster, we lay the groundwork for our analysis.

First, we briefly define what we mean by "information need" and offer some context for considering information needs in disasters. We then introduce our framework for making meaningful comparisons between different kinds of resources that are called into play in meeting information needs in disaster-affected communities—our particular notion of how social and technical infrastructures come together to facilitate information work in crises. After giving an example of how such infrastructures come into play to address a particular information need, we conclude with some considerations for policymakers that follow from our findings.

The Spectrum of Information Needs in Disasters

To understand how actionable, useful information is created, shaped, and diffused in a crisis, our first task is to identify what information is *needed* by members of the affected public, as opposed to general information in circulation about the event. In a newsworthy, large-scale crisis, such as a hurricane that is destined to sweep over the homes of 65 million individuals, discerning need-to-know information from good-to-know information is a non-trivial task. For example, when we review Twitter data about a crisis, it is not unusual for the most shared tweets to be non-actionable news items. We do not dismiss the importance of raising general awareness about current events. We only wish to refine our understanding of the value of general information by distinguishing it in our analysis from information that an affected public needs to have to make decisions in the disaster context. Such *actionable information* includes evacuation warnings, calls for assistance, and practical information about giving or receiving aid. Thus, to understand *information needs*, we strive to distinguish the affected publics from the public at large and to distinguish the specific diffusion pattern of particular kinds of information. We are able to make these distinctions by triangulating data derived from intensive interviews, site visits to disaster-affected communities, and extensive reviews of publicly available digital trace data such as collections of tweets, liveblogs chats, news sites, Facebook pages, YouTube videos, Wikpedia pages, Reddit threads, and so forth. We use these data to determine empirically what constitutes an information need during a specific event.

The chart above Fig. 18.1 gives an example of some information needs that community members identified in relation to Hurricane Irene's impact in one impacted region, the Catskill Mountains in New York State. The chart illustrates how different information needs are associated with each phase of the disaster. Once we identify a specific information need, we can then look for evidence of how it was addressed, by whom, and with what resources. As the chart illustrates, a disaster response requires timely, actionable information of many different kinds. The resources employed in creating, shaping, and sharing each specific kind of information will likely differ. Patterns of diffusion will likely also be distinct for each one.

For example, individuals in the Catskills were first warned about Hurricane Irene about a week before it arrived in the area. Those we interviewed learned of it by monitoring traditional news sources and from discussions with friends, coworkers, and family. Ultimately, the news outlets

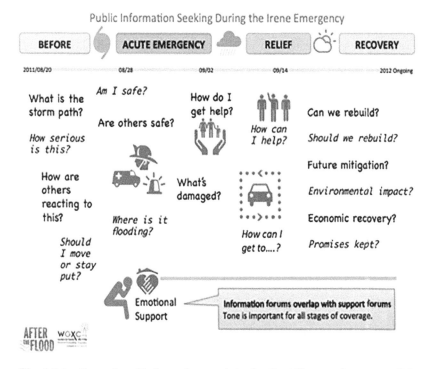

Fig. 18.1 Examples of information needs in the Catskills over the course of the Irene crisis

were reporting information that came from the National Hurricane Center (NHC), a government agency that monitors hurricane activity. Thus, in this instance, we might consider that warning information was diffused from the "top down," first originating from an authoritative source (the NHC), then reaching members of the public primarily through news organizations, and diffusing to a wider public through discussion of the news reports.

While the "top down" hurricane warnings helped the public in the Catskills to prepare for a potential disaster, once flooding and wind damage occurred, the pattern of information diffusion changed. Described in more detail below, damage assessment information filtered up from affected areas. Instead of one source, like NHC, information from perhaps thousands of individuals was collated into a coherent picture of where damage was greatest. Thus, in the acute emergency, the diffusion pattern of actionable information was, to some extent, an inversion of that in the warning phase. Information was moving from the "bottom up," originating from countless sources of those on the ground, then making its way through regional hubs to national actors who synthesized disparate bits of information into a broader understanding.

Our research focuses on information behaviors in the acute emergency phase of crises. Yet, interviewees rarely report that their disaster-related information work has concluded with the end of the emergency (e.g. Shklovski et al. 2010).[1] Pressing information needs persisted long after Irene. Difficult-to-answer questions about where to rebuild (or not), how to rebuild, how to resource rebuilding, and accountability around the resources needed to rebuild lingered long after the emergency. How these information gaps were addressed and their subsequent patterns of information diffusion look very different from those associated with the other phases of the disaster.

HOW ARE INFORMATION NEEDS ADDRESSED IN DISASTERS?

It is true that crowds empowered through social media and related ICTs can do important information work during crises (e.g. see Starbird and Palen 2013). Yet, it is also true that legacy media has a strong presence on social media platforms. To clarify the relationship between traditional media and the ICT-enabled crowd, we seek to identify the key resources that support essential information work in crises. That is, we aim to disaggregate the technologies, social arrangements, individual skills, expertise, and relations that are commonly conflated by the word "media" so that we may make meaningful comparisons about specific arrangements such as "legacy media" or "social media." Our approach to such disaggregation is empirical. Starting with a data-derived information need, we attempt to identify specific resources that came into play to fulfill that need.

Once we identify key resources, we need a way to clearly describe the relationships between these resources when they exist and to clearly delineate where relationships do not exist. We consider any resource for which we have evidence of helping to create, shape, or share actionable information to be a component of an "infrastructure" that existed to meet a specific information need. Following other scholars in infrastructure studies, the infrastructures we describe are dynamic and reflexive (Star and Ruhleder 1996). Our infrastructure models are reflexive in the sense that they describe how specific information needs were addressed in specific crises. That is, we consider only those resources that we see evidence for having contributed to closing an information gap to be a part of the infrastructure that addressed that gap. While the resulting analysis often yields a complex picture of how a given information need was addressed, it simplifies the analysis in that many potential resources that did not come into play are left out of the empirical model.

What remains available for analysis are any tools, technologies, practices, skills, knowledge, or human relationships that contributed to bridging an information gap. These assets can be examined through two perspectives that highlight their different components: as technical infrastructures and as social infrastructures. Though analytically it can be helpful to consider social and technical infrastructures separately, in practice, it is the interplay between them that culminates in an information need being addressed.

Technical Infrastructures

Like many rural areas in the USA, the Catskills has a relatively uneven telecommunications infrastructure. Several areas lack cell service, Internet service, or both (Cairns 2015; Reischel 2015). County emergency managers have been slowly improving emergency radio service as grant monies become available. Internet outages frequently accompany inclement weather due to the aging electrical grid.[2] These gaps were exacerbated by Irene, which knocked out power and telecommunications for an extended period in several parts of the region. Given the patchwork nature of infrastructure in the area, it should be no surprise that interviewees from the region reported relying on different kinds of technical infrastructures to share and receive information. Depending on the individual involved, technical infrastructures included emergency services radio, terrestrial radio, Internet over cellular network, Internet over cable network, SMS, cable television, landline phone, and cellular phone. Another layer of technical infrastructure that was also important was the many network-enabled services that many (but not all) people employed. A non-exhaustive list of these services includes social media services, such as Twitter, Facebook, YouTube, and Google Maps, as well as news, government, and aid websites.

Social Infrastructures
Actionable information is typically the result of individuals working in a coordinated fashion. The non-technical resources that close information gaps in crises are even broader and more diverse than the many technologies involved. Two of the most visible kinds of social infrastructures are organizations and professional practices. While news organizations can be quite different from one another, our notion of what constitutes a news organization is based upon shared conceptions of the purpose they serve and how they work. For example, "reporters" typically work with "editors." The work of an "editor" is different than that of the "reporter." The difference in job title denotes established professional practices. Social infrastructures also include the contributions made by individuals—their knowledge, skills, practices, and relationships to others.

We examined several of the social infrastructures that appeared to play a significant role in meeting public information needs in the Catskills after Irene. This included several media organizations within the affected region or just outside of it. The media landscape of the Catskills is being shaped by the same financial pressures as the rest of the USA. Like many rural areas, there were comparatively fewer media professionals working in comparatively fewer news organizations prior to Irene than a decade before.[3] The region has a patchwork of relatively small outlets mostly covering one town or one county, respectively. The larger outlets are on the periphery of the region. Television news outlets and papers from the more populated areas adjacent to the Catskills—the Albany and Hudson Valley markets—make coverage forays into the Catskills. The financial pressure on newsrooms in recent years has made these forays less frequent. However, throughout the 2000s, even as traditional newspapers in Catskill towns closed their doors, the demand for news coverage led to the formation of several new media outlets in the region. These new outlets introduced different technical, social, and financial arrangements to news coverage in the region. For example, the Watershed Post, a commercial online-only "information hub" run by two former print editors, Lissa Harris and Julia Reischel, grew from a Twitter account that aggregated news outlets throughout the region. Two community radio stations were launched shortly before Irene, WIOX and WGXC. Both were attempting to use volunteers to produce news. Whether new or old, it is in such small, lightly resourced organizations where much of the day-to-day public information work in the region takes place.

Emergent Infrastructures

We normally think of information work as occurring within organizations. However, in the acute emergency phase of a disaster, information work is highly diffused. Nearly everyone in an affected area is typically assessing the situation in their vicinity, seeking information, and sharing what they know in order to act accordingly. In such circumstances, people come together in temporary and novel arrangements to fill information gaps (Dynes, 1970). These emergent social infrastructures are dynamic and amorphous. They often come together just long enough to fill a gap, and then dissolve once the need is deemed resolved. Such temporary infrastructures can draw on the resources of more established and visible social infrastructures (e.g. see Lee et al. 2006).

In the Catskills after Irene, we see evidence of such emergent infrastructures forming to fill information gaps (Dailey and Starbird 2014a, b). Similar to what takes place in traditional organizations, individuals take on specific kinds of work that fill different niches. For example, a remote volunteer can moderate an Internet forum, while another may post information about damage in their immediate area. Yet another might collate the moderated information into a map. Yet another might embed the map onto a web page where it is likely to reach a wider audience who can use it. Still another may tweet a link to that website. Like work that occurs in traditional organizations, where individuals take on distinct and complementary kinds of work, the act of each individual in the network-enabled crowd contributes to the whole.

The *interplay* between emergent infrastructures and established ones is an important success factor in complex large-scale collaborations (Lee et al. 2006). In our study of the infrastructures that served the Catskills public after Irene, the most commonly identified information resources tended to be "information hubs" that played a role both in accumulating information from the public and in diffusing it to them. These information hubs were local and regional media organizations. Yet, the information that was accumulated and diffused through these hubs was often the result of emergent efforts that bridged specific information gaps.

ONE INFORMATION NEED, MANY MAPS

To illustrate the interplay between legacy media and social media in terms of meeting information needs in a crisis, we now give an extended example of how one specific information need was addressed in the Catskills after Irene. We briefly introduce a few of the solutions that emerged in the Catskills to address this particular information challenge.

Among many forms of damage, thousands of miles of New York roads and hundreds of bridges incurred obstructions and damage. Thus, one pressing information challenge for all those in the region and all those drawn into the response was to identify passable roadways. For the first few weeks of the crisis, this was a very dynamic information need. On the one hand, debris was continuously being pulled from roadways, making them passable, while on the other hand, as engineers deployed to inspect bridges made their way through the area, they declared seemingly passable roads and bridges to be structurally unsound. In the nearby state of Vermont—which was also severely impacted by Irene—the state partnered with Google to provide a single, publically available map identifying all obstructed roadways in the state (VT Office of the Governor 2011). No single resource was available for all of New York State. In the Catskills, some counties published damage maps, while others did not. In lieu of an official resource, a patchwork of localized solutions appeared. For example, the Red Cross developed and maintained their own map of the region.

FROM AUDIENCE MEMBER TO CRISIS MAPPER

One of the most frequently mentioned—and lauded—information resources respective to the acute crisis in the Catskills was a crisis map instigated by a geographic information system (GIS) professional. His story exemplifies many of the patterns that we have observed across several disasters, illustrating how concerned individuals identify and then move to address an information gap, bringing their specific skills and resources to bear upon it. Don Meltz is a GIS consultant who has worked for several towns in the Catskills. By monitoring news outlets via Twitter on the night that Irene arrived in the Catskills, he learned that damage in the region was expected to be severe. Though he lives outside of the region, his

personal and professional connections to the area drove him to follow the
storm's progress in the Catskills in real time. He sought a reliable source
that could give more in-depth information specific to the Catskills as the
crisis developed. This led him to discover the Watershed Post's Twitter
account, which was aggregating information from around the region in
collaboration with journalists from several other regional outlets. Though
he was not familiar with the Watershed Post before that night, by following the Twitter feed for several hours, he determined that it was the
best information available for the Catskills. The following morning after
flooding and heavy winds had hit the region, Meltz observed that many
members of the public were posting into a liveblog chat forum run by
the Watershed Post. These posts included requests for information about
what roads were passable or not passable. Meltz used his knowledge of the
government agencies that might produce maps and his personal connections within those agencies to assess whether official maps were likely to
become available. Once he determined they would not become available,
he contacted the Watershed Post and offered to create a map that they
could publish.

The Watershed Post was acting as an aggregator for several media
outlets around the Catskills. During the storm, many of the respective
audiences of those hyperlocal outlets had also found their way to the
Watershed Post and were alternatively seeking or sharing information
about road closures in a liveblog forum hosted by the Watershed Post.
The Post's editors used the forum and Twitter to request volunteers work
with Meltz. Some participants in the liveblog forum or in hashtag-curated
conversations on Twitter helped to curate, share, and verify information
about road closures. Others worked directly with Meltz, coordinating the
work of verifying and vetting information for the map through private,
direct messages over Twitter.

What does this brief example tell us about the interplay between
traditional legacy media and social media? What does it say about the
infrastructures that support the flow of essential information in a crisis?
In terms of technical infrastructure, we see how networked ICTs can
enable a concerned individual outside of an affected area to make a significant contribution to a community's response. The individuals who
helped Meltz to curate, verify, and update crisis information formed
an emergent infrastructure (both social and technical) that relied on
coordination of individuals outside of a traditionally organized structure. However, these emergent efforts benefited in several ways from

more persistent social infrastructures. As a GIS professional, Meltz had observed the work of other "crisis mappers" who contributed their expertise in a similar fashion in other disasters. This is but one example of the professional practices that he drew on to create the Catskills crisis map. The map also benefitted from direct collaboration with the Watershed Post editors and their "information hub," which spread across their website, a liveblog chat forum, Twitter, and Facebook. Several features of this "hub" enabled it to become one of the primary information resources about the crisis for those in the region. This included the journalistic practices its editors had honed over years of reporting and editing, specific knowledge of the Catskill region and its audiences, and established relationships the editors had with other media outlets in the region and with the official responders in their county. In turn, the Watershed Post's ability to serve their community was enhanced by emergent infrastructures (social and technical) that sprung up around them to address specific information needs like how to route around damaged roadways.

While the Watershed Post itself may not be characterized as a "legacy" media organization, it draws on legacy media organizations in two important ways. First, its editors were trained and worked in print publications for many years before they started the Watershed Post. We detail elsewhere how they diverged from traditional news practices to better fit into the current media environment to meet the information demands of the Irene crisis. Nevertheless, an intensive interview with one of the editors revealed that they continue to draw on the concepts of the traditional newsroom for their notions of what good reporting is and how to achieve it. That is the starting point for their innovation.

A second, less directly obvious way that legacy media was involved in this collaboration is that many individuals associated with legacy outlets were active members of the online crowd, both following and being followed by people directly contributing to the crisis map. For example, Ivan Lajara, who was the social media editor at *The Daily Freeman*—one of the larger newspapers to cover a portion of the Catskills—was aware of the crisis map and became one of the most active participants in social media in the region throughout the event. His knowledge and awareness of the map contributed to the *Freeman*'s most visited Irene-related story, a simple text list of road closures.

The Less Connected and Most Affected

While networked ICTs are a powerful tool for coordinating information work in disasters, it is important to recognize their limitations. As has been observed in many other crises, we have ample evidence of individuals in the Catskills who appear to be sharing directly observed information about damage as it occurred through network-enabled ICTs. However, there is a reason to suspect that even widely useful and widely disseminated information resources like Meltz's crisis map do not always reach the most affected portions of a community. For example, other researchers have pointed out that those who are most affected by a disaster are least likely to have access to networked ICTs (Burns 2014). Conversely, those who do have access to networked ICTs and contribute information through them may be different in important ways from those who are affected (Crawford and Finn 2014; Crutcher and Zook 2009; Shelton et al. 2014). Further, it has been suggested that much online data are inherently biased against rural users (Hecht and Stephens 2014), likely due to the fact that rural communication patterns have been shown to differ in many ways from urban ones (e.g. Gilbert et al. 2008, 2010). However, it should be noted that these observations about affected publics are still provisional. There is much work to do to relate the users of particular online platforms to specific populations or even specific demographic characteristics (Hargittai 2015; Tufekci 2014). With these limitations in mind, we offer a second example of how another important information hub addressed the same information gap in somewhat different ways. By offering another example from the same crisis, we hope to highlight the importance of assuring that telecommunication infrastructures are designed around the expectation that disaster-affected communities will need to scaffold site-specific solutions based on hyperlocal needs and resources at hand.

WRIP is a commercial FM radio station that played a very important role in the area of the Catskills that was most intensely impacted by Irene. Described by Operations Manager and DJ Joe Loverro as an "industry dinosaur," WRIP in many ways squarely embodies the characterization of a "legacy media" outlet. Its terrestrial broadcast reaches the more rural Catskill Mountain portion of Greene County, New York (population 49,221). It relies entirely on advertisers in its listening area. Most broadcast hours are devoted to music meant to appeal to full-time residents and tourists. Its small staff of two and a handful of part-time DJs regularly broadcast at community events, such as fire station fund-raisers.

All live in the area they serve. The station takes seriously its public service role during emergencies. For example, Loverro described sleeping under his desk so he could be in the studio to announce a snow day. While it is still true that emergency-oriented announcements can be imposed on terrestrial broadcasters by government response organizations, changes in the broadcast industry over the last several decades have led to less outlets that are demonstrably committed and capable of playing this role. Bucking this trend, WRIP has a long-standing trusted relationship with local government. Prior to Irene, the county legislature purchased backup generators for WRIPs transmitters and studio. When Irene struck, emergency radio towers in the most impacted region, the Catskills, were washed away as damage to roadways made those areas difficult to reach. It took three days to reach the most affected areas. Fortunately, nearby WRIP was able to maintain broadcasting. County Emergency Services Director John Farrell described WRIP as the "primary communication" with the most affected area in the 72 hours when emergency service communication was lost. In this critical period, responders and community members converged on WRIP studios for information, and broadcasts became a hybrid of official emergency communication and the traditional emergency communication that stations like WRIP have performed for decades.

While performing two important communication roles simultaneously from an intensely impacted area, it may not be surprising that those at WRIP were too busy to learn of the existence of Meltz's crisis map. Instead, they relied on a map that someone taped to the door of the studio. It was marked and re-marked with pen and pencil as information made its way into the studio through visitors, landline phone calls (the station has three), or Facebook posts. Though its staff strongly associate with legacy media, like most legacy media outlets, they maintain a presence on multiple platforms. They have a website that is maintained by someone outside the listening area. The website has primarily static information but does help people connect to a webstream that occurs through a third-party platform. These services typically charge stations by the number of listeners. Like most small outlets, WRIP caps the number of people who can listen to their streams to reduce costs. Thus, to get information into or out of this important information hub beyond the immediate area took some improvisation.

The Watershed Post made a plea for people participating in their liveblog or on Twitter who were also able to hear the WRIP terrestrial broadcast to listen and report back what they heard. Though Loverro reported that one computer in the studio was open to Facebook at all times, those in the studio had little time to consistently monitor or contribute to the requests for information occurring through their Facebook pages. Observing that this was creating an information gap, Alex Tighe, a local woman following WRIP's Facebook page, took on the work of moderating it and responding to questions. As we have observed in many instances of successful information work in crises, the person who stepped out of the crowd to fill this information gap brought specific skills to the task. In this instance, Tighe is a public relations professional who specializes in social media communication. Tighe drew on both her knowledge of the community in which she lived and her knowledge of effective communication through social media to make WRIP's Facebook page more useful to information seekers and sharers in the days after the disaster. Through Tighe's involvement, we can see the significant amount of work that is involved in diffusing information to multiple publics across multiple platforms. Diffusion happens through the effort of many helping hands.

Though it may be relatively new for Facebook to scaffold the social infrastructures populated by Tighe and other spontaneous volunteers, the work that Tighe took on is a very old part of disaster response. Spontaneous coordination between community members in crisis contexts is a feature of disaster response regularly observed since the earliest sociological studies of disasters 100 years ago. What is new is that such work is now more visible to researchers and to an extended audience of observers—and potential collaborators—on these platforms.

In this example, we see the same *kinds* of infrastructures contributed to the diffusion of actionable information, but the particular arrangements differed due to differences in need and differences in resources. When emergency radio communication was washed away by the storm, WRIP's combined socio-technical infrastructure was called upon to act as emergency communication until official response channels could be re-established with the most intensely impacted areas. This was possible because of the strongly established relationships in place between local responders and the station—and the station's ability to take on this additional role. This aligns with other research that demonstrates how information sharing in crises flows most easily among those with established, trusted relationships (e.g. see Tapia and Moore 2014). However, along with these established relations, new human infrastructures sprung up to aid the flow of information into and out of WRIP in the form of volunteer moderators who helped to communicate to individuals on WRIP's

Facebook page and even individuals who took on the work of listening to its terrestrial broadcasts and tweeting what they heard.

DESIGNING TECHNICAL INFRASTRUCTURES TO SUPPORT THE DISASTER-AFFECTED

We describe several key resources that were important for surfacing and sharing useful, actionable information in an affected rural area in the immediate aftermath of a disaster. These resources were intentionally arranged into socio-technical infrastructures—some established, some emergent and temporary. We find that *interplay* between *traditional legacy media organizations* and the *crowd empowered to act through social media* is not a simple one of displacement. Actionable information comes to light through specific kinds of interplay between these groups. Affected people are searching for (and in some cases finding) needed actionable information through these resources in combination. This suggests that the socio-technical infrastructures relied upon for disaster response need to be designed to support a plurality of potentially different arrangements. Our research supports the view that information actors—those sharing, seeking, and processing information—in affected communities are, in a real sense, also designers (Pipek and Wulf 2009; Le Dantec and DiSalvo 2013) who dynamically and tactically bridge technical, social, and information gaps through the arrangements they create.

When considering the communication infrastructures that support communities in crisis, telecommunications policy often focuses on meeting the needs of official response organizations. This case study illustrates the important interplay between community response (including formal and informal actors) and official response. The creation and distribution of a crisis map and the use of a radio station for official emergency communication are two examples of community resources filling a pressing gap in the official response. This suggests the need to evaluate community preparedness in light of technical infrastructures that are specific to the formal response along with those that serve the general public. For the Catskills, this means continued improvement to emergency radio services, cellular, and broadband services.

A patchwork of different technologies were used after Irene. The reliance on legacy technologies like terrestrial broadcasts and landline phones raises several questions about the relationship between legacy infrastructures and broadband for crisis communication. For example, would WRIP have been able to play the role it did if it was online-only? Yet, even legacy media outlets like WRIP are increasingly reliant on networked ICTs. One computer in their broadcast studio was dedicated to Facebook. They maintain a website and use a third-party service to stream audio to web listeners. Other than a landline phone, the Watershed Post's entire operation is dependent on networked services.

As networked ICTs take an increasingly prominent role in crisis communication in disaster-affected communities, their position in the broad socio-technical infrastructure deserves closer inspection. At the network level, there are questions around how to quickly scale the amount of bandwidth needed to keep pace with the demand for information from such local information hubs during an emergency. Scaling has both logistical and cost implications. Can logistical support be set up in advance for local hubs? If not, can those shaping traffic in real time identify these "bottom-up" resources? Who should pay for the surge in service?

Third-party services were woven into the information work of individuals and organizations throughout this emergency. The Watershed Post was able to act as a community-based information hub through its website (which relies on a hosting service), the social media platforms Twitter, Facebook, and CoverItLive, a liveblog service that was a core tool for communicating with the affected public. The reliance on third-party services raises an additional set of concerns. Many of these services are not designed for use in crises. As business needs change, web services change their offerings. This can happen quickly and without notice. At the time of Irene, CoverItLive offered a free, ad-supported version of their service, but they no longer do. Now they charge by the viewer/reader load. This is also the case with webhosting services and webstreaming services, which means that an emergent, community-based information hub in a disaster that is doing its job to fill information gaps by using such services is likely to see many costs rise simultaneously. The more important their role, the more expensive it becomes. For this reason, the Watershed Post's editors are uncertain if they would be able to play the same role in future crises that they played during Irene.

We end by pointing out a limitation of our research. We focus on information behaviors in the acute emergency phase of crises. Yet, interviewees rarely report that their disaster-related information work has concluded with the end of the emergency. Post-emergency information needs tend to be resource-intensive to address. Though there are many experiments that aim to crowdsource portions of investigative journalism (e.g. Aitamurto 2015), so far these efforts have not been demonstrated to fill post-disaster information gaps. As community news organizations become leaner and sparser, we see the need to proactively identify and support social and technical solutions that can fill important, yet resource-intensive, post-disaster information gaps.

NOTES

1. Based on 36 intensive interviews with those doing various forms of information work during two disasters.
2. This summarizes information Dailey learned during interviews with the Greene County Emergency Manager for the WGXC's Forum on Flood Coverage in 2011, interviews with local infrastructure experts for the Broadband Adoption in Low-Income Communities study for the FCC in 2010, and from being on the WGXC work team during planning and build-out of the station.
3. This summarizes Dailey's impressions of the media environment based on interviews with media professionals in the region for the WGXC's Forum on Flood Coverage in 2011, four years of participatory community research leading up to WGXC launch in 2011, and the FCC's Hudson Valley hearing on November 21, 2006.

REFERENCES

Aitamurto, Tanja. 2015. Crowdsourcing as a knowledge-search method in digital journalism: Ruptured ideals and blended responsibility. *Digital Journalism*: 1–18 (ahead-of-print).

Burns, Ryan. 2014. Rethinking big data in digital humanitarianism: Practices, epistemologies, and social relations. *GeoJournal*: 1–14.

Cairns, Robert. 2015. Broadband partnership targets rural areas in three Catskills counties. *Watershed Post*, August 7.

Crawford, Kate, and Megan Finn. 2014. The limits of crisis data: Analytical and ethical challenges of using social and mobile data to understand disasters. *GeoJournal*: 1–12.

Crutcher, Michael, and Matthew Zook. 2009. Placemarks and waterlines: Racialized cyberscapes in post-Katrina Google Earth. *Geoforum* 40(4): 523–534.

Dailey, Dharma, and Kate Starbird. 2014a. Visible skepticism: Community vetting after Hurricane Irene. In *Proceedings of information systems for crisis response and management conference (ISCRAM)*. Penn State University.

Dailey, Dharma, and Kate Starbird. 2014b. Journalists as crowdsourcerers: Responding to crisis by reporting with a crowd. *Computer Supported Cooperative Work (CSCW)* 23(4–6): 445–481.

Dantec, Le, A. Christopher, and Carl DiSalvo. 2013. Infrastructuring and the formation of publics in participatory design. *Social Studies of Science* 43(2): 241–264.

Dynes, Russell Rowe. 1970. *Organized behavior in disaster*. Lexington, Massachusetts: Heath Lexington Books.

Gilbert, Eric, Karrie Karahalios, and Christian Sandvig. 2008. The network in the garden: An empirical analysis of social media in rural life. In *Proceedings of the ACM SIGCHI Conference on Human Factors in Computing Systems*, 1603–1612.

Gilbert, Eric, Karrie Karahalios, and Christian Sandvig. 2010. The network in the garden: Designing social media for rural life. *American Behavioral Scientist* 53(9): 1367–1388.

Hargittai, Eszter. 2015. Is bigger always better? Potential biases of big data derived from social network sites. *The ANNALS of the American Academy of Political and Social Science* 659(1): 63–76.

Hecht, Brent, and Monica Stephens. 2014. A tale of cities: Urban biases in volunteered geographic information. *In Proceedings of ICWSM*.

Lee, Charlotte P., Paul Dourish, and Gloria Mark. 2006. The human infrastructure of cyberinfrastructure. In *Proceedings of the 2006 20th anniversary conference on computer supported cooperative work*, ACM, 483–492.

New York Office of the Governor. 2012. New York State responds: Hurricane Irene and tropical storm Lee one year later. Available at http://www.governor.ny.gov/sites/governor.ny.gov/files/archive/assets/documents/Irene-Lee-One-Year-Report.pdf

Pipek, Volkmar, and Volker Wulf. 2009. Infrastructuring: Toward an integrated perspective on the design and use of information technology. *Journal of the Association for Information Systems* 10(5): 1.

Reischel, Julia. 2015. In visit to Roxbury, state officials vow faster Internet for rural New York. *Watershed Post*, March 2.

Shelton, T., A. Poorthuis, M. Graham, and M. Zook. 2014. Mapping the data shadows of Hurricane Sandy: Uncovering the sociospatial dimensions of 'big data'. *Geoforum* 52: 167–179.

Shklovski, Irina, Moira Burke, Sara Kiesler, and Robert Kraut. 2010. Technology adoption and use in the aftermath of Hurricane Katrina in New Orleans. *American Behavioral Scientist* 53(8): 1228–1246.

Star, Susan Leigh, and Karen Ruhleder. 1996. Steps toward an ecology of infrastructure: Design and access for large information spaces. *Information Systems Research* 7(1): 111–134.

Starbird, Kate, and Leysia Palen. 2013. Working and sustaining the virtual Disaster Desk. In *Proceedings of the 2013 ACM conference on computer supported cooperative work*, 491–502.

Tapia, Andrea H., and Kathleen Moore. 2014. Good enough is good enough: Overcoming disaster response organizations' slow social media data adoption. *Computer Supported Cooperative Work (CSCW)* 23(4–6): 483–512.

Tufekci, Zeynep. 2014. Big questions for social media big data: Representativeness, validity and other methodological pitfalls. *arXiv preprint* arXiv:1403.7400.

Vermont Office of the Governor. 2011. VTRANS enhances public information through Google Maps. Available at http://governor.vermont.gov/newsroom-aot-google-map

CHAPTER 19

Conclusion: The Fierce Urgency of Now

Mark Lloyd and Lewis Friedland

The debate between advocates of a limited federal government and advocates of an active federal government goes back to the founding of our nation. Over the course of nearly two centuries, there has been an agreement on both sides of this divide that even a limited federal government has a responsibility to protect the public and to make possible what Lincoln called a government of the people, by the people, and for the people. We believe that the vast majority of the American public continues to believe that our current government continues to bear basic responsibilities for the common protection and general welfare.

The failure of our current government to ensure that the critical information needs of the public are met will affect the wealthy Wall Street banker and the poor schoolchild in Los Angeles, the independent rancher in Montana and the young hipster in Miami. Weather-related disasters are not limited to either the Gulf Coast or the Great Lakes, the Rocky Mountains or the Mississippi Delta. All of us need to know the trouble

M. Lloyd (✉)
University of Southern California, Los Angeles, CA, USA

L. Friedland
University of Wisconsin, Madison, WI, USA

© The Editor(s) (if applicable) and The Author(s) 2016   305
M.I. Lloyd, L.A. Friedland (eds.), *The Communication Crisis in America, And How to Fix It*, DOI 10.1057/978-1-349-94925-0_19

coming our way. All of us need access to basic information to care for our children and parents and to participate as responsible citizens in our democracy. Addressing the critical information needs of the public should not be a partisan issue.

The failure to establish communication policy that recognizes our collective need for information about the coming storm or to honor our democratic form of government is not the fault of one party or another. This is not to say that the resolution of this issue should not be a part of our political conversation. If this collective effort succeeds, it will generate partisan debate. Because our recommendations touch on the power of established media and telecommunications corporations, our proposals here will be subject to the same sort of distortions that warp the debate over climate change, market regulation, and gun control. But the crisis in communication in the USA is too great for us not to try to bring some attention to this issue to the American public. And so we offer some recommendations about how to fix our communication crisis.

While much of what follows is drawn from the contributors to this volume, the editors here do not suggest universal agreement among our contributors regarding priorities.

1. *Our thinking about communication must change*
     The first recommendation is to shift our collective way of thinking about what we commonly call media. We all live in a complex, interactive, interdependent, and dynamic communication environment. Creating rules for one system, or failing to create rules for another, has an impact, intended or not, on this environment. Focusing exclusively on one aspect or technology of the communication environment (broadband, for example) fails to appreciate the whole. Compartmental thinking fails to understand that different American communities rationally rely upon different media (like radio or printed newspapers) for different purposes. Policymakers, and those who influence policymakers, must become at least as insightful as the business community and embrace the reality of our current merged media environment. The first recommendation is that we must all change the way we think about communication.

     Communication is, as the Founders understood, instrumental to the basic functioning of our republic. Communication was not left to the market, or any new technology. The Founders put the facilitation of democratic discourse before the establishment of a standing army, or the needs of the treasury, or the establishment of a public education system, or any of the other priorities that dominate our current politics.

We must change the way we think about communication if we are to address all of our other common challenges.

2. *Fund better research*

The second recommendation is that we must do much better research on how our media ecologies, at the national, state, and local level, serve or fail to serve our communities. This means more federal money and more foundation funding to understand how best to communicate to the public about the next hurricane, toxic waste disaster, or election. We need to better understand the unintended consequences of the communications transformation, including the market failure to support journalism, particularly in local communities, low-income areas, and diverse communities. And, without diminishing the importance of either markets or technologies, the government must commit to research that focuses on the critical information needs of the public. We need to move beyond and deeper into the categories of "race" and ethnicity and recognize and respect both the diversity of choices and the common challenges faced by the all the different people that make up our nation. Because our communication ecology and our population shifts are dynamic, not static, we must commit to ongoing research to make sure that our policies are actually serving the needs of communities.

This ongoing research should include a focus on better understanding the unequal distribution of communication opportunities and participation. This research needs to be cumulative and periodically reviewed at the highest levels of research policy, including the National Science Foundation, Federal Communications Commission (FCC), National Telecommunications and Information Administration, Federal Trade Commission (FTC), Consumer Financial Protection Bureau, and Corporation for Public Broadcasting (CPB). This will require moving beyond narrow quantitative methodologies to embrace a multidisciplinary approach to understanding our communication ecology.

3. *Establish stronger public policy regarding private communication companies*

Create stronger incentives aimed at private industry to serve the critical information needs of communities, and create disincentives from stripping the communication commons either for private gain or as unintended consequences of market action. We recognize that we live in a capitalist economy and that commercial privately owned media and telecommunications corporations will be an important part of our communication system for the indefinite future. But Fox News and *The New York Times* and Comcast/NBC and Google all have a stake in our society. And all of these corporations are subject to the discipline of shareholders and the government officials who give them license to operate. That license, whether a franchise agreement, FCC license, or corporate charter, needs to ensure that the general welfare is advanced along with the private interest.

Because we know policymakers look for bullet points, we suggest:

- Maintaining current DOJ, FTC, and FCC oversight of anti-competitive arrangements, such as Shared Services Agreements and proposed mergers.
- Reestablishing tax certificates to spur the disinvestment of "grandfa-thered" combinations that limit local, diverse ownership.
- In the event of emergencies, the federal government should prohibit any data caps imposed on digital services.
- Requiring all media and telecommunications companies licensed to use the spectrum to pay into a fund to support emergency communication services.
- Stopping any potential sale of spectrum used for public media.
- Putting hard limits on the revolving door that allows former regulators to work for the companies they regulate.

4. *Support public communication*

The USA needs a strong public communication service that is not subject to either political whim or commercial/corporate influence. And this public communication must provide both content and telecommunication services. It must operate across all media platforms and provide national, state, and local service with a focus on serving the critical information needs of the diverse American public. A trust fund established by government, foundations, and the communication industry must be put in place, along with a sustainable source of funding derived from all private communication companies licensed to use the spectrum or who have a franchise to use public streets to access customers. A reshaped, more democratic, and accountable Corporation for Public Communication needs to be created.

Because we know our recommendations will be distorted in the current partisan environment, let us make clear what we are not calling for. We are not calling for a return of the Fairness Doctrine. We are not calling for government monitoring of news media. We are not calling for an end to Rush Limbaugh or Bill O'Reilly or "Saturday Night Live."

Many years before terrorists attacked the World Trade Center and the Pentagon on September 11, 2001, and years before Hurricane Katrina, Hurricane Sandy, or Hurricane Irene, public officials understood that US communications networks were not prepared to protect the American public in the event of a disaster. Neither the market nor new technologies have stepped up to address this problem, but it is not a failure of the business community, or the technologists. It is a failure of US public policy. By that we do not mean that it is a failure of government alone, for we understand that business leaders and foundation leaders and community leaders and academic leaders have a strong role to play in US public policy. And the same is true of you the reader.

We must all speak up, now—before the next environmental disaster strikes. We must ask our elected leaders where they stand on these issues, and if they do not have a stand, we must insist they make one clear to us before we next go to the voting booth. We must ask all those media and telecommunications companies where they stand, and if they do not have a stand, we must use whatever consumer power we have to get them to address our critical information needs. We must take a stand to address the communication crisis in our country.

INDEX

A

advertising, 19–21, 24, 34, 88–91, 92n3, 99, 114, 129, 135, 138, 156, 159n7, 166, 184, 185, 194, 195, 215, 217–19, 243, 271, 274

African Americans (Black Americans), 50, 82, 110, 202, 253, 254

algorithms, 21–4, 39, 40, 221

American Society of News Editors (ASNE), 36, 216, 250, 252, 253

America's Public Television Stations or Association of Public Television Stations (APTS), 274, 276

Anti-Trust
Clayton Act, 145, 158n5, 158n6, 159n6
Sherman Act, 145, 158n4

Associated Press v. United States, 138n6, 239, 244

AT&T, 134, 144, 154–6, 160

audience, 17–28, 34–5, 37, 38, 40, 81–91, 95, 97–103, 122–3, 129, 169, 175, 183, 185, 201, 203, 205, 217, 251, 272, 292–5, 298

B

BBC, 271–3, 275

behavioral economics, 184–6, 189–91, 194, 195

big data, 21, 184–6, 191–5, 208

Black Lives Matter, 249, 262

blogs, 12, 38, 200, 201, 203, 204, 253

broadband, xxviii, 4, 9, 12–14, 23, 36, 56, 82, 84, 85, 87, 91, 127, 134, 135, 139n9, 152, 154, 156, 195, 206, 217, 221, 229, 233, 255, 262, 269, 278, 299, 300, 301n2

adoption, 56, 91, 301n2

broadcasting
radio, xxvii, 6, 8, 53, 54, 66, 67, 73–6, 81, 84–6, 88, 89, 97, 98, 100–3, 103n2, 103n3, 127, 134, 136, 137, 145, 146, 148, 149, 158n2, 158n6, 169, 239, 245, 252, 256, 268, 270–4, 276, 277, 280–2, 285, 290, 292, 296–9, 306

television, xxvii, xxviii, 6, 11, 14, 19, 53–6, 73, 76, 81, 84–6, 88, 89, 97, 98, 103, 103n3, 111, 115,

© The Editor(s) (if applicable) and The Author(s) 2016
M.I. Lloyd, L.A. Friedland (eds.), *The Communication Crisis in America, And How to Fix It*, DOI 10.1057/978-1-349-94925-0

125, 137, 146, 148, 149, 152,
158n2, 165–80, 185, 220, 243,
252, 255, 268, 271–82, 291
bundling, 20, 51, 184–9, 194, 195

C
Carnegie Commission, 268, 283
census, 51, 52, 57–9, 84, 89–91,
92n1, 92n2, 119, 216, 222, 223,
226, 228, 250, 252, 254
circulation, xxviii, 51, 88–91, 115,
117, 219–24, 226–9
Citizens United, 240
civic engagement, 32, 37, 72, 108,
109, 116, 245
civic information, 3, 5, 10–11, 40,
84, 239
civic mandate of communication, 236
COMCAST/NBC, 144, 308
commercial media, 34, 140, 229
Communications Act of 1934, 145,
262, 268
communications economy, 17–28
communications/media ecology, 32,
233, 237, 245, 249, 250, 252,
256, 257, 259–62
Communications Policy Research
Network (CPRN), 4, 5, 7, 14
Communities
Catskills, 286, 296, 299
Los Angeles, 52, 85, 107–23
New York, 52, 90–1, 286, 288
Texas, 52
constitution, xxx, 58, 233, 235–45
content farms, 22
corporate libertarianism, 137–8
Corporation for Public Broadcasting
(CPB), 252, 262n4, 268, 269,
272–6, 278, 281

critical information needs, xxvii, xxix,
xxx, 1, 4–5, 11, 12, 14, 17, 33,
35, 48–60, 65–76, 82, 117, 125,
126, 165, 217, 235–45, 267,
280, 305–9
CTIA, 132

D
data standards, 6
democracy, 1, 10, 11, 15, 18, 35, 103,
128, 138, 143, 217, 218, 233,
235, 242, 262, 279, 306
Department of Agriculture's (USDA),
220, 221
Department of Commerce, 278
Department of Justice (DOJ), 69,
143–59, 167, 308
digital divide, xxviii, 36, 56, 59, 135,
183, 195, 199, 200, 205, 250,
260, 262n1
digital inclusion, 250
digital literacy, 36
disabilities, xxviii, 36, 56, 187
women, 70, 71, 73
discrimination
ethnic, 51
gender, 75, 245
racial, 59, 245
women, 69, 75
diversity
ethnicity, xxviii, 50–2, 57, 109,
111, 116, 117, 201,
261, 307
gender, 76, 201, 261
geographic, 185
language, 5, 47
race, 50–2, 76, 109, 111, 201, 259,
261, 307
socio-economic, 201

E
Earned Income Tax Credit, 184, 187
economic information, 4, 9. 38
ecosystem, 21–7, 215–30, 256
education, 5, 7–8, 10, 14, 24, 36, 51,
    65, 71, 82–4, 86, 110, 130, 131,
    158n2, 185, 187, 188, 194, 206,
    215, 223, 228, 229, 251, 307
emergency communication, 101, 102,
    103n3, 281, 297–9, 308
Emergency Planning and Community
    Right-to-Know Act (EPCRA),
    241
environmental information, 8, 9
Equal Protection Clause–Fourteenth
    Amendment, 236, 238, 244
ethnicity, xxviii, 14, 36, 50–2, 57, 59,
    109, 111, 114, 116, 117, 122,
    201, 204, 223, 252, 261, 307
ethnic media, 48, 50, 81–92, 111,
    116, 117, 122

F
Fairness Doctrine, 239, 240, 309
Federal Communications Commission
    (FCC), 1, 4, 11, 13, 14, 33, 35,
    74–6, 85, 88, 91, 101, 102,
    103n4, 132, 134, 143–59,
    159n8, 159n13, 166–8, 177,
    179, 195, 217, 233, 240, 243–5,
    251, 252, 255, 256, 261, 262,
    271, 272, 278, 283, 301n2,
    301n3, 307, 308
Federal Election Commission (FEC),
    240
Federal Radio Commission (FRC),
    271
Federal Trade Commission, 144–7,
    158n4, 240, 307
    T-Mobile merger, 144, 154–6
feminist media, 66, 67

First Amendment, 75, 128, 133,
    138n5, 233, 235, 237, 239,
    243–5
Food and Drug Administration
    (FDA), 240
foundations, xxx, 1, 20, 27, 71,
    103n3, 107, 136, 156, 220, 230,
    239, 261, 273, 275, 279, 280,
    282, 283, 307–9
Free Press, 132, 138n4, 158n1

G
Geospatial media analytics (GIS),
    219–21, 223, 224, 293, 295
Global Media Monitoring Project, 73

H
health
    insurance, 6, 69, 194
    risks, 6
    services, 7, 83, 138
Hurricane Irene, 286, 288, 309
Hurricane Katrina, 5, 52, 70, 309
Hurricane Sandy, xxvii, 70, 309

I
immigrant media, 50, 81, 82, 87, 90,
    116
immigrants (New Americans), 81–7,
    90–2
income inequality, 69, 183
individuals, 2, 3, 5, 9, 13, 20, 22, 27,
    31–4, 36–40, 55, 69, 74, 82–90,
    98, 100, 115, 125, 129, 131,
    138n2, 172, 183–8, 190–2, 194,
    195, 203, 237, 238, 255, 256,
    262, 262n2, 273, 277, 288–95,
    298–300
information actors, 299

information and communication
    technologies (ICTs), 36, 285,
    286, 289, 294, 296, 300
information environment, 41, 55,
    186, 217
    households, 55
Information Needs of Communities:
    The Changing Media Landscape
    in a Broadband Age, 217
Informing Communities: Sustaining
    Democracy in a Digital Age, 217,
    218
Institute for Women's Policy Research,
    68

J
job information, 5
journalism, xxix, xxx, 4, 10, 17–28,
    33, 38, 72, 88, 102, 107, 109,
    118, 125, 127–30, 135–8, 165,
    168, 216, 217, 219, 220, 224,
    254, 256, 261, 280, 281, 285,
    301, 307

K
Knight Commission, 1, 18, 33, 217, 218

L
Latino/Hispanic, 48, 50–3, 56, 68,
    69, 72, 82, 84, 85, 89, 95–103,
    103n2, 110–13, 115, 118,
    253–5, 262n2
Lifeline, 184, 195
Local Initiatives Support Corporation,
    187
low-income communities, 12–14, 36,
    183–95, 301n2

M
Mail Fraud Act, 240
mapping, 121, 218–23, 229
market capitalism, 67
market failure, xxx, 11, 125–39, 307
media consolidation, 75, 143, 255
media deserts, 215–30
mergers, xxvii, 132, 144–57, 158n5,
    159n11, 159n13, 159n15,
    159n16, 167, 177, 308
Metamorphosis Project, 108, 109,
    111–14, 118–20, 123
Metcalfe's Law, 233, 257, 258

N
National Association of Broadcasters
    (NAB), 14, 179
National Broadband Plan, 278
National Cable Telecommunications
    Association (NCTA), 132
National Hurricane Center (NHC),
    288–9
National Public Radio (NPR), 67,
    137, 169, 268, 272, 274–6
National Telecommunications and
    Information Administration
    (NTIA), 53, 307
Native Americans (American Indians),
    51, 56, 253, 254
neighborhood, 1, 5–12, 31, 32, 48,
    55, 56, 59, 70, 74, 117, 119,
    120, 185, 217
neoliberalism, 67, 68
network neutrality, 13, 262
New Americans (immigrants), 81–7, 90–2
news
    advertising, 19–21, 138, 218, 219
    business models, 17, 18, 130, 136
    employment, 216, 253

Internet impact on news, 37
  local *vs.* national, 102, 280–2
  public good, 25, 128–9, 138
news deserts, 11, 12, 14, 125, 221
  production and dissemination, 17, 18
newspapers, xxvii, xxviii, 11, 14,
  18–20, 26, 38, 50, 55, 56,
  66, 70, 72, 73, 81, 82, 84,
  89, 111, 115, 127, 129, 130,
  136, 139n11, 139n12, 149,
  158n2, 169, 184, 203, 215–19,
  221–30, 236, 238, 255, 256, 291,
  295, 306
Nextar, 166, 167
noncommercial, educational stations
  (NCE), 268, 272

O
Occupational Safety and Health
  Administration (OSHA), 240, 241
online participation, 199–208

P
Pew Research Center, 21, 33, 38, 168,
  169, 201, 216, 217, 219, 224,
  229, 255, 256
policy failure, 126, 128, 130, 131,
  133, 134
political information, 38, 86, 168
postal service, 222, 236, 238
Prometheus v. FCC, 74
Public Broadcasting Act of 1967, 268,
  272–7
Public Broadcasting leaders-G-4, 267
Public Broadcasting Service (PBS),
  137, 139n14, 244, 268, 269,
  272, 274–8, 281, 282
public interest review, 144, 148
public media, 234, 267–83, 308
  Latino, 100, 102, 103n2

public safety, 5–6, 85–6, 236, 245

R
race
  American Anthropological
    Association, 58
  category making, 57
Radio Act of 1927, 271
Radio-Television News Directors
  Association (RTNDA), 252
ratings, 22, 88, 90, 91, 96, 272, 281
regulatory capture, 132
research
  Communications Infrastructure,
    285
  Content Analysis, 31, 37–9, 41,
    170; agenda setting, 38
  ecological community, 32
  economic approaches, 31, 34–5
  market structure, 34, 41
  mass communication, 31, 37–9, 41
  media ownership, 35
  mixed-method, 32, 41
  multilevel, 31, 32, 41
  neighborhood storytelling, 32
  network analysis, 31, 32, 39–40
revolving door, 132, 143, 144, 149,
  157, 158, 308

S
schools, 5–8, 11, 12, 32, 40, 59, 72,
  85, 97, 107–9, 114, 119, 121,
  137, 152, 187, 188, 192–4, 206,
  208, 217, 242, 251, 271
seniors, 6, 36, 56, 188, 192, 194
Shared Services Agreement (SSAs)
  Local Marketing Agreement, 166
  Local News Sharing Agreement, 166
Sinclair Broadcasting, 167
social infrastructures, 290–2, 295, 298

social media, xxviii, 6, 21–3, 33,
    38–40, 50, 51, 85, 101, 103,
    115, 122, 199, 202, 216, 222,
    249, 253, 254, 277, 281,
    285–301
social network sites (SNS), 201–3
strict scrutiny
    compelling interest, 242
    narrowly tailored, 237

T
Telecommunications Act of 1996, 74,
    145, 251
telecommunication service, 233, 308
telephone, 13, 14, 53–5, 120, 148,
    158n2, 257, 271
    adoption, 53
television, xxvii, xxviii, 6, 11, 14, 19,
    53–6, 73, 76, 81, 84–6, 88, 89,
    97, 98, 103, 103n3, 111, 115,
    125, 137, 146, 148, 149, 152,

    158n2, 165–80, 185, 220, 243,
    252, 255, 268, 271–82, 291
    adoption, 53
transportation, 5, 8, 14, 97, 113, 220,
    241, 271
Tropical Storm Lee, 286

V
venture capital, 254, 261

W
Wikipedia, 200, 204–5, 207
Wilson–Tongia formulation, 250,
    257–60
wireless technology, 278
women, 36, 40, 47, 48,
    65–76, 83, 203–7, 236,
    244, 251
women's movement, 66, 72
World Gender Gap Report, 68

Made in the USA
Las Vegas, NV
15 October 2022

57303500R00193